SELECTED FEDERAL AND STATE ADMINISTRATIVE AND REGULATORY LAWS

2007 Edition

Selected and Edited By

William F. Funk
Professor of Law
Lewis and Clark Law School

Sidney A. Shapiro
University Distinguished Professor in Law
Wake Forest University
School of Law

Russell L. Weaver
Professor of Law & Distinguished University Scholar
University of Louisville
School of Law

Mat #40617200

American Casebook Series and West Group are trademarks registered in the U.S. Patent and Trademark Office.

© West, a Thomson business, 1997, 1999, 2002, 2004, 2006
© 2007 Thomson/West
      610 Opperman Drive
      P.O. Box 64526
      St. Paul, MN 55164–0526
      1–800–328–9352
Printed in the United States of America

ISBN: 978–0–314–18355–2

TEXT IS PRINTED ON 10% POST CONSUMER RECYCLED PAPER

Table of Contents

*

SELECTED
FEDERAL AND STATE
ADMINISTRATIVE
AND
REGULATORY LAWS

2007 Edition

*

THE CONSTITUTION OF THE UNITED STATES

Article I

Section 1.

All legislative powers herein granted shall be vested in a Congress of the United States, which shall consist of a Senate and House of Representatives.

Section 2.

The House of Representatives shall be composed of Members chosen every second Year by the People of the several States, and the Electors in each State shall have the Qualifications requisite for Electors of the most numerous Branch of the State Legislature.

No Person shall be a Representative who shall not have attained to the Age of twenty five Years, and been seven Years a Citizen of the United States, and who shall not, when elected, be an Inhabitant of that State in which he shall be chosen.

[Representatives and direct Taxes shall be apportioned among the several States which may be included within this Union, according to their respective Numbers, which shall be determined by adding to the whole Number of free Persons, including those bound to Service for a Term of Years, and excluding Indians not taxed, three fifths of all other Persons.] The actual Enumeration shall be made within three Years after the first Meeting of the Congress of the United States, and within every subsequent Term of ten Years, in such Manner as they shall by Law direct....

When vacancies happen in the Representation from any State, the Executive Authority thereof shall issue Writs of Election to fill such Vacancies.

The House of Representatives shall chuse their Speaker and other Officers; and shall have the sole Power of Impeachment.

Section 3.

The Senate of the United States shall be composed of two Senators from each State, [chosen by the Legislature thereof,] for six Years; and each Senator shall have one Vote....

The Vice President of the United States shall be President of the Senate, but shall have no Vote, unless they be equally divided.

1

The Senate shall chuse their other Officers, and also a President pro tempore, in the Absence of the Vice President, or when he shall exercise the Office of President of the United States.

The Senate shall have the sole Power to try all Impeachments. When sitting for that Purpose, they shall be on Oath or Affirmation. When the President of the United States is tried, the Chief Justice shall preside: And no Person shall be convicted without the Concurrence of two thirds of the Members present.

Judgment in Cases of Impeachment shall not extend further than to removal from Office, and disqualification to hold and enjoy any Office of honor, Trust or Profit under the United States: but the Party convicted shall nevertheless be liable and subject to Indictment, Trial, Judgment and Punishment, according to Law.

Section 4.

The Times, Places and Manner of holding Elections for Senators and Representatives, shall be prescribed in each State by the Legislature thereof; but the Congress may at any time by Law make or alter such Regulations, except as to the Places of chusing Senators....

Section 5.

Each House shall be the Judge of the Elections, Returns and Qualifications of its own Members, and a Majority of each shall constitute a Quorum to do Business; but a smaller Number may adjourn from day to day, and may be authorized to compel the Attendance of absent Members, in such Manner, and under such Penalties as each House may provide.

Each House may determine the Rules of its Proceedings, punish its Members for disorderly Behaviour, and, with the Concurrence of two thirds, expel a Member.

Each House shall keep a Journal of its Proceedings, and from time to time publish the same, excepting such Parts as may in their Judgment require Secrecy; and the Yeas and Nays of the Members of either House on any question shall, at the Desire of one fifth of those Present, be entered on the Journal....

Section 6.

The Senators and Representatives shall receive a Compensation for their Services, to be ascertained by Law, and paid out of the Treasury of the United States. They shall in all Cases, except Treason, Felony and Breach of the Peace, be privileged from Arrest during their Attendance at the Session of their respective Houses, and in going to and returning from the same; and for any Speech or Debate in either House, they shall not be questioned in any other Place.

No Senator or Representative shall, during the Time for which he was elected, be appointed to any civil Office under the Authority of the United States, which shall have been created, or the Emoluments whereof shall have been encreased during such time; and no Person holding any Office under the United States, shall be a Member of either House during his Continuance in Office.

Section 7.

All Bills for raising Revenue shall originate in the House of Representatives; but the Senate may propose or concur with Amendments as on other Bills.

Every Bill which shall have passed the House of Representatives and the Senate, shall, before it become a Law, be presented to the President of the United States; if he approve he shall sign it, but if not he shall return it, with his Objections to that House in which it shall have originated, who shall enter the Objections at large on their Journal, and proceed to reconsider it. If after such Reconsideration two thirds of that House shall agree to pass the Bill, it shall be sent, together with the Objections, to the other House, by which it shall likewise be reconsidered, and if approved by two thirds of that House, it shall become a Law. But in all such Cases the Votes of both Houses shall be determined by Yeas and Nays, and the Names of the Persons voting for and against the Bill shall be entered on the Journal of each House respectively. If any Bill shall not be returned by the President within ten Days (Sundays excepted) after it shall have been presented to him, the Same shall be a Law, in like Manner as if he had signed it, unless the Congress by their Adjournment prevent its Return, in which case it shall not be a Law.

Every Order, Resolution, or Vote to Which the Concurrence of the Senate and House of Representatives may be necessary (except on a question of Adjournment) shall be presented to the President of the United States; and before the Same shall take Effect, shall be approved by him, or being disapproved by him, shall be repassed by two thirds of the Senate and House of Representatives, according to the Rules and Limitations prescribed in the Case of a Bill.

Section 8.

The Congress shall have Power To lay and collect Taxes, Duties, Imposts and Excises, to pay the Debts and provide for the common Defense and general Welfare of the United States; but all Duties, Imposts and Excises shall be uniform throughout the United States;

To borrow Money on the credit of the United States;

To regulate Commerce with foreign Nations, and among the several States, and with the Indian Tribes;

To establish a uniform Rule of Naturalization, and uniform Laws on the subject of Bankruptcies throughout the United States;

To coin Money, regulate the Value thereof, and of foreign Coin, and fix the Standard of Weights and Measures;

To provide for the Punishment of counterfeiting the Securities and current Coin of the United States;

To establish Post Offices and post Roads;

To promote the Progress of Science and useful Arts, by securing for limited Times to Authors and Inventors the exclusive Right to their respective Writings and Discoveries;

To constitute Tribunals inferior to the supreme Court;

To define and punish Piracies and Felonies committed on the high Seas, and Offences against the Law of Nations;

To declare War, grant Letters of Marque and Reprisal, and make Rules concerning Captures on Land and Water;

To raise and support Armies, but no Appropriation of Money to that use shall be for a longer Term than two Years;

To provide and maintain a Navy;

To make Rules for the Government and Regulation of the land and naval Forces;

To provide for calling forth the Militia to execute the Laws of the Union, suppress Insurrections and repel Invasions;

To provide for organizing, arming, and disciplining, the Militia, and for governing such Part of them as may be employed in the Service of the United States, reserving to the States respectively, the Appointment of the Officers, and the Authority of training the Militia according to the discipline prescribed by Congress;

To exercise exclusive Legislation in all Cases whatsoever, over such District (not exceeding ten Miles square) as may, by Cession of Particular States, and the Acceptance of Congress, become the Seat of the Government of the United States, and to exercise like Authority over all Places purchased by the Consent of the Legislature of the State in which the Same shall be, for the Erection of Forts, Magazines, Arsenals, dock-Yards, and other needful Buildings;—And

To make all Laws which shall be necessary and proper for carrying into Execution the foregoing Powers, and all other Powers vested by this Constitution in the Government of the United States, or in any Department or Officer thereof.

* * *

Article II

Section 1.

The executive Power shall be vested in a President of the United States of America. He shall hold his Office during the Term of four Years. . . .

Before he enter on the Execution of his Office, he shall take the following Oath or Affirmation:—"I do solemnly swear (or affirm) that I will faithfully execute the Office of President of the United States, and will to the best of my Ability, preserve, protect and defend the Constitution of the United States."

Section 2.

The President shall be the Commander in Chief of the Army and Navy of the United States, and of the Militia of the several States, when called into the actual Service of the United States; may require the Opinion, in writing, of the principal Officer in each of the executive Departments, upon any Subject relating to the Duties of their respective Offices, and he shall have Power to Grant Reprieves and Pardons for Offences against the United States, except in Cases of Impeachment.

He shall have Power, by and with the Advice and Consent of the Senate, to make Treaties, provided two-thirds of the Senators present concur; and he shall nominate, and by and with the Advice and Consent of the Senate, shall appoint Ambassadors, other public Ministers and Consuls, Judges of the supreme Court, and all other Officers of the United States, whose Appointments are not herein otherwise provided for, and which shall be established by Law: but the Congress may by Law vest the Appointment of such inferior Officers, as they think proper, in the President alone, in the Courts of Law, or in the Heads of Departments.

The President shall have Power to fill up all Vacancies that may happen during the Recess of the Senate, by granting Commissions which shall expire at the End of their next Session.

Section 3.

He shall from time to time give to Congress Information of the State of the Union, and recommend to their Consideration, such Measures as he shall judge necessary and expedient; he may, on extraordinary Occasions, convene both Houses, or either of them, and in Case of Disagreement between them, with Respect to the Time of Adjournment, he may adjourn them to such Time as he shall think proper; he shall receive Ambassadors and other public Ministers; he shall take Care that the Laws be faithfully executed, and shall Commission all the Officers of the United States.

Section 4.

The President, Vice President, and all Civil Officers of the United States shall be removed from Office on Impeachment for, and Conviction of, Treason, Bribery, or other high Crimes and Misdemeanors.

UNITED STATES CONSTITUTION

Article III

Section 1.

The judicial Power of the United States, shall be vested in one supreme Court, and in such inferior courts as the Congress may from time to time ordain and establish.

Section 2.

The judicial Power shall extend to all Cases, in Law and Equity, arising under this Constitution, the Laws of the United States, and Treaties made, or which shall be made, under their Authority;—to all Cases affecting Ambassadors, other public ministers and Consuls;—to all Cases of admiralty and maritime Jurisdiction;—to Controversies to which the United States shall be a Party;—to Controversies between two or more States;—between a State and Citizens of another State;—between Citizens of different States;—between Citizens of the same State claiming Lands under Grants of different States, and between a State, or the Citizens thereof, and foreign States, Citizens or Subjects.

* * *

Amendments to the Constitution of the United States
Amendment I (1791)

Congress shall make no law respecting an establishment of religion, or prohibiting the free exercise thereof; or abridging the freedom of speech, or of the press; or the right of the people peaceably to assemble, and to petition the government for a redress of grievances.

Amendment IV (1791)

The right of the people to be secure in their persons, houses, papers, and effects, against unreasonable searches and seizures, shall not be violated, and no Warrants shall issue, but upon probable cause, supported by Oath or affirmation, and particularly describing the place to be searched, and the persons or things to be seized.

Amendment V (1791)

No person shall be ... compelled in any criminal case to be a witness against himself, nor be deprived of life, liberty, or property, without due process of law; nor shall private property be taken for public use, without just compensation.

Amendment VII (1791)

In Suits at common law, where the value in controversy shall exceed twenty dollars, the right of trial by jury shall be preserved, and no fact tried by a jury, shall be otherwise reexamined in any Court of the United States, than according to the rules of the common law.

UNITED STATES CONSTITUTION

Amendment XIV (1868)

Section 1.

All persons born or naturalized in the United States, and subject to the jurisdiction thereof, are citizens of the United States and of the State wherein they reside. No State shall make or enforce any law which shall abridge the privileges or immunities of citizens of the United States; nor shall any State deprive any person of life, liberty, or property, without due process of law; nor deny to any person within its jurisdiction the equal protection of the laws.

ADMINISTRATIVE PROCEDURE ACT

TITLE 5. GOVERNMENT ORGANIZATION AND EMPLOYEES
PART I—THE AGENCIES GENERALLY
CHAPTER 5—ADMINISTRATIVE PROCEDURE
SUBCHAPTER II—ADMINISTRATIVE PROCEDURE

§ 551. Definitions

For the purpose of this subchapter—

(1) "agency" means each authority of the Government of the United States, whether or not it is within or subject to review by another agency, but does not include—

(A) the Congress;

(B) the courts of the United States;

(C) the governments of the territories or possessions of the United States;

(D) the government of the District of Columbia; or except as to the requirements of section 552 of this title—

(E) agencies composed of representatives of the parties or of representatives of organizations of the parties to the disputes determined by them;

(F) courts martial and military commissions;

(G) military authority exercised in the field in time of war or in occupied territory; or

(H) functions conferred by sections 1738, 1739, 1743, and 1744 of title 12; chapter 2 of title 41; subchapter II of chapter 471 of title 49; or sections 1884, 1891–1902, and former section 1641(b)(2), of title 50, appendix;

(2) "person" includes an individual, partnership, corporation, association, or public or private organization other than an agency;

(3) "party" includes a person or agency named or admitted as a party, or properly seeking and entitled as of right to be admitted as a party, in an agency proceeding, and a person or agency admitted by an agency as a party for limited purposes;

(4) "rule" means the whole or a part of an agency statement of general or particular applicability and future effect designed to implement, interpret, or prescribe law or policy or describing the organization, procedure, or practice requirements of an agency and includes the approval or prescription for the future of rates, wages, corporate or financial structures or reorganizations thereof, prices, facilities, appliances, services or allowances therefor or of valuations, costs, or accounting, or practices bearing on any of the foregoing;

(5) "rule making" means agency process for formulating, amending, or repealing a rule;

(6) "order" means the whole or a part of a final disposition, whether affirmative, negative, injunctive, or declaratory in form, of an agency in a matter other than rule making but including licensing;

(7) "adjudication" means agency process for the formulation of an order;

(8) "license" includes the whole or a part of an agency permit, certificate, approval, registration, charter, membership, statutory exemption or other form of permission;

(9) "licensing" includes agency process respecting the grant, renewal, denial, revocation, suspension, annulment, withdrawal, limitation, amendment, modification, or conditioning of a license;

(10) "sanction" includes the whole or a part of an agency—

(A) prohibition, requirement, limitation, or other condition affecting the freedom of a person;

(B) withholding of relief;

(C) imposition of penalty or fine;

(D) destruction, taking, seizure, or withholding of property;

(E) assessment of damages, reimbursement, restitution, compensation, costs, charges, or fees;

(F) requirement, revocation, or suspension of a license; or

(G) taking other compulsory or restrictive action;

(11) "relief" includes the whole or a part of an agency—

(A) grant of money, assistance, license, authority, exemption, exception, privilege, or remedy;

(B) recognition of a claim, right, immunity, privilege, exemption, or exception; or

(C) taking of other action on the application or petition of, and beneficial to, a person;

(12) "agency proceeding" means an agency process as defined by paragraphs (5), (7), and (9) of this section;

(13) "agency action" includes the whole or a part of an agency rule, order, license, sanction, relief, or the equivalent or denial thereof, or failure to act; and

(14) "ex parte communication" means an oral or written communication not on the public record with respect to which reasonable prior notice to all parties is not given, but it shall not include requests for status reports on any matter or proceeding covered by this subchapter.

§ 552. Public Information; agency rules, opinions, orders, records, and proceedings [Freedom of Information Act—infra]

§ 552a. Records maintained on individuals [Privacy Act of 1974—infra]

§ 552b. Open meetings [Government in the Sunshine Act—infra]

§ 553. Rulemaking

(a) This section applies, according to the provisions thereof, except to the extent that there is involved—

(1) a military or foreign affairs function of the United States; or

(2) a matter relating to agency management or personnel or to public property, loans, grants, benefits, or contracts.

(b) General notice of proposed rule making shall be published in the Federal Register, unless persons subject thereto are named and either personally served or otherwise have actual notice thereof in accordance with law. The notice shall include—

(1) a statement of the time, place, and nature of public rule making proceedings;

(2) reference to the legal authority under which the rule is proposed; and

(3) either the terms or substance of the proposed rule or a description of the subjects and issues involved.

Except when notice or hearing is required by statute, this subsection does not apply—

    (A) to interpretative rules, general statements of policy, or rules of agency organization, procedure, or practice; or

    (B) when the agency for good cause finds (and incorporates the finding and a brief statement of reasons therefor in the rules issued) that notice and public procedure thereon are impracticable, unnecessary, or contrary to the public interest.

(c) After notice required by this section, the agency shall give interested persons an opportunity to participate in the rule making through submission of written data, views, or arguments with or without opportunity for oral presentation. After consideration of the relevant matter presented, the agency shall incorporate in the rules adopted a concise general statement of their basis and purpose. When rules are required by statute to be made on the record after opportunity for an agency hearing, sections 556 and 557 of this title apply instead of this subsection.

(d) The required publication or service of a substantive rule shall be made not less than 30 days before its effective date, except—

    (1) a substantive rule which grants or recognizes an exemption or relieves a restriction;

    (2) interpretative rules and statements of policy; or

    (3) as otherwise provided by the agency for good cause found and published with the rule.

(e) Each agency shall give an interested person the right to petition for the issuance, amendment, or repeal of a rule.

§ 554. Adjudications

(a) This section applies, according to the provisions thereof, in every case of adjudication required by statute to be determined on the record after opportunity for an agency hearing, except to the extent that there is involved—

    (1) a matter subject to a subsequent trial of the law and the facts de novo in a court;

    (2) the selection or tenure of an employee, except a administrative law judge appointed under section 3105 of this title;

    (3) proceedings in which decisions rest solely on inspections, tests, or elections;

(4) the conduct of military or foreign affairs functions;

(5) cases in which an agency is acting as an agent for a court; or

(6) the certification of worker representatives.

(b) Persons entitled to notice of an agency hearing shall be timely informed of—

(1) the time, place, and nature of the hearing;

(2) the legal authority and jurisdiction under which the hearing is to be held; and

(3) the matters of fact and law asserted.

When private persons are the moving parties, other parties to the proceeding shall give prompt notice of issues controverted in fact or law; and in other instances agencies may by rule require responsive pleading. In fixing the time and place for hearings, due regard shall be had for the convenience and necessity of the parties or their representatives.

(c) The agency shall give all interested parties opportunity for—

(1) the submission and consideration of facts, arguments, offers of settlement, or proposals of adjustment when time, the nature of the proceeding, and the public interest permit; and

(2) to the extent that the parties are unable so to determine a controversy by consent, hearing and decision on notice and in accordance with sections 556 and 557 of this title.

(d) The employee who presides at the reception of evidence pursuant to section 556 of this title shall make the recommended decision or initial decision required by section 557 of this title, unless he becomes unavailable to the agency. Except to the extent required for the disposition of ex parte matters as authorized by law, such an employee may not—

(1) consult a person or party on a fact in issue, unless on notice and opportunity for all parties to participate; or

(2) be responsible to or subject to the supervision or direction of an employee or agent engaged in the performance of investigative or prosecuting functions for an agency.

An employee or agent engaged in the performance of investigative or prosecuting functions for an agency in a case may not, in that or a factually related case, participate or advise in the decision, recommended decision, or agency review pursuant to section 557 of this title, except as witness or counsel in public proceedings. This subsection does not apply—

(A) in determining applications for initial licenses;

(B) to proceedings involving the validity or application of rates, facilities, or practices of public utilities or carriers; or

(C) to the agency or a member or members of the body comprising the agency.

(e) The agency, with like effect as in the case of other orders, and in its sound discretion, may issue a declaratory order to terminate a controversy or remove uncertainty.

§ 555. Ancillary matters

(a) This section applies, according to the provisions thereof, except as otherwise provided by this subchapter.

(b) A person compelled to appear in person before an agency or representative thereof is entitled to be accompanied, represented, and advised by counsel or, if permitted by the agency, by other qualified representative. A party is entitled to appear in person or by or with counsel or other duly qualified representative in an agency proceeding. So far as the orderly conduct of public business permits, an interested person may appear before an agency or its responsible employees for the presentation, adjustment, or determination of an issue, request, or controversy in a proceeding, whether interlocutory, summary, or otherwise, or in connection with an agency function. With due regard for the convenience and necessity of the parties or their representatives and within a reasonable time, each agency shall proceed to conclude a matter presented to it. This subsection does not grant or deny a person who is not a lawyer the right to appear for or represent others before an agency or in an agency proceeding.

(c) Process, requirement of a report, inspection, or other investigative act or demand may not be issued, made, or enforced except as authorized by law. A person compelled to submit data or evidence is entitled to retain or, on payment of lawfully prescribed costs, procure a copy or transcript thereof, except that in a nonpublic investigatory proceeding the witness may for good cause be limited to inspection of the official transcript of his testimony.

(d) Agency subpenas authorized by law shall be issued to a party on request and, when required by rules of procedure, on a statement or showing of general relevance and reasonable scope of the evidence sought. On contest, the court shall sustain the subpena or similar process or demand to the extent that it is found to be in accordance with law. In a proceeding for enforcement, the court shall issue an order requiring the appearance of the witness or the production of the evidence or data within a reasonable time under penalty of punishment for contempt in case of contumacious failure to comply.

(e) Prompt notice shall be given of the denial in whole or in part of a written application, petition, or other request of an interested person made in connection with any agency proceeding. Except in affirming a prior denial or when the denial is self-explanatory, the notice shall be accompanied by a brief statement of the grounds for denial.

Formal

§ 556. Hearings; presiding employees; powers and duties; burden of proof; evidence; record as basis of decision

(a) This section applies, according to the provisions thereof, to hearings required by section 553 or 554 of this title to be conducted in accordance with this section.

(b) There shall preside at the taking of evidence—

(1) the agency;

(2) one or more members of the body which comprises the agency; or

(3) one or more administrative law judges appointed under section 3105 of this title.

This subchapter does not supersede the conduct of specified classes of proceedings, in whole or in part, by or before boards or other employees specially provided for by or designated under statute. The functions of presiding employees and of employees participating in decisions in accordance with section 557 of this title shall be conducted in an impartial manner. A presiding or participating employee may at any time disqualify himself. On the filing in good faith of a timely and sufficient affidavit of personal bias or other disqualification of a presiding or participating employee, the agency shall determine the matter as a part of the record and decision in the case.

(c) Subject to published rules of the agency and within its powers, employees presiding at hearings may—

(1) administer oaths and affirmations;

(2) issue subpoenas authorized by law;

(3) rule on offers of proof and receive relevant evidence;

(4) take depositions or have depositions taken when the ends of justice would be served;

(5) regulate the course of the hearing;

(6) hold conferences for the settlement or simplification of the issues by consent of the parties or by the use of alternative means of dispute resolution as provided in subchapter IV of this chapter;

(7) inform the parties as to the availability of one or more alternative means of dispute resolution, and encourage use of such methods;

(8) require the attendance at any conference held pursuant to paragraph (6) of at least one representative of each party who has authority to negotiate concerning resolution of issues in controversy;

(9) dispose of procedural requests or similar matters;

(10) make or recommend decisions in accordance with section 557 of this title; and

(11) take other action authorized by agency rule consistent with this subchapter.

(d) Except as otherwise provided by statute, the proponent of a rule or order has the burden of proof. Any oral or documentary evidence may be received, but the agency as a matter of policy shall provide for the exclusion of irrelevant, immaterial, or unduly repetitious evidence. A sanction may not be imposed or rule or order issued except on consideration of the whole record or those parts thereof cited by a party and supported by and in accordance with the reliable, probative, and substantial evidence. The agency may, to the extent consistent with the interests of justice and the policy of the underlying statutes administered by the agency, consider a violation of section 557(d) of this title sufficient grounds for a decision adverse to a party who has knowingly committed such violation or knowingly caused such violation to occur. A party is entitled to present his case or defense by oral or documentary evidence, to submit rebuttal evidence, and to conduct such cross-examination as may be required for a full and true disclosure of the facts. In rule making or determining claims for money or benefits or applications for initial licenses an agency may, when a party will not be prejudiced thereby, adopt procedures for the submission of all or part of the evidence in written form.

(e) The transcript of testimony and exhibits, together with all papers and requests filed in the proceeding, constitutes the exclusive record for decision in accordance with section 557 of this title and, on payment of lawfully prescribed costs, shall be made available to the parties. When an agency decision rests on official notice of a material fact not appearing in the evidence in the record, a party is entitled, on timely request, to an opportunity to show the contrary.

§ 557. Initial decisions; conclusiveness; review by agency; submissions by parties; contents of decisions; record

(a) This section applies, according to the provisions thereof, when a hearing is required to be conducted in accordance with section 556 of this title.

(b) When the agency did not preside at the reception of the evidence, the presiding employee or, in cases not subject to section 554(d) of this title, an employee qualified to preside at hearings pursuant to section 556 of this title, shall initially decide the case unless the agency requires, either in specific cases or by general rule, the entire record to be certified to it for decision. When the presiding employee makes an initial decision, that decision then becomes the decision of the agency without further proceedings unless there is an appeal to, or review on motion of, the agency within time provided by rule. On appeal from or review of the initial decision, the agency has all the powers which it would have in making the initial decision except as it may limit the issues on notice or by rule. When the agency makes the decision without having presided at the reception of the evidence, the presiding employee or an employee qualified to preside at hearings pursuant to section 556 of this title shall first recommend a decision, except that in rule making or determining applications for initial licenses—

(1) instead thereof the agency may issue a tentative decision or one of its responsible employees may recommend a decision; or

(2) this procedure may be omitted in a case in which the agency finds on the record that due and timely execution of its functions imperatively and unavoidably so requires.

(c) Before a recommended, initial, or tentative decision, or a decision on agency review of the decision of subordinate employees, the parties are entitled to a reasonable opportunity to submit for the consideration of the employees participating in the decisions—

(1) proposed findings and conclusions; or

(2) exceptions to the decisions or recommended decisions of subordinate employees or to tentative agency decisions; and

(3) supporting reasons for the exceptions or proposed findings or conclusions. The record shall show the ruling on each finding, conclusion, or exception presented. All decisions, including initial, recommended, and tentative decisions, are a part of the record and shall include a statement of—

(A) findings and conclusions, and the reasons or basis therefor, on all the material issues of fact, law, or discretion presented on the record; and

(B) the appropriate rule, order, sanction, relief, or denial thereof.

(d)(1) In any agency proceeding which is subject to subsection (a) of this section, except to the extent required for the disposition of ex parte matters as authorized by law—

(A) no interested person outside the agency shall make or knowingly cause to be made to any member of the body comprising the agency, administrative law judge, or other employee who is or may reasonably be expected to be involved in the decisional process of the proceeding, an ex parte communication relevant to the merits of the proceeding;

(B) no member of the body comprising the agency, administrative law judge, or other employee who is or may reasonably be expected to be involved in the decisional process of the proceeding, shall make or knowingly cause to be made to any interested

16

person outside the agency an ex parte communication relevant to the merits of the proceeding;

(C) a member of the body comprising the agency, administrative law judge, or other employee who is or may reasonably be expected to be involved in the decisional process of such proceeding who receives, or who makes or knowingly causes to be made, a communication prohibited by this subsection shall place on the public record of the proceeding:

(i) all such written communications;

(ii) memoranda stating the substance of all such oral communications; and

(iii) all written responses, and memoranda stating the substance of all oral responses, to the materials described in clauses (i) and (ii) of this subparagraph;

(D) upon receipt of a communication knowingly made or knowingly caused to be made by a party in violation of this subsection, the agency, administrative law judge, or other employee presiding at the hearing may, to the extent consistent with the interests of justice and the policy of the underlying statutes, require the party to show cause why his claim or interest in the proceeding should not be dismissed, denied, disregarded, or otherwise adversely affected on account of such violation; and

(E) the prohibitions of this subsection shall apply beginning at such time as the agency may designate, but in no case shall they begin to apply later than the time at which a proceeding is noticed for hearing unless the person responsible for the communication has knowledge that it will be noticed, in which case the prohibitions shall apply beginning at the time of his acquisition of such knowledge.

(2) This subsection does not constitute authority to withhold information from Congress.

§ 558. Imposition of sanctions; determination of applications for licenses; suspension, revocation, and expiration of licenses

(a) This section applies, according to the provisions thereof, to the exercise of a power or authority.

(b) A sanction may not be imposed or a substantive rule or order issued except within jurisdiction delegated to the agency and as authorized by law.

(c) When application is made for a license required by law, the agency, with due regard for the rights and privileges of all the interested parties or adversely affected persons and within a reasonable time, shall set and complete proceedings required to be conducted in accordance with sections 556 and 557 of this title or other proceedings required by law and shall make its decision. Except in cases of willfulness or those in which public health, interest, or safety requires otherwise, the withdrawal, suspension, revocation, or annulment of a license is lawful only if, before the institution of agency proceedings therefore, the licensee has been given—

(1) notice by the agency in writing of the facts or conduct which may warrant the action; and

(2) opportunity to demonstrate or achieve compliance with all lawful requirements. When the licensee has made timely and sufficient application for a renewal or a new license in accordance with agency rules, a license with reference to an activity of a continuing nature does not expire until the application has been finally determined by the agency.

§ 559. Effect on other laws; effect of subsequent statute

This subchapter, chapter 7, and sections 1305, 3105, 3344, 4301(2)(E), 5372, and 7521 of this title, and the provisions of section 5335(a)(B) of this title that relate to administrative law judges, do not limit or repeal additional requirements imposed by statute or otherwise recognized by law. Except as otherwise required by law, requirements or privileges relating to evidence or procedure apply equally to agencies and persons. Each agency is granted the authority necessary to comply with the requirements of this subchapter through the issuance of rules or otherwise. Subsequent statute may not be held to supersede or modify this subchapter, chapter 7, sections 1305, 3105, 3344, 4301(2)(E), 5372, or 7521 of this title, or the provisions of section 5335(a)(B) of this title that relate to administrative law judges, except to the extent that it does so expressly.

Chapter 7—Judicial Review

§ 701. Application; definitions

(a) This chapter applies, according to the provisions thereof, except to the extent that—

(1) statutes preclude judicial review; or

(2) agency action is committed to agency discretion by law.

(b) For the purpose of this chapter—

(1) "agency" means each authority of the Government of the United States, whether or not it is within or subject to review by another agency, but does not include—

(A) the Congress;

(B) the courts of the United States;

(C) the governments of the territories or possessions of the United States;

(D) the government of the District of Columbia;

(E) agencies composed of representatives of the parties or of representatives of organizations of the parties to the disputes determined by them;

(F) courts martial and military commissions;

(G) military authority exercised in the field in time of war or in occupied territory; or

(H) functions conferred by sections 1738, 1739, 1743, and 1744 of title 12; chapter 2 of title 41; subchapter II of chapter 471 of title 49; or sections 1884, 1891–1902, and former section 1641(b)(2), of title 50, appendix; and

(2) "person", "rule", "order", "license", "sanction", "relief", and "agency action" have the meanings given them by section 551 of this title.

§ 702. Right of review

A person suffering legal wrong because of agency action, or adversely affected or aggrieved by agency action within the meaning of a relevant statute, is entitled to judicial review thereof. An action in a court of the United States seeking relief other than money damages and stating a claim that an agency or an officer or employee thereof acted or failed to act in an official capacity or under color of legal authority shall not be dismissed nor relief therein be denied on the ground that it is against the United States or that the United States is an indispensable party. The United States may be named as a defendant in any such action, and a judgment or decree may be entered against the United States: Provided, That any mandatory or injunctive decree shall specify the Federal officer or officers (by name or by title), and their successors in office, personally responsible for compliance. Nothing herein (1) affects other limitations on judicial review or the power or duty of the court to dismiss any action or deny relief on any other appropriate legal or equitable ground; or (2) confers authority to grant relief if any other statute that grants consent to suit expressly or impliedly forbids the relief which is sought.

§ 703. Form and venue of proceeding

The form of proceeding for judicial review is the special statutory review proceeding relevant to the subject matter in a court specified by statute or, in the absence or inadequacy thereof, any applicable form of legal action, including actions for declaratory judgments or writs of prohibitory or mandatory injunction or habeas corpus, in a court of competent jurisdiction. If no special statutory review proceeding is applicable, the action for judicial review may be brought against the United States, the agency by its official title, or the appropriate officer. Except to the extent that prior, adequate, and exclusive opportunity for judicial review is provided by law, agency action is subject to judicial review in civil or criminal proceedings for judicial enforcement.

§ 704. Actions reviewable

Agency action made reviewable by statute and final agency action for which there is no other adequate remedy in a court are subject to judicial review. A preliminary, procedural, or intermediate agency action or ruling not directly reviewable is subject to review on the review of the final agency action. Except as otherwise expressly required by statute, agency action otherwise final is final for the purposes of this section whether or not there has been presented or determined an application for a declaratory order, for any form of reconsideration, or, unless the agency otherwise requires by rule and provides that the action meanwhile is inoperative, for an appeal to superior agency authority.

§ 705. Relief pending review

When an agency finds that justice so requires, it may postpone the effective date of action taken by it, pending judicial review. On such conditions as may be required and to the extent necessary to prevent irreparable injury, the reviewing court, including the court to which a case may be taken on appeal from or on application for certiorari or other writ to a reviewing court, may issue all necessary and appropriate process to postpone the effective date of an agency action or to preserve status or rights pending conclusion of the review proceedings.

§ 706. Scope of review

To the extent necessary to decision and when presented, the reviewing court shall decide all relevant questions of law, interpret constitutional and statutory provisions, and determine the meaning or applicability of the terms of an agency action. The reviewing court shall—

    (1) compel agency action unlawfully withheld or unreasonably delayed; and

    (2) hold unlawful and set aside agency action, findings, and conclusions found to be—

        (A) arbitrary, capricious, an abuse of discretion, or otherwise not in accordance with law;

        (B) contrary to constitutional right, power, privilege, or immunity;

        (C) in excess of statutory jurisdiction, authority, or limitations, or short of statutory right;

(D) without observance of procedure required by law;

(E) unsupported by substantial evidence in a case subject to sections 556 and 557 of this title or otherwise reviewed on the record of an agency hearing provided by statute; or

(F) unwarranted by the facts to the extent that the facts are subject to trial de novo by the reviewing court.

In making the foregoing determinations, the court shall review the whole record or those parts of it cited by a party, and due account shall be taken of the rule of prejudicial error.

§ 3105. Appointment of administrative law judges

Each agency shall appoint as many administrative law judges as are necessary for proceedings required to be conducted in accordance with sections 556 and 557 of this title. Administrative law judges shall be assigned to cases in rotation so far as practicable, and may not perform duties inconsistent with their duties and responsibilities as administrative law judges.

§ 3344. Details; administrative law judges

An agency as defined by section 551 of this title which occasionally or temporarily is insufficiently staffed with administrative law judges appointed under section 3105 of this title may use administrative law judges selected by the Office of Personnel Management from and with the consent of other agencies.

§ 7521. Actions against administrative law judges

(a) An action may be taken against an administrative law judge appointed under section 3105 of this title by the agency in which the administrative law judge is employed only for good cause established and determined by the Merit Systems Protection Board on the record after opportunity for hearing before the Board.

(b) The actions covered by this section are—

(1) a removal;

(2) a suspension;

(3) a reduction in grade;

(4) a reduction in pay; and

(5) a furlough of 30 days or less; but do not include—

(A) a suspension or removal under section 7532 of this title;

(B) a reduction-in-force action under section 3502 of this title; or

(C) any action initiated under section 1215 of this title.

EXECUTIVE ORDER 12866

(September 30, 1993, 58 F.R. 51735, as amended by Executive Order 13258, 67 F.R. 9385 (February 26, 2002), and by Executive Order 13422, 72 F.R. 2763 (January 23, 2007))

Regulatory Planning and Review

The American people deserve a regulatory system that works for them, not against them: a regulatory system that protects and improves their health, safety, environment, and well-being and improves the performance of the economy without imposing unacceptable or unreasonable costs on society; regulatory policies that recognize that the private sector and private markets are the best engine for economic growth; regulatory approaches that respect the role of State, local, and tribal governments; and regulations that are effective, consistent, sensible, and understandable. We do not have such a regulatory system today. With this Executive order, the Federal Government begins a program to reform and make more efficient the regulatory process. The objectives of this Executive order are to enhance planning and coordination with respect to both new and existing regulations; to reaffirm the primacy of Federal agencies in the regulatory decision-making process; to restore the integrity and legitimacy of regulatory review and oversight; and to make the process more accessible and open to the public. In pursuing these objectives, the regulatory process shall be conducted so as to meet applicable statutory requirements and with due regard to the discretion that has been entrusted to the Federal agencies. Accordingly, by the authority vested in me as President by the Constitution and the laws of the United States of America, it is hereby ordered as follows:

Section 1. Statement of Regulatory Philosophy and Principles.

(a) The Regulatory Philosophy. Federal agencies should promulgate only such regulations as are required by law, are necessary to interpret the law, or are made necessary by compelling public need, such as material failures of private markets to protect or improve the health and safety of the public, the environment, or the well-being of the American people. In deciding whether and how to regulate, agencies should assess all costs and benefits of available regulatory alternatives, including the alternative of not regulating. Costs and benefits shall be understood to include both quantifiable measures (to the fullest extent that these can be usefully estimated) and qualitative measures of costs and benefits that are difficult to quantify, but nevertheless essential to consider. Further, in choosing among alternative regulatory approaches, agencies should select those approaches that maximize net benefits (including potential economic, environmental, public health and safety, and other advantages; distributive impacts; and equity), unless a statute requires another regulatory approach.

(b) The Principles of Regulation. To ensure that the agencies' regulatory programs are consistent with the philosophy set forth above, agencies should adhere to the following principles, to the extent permitted by law and where applicable:

(1) Each agency shall identify in writing the specific market failure (such as externalities, market power, lack of information) or other specific problem that it intends to address (including, where applicable, the failures of public institutions) that warrant new agency action, as well as assess the significance of that problem, to enable assessment of whether any new regulation is warranted.

(2) Each agency shall examine whether existing regulations (or other law) have created, or contributed to, the problem that a new regulation is intended to correct and whether those regulations (or other law) should be modified to achieve the intended goal of regulation more effectively.

(3) Each agency shall identify and assess available alternatives to direct regulation, including providing economic incentives to encourage the desired behavior, such as user fees or marketable permits, or providing information upon which choices can be made by the public.

(4) In setting regulatory priorities, each agency shall consider, to the extent reasonable, the degree and nature of the risks posed by various substances or activities within its jurisdiction.

(5) When an agency determines that a regulation is the best available method of achieving the regulatory objective, it shall design its regulations in the most cost-effective manner to achieve the regulatory objective. In doing so, each agency shall consider incentives for innovation, consistency, predictability, the costs of enforcement and compliance (to the government, regulated entities, and the public), flexibility, distributive impacts, and equity.

(6) Each agency shall assess both the costs and the benefits of the intended regulation and, recognizing that some costs and benefits are difficult to quantify, propose or adopt a regulation only upon a reasoned determination that the benefits of the intended regulation justify its costs.

(7) Each agency shall base its decisions on the best reasonably obtainable scientific, technical, economic, and other information concerning the need for, and consequences of, the intended regulation or guidance document.

(8) Each agency shall identify and assess alternative forms of regulation and shall, to the extent feasible, specify performance objec-

tives, rather than specifying the behavior or manner of compliance that regulated entities must adopt.

(9) Wherever feasible, agencies shall seek views of appropriate State, local, and tribal officials before imposing regulatory requirements that might significantly or uniquely affect those governmental entities. Each agency shall assess the effects of Federal regulations on State, local, and tribal governments, including specifically the availability of resources to carry out those mandates, and seek to minimize those burdens that uniquely or significantly affect such governmental entities, consistent with achieving regulatory objectives. In addition, as appropriate, agencies shall seek to harmonize Federal regulatory actions with related State, local, and tribal regulatory and other governmental functions.

(10) Each agency shall avoid regulations and guidance documents that are inconsistent, incompatible, or duplicative with its other regulations and guidance documents or those of other Federal agencies.

(11) Each agency shall tailor its regulations and guidance documents to impose the least burden on society, including individuals, businesses of differing sizes, and other entities (including small communities and governmental entities), consistent with obtaining the regulatory objectives, taking into account, among other things, and to the extent practicable, the costs of cumulative regulations.

(12) Each agency shall draft its regulations and guidance documents to be simple and easy to understand, with the goal of minimizing the potential for uncertainty and litigation arising from such uncertainty.

§ 2. *Organization.* An efficient regulatory planning and review process is vital to ensure that the Federal Government's regulatory system best serves the American people.

(a) The Agencies. Because Federal agencies are the repositories of significant substantive expertise and experience, they are responsible for developing regulations and guidance documents and assuring that the regulations and guidance documents are consistent with applicable law, the President's priorities, and the principles set forth in this Executive order.

(b) The Office of Management and Budget. Coordinated review of agency rulemaking is necessary to ensure that regulations and guidance documents are consistent with applicable law, the President's priorities, and the principles set forth in this Executive order, and that decisions made by one agency do not conflict with the policies or actions taken or planned by another agency. The Office of Management and Budget (OMB) shall carry out that review function. Within OMB, the Office of Information and Regulatory Affairs (OIRA) is the repository of expertise concerning regulatory issues, including methodologies and procedures that affect more than one agency, this Executive order, and the President's regulatory policies. To the extent permitted by law, OMB shall provide guidance to agencies and assist the President and regulatory policy advisors to the President in regulatory planning and shall be the entity that reviews individual regulations and guidance documents, as provided by this Executive order.

(c) Assistance. In fulfilling his responsibilities under this Executive order, the President shall be assisted by the regulatory policy advisors within the Executive Office of the President and by such agency officials and personnel as the President may, from time to time, consult.

§ 3. *Definitions.* **For purposes of this Executive order:**

(a) "Advisors" refers to such regulatory policy advisors to the President as the President may from time to time consult, including, among others: (1) the Director of OMB; (2) the Chair (or another member) of the Council of Economic Advisers; (3) the Assistant to the President for Economic Policy; (4) the Assistant to the President for Domestic Policy; (5) the Assistant to the President for National Security Affairs; (6) the Director of the Office of Science and Technology Policy; (7) the Deputy Assistant to the President and Director for Intergovernmental Affairs; (8) the Assistant to the President and Staff Secretary; (9) the Assistant to the President and Chief of Staff to the Vice President; (10) the Assistant to the President and Counsel to the President; (11) the Chairman of the Council on Environmental Quality and Director of the Office of Environmental Quality; (12) the Assistant to the President for Homeland Security; and (13) the Administrator of OIRA, who also shall coordinate communications relating to this Executive order among the agencies, OMB, the other Advisors, and the Office of the Vice President.

(b) "Agency," unless otherwise indicated, means any authority of the United States that is an "agency" under 44 U.S.C. 3502(1), other than those considered to be independent regulatory agencies, as defined in 44 U.S.C. 3502(10).

(c) "Director" means the Director of OMB.

(d) "Regulation" means an agency statement of general applicability and future effect, which the agency intends to have the force and effect of law, that is designed to implement, interpret, or prescribe law or policy or to describe the procedure or practice requirements of an agency. It does not, however, include:

   (1) Regulations issued in accordance with the formal rulemaking provisions of 5 U.S.C. 556, 557;

   (2) Regulations that pertain to a military or foreign affairs function of the United States, other than procurement regulations and regu-

lations involving the import or export of non-defense articles and services;

(3) Regulations that are limited to agency organization, management, or personnel matters; or

(4) Any other category of regulations exempted by the Administrator of OIRA.

(e) "Regulatory action" means any substantive action by an agency (normally published in the Federal Register) that promulgates or is expected to lead to the promulgation of a final regulation, including notices of inquiry, advance notices of proposed rulemaking, and notices of proposed rulemaking.

(f) "Significant regulatory action" means any regulatory action that is likely to result in a regulation that may:

(1) Have an annual effect on the economy of $100 million or more or adversely affect in a material way the economy, a sector of the economy, productivity, competition, jobs, the environment, public health or safety, or State, local, or tribal governments or communities;

(2) Create a serious inconsistency or otherwise interfere with an action taken or planned by another agency;

(3) Materially alter the budgetary impact of entitlements, grants, user fees, or loan programs or the rights and obligations of recipients thereof; or

(4) Raise novel legal or policy issues arising out of legal mandates, the President's priorities, or the principles set forth in this Executive order.

(g) "Guidance document" means an agency statement of general applicability and future effect other than a regulatory action, that sets forth a policy on a statutory, regulatory, or technical issue or an interpretation of a statutory or regulatory issue.

(h) "Significant guidance document"—

(1) Means a guidance document disseminated to regulated entities or the general public that, for purposes of this order, may reasonably be anticipated to:

(A) Lead to an annual effect of $100 million or more or adversely affect in a material way the economy, a sector of the economy, productivity, competition, jobs, the environment, public health or safety, or State, local, or tribal governments or communities;

(B) Create a serious inconsistency or otherwise interfere with an action taken or planned by another agency;

(C) Materially alter the budgetary impact of entitlements, grants, user fees, or loan programs or the rights or obligations of recipients thereof; or

(D) Raise novel legal or policy issues arising out of legal mandates, the President's priorities, or the principles set forth in this Executive order; and

(2) Does not include:

(A) Guidance documents on regulations issued in accordance with the formal rulemaking provisions of 5 U.S.C. 556, 557;

(B) Guidance documents that pertain to a military or foreign affairs function of the United States, other than procurement regulations and regulations involving the import or export of non-defense articles and services;

(C) Guidance documents on regulations that are limited to agency organization, management, or personnel matters; or

(D) Any other category of guidance documents exempted by the Administrator of OIRA.

§ 4. *Planning Mechanism.* In order to have an effective regulatory program, to provide for coordination of regulations, to maximize consultation and the resolution of potential conflicts at an early stage, to involve the public and its State, local, and tribal officials in regulatory planning, and to ensure that new or revised regulations promote the President's priorities and the principles set forth in this Executive order, these procedures shall be followed, to the extent permitted by law:

(a) Agencies' Policy Meeting. The Director may convene a meeting of agency heads and other government personnel as appropriate to seek a common understanding of priorities and to coordinate regulatory efforts to be accomplished in the upcoming year.

(b) Unified Regulatory Agenda. For purposes of this subsection, the term "agency" or "agencies" shall also include those considered to be independent regulatory agencies, as defined in 44 U.S.C. 3502(10). Each agency shall prepare an agenda of all regulations under development or review, at a time and in a manner specified by the Administrator of OIRA. The description of each regulatory action shall contain, at a minimum, a regulation identifier number, a brief summary of the action, the legal authority for the action, any legal deadline for the action, and the name and telephone number of a knowledgeable agency official. Agencies may incorporate the information required under 5 U.S.C. 602 and 41 U.S.C. 402 into these agendas.

(c) The Regulatory Plan. For purposes of this subsection, the term "agency" or "agencies" shall also include those considered to be independent regulatory agencies, as defined in 44 U.S.C. 3502(10).

EXECUTIVE ORDER 12866

(1) As part of the Unified Regulatory Agenda, beginning in 1994, each agency shall prepare a Regulatory Plan (Plan) of the most important significant regulatory actions that the agency reasonably expects to issue in proposed or final form in that fiscal year or thereafter. Unless specifically authorized by the head of the agency, no rulemaking shall commence nor be included on the Plan without the approval of the agency's Regulatory Policy Office, and the Plan shall contain at a minimum:

(A) A statement of the agency's regulatory objectives and priorities and how they relate to the President's priorities;

(B) A summary of each planned significant regulatory action including, to the extent possible, alternatives to be considered and preliminary estimates of the anticipated costs and benefits of each rule as well as the agency's best estimate of the combined aggregate costs and benefits of all its regulations planned for that calendar year to assist with the identification of priorities;

(C) A summary of the legal basis for each such action, including whether any aspect of the action is required by statute or court order, and specific citation to such statute, order, or other legal authority;

(D) A statement of the need for each such action and, if applicable, how the action will reduce risks to public health, safety, or the environment, as well as how the magnitude of the risk addressed by the action relates to other risks within the jurisdiction of the agency;

(E) The agency's schedule for action, including a statement of any applicable statutory or judicial deadlines; and

(F) The name, address, and telephone number of a person the public may contact for additional information about the planned regulatory action.

(2) Each agency shall forward its Plan to OIRA by June 1st of each year.

(3) Within 10 calendar days after OIRA has received an agency's Plan, OIRA shall circulate it to other affected agencies and the Advisors.

(4) An agency head who believes that a planned regulatory action of another agency may conflict with its own policy or action taken or planned shall promptly notify, in writing, the Administrator of OIRA, who shall forward that communication to the issuing agency and the Advisors.

(5) If the Administrator of OIRA believes that a planned regulatory action of an agency may be inconsistent with the President's priori-

ties or the principles set forth in this Executive order or may be in conflict with any policy or action taken or planned by another agency, the Administrator of OIRA shall promptly notify, in writing, the affected agencies and the Advisors.

(6) The Director may consult with the heads of agencies with respect to their Plans and, in appropriate instances, request further consideration or inter-agency coordination.

(7) The Plans developed by the issuing agency shall be published annually in the October publication of the Unified Regulatory Agenda. This publication shall be made available to the Congress; State, local, and tribal governments; and the public. Any views on any aspect of any agency Plan, including whether any planned regulatory action might conflict with any other planned or existing regulation, impose any unintended consequences on the public, or confer any unclaimed benefits on the public, should be directed to the issuing agency, with a copy to OIRA.

(d) Regulatory Working Group. Within 30 days of the date of this Executive order, the Administrator of OIRA shall convene a Regulatory Working Group ("Working Group"), which shall consist of representatives of the heads of each agency that the Administrator determines to have significant domestic regulatory responsibility and the Advisors. The Administrator of OIRA shall chair the Working Group and shall periodically advise the Director on the activities of the Working Group. The Working Group shall serve as a forum to assist agencies in identifying and analyzing important regulatory issues (including, among others (1) the development of innovative regulatory techniques, (2) the methods, efficacy, and utility of comparative risk assessment in regulatory decision-making, and (3) the development of short forms and other streamlined regulatory approaches for small businesses and other entities). The Working Group shall meet at least quarterly and may meet as a whole or in subgroups of agencies with an interest in particular issues or subject areas. To inform its discussions, the Working Group may commission analytical studies and reports by OIRA, the Administrative Conference of the United States, or any other agency.

(e) Conferences. The Administrator of OIRA shall meet quarterly with representatives of State, local, and tribal governments to identify both existing and proposed regulations that may uniquely or significantly affect those governmental entities. The Administrator of OIRA shall also convene, from time to time, conferences with representatives of businesses, nongovernmental organizations, and the public to discuss regulatory issues of common concern.

§ 5. *Existing Regulations.* In order to reduce the regulatory burden on the American people, their families, their communities, their State, local, and tribal governments, and their industries; to determine whether regulations promulgated by the executive branch of the Federal Government have become unjustified or unnecessary as a result of changed circumstances; to confirm that regulations are both compatible with each other and not duplicative or inappropriately burdensome in the aggregate; to ensure that all regulations are consistent with the President's priorities and the principles set forth in this Executive order, within applicable law; and to otherwise improve the effectiveness of existing regulations:

(a) Within 90 days of the date of this Executive order, each agency shall submit to OIRA a program, consistent with its resources and regulatory priorities, under which the agency will periodically review its existing significant regulations to determine whether any such regulations should be modified or eliminated so as to make the agency's regulatory program more effective in achieving the regulatory objectives, less burdensome, or in greater alignment with the President's priorities and the principles set forth in this Executive order. Any significant regulations selected for review shall be included in the agency's annual Plan. The agency shall also identify any legislative mandates that require the agency to promulgate or continue to impose regulations that the agency believes are unnecessary or outdated by reason of changed circumstances.

(b) The Administrator of OIRA shall work with the Regulatory Working Group and other interested entities to pursue the objectives of this section. State, local, and tribal governments are specifically encouraged to assist in the identification of regulations that impose significant or unique burdens on those governmental entities and that appear to have outlived their justification or be otherwise inconsistent with the public interest.

(c) The Director, in consultation with the Advisors, may identify for review by the appropriate agency or agencies other existing regulations of an agency or groups of regulations of more than one agency that affect a particular group, industry, or sector of the economy, or may identify legislative mandates that may be appropriate for reconsideration by the Congress.

§ 6. *Centralized Review of Regulations.* The guidelines set forth below shall apply to all regulatory actions, for both new and existing regulations, by agencies other than those agencies specifically exempted by the Administrator of OIRA:

(a) **Agency Responsibilities.** (1) Each agency shall (consistent with its own rules, regulations, or procedures) provide the public with meaningful participation in the regulatory process. In particular, before issuing a notice of proposed rulemaking, each agency should, where appropriate, seek the involvement of those who are intended to benefit from and those expected to be burdened by any regulation (including, specifically, State, local, and tribal officials). In addition, each agency should afford the public a meaningful opportunity to comment on any proposed regulation, which in most cases should include a comment period of not less than 60 days. In consultation with OIRA, each agency may also consider whether to utilize formal rulemaking procedures under 5 U.S.C. 556 and 557 for the resolution of complex determinations. Each agency also is directed to explore and, where appropriate, use consensual mechanisms for developing regulations, including negotiated rulemaking.

(2) Within 60 days of the date of this Executive order, each agency head shall designate one of the agency's Presidential Appointees to be its Regulatory Policy Officer, advise OMB of such designation, and annually update OMB on the status of this designation. The Regulatory Policy Officer shall be involved at each stage of the regulatory process to foster the development of effective, innovative, and least burdensome regulations and to further the principles set forth in this Executive order.

(3) In addition to adhering to its own rules and procedures and to the requirements of the Administrative Procedure Act, the Regulatory Flexibility Act, the Paperwork Reduction Act, and other applicable law, each agency shall develop its regulatory actions in a timely fashion and adhere to the following procedures with respect to a regulatory action:

(A) Each agency shall provide OIRA, at such times and in the manner specified by the Administrator of OIRA, with a list of its planned regulatory actions, indicating those which the agency believes are significant regulatory actions within the meaning of this Executive order. Absent a material change in the development of the planned regulatory action, those not designated as significant will not be subject to review under this section unless, within 10 working days of receipt of the list, the Administrator of OIRA notifies the agency that OIRA has determined that a planned regulation is a significant regulatory action within the meaning of this Executive order. The Administrator of OIRA may waive review of any planned regulatory action designated by the agency as significant, in which case the agency need not further comply with subsection (a)(3)(B) or subsection (a)(3)(C) of this section.

(B) For each matter identified as, or determined by the Administrator of OIRA to be, a significant regulatory action, the issuing agency shall provide to OIRA:

(i) The text of the draft regulatory action, together with a reasonably detailed description of the need for the regulatory action and an explanation of how the regulatory action will meet that need; and

(ii) An assessment of the potential costs and benefits of the regulatory action, including an explanation of the manner in which the regulatory action is consistent with a statutory mandate and, to the extent permitted by law, promotes the

President's priorities and avoids undue interference with State, local, and tribal governments in the exercise of their governmental functions.

(C) For those matters identified as, or determined by the Administrator of OIRA to be, a significant regulatory action within the scope of section 3(f)(1), the agency shall also provide to OIRA the following additional information developed as part of the agency's decision-making process (unless prohibited by law):

(i) An assessment, including the underlying analysis, of benefits anticipated from the regulatory action (such as, but not limited to, the promotion of the efficient functioning of the economy and private markets, the enhancement of health and safety, the protection of the natural environment, and the elimination or reduction of discrimination or bias) together with, to the extent feasible, a quantification of those benefits;

(ii) An assessment, including the underlying analysis, of costs anticipated from the regulatory action (such as, but not limited to, the direct cost both to the government in administering the regulation and to businesses and others in complying with the regulation, and any adverse effects on the efficient functioning of the economy, private markets (including productivity, employment, and competitiveness), health, safety, and the natural environment), together with, to the extent feasible, a quantification of those costs; and

(iii) An assessment, including the underlying analysis, of costs and benefits of potentially effective and reasonably feasible alternatives to the planned regulation, identified by the agencies or the public (including improving the current regulation and reasonably viable nonregulatory actions), and an explanation why the planned regulatory action is preferable to the identified potential alternatives.

(D) In emergency situations or when an agency is obligated by law to act more quickly than normal review procedures allow, the agency shall notify OIRA as soon as possible and, to the extent practicable, comply with subsections (a)(3)(B) and (C) of this section. For those regulatory actions that are governed by a statutory or court-imposed deadline, the agency shall, to the extent practicable, schedule rulemaking proceedings so as to permit sufficient time for OIRA to conduct its review, as set forth below in subsection (b)(2) through (4) of this section.

(E) After the regulatory action has been published in the Federal Register or otherwise issued to the public, the agency shall:

(i) Make available to the public the information set forth in subsections (a)(3)(B) and (C);

(ii) Identify for the public, in a complete, clear, and simple manner, the substantive changes between the draft submitted to OIRA for review and the action subsequently announced; and

(iii) Identify for the public those changes in the regulatory action that were made at the suggestion or recommendation of OIRA.

(F) All information provided to the public by the agency shall be in plain, understandable language.

(b) OIRA Responsibilities. The Administrator of OIRA shall provide meaningful guidance and oversight so that each agency's regulatory actions are consistent with applicable law, the President's priorities, and the principles set forth in this Executive order and do not conflict with the policies or actions of another agency. OIRA shall, to the extent permitted by law, adhere to the following guidelines:

(1) OIRA may review only actions identified by the agency or by OIRA as significant regulatory actions under subsection (a)(3)(A) of this section.

(2) OIRA shall waive review or notify the agency in writing of the results of its review within the following time periods:

(A) For any notices of inquiry, advance notices of proposed rulemaking, or other preliminary regulatory actions prior to a Notice of Proposed Rulemaking, within 10 working days after the date of submission of the draft action to OIRA;

(B) For all other regulatory actions, within 90 calendar days after the date of submission of the information set forth in subsections (a)(3)(B) and (C) of this section, unless OIRA has previously reviewed this information and, since that review, there has been no material change in the facts and circumstances upon which the regulatory action is based, in which case, OIRA shall complete its review within 45 days; and

(C) The review process may be extended (1) once by no more than 30 calendar days upon the written approval of the Director and (2) at the request of the agency head.

(3) For each regulatory action that the Administrator of OIRA returns to an agency for further consideration of some or all of its provisions, the Administrator of OIRA shall provide the issuing agency a written explanation for such return, setting forth the pertinent provision of this Executive order on which OIRA is relying. If the agency head disagrees with some or all of the bases for

the return, the agency head shall so inform the Administrator of OIRA in writing.

(4) Except as otherwise provided by law or required by a Court, in order to ensure greater openness, accessibility, and accountability in the regulatory review process, OIRA shall be governed by the following disclosure requirements:

(A) Only the Administrator of OIRA (or a particular designee) shall receive oral communications initiated by persons not employed by the executive branch of the Federal Government regarding the substance of a regulatory action under OIRA review;

(B) All substantive communications between OIRA personnel and persons not employed by the executive branch of the Federal Government regarding a regulatory action under review shall be governed by the following guidelines:

(i) A representative from the issuing agency shall be invited to any meeting between OIRA personnel and such person(s);

(ii) OIRA shall forward to the issuing agency, within 10 working days of receipt of the communication(s), all written communications, regardless of format, between OIRA personnel and any person who is not employed by the executive branch of the Federal Government, and the dates and names of individuals involved in all substantive oral communications (including meetings to which an agency representative was invited, but did not attend, and telephone conversations between OIRA personnel and any such persons); and

(iii) OIRA shall publicly disclose relevant information about such communication(s), as set forth below in subsection (b)(4)(C) of this section.

(C) OIRA shall maintain a publicly available log that shall contain, at a minimum, the following information pertinent to regulatory actions under review:

(i) The status of all regulatory actions, including if (and if so, when and by whom) Presidential consideration was requested;

(ii) A notation of all written communications forwarded to an issuing agency under subsection (b)(4)(B)(ii) of this section; and

(iii) The dates and names of individuals involved in all substantive oral communications, including meetings and telephone conversations, between OIRA personnel and any person not employed by the executive branch of the Federal Government, and the subject matter discussed during such communications.

(D) After the regulatory action has been published in the Federal Register or otherwise issued to the public, or after the agency has announced its decision not to publish or issue the regulatory action, OIRA shall make available to the public all documents exchanged between OIRA and the agency during the review by OIRA under this section.

(5) All information provided to the public by OIRA shall be in plain, understandable language.

§ 7. *Resolution of Conflicts.*

(a) To the extent permitted by law, disagreements or conflicts between or among agency heads or between OMB and any agency that cannot be resolved by the Administrator of OIRA shall be resolved by the President, with the assistance of the Chief of Staff to the President ("Chief of Staff"), with the relevant agency head (and, as appropriate, other interested government officials). Presidential consideration of such disagreements may be initiated only by the Director, by the head of the issuing agency, or by the head of an agency that has a significant interest in the regulatory action at issue. Such review will not be undertaken at the request of other persons, entities, or their agents.

(b) Resolution of such conflicts shall be informed by recommendations developed by the Chief of Staff, after consultation with the Advisors (and other executive branch officials or personnel whose responsibilities to the President include the subject matter at issue). The development of these recommendations shall be concluded within 60 days after review has been requested.

(c) During the Presidential review period, communications with any person not employed by the Federal Government relating to the substance of the regulatory action under review and directed to the Advisors or their staffs or to the staff of the Chief of Staff shall be in writing and shall be forwarded by the recipient to the affected agency(ies) for inclusion in the public docket(s). When the communication is not in writing, such Advisors or staff members shall inform the outside party that the matter is under review and that any comments should be submitted in writing.

(d) At the end of this review process, the President, or the Chief of Staff acting at the request of the President, shall notify the affected agency and the Administrator of OIRA of the President's decision with respect to the matter.

§ 8. *Publication.* Except to the extent required by law, an agency shall not publish in the Federal Register or otherwise issue to the public any regulatory action that is subject to review under section 6 of this

Executive order until (1) the Administrator of OIRA notifies the agency that OIRA has waived its review of the action or has completed its review without any requests for further consideration, or (2) the applicable time period in section 6(b)(2) expires without OIRA having notified the agency that it is returning the regulatory action for further consideration under section 6(b)(3), whichever occurs first. If the terms of the preceding sentence have not been satisfied and an agency wants to publish or otherwise issue a regulatory action, the head of that agency may request Presidential consideration through the Director, as provided under section 7 of this order. Upon receipt of this request, the Director shall notify OIRA and the Advisors. The guidelines and time period set forth in section 7 shall apply to the publication of regulatory actions for which Presidential consideration has been sought.

§ 9. *Significant Guidance Documents.* Each agency shall provide OIRA, at such times and in the manner specified by the Administrator of OIRA, with advance notification of any significant guidance documents. Each agency shall take such steps as are necessary for its Regulatory Policy Officer to ensure the agency's compliance with the requirements of this section. Upon the request of the Administrator, for each matter identified as, or determined by the Administrator to be, a significant guidance document, the issuing agency shall provide to OIRA the content of the draft guidance document, together with a brief explanation of the need for the guidance document and how it will meet that need. The OIRA Administrator shall notify the agency when additional consultation will be required before the issuance of the significant guidance document.

§ 10. *Preservation of Agency Authority.* Nothing in this order shall be construed to impair or otherwise affect the authority vested by law in an agency or the head thereof, including the authority of the Attorney General relating to litigation.

§ 11. *Judicial Review.* Nothing in this Executive order shall affect any otherwise available judicial review of agency action. This Executive order is intended only to improve the internal management of the Federal Government and does not create any right or benefit, substantive or procedural, enforceable at law or equity by a party against the United States, its agencies or instrumentalities, its officers or employees, or any other person.

§ 12. *Revocations.* Executive Orders Nos. 12291 and 12498; all amendments to those Executive orders; all guidelines issued under those orders; and any exemptions from those orders heretofore granted for any category of rule are revoked.

WILLIAM CLINTON
THE WHITE HOUSE
September 30, 1993.

FREEDOM OF INFORMATION ACT

5 U.S.C. § 552

§ 552. Public information; agency rules, opinions, orders, records, and proceedings

(a) Each agency shall make available to the public information as follows:

(1) Each agency shall separately state and currently publish in the Federal Register for the guidance of the public—

(A) descriptions of its central and field organization and the established places at which, the employees (and in the case of a uniformed service, the members) from whom, and the methods whereby, the public may obtain information, make submittals or requests, or obtain decisions;

(B) statements of the general course and method by which its functions are channeled and determined, including the nature and requirements of all formal and informal procedures available;

(C) rules of procedure, descriptions of forms available or the places at which forms may be obtained, and instructions as to the scope and contents of all papers, reports, or examinations;

(D) substantive rules of general applicability adopted as authorized by law, and statements of general policy or interpretations of general applicability formulated and adopted by the agency; and

(E) each amendment, revision, or repeal of the foregoing.

Except to the extent that a person has actual and timely notice of the terms thereof, a person may not in any manner be required to resort to, or be adversely affected by, a matter required to be published in the Federal Register and not so published. For the purpose of this paragraph, matter reasonably available to the class of persons affected thereby is deemed published in the Federal Register when incorporated by reference therein with the approval of the Director of the Federal Register.

(2) Each agency, in accordance with published rules, shall make available for public inspection and copying—

(A) final opinions, including concurring and dissenting opinions, as well as orders, made in the adjudication of cases;

(B) those statements of policy and interpretations which have been adopted by the agency and are not published in the Federal Register;

(C) administrative staff manuals and instructions to staff that affect a member of the public;

(D) copies of all records, regardless of form or format, which have been released to any person under paragraph (3) and which, because of the nature of their subject matter, the agency determines have become or are likely to become the subject of subsequent requests for substantially the same records; and

(E) a general index of the records referred to under subparagraph (D);

unless the materials are promptly published and copies offered for sale. For records created on or after November 1, 1996, within one year after such date, each agency shall make such records available, including by computer telecommunications or, if computer telecommunications means have not been established by the agency, by other electronic means. To the extent required to prevent a clearly unwarranted invasion of personal privacy, an agency may delete identifying details when it makes available or publishes an opinion, statement of policy, interpretation, staff manual, instruction, or copies of records referred to in subparagraph (D). However, in each case the justification for the deletion shall be explained fully in writing, and the extent of such deletion shall be indicated on the portion of the record which is made available or published, unless including that indication would harm an interest protected by the exemption in subsection (b) under which the deletion is made. If technically feasible, the extent of the deletion shall be indicated at the place in the record where the deletion was made. Each agency shall also maintain and make available for public inspection and copying current indexes providing identifying information for the public as to any matter issued, adopted, or promulgated after July 4, 1967, and required by this paragraph to be made available or published. Each agency shall promptly publish, quarterly or more frequently, and distribute (by sale or otherwise) copies of each index or supplements thereto unless it determines by order published in the Federal Register that the publication would be unnecessary and impracticable, in which case the agency shall nonetheless provide copies of such index on request at a cost not to exceed the direct cost of duplication. Each agency shall make the index referred to in subparagraph (E) available by computer telecommunications by December 31, 1999. A final order, opinion, statement of policy, interpretation, or staff manual or instruction that affects a member of the public may be relied on, used, or cited as precedent by an agency against a party other than an agency only if—

(i) it has been indexed and either made available or published as provided by this paragraph; or

(ii) the party has actual and timely notice of the terms thereof.

(3)(A) Except with respect to the records made available under paragraphs (1) and (2) of this subsection, and except as provided in subparagraph (E), each agency, upon any request for records which (i) reasonably describes such records and (ii) is made in accordance with published rules stating the time, place, fees (if any), and procedures to be followed, shall make the records promptly available to any person.

(B) In making any record available to a person under this paragraph, an agency shall provide the record in any form or format requested by the person if the record is readily reproducible by the agency in that form or format. Each agency shall make reasonable efforts to maintain its records in forms or formats that are reproducible for purposes of this section.

(C) In responding under this paragraph to a request for records, an agency shall make reasonable efforts to search for the records in electronic form or format, except when such efforts would significantly interfere with the operation of the agency's automated information system.

(D) For purposes of this paragraph, the term "search" means to review, manually or by automated means, agency records for the purpose of locating those records which are responsive to a request.

(E) An agency, or part of an agency, that is an element of the intelligence community (as that term is defined in section 3(4) of the National Security Act of 1947 (50 U.S.C. 401a(4))) shall not make any record available under this paragraph to—

(i) any government entity, other than a State, territory, commonwealth, or district of the United States, or any subdivision thereof; or

(ii) a representative of a government entity described in clause (i).

(4)(A)(i) In order to carry out the provisions of this section, each agency shall promulgate regulations, pursuant to notice and receipt of public comment, specifying the schedule of fees applicable to the processing of requests under this section and establishing procedures and guidelines for determining when such fees should be waived or reduced. Such schedule shall conform to the guidelines which shall be promulgated, pursuant to notice and receipt of public comment, by the Director of the Office of Management and Budget and which shall provide for a uniform schedule of fees for all agencies.

(ii) Such agency regulations shall provide that—

(I) fees shall be limited to reasonable standard charges for document search, duplication, and review, when records are requested for commercial use;

(II) fees shall be limited to reasonable standard charges for document duplication when records are not sought for commercial use and the request is made by an educational or noncommercial scientific institution, whose purpose is scholarly or scientific research; or a representative of the news media; and

(III) for any request not described in (I) or (II), fees shall be limited to reasonable standard charges for document search and duplication.

(iii) Documents shall be furnished without any charge or at a charge reduced below the fees established under clause (ii) if disclosure of the information is in the public interest because it is likely to contribute significantly to public understanding of the operations or activities of the government and is not primarily in the commercial interest of the requester.

(iv) Fee schedules shall provide for the recovery of only the direct costs of search, duplication, or review. Review costs shall include only the direct costs incurred during the initial examination of a document for the purposes of determining whether the documents must be disclosed under this section and for the purposes of withholding any portions exempt from disclosure under this section. Review costs may not include any costs incurred in resolving issues of law or policy that may be raised in the course of processing a request under this section. No fee may be charged by any agency under this section—

(I) if the costs of routine collection and processing of the fee are likely to equal or exceed the amount of the fee; or

(II) for any request described in clause (ii)(II) or (III) of this subparagraph for the first two hours of search time or for the first one hundred pages of duplication.

(v) No agency may require advance payment of any fee unless the requester has previously failed to pay fees in a timely fashion, or the agency has determined that the fee will exceed $250.

(vi) Nothing in this subparagraph shall supersede fees chargeable under a statute specifically providing for setting the level of fees for particular types of records.

(vii) In any action by a requester regarding the waiver of fees under this section, the court shall determine the matter de novo: Provided, That the court's review of the matter shall be limited to the record before the agency.

(B) On complaint, the district court of the United States in the district in which the complainant resides, or has his principal place of business, or in which the agency records are situated, or in the District of Columbia, has jurisdiction to enjoin the agency from withholding agency records and to order the production of any agency records improperly withheld from the complainant. In such a case the court shall determine the matter de novo, and may examine the contents of such agency records in camera to determine whether such records or any part thereof shall be withheld under any of the exemptions set forth in subsection (b) of this section, and the burden is on the agency to sustain its action. In addition to any other matters to which a court accords substantial weight, a court shall accord substantial weight to an affidavit of an agency concerning the agency's determination as to technical feasibility under paragraph (2)(C) and subsection (b) and reproducibility under paragraph (3)(B).

(C) Notwithstanding any other provision of law, the defendant shall serve an answer or otherwise plead to any complaint made under this subsection within thirty days after service upon the defendant of the pleading in which such complaint is made, unless the court otherwise directs for good cause shown.

[(D) Repealed. Pub.L. 98–620, Title IV, § 402(2), Nov. 8, 1984, 98 Stat. 3357]

(E) The court may assess against the United States reasonable attorney fees and other litigation costs reasonably incurred in any case under this section in which the complainant has substantially prevailed.

(F) Whenever the court orders the production of any agency records improperly withheld from the complainant and assesses against the United States reasonable attorney fees and other litigation costs, and the court additionally issues a written finding that the circumstances surrounding the withholding raise questions whether agency personnel acted arbitrarily or capriciously with respect to the withholding, the Special Counsel shall promptly initiate a proceeding to determine whether disciplinary action is warranted against the officer or employee who was primarily responsible for the withholding. The Special Counsel, after investigation and consideration of the evidence submitted, shall submit his findings and recommendations to the administrative authority of the agency concerned and shall send copies of the findings and recommendations to the officer or employee or his representative. The administrative authority shall take the corrective action that the Special Counsel recommends.

(G) In the event of noncompliance with the order of the court, the district court may punish for contempt the responsible employee, and in the case of a uniformed service, the responsible member.

(5) Each agency having more than one member shall maintain and make available for public inspection a record of the final votes of each member in every agency proceeding.

(6)(A) Each agency, upon any request for records made under paragraph (1), (2), or (3) of this subsection, shall—

>(i) determine within 20 days (excepting Saturdays, Sundays, and legal public holidays) after the receipt of any such request whether to comply with such request and shall immediately notify the person making such request of such determination and the reasons therefor, and of the right of such person to appeal to the head of the agency any adverse determination; and

>(ii) make a determination with respect to any appeal within ten days (excepting Saturdays, Sundays, and legal public holidays) after the receipt of such appeal. If on appeal the denial of the request for records is in whole or in part upheld, the agency shall notify the person making such request of the provisions for judicial review of that determination under paragraph (4) of this subsection.

(B)(i) In unusual circumstances as specified in this subparagraph, the time limits prescribed in either clause (i) or clause (ii) of subparagraph (A) may be extended by written notice to the person making such request setting forth the unusual circumstances for such extension and the date on which a determination is expected to be dispatched. No such notice shall specify a date that would result in an extension for more than ten working days, except as provided in clause (ii) of this subparagraph.

>(ii) With respect to a request for which a written notice under clause (i) extends the time limits prescribed under clause (i) of subparagraph (A), the agency shall notify the person making the request if the request cannot be processed within the time limit specified in that clause and shall provide the person an opportunity to limit the scope of the request so that it may be processed within that time limit or an opportunity to arrange with the agency an alternative time frame for processing the request or a

modified request. Refusal by the person to reasonably modify the request or arrange such an alternative time frame shall be considered as a factor in determining whether exceptional circumstances exist for purposes of subparagraph (C).

(iii) As used in this subparagraph, "unusual circumstances" means, but only to the extent reasonably necessary to the proper processing of the particular requests—

(I) the need to search for and collect the requested records from field facilities or other establishments that are separate from the office processing the request;

(II) the need to search for, collect, and appropriately examine a voluminous amount of separate and distinct records which are demanded in a single request; or

(III) the need for consultation, which shall be conducted with all practicable speed, with another agency having a substantial interest in the determination of the request or among two or more components of the agency having substantial subject-matter interest therein.

(iv) Each agency may promulgate regulations, pursuant to notice and receipt of public comment, providing for the aggregation of certain requests by the same requestor, or by a group of requestors acting in concert, if the agency reasonably believes that such requests actually constitute a single request, which would otherwise satisfy the unusual circumstances specified in this subparagraph, and the requests involve clearly related matters. Multiple requests involving unrelated matters shall not be aggregated.

(C)(i) Any person making a request to any agency for records under paragraph (1), (2), or (3) of this subsection shall be deemed to have exhausted his administrative remedies with respect to such request if the agency fails to comply with the applicable time limit provisions of this paragraph. If the Government can show exceptional circumstances exist and that the agency is exercising due diligence in responding to the request, the court may retain jurisdiction and allow the agency additional time to complete its review of the records. Upon any determination by an agency to comply with a request for records, the records shall be made promptly available to such person making such request. Any notification of denial of any request for records under this subsection shall set forth the names and titles or positions of each person responsible for the denial of such request.

(ii) For purposes of this subparagraph, the term "exceptional circumstances" does not include a delay that results from a predictable agency workload of requests under this section, unless the agency demonstrates reasonable progress in reducing its backlog of pending requests.

(iii) Refusal by a person to reasonably modify the scope of a request or arrange an alternative time frame for processing a request (or a modified request) under clause (ii) after being given an opportunity to do so by the agency to whom the person made the request shall be considered as a factor in determining whether exceptional circumstances exist for purposes of this subparagraph.

(D)(i) Each agency may promulgate regulations, pursuant to notice and receipt of public comment, providing for multitrack processing of requests for records based on the amount of work or time (or both) involved in processing requests.

(ii) Regulations under this subparagraph may provide a person making a request that does not qualify for the fastest multitrack processing an opportunity to limit the scope of the request in order to qualify for faster processing.

(iii) This subparagraph shall not be considered to affect the requirement under subparagraph (C) to exercise due diligence.

(E)(i) Each agency shall promulgate regulations, pursuant to notice and receipt of public comment, providing for expedited processing of requests for records—

(I) in cases in which the person requesting the records demonstrates a compelling need; and

(II) in other cases determined by the agency.

(ii) Notwithstanding clause (i), regulations under this subparagraph must ensure—

(I) that a determination of whether to provide expedited processing shall be made, and notice of the determination shall be provided to the person making the request, within 10 days after the date of the request; and

(II) expeditious consideration of administrative appeals of such determinations of whether to provide expedited processing.

(iii) An agency shall process as soon as practicable any request for records to which the agency has granted expedited processing under this subparagraph. Agency action to deny or affirm denial of a request for expedited processing pursuant to this subparagraph, and failure by an agency to respond in a timely manner to such a request shall be subject to judicial review under paragraph (4), except that the judicial review shall be based on the record before the agency at the time of the determination.

(iv) A district court of the United States shall not have jurisdiction to review an agency denial of expedited processing of a request for records after the agency has provided a complete response to the request.

(v) For purposes of this subparagraph, the term "compelling need" means—

(I) that a failure to obtain requested records on an expedited basis under this paragraph could reasonably be expected to pose an imminent threat to the life or physical safety of an individual; or

(II) with respect to a request made by a person primarily engaged in disseminating information, urgency to inform the public concerning actual or alleged Federal Government activity.

(vi) A demonstration of a compelling need by a person making a request for expedited processing shall be made by a statement certified by such person to be true and correct to the best of such person's knowledge and belief.

(F) In denying a request for records, in whole or in part, an agency shall make a reasonable effort to estimate the volume of any requested matter the provision of which is denied, and shall provide any such estimate to the person making the request, unless providing such estimate would harm an interest protected by the exemption in subsection (b) pursuant to which the denial is made.

(b) This section does not apply to matters that are—

(1)(A) specifically authorized under criteria established by an Executive order to be kept secret in the interest of national defense or foreign policy and (B) are in fact properly classified pursuant to such Executive order;

(2) related solely to the internal personnel rules and practices of an agency;

(3) specifically exempted from disclosure by statute (other than section 552b of this title), provided that such statute (A) requires that the matters be withheld from the public in such a manner as to leave no discretion on the issue, or (B) establishes particular criteria

for withholding or refers to particular types of matters to be withheld;

(4) trade secrets and commercial or financial information obtained from a person and privileged or confidential;

(5) inter-agency or intra-agency memorandums or letters which would not be available by law to a party other than an agency in litigation with the agency;

(6) personnel and medical files and similar files the disclosure of which would constitute a clearly unwarranted invasion of personal privacy;

(7) records or information compiled for law enforcement purposes, but only to the extent that the production of such law enforcement records or information (A) could reasonably be expected to interfere with enforcement proceedings, (B) would deprive a person of a right to a fair trial or an impartial adjudication, (C) could reasonably be expected to constitute an unwarranted invasion of personal privacy, (D) could reasonably be expected to disclose the identity of a confidential source, including a State, local, or foreign agency or authority or any private institution which furnished information on a confidential basis, and, in the case of a record or information compiled by criminal law enforcement authority in the course of a criminal investigation or by an agency conducting a lawful national security intelligence investigation, information furnished by a confidential source, (E) would disclose techniques and procedures for law enforcement investigations or prosecutions, or would disclose guidelines for law enforcement investigations or prosecutions if such disclosure could reasonably be expected to risk circumvention of the law, or (F) could reasonably be expected to endanger the life or physical safety of any individual;

(8) contained in or related to examination, operating, or condition reports prepared by, on behalf of, or for the use of an agency responsible for the regulation or supervision of financial institutions; or

(9) geological and geophysical information and data, including maps, concerning wells.

Any reasonably segregable portion of a record shall be provided to any person requesting such record after deletion of the portions which are exempt under this subsection. The amount of information deleted shall be indicated on the released portion of the record, unless including that indication would harm an interest protected by the exemption in this subsection under which the deletion is made. If technically feasible, the amount of the information deleted shall be indicated at the place in the record where such deletion is made.

(c)(1) Whenever a request is made which involves access to records described in subsection (b)(7)(A) and—

    (A) the investigation or proceeding involves a possible violation of criminal law; and

    (B) there is reason to believe that (i) the subject of the investigation or proceeding is not aware of its pendency, and (ii) disclosure of the existence of the records could reasonably be expected to interfere with enforcement proceedings, the agency may, during only such time as that circumstance continues, treat the records as not subject to the requirements of this section.

(2) Whenever informant records maintained by a criminal law enforcement agency under an informant's name or personal identifier are requested by a third party according to the informant's name or personal identifier, the agency may treat the records as not subject to the requirements of this section unless the informant's status as an informant has been officially confirmed.

(3) Whenever a request is made which involves access to records maintained by the Federal Bureau of Investigation pertaining to foreign intelligence or counterintelligence, or international terrorism, and the existence of the records is classified information as provided in subsection (b)(1), the Bureau may, as long as the existence of the records remains classified information, treat the records as not subject to the requirements of this section.

(d) This section does not authorize withholding of information or limit the availability of records to the public, except as specifically stated in this section. This section is not authority to withhold information from Congress.

(e)(1) On or before February 1 of each year, each agency shall submit to the Attorney General of the United States a report which shall cover the preceding fiscal year and which shall include—

    (A) the number of determinations made by the agency not to comply with requests for records made to such agency under subsection (a) and the reasons for each such determination;

    (B)(i) the number of appeals made by persons under subsection (a)(6), the result of such appeals, and the reason for the action upon each appeal that results in a denial of information; and

        (ii) a complete list of all statutes that the agency relies upon to authorize the agency to withhold information under subsection (b)(3), a description of whether a court has upheld the decision of the agency to withhold information under each such statute, and a concise description of the scope of any information withheld;

(C) the number of requests for records pending before the agency as of September 30 of the preceding year, and the median number of days that such requests had been pending before the agency as of that date;

(D) the number of requests for records received by the agency and the number of requests which the agency processed;

(E) the median number of days taken by the agency to process different types of requests;

(F) the total amount of fees collected by the agency for processing requests; and

(G) the number of full-time staff of the agency devoted to processing requests for records under this section, and the total amount expended by the agency for processing such requests.

(2) Each agency shall make each such report available to the public including by computer telecommunications, or if computer telecommunications means have not been established by the agency, by other electronic means.

(3) The Attorney General of the United States shall make each report which has been made available by electronic means available at a single electronic access point. The Attorney General of the United States shall notify the Chairman and ranking minority member of the Committee on Government Reform and Oversight of the House of Representatives and the Chairman and ranking minority member of the Committees on Governmental Affairs and the Judiciary of the Senate, no later than April 1 of the year in which each such report is issued, that such reports are available by electronic means.

(4) The Attorney General of the United States, in consultation with the Director of the Office of Management and Budget, shall develop reporting and performance guidelines in connection with reports required by this subsection by October 1, 1997, and may establish additional requirements for such reports as the Attorney General determines may be useful.

(5) The Attorney General of the United States shall submit an annual report on or before April 1 of each calendar year which shall include for the prior calendar year a listing of the number of cases arising under this section, the exemption involved in each case, the disposition of such case, and the cost, fees, and penalties assessed under subparagraphs (E), (F), and (G) of subsection (a)(4). Such report shall also include a description of the efforts undertaken by the Department of Justice to encourage agency compliance with this section.

(f) For purposes of this section, the term—

(1) "agency" as defined in section 551(1) of this title includes any executive department, military department, Government corporation, Government controlled corporation, or other establishment in the executive branch of the Government (including the Executive Office of the President), or any independent regulatory agency; and

(2) "record" and any other term used in this section in reference to information includes any information that would be an agency record subject to the requirements of this section when maintained by an agency in any format, including an electronic format.

(g) The head of each agency shall prepare and make publicly available upon request, reference material or a guide for requesting records or information from the agency, subject to the exemptions in subsection (b), including—

(1) an index of all major information systems of the agency;

(2) a description of major information and record locator systems maintained by the agency; and

(3) a handbook for obtaining various types and categories of public information from the agency pursuant to chapter 35 of title 44, and under this section.

CRITICAL INFORMATION INFRASTRUCTURE ACT

TITLE 6. DOMESTIC SECURITY
CHAPTER 1—HOMELAND SECURITY ORGANIZATION
SUBCHAPTER II—INFORMATION ANALYSIS AND INFRASTRUCTURE PROTECTION
PART B—Critical Infrastructure Information

§ 131. Definitions

In this part:

(1) AGENCY. The term "agency" has the meaning given it in section 551 of Title 5.

(2) COVERED FEDERAL AGENCY. The term "covered Federal agency" means the Department of Homeland Security.

(3) CRITICAL INFRASTRUCTURE INFORMATION. The term "critical infrastructure information" means information not customarily in the public domain and related to the security of critical infrastructure or protected systems—

(A) actual, potential, or threatened interference with, attack on, compromise of, or incapacitation of critical infrastructure or protected systems by either physical or computer-based attack or other similar conduct (including the misuse of or unauthorized access to all types of communications and data transmission systems) that violates Federal, State, or local law, harms interstate commerce of the United States, or threatens public health or safety;

(B) the ability of any critical infrastructure or protected system to resist such interference, compromise, or incapacitation, including any planned or past assessment, projection, or estimate of the vulnerability of critical infrastructure or a protected system, including security testing, risk evaluation thereto, risk management planning, or risk audit; or

(C) any planned or past operational problem or solution regarding critical infrastructure or protected systems, including repair, recovery, reconstruction, insurance, or continuity, to the extent it is related to such interference, compromise, or incapacitation.

(4) CRITICAL INFRASTRUCTURE PROTECTION PROGRAM. The term "critical infrastructure protection program" means any component or bureau of a covered Federal agency that has been designated by the President or any agency head to receive critical infrastructure information.

(5). INFORMATION SHARING AND ANALYSIS ORGANIZATION. The term "Information Sharing and Analysis Organization" means any formal or informal entity or collaboration created or employed by public or private sector organizations, for purposes of—

(A) gathering and analyzing critical infrastructure information in order to better understand security problems and interdependencies related to critical infrastructure and protected systems, so as to ensure the availability, integrity, and reliability thereof;

(B) communicating or disclosing critical infrastructure information to help prevent, detect, mitigate, or recover from the effects of a[1] interference, compromise, or a[2] incapacitation problem related to critical infrastructure or protected systems; and

(C) voluntarily disseminating critical infrastructure information to its members, State, local, and Federal Governments, or any other entities that may be of assistance in carrying out the purposes specified in subparagraphs (A) and (B).

(6) PROTECTED SYSTEM. The term "protected system"—

(A) means any service, physical or computer-based system, process, or procedure that directly or indirectly affects the viability of a facility of critical infrastructure; and

(B) includes any physical or computer-based system, including a computer, computer system, computer or communications network, or any component hardware or element thereof, software program, processing instructions, or information or data in transmission or storage therein, irrespective of the medium of transmission or storage.

(7) VOLUNTARY

(A) IN GENERAL. The term "voluntary", in the case of any submittal of critical infrastructure information to a covered Federal agency, means the submittal thereof in the absence of such agency's exercise of legal authority to compel access to or submission of such information and may be accomplished by a

1. So in original. Probably should be "an".

2. So in original. The word "a" probably should not appear.

single entity or an Information Sharing and Analysis Organization on behalf of itself or its members.

(B) EXCLUSIONS. The term "voluntary"—

(i) in the case of any action brought under the securities laws as is defined in section 78c(a)(47) of Title 15—

(I) does not include information or statements contained in any documents or materials filed with the Securities and Exchange Commission, or with Federal banking regulators, pursuant to section 78l(i) of Title 15; and

(II) with respect to the submittal of critical infrastructure information, does not include any disclosure or writing that when made accompanied the solicitation of an offer or a sale of securities; and

(ii) does not include information or statements submitted or relied upon as a basis for making licensing or permitting determinations, or during regulatory proceedings.

§ 132. Designation of critical infrastructure protection program

A critical infrastructure protection program may be designated as such by one of the following:

(1) The President.

(2) The Secretary of Homeland Security.

§ 133. Protection of voluntarily shared critical infrastructure information

(a) PROTECTION

(1) IN GENERAL. Notwithstanding any other provision of law, critical infrastructure information (including the identity of the submitting person or entity) that is voluntarily submitted to a covered Federal agency for use by that agency regarding the security of critical infrastructure and protected systems, analysis, warning, interdependency study, recovery, reconstitution, or other informational purpose, when accompanied by an express statement specified in paragraph (2)—

(A) shall be exempt from disclosure under section 552 of Title 5 (commonly referred to as the Freedom of Information Act);

(B) shall not be subject to any agency rules or judicial doctrine regarding ex parte communications with a decision making official;

(C) shall not, without the written consent of the person or entity submitting such information, be used directly by such agency, any other Federal, State, or local authority, or any third party, in any civil action arising under Federal or State law if such information is submitted in good faith;

(D) shall not, without the written consent of the person or entity submitting such information, be used or disclosed by any officer or employee of the United States for purposes other than the purposes of this part, except—

(i) in furtherance of an investigation or the prosecution of a criminal act; or

(ii) when disclosure of the information would be—

(I) to either House of Congress, or to the extent of matter within its jurisdiction, any committee or subcommittee thereof, any joint committee thereof or subcommittee of any such joint committee; or

(II) to the Comptroller General, or any authorized representative of the Comptroller General, in the course of the performance of the duties of the Government Accountability Office.[3]

(E) shall not, if provided to a State or local government or government agency—

(i) be made available pursuant to any State or local law requiring disclosure of information or records;

(ii) otherwise be disclosed or distributed to any party by said State or local government or government agency without the written consent of the person or entity submitting such information; or

(iii) be used other than for the purpose of protecting critical infrastructure or protected systems, or in furtherance of an investigation or the prosecution of a criminal act; and

(F) does not constitute a waiver of any applicable privilege or protection provided under law, such as trade secret protection.

(2) EXPRESS STATEMENT. For purposes of paragraph (1), the term "express statement", with respect to information or records, means—

(A) in the case of written information or records, a written marking on the information or records substantially similar to the following: "This information is voluntarily submitted to the Federal Government in expectation of protection from disclo-

3. So in original. The period probably should be a semicolon.

sure as provided by the provisions of the Critical Infrastructure Information Act of 2002."; or

(B) in the case of oral information, a similar written statement submitted within a reasonable period following the oral communication.

(b) LIMITATION. No communication of critical infrastructure information to a covered Federal agency made pursuant to this subtitle shall be considered to be an action subject to the requirements of the Federal Advisory Committee Act (5 U.S.C. App. 2).

(c) INDEPENDENTLY OBTAINED INFORMATION. Nothing in this section shall be construed to limit or otherwise affect the ability of a State, local, or Federal Government entity, agency, or authority, or any third party, under applicable law, to obtain critical infrastructure information in a manner not covered by subsection (a) of this section, including any information lawfully and properly disclosed generally or broadly to the public and to use such information in any manner permitted by law.

(d) TREATMENT OF VOLUNTARILY SUBMITTAL OF INFORMATION. The voluntary submittal to the Government of information or records that are protected from disclosure by this subtitle shall not be construed to constitute compliance with any requirement to submit such information to a Federal agency under any other provision of law.

(e) PROCEDURES

(1) IN GENERAL. The Secretary of the Department of Homeland Security shall, in consultation with appropriate representatives of the National Security Council and the Office of Science and Technology Policy, establish uniform procedures for the receipt, care, and storage by Federal agencies of critical infrastructure information that is voluntarily submitted to the Government. The procedures shall be established not later than 90 days after November 25, 2002.

(2) ELEMENTS. The procedures established under paragraph (1) shall include mechanisms regarding—

(A) the acknowledgement of receipt by Federal agencies of critical infrastructure information that is voluntarily submitted to the Government;

(B) the maintenance of the identification of such information as voluntarily submitted to the Government for purposes of and subject to the provisions of this subtitle;

(C) the care and storage of such information; and

(D) the protection and maintenance of the confidentiality of such information so as to permit the sharing of such information within the Federal Government and with State and local governments, and the issuance of notices and warnings related to the protection of critical infrastructure and protected systems, in such manner as to protect from public disclosure the identity of the submitting person or entity, or information that is proprietary, business sensitive, relates specifically to the submitting person or entity, and is otherwise not appropriately in the public domain.

(f) PENALTIES. Whoever, being an officer or employee of the United States or of any department or agency thereof, knowingly publishes, divulges, discloses, or makes known in any manner or to any extent not authorized by law, any critical infrastructure information protected from disclosure by this subtitle coming to him in the course of this employment or official duties or by reason of any examination or investigation made by, or return, report, or record made to or filed with, such department or agency or officer or employee thereof, shall be fined under Title 18, imprisoned not more than 1 year, or both, and shall be removed from office or employment.

(g) AUTHORITY TO ISSUE WARNINGS. The Federal Government may provide advisories, alerts, and warnings to relevant companies, targeted sectors, other governmental entities, or the general public regarding potential threats to critical infrastructure as appropriate. In issuing a warning, the Federal Government shall take appropriate actions to protect from disclosure—

(1) the source of any voluntarily submitted critical infrastructure information that forms the basis for the warning; or

(2) information that is proprietary, business sensitive, relates specifically to the submitting person or entity, or is otherwise not appropriately in the public domain.

(h) AUTHORITY TO DELEGATE. The President may delegate authority to a critical infrastructure protection program, designated under section 132 of this title, to enter into a voluntary agreement to promote critical infrastructure security, including with any Information Sharing and Analysis Organization, or a plan of action as otherwise defined in section 2158 of the Appendix to Title 50.

§ 134. No private right of action

Nothing in this part may be construed to create a private right of action for enforcement of any provision of this Act.

PRIVACY ACT OF 1974

5 U.S.C. § 552a

§ 552a. Records maintained on individuals

(a) Definitions.—For purposes of this section—

(1) the term "agency" means agency as defined in section 552(e) of this title;

(2) the term "individual" means a citizen of the United States or an alien lawfully admitted for permanent residence;

(3) the term "maintain" includes maintain, collect, use, or disseminate;

(4) the term "record" means any item, collection, or grouping of information about an individual that is maintained by an agency, including, but not limited to, his education, financial transactions, medical history, and criminal or employment history and that contains his name, or the identifying number, symbol, or other identifying particular assigned to the individual, such as a finger or voice print or a photograph;

(5) the term "system of records" means a group of any records under the control of any agency from which information is retrieved by the name of the individual or by some identifying number, symbol, or other identifying particular assigned to the individual;

(6) the term "statistical record" means a record in a system of records maintained for statistical research or reporting purposes only and not used in whole or in part in making any determination about an identifiable individual, except as provided by section 8 of title 13;

(7) the term "routine use" means, with respect to the disclosure of a record, the use of such record for a purpose which is compatible with the purpose for which it was collected;

(8) the term "matching program"—

(A) means any computerized comparison of—

(i) two or more automated systems of records or a system of records with non-Federal records for the purpose of—

(I) establishing or verifying the eligibility of, or continuing compliance with statutory and regulatory requirements by, applicants for, recipients or beneficiaries of, participants in, or providers of services with respect to, cash or in-kind assistance or payments under Federal benefit programs, or

(II) recouping payments or delinquent debts under such Federal benefit programs, or

(ii) two or more automated Federal personnel or payroll systems of records or a system of Federal personnel or payroll records with non-Federal records,

(B) but does not include—

(i) matches performed to produce aggregate statistical data without any personal identifiers;

(ii) matches performed to support any research or statistical project, the specific data of which may not be used to make decisions concerning the rights, benefits, or privileges of specific individuals;

(iii) matches performed, by an agency (or component thereof) which performs as its principal function any activity pertaining to the enforcement of criminal laws, subsequent to the initiation of a specific criminal or civil law enforcement investigation of a named person or persons for the purpose of gathering evidence against such person or persons;

(iv) matches of tax information (I) pursuant to section 6103(d) of the Internal Revenue Code of 1986, (II) for purposes of tax administration as defined in section 6103(b)(4) of such Code, (III) for the purpose of intercepting a tax refund due an individual under authority granted by section 404(e), 464, or 1137 of the Social Security Act; or (IV) for the purpose of intercepting a tax refund due an individual under any other tax refund intercept program authorized by statute which has been determined by the Director of the Office of Management and Budget to contain verification, notice, and hearing requirements that are substantially similar to the procedures in section 1137 of the Social Security Act;

(v) matches—

(I) using records predominantly relating to Federal personnel, that are performed for routine administrative purposes (subject to guidance provided by the Director of the Office of Management and Budget pursuant to subsection (v)); or

(II) conducted by an agency using only records from systems of records maintained by that agency;

if the purpose of the match is not to take any adverse financial, personnel, disciplinary, or other adverse action against Federal personnel[1]

(vi) matches performed for foreign counterintelligence purposes or to produce background checks for security clearances of Federal personnel or Federal contractor personnel; or

(vii) matches performed incident to a levy described in section 6103(k)(8) of the Internal Revenue Code of 1986;

(9) the term "recipient agency" means any agency, or contractor thereof, receiving records contained in a system of records from a source agency for use in a matching program;

(10) the term "non-Federal agency" means any State or local government, or agency thereof, which receives records contained in a system of records from a source agency for use in a matching program;

(11) the term "source agency" means any agency which discloses records contained in a system of records to be used in a matching program, or any State or local government, or agency thereof, which discloses records to be used in a matching program;

(12) the term "Federal benefit program" means any program administered or funded by the Federal Government, or by any agent or State on behalf of the Federal Government, providing cash or in-kind assistance in the form of payments, grants, loans, or loan guarantees to individuals; and

(13) the term "Federal personnel" means officers and employees of the Government of the United States, members of the uniformed services (including members of the Reserve Components), individuals[2] entitled to receive immediate or deferred retirement benefits under any retirement program of the Government of the United States (including survivor benefits).

(b) Conditions of disclosure.—No agency shall disclose any record which is contained in a system of records by any means of communication to any person, or to another agency, except pursuant to a written request by, or with the prior written consent of, the individual to whom the record pertains, unless disclosure of the record would be—

(1) to those officers and employees of the agency which maintains the record who have a need for the record in the performance of their duties;

(2) required under section 552 of this title;

(3) for a routine use as defined in subsection (a)(7) of this section and described under subsection (e)(4)(D) of this section;

---

1. So in original. Probably should be "personnel;".

2. So in original. Probably should be "and individuals".

(4) to the Bureau of the Census for purposes of planning or carrying out a census or survey or related activity pursuant to the provisions of title 13;

(5) to a recipient who has provided the agency with advance adequate written assurance that the record will be used solely as a statistical research or reporting record, and the record is to be transferred in a form that is not individually identifiable;

(6) to the National Archives and Records Administration as a record which has sufficient historical or other value to warrant its continued preservation by the United States Government, or for evaluation by the Archivist of the United States or the designee of the Archivist to determine whether the record has such value;

(7) to another agency or to an instrumentality of any governmental jurisdiction within or under the control of the United States for a civil or criminal law enforcement activity if the activity is authorized by law, and if the head of the agency or instrumentality has made a written request to the agency which maintains the record specifying the particular portion desired and the law enforcement activity for which the record is sought;

(8) to a person pursuant to a showing of compelling circumstances affecting the health or safety of an individual if upon such disclosure notification is transmitted to the last known address of such individual;

(9) to either House of Congress, or, to the extent of matter within its jurisdiction, any committee or subcommittee thereof, any joint committee of Congress or subcommittee of any such joint committee;

(10) to the Comptroller General, or any of his authorized representatives, in the course of the performance of the duties of the Government Accountability Office;

(11) pursuant to the order of a court of competent jurisdiction; or

(12) to a consumer reporting agency in accordance with section 3711(e) of title 31.

(c) Accounting of certain disclosures.—Each agency, with respect to each system of records under its control, shall—

(1) except for disclosures made under subsections (b)(1) or (b)(2) of this section, keep an accurate accounting of—

(A) the date, nature, and purpose of each disclosure of a record to any person or to another agency made under subsection (b) of this section; and

(B) the name and address of the person or agency to whom the disclosure is made;

(2) retain the accounting made under paragraph (1) of this subsection for at least five years or the life of the record, whichever is longer, after the disclosure for which the accounting is made;

(3) except for disclosures made under subsection (b)(7) of this section, make the accounting made under paragraph (1) of this subsection available to the individual named in the record at his request; and

(4) inform any person or other agency about any correction or notation of dispute made by the agency in accordance with subsection (d) of this section of any record that has been disclosed to the person or agency if an accounting of the disclosure was made.

(d) Access to records.—Each agency that maintains a system of records shall—

(1) upon request by any individual to gain access to his record or to any information pertaining to him which is contained in the system, permit him and upon his request, a person of his own choosing to accompany him, to review the record and have a copy made of all or any portion thereof in a form comprehensible to him, except that the agency may require the individual to furnish a written statement authorizing discussion of that individual's record in the accompanying person's presence;

(2) permit the individual to request amendment of a record pertaining to him and—

    (A) not later than 10 days (excluding Saturdays, Sundays, and legal public holidays) after the date of receipt of such request, acknowledge in writing such receipt; and

    (B) promptly, either—

        (i) make any correction of any portion thereof which the individual believes is not accurate, relevant, timely, or complete; or

        (ii) inform the individual of its refusal to amend the record in accordance with his request, the reason for the refusal, the procedures established by the agency for the individual to request a review of that refusal by the head of the agency or an officer designated by the head of the agency, and the name and business address of that official;

(3) permit the individual who disagrees with the refusal of the agency to amend his record to request a review of such refusal, and not later than 30 days (excluding Saturdays, Sundays, and legal public holidays) from the date on which the individual requests such review, complete such review and make a final determination unless, for good cause shown, the head of the agency extends such 30–day period; and if, after his review, the reviewing official also refuses to

amend the record in accordance with the request, permit the individual to file with the agency a concise statement setting forth the reasons for his disagreement with the refusal of the agency, and notify the individual of the provisions for judicial review of the reviewing official's determination under subsection (g)(1)(A) of this section;

(4) in any disclosure, containing information about which the individual has filed a statement of disagreement, occurring after the filing of the statement under paragraph (3) of this subsection, clearly note any portion of the record which is disputed and provide copies of the statement and, if the agency deems it appropriate, copies of a concise statement of the reasons of the agency for not making the amendments requested, to persons or other agencies to whom the disputed record has been disclosed; and

(5) nothing in this section shall allow an individual access to any information compiled in reasonable anticipation of a civil action or proceeding.

(e) Agency requirements.—Each agency that maintains a system of records shall—

(1) maintain in its records only such information about an individual as is relevant and necessary to accomplish a purpose of the agency required to be accomplished by statute or by executive order of the President;

(2) collect information to the greatest extent practicable directly from the subject individual when the information may result in adverse determinations about an individual's rights, benefits, and privileges under Federal programs;

(3) inform each individual whom it asks to supply information, on the form which it uses to collect the information or on a separate form that can be retained by the individual—

(A) the authority (whether granted by statute, or by executive order of the President) which authorizes the solicitation of the information and whether disclosure of such information is mandatory or voluntary;

(B) the principal purpose or purposes for which the information is intended to be used;

(C) the routine uses which may be made of the information, as published pursuant to paragraph (4)(D) of this subsection; and

(D) the effects on him, if any, of not providing all or any part of the requested information;

(4) subject to the provisions of paragraph (11) of this subsection, publish in the Federal Register upon establishment or revision a

notice of the existence and character of the system of records, which notice shall include—

(A) the name and location of the system;

(B) the categories of individuals on whom records are maintained in the system;

(C) the categories of records maintained in the system;

(D) each routine use of the records contained in the system, including the categories of users and the purpose of such use;

(E) the policies and practices of the agency regarding storage, retrievability, access controls, retention, and disposal of the records;

(F) the title and business address of the agency official who is responsible for the system of records;

(G) the agency procedures whereby an individual can be notified at his request if the system of records contains a record pertaining to him;

(H) the agency procedures whereby an individual can be notified at his request how he can gain access to any record pertaining to him contained in the system of records, and how he can contest its content; and

(I) the categories of sources of records in the system;

(5) maintain all records which are used by the agency in making any determination about any individual with such accuracy, relevance, timeliness, and completeness as is reasonably necessary to assure fairness to the individual in the determination;

(6) prior to disseminating any record about an individual to any person other than an agency, unless the dissemination is made pursuant to subsection (b)(2) of this section, make reasonable efforts to assure that such records are accurate, complete, timely, and relevant for agency purposes;

(7) maintain no record describing how any individual exercises rights guaranteed by the First Amendment unless expressly authorized by statute or by the individual about whom the record is maintained or unless pertinent to and within the scope of an authorized law enforcement activity;

(8) make reasonable efforts to serve notice on an individual when any record on such individual is made available to any person under compulsory legal process when such process becomes a matter of public record;

(9) establish rules of conduct for persons involved in the design, development, operation, or maintenance of any system of records, or in maintaining any record, and instruct each such person with

respect to such rules and the requirements of this section, including any other rules and procedures adopted pursuant to this section and the penalties for noncompliance;

(10) establish appropriate administrative, technical, and physical safeguards to insure the security and confidentiality of records and to protect against any anticipated threats or hazards to their security or integrity which could result in substantial harm, embarrassment, inconvenience, or unfairness to any individual on whom information is maintained;

(11) at least 30 days prior to publication of information under paragraph (4)(D) of this subsection, publish in the Federal Register notice of any new use or intended use of the information in the system, and provide an opportunity for interested persons to submit written data, views, or arguments to the agency; and

(12) if such agency is a recipient agency or a source agency in a matching program with a non-Federal agency, with respect to any establishment or revision of a matching program, at least 30 days prior to conducting such program, publish in the Federal Register notice of such establishment or revision.

(f) Agency rules.—In order to carry out the provisions of this section, each agency that maintains a system of records shall promulgate rules, in accordance with the requirements (including general notice) of section 553 of this title, which shall—

(1) establish procedures whereby an individual can be notified in response to his request if any system of records named by the individual contains a record pertaining to him;

(2) define reasonable times, places, and requirements for identifying an individual who requests his record or information pertaining to him before the agency shall make the record or information available to the individual;

(3) establish procedures for the disclosure to an individual upon his request of his record or information pertaining to him, including special procedure, if deemed necessary, for the disclosure to an individual of medical records, including psychological records, pertaining to him;

(4) establish procedures for reviewing a request from an individual concerning the amendment of any record or information pertaining to the individual, for making a determination on the request, for an appeal within the agency of an initial adverse agency determination, and for whatever additional means may be necessary for each individual to be able to exercise fully his rights under this section; and

(5) establish fees to be charged, if any, to any individual for making copies of his record, excluding the cost of any search for and review of the record.

The Office of the Federal Register shall biennially compile and publish the rules promulgated under this subsection and agency notices published under subsection (e)(4) of this section in a form available to the public at low cost.

(g)(1) Civil remedies.—Whenever any agency

(A) makes a determination under subsection (d)(3) of this section not to amend an individual's record in accordance with his request, or fails to make such review in conformity with that subsection;

(B) refuses to comply with an individual request under subsection (d)(1) of this section;

(C) fails to maintain any record concerning any individual with such accuracy, relevance, timeliness, and completeness as is necessary to assure fairness in any determination relating to the qualifications, character, rights, or opportunities of, or benefits to the individual that may be made on the basis of such record, and consequently a determination is made which is adverse to the individual; or

(D) fails to comply with any other provision of this section, or any rule promulgated thereunder, in such a way as to have an adverse effect on an individual,

the individual may bring a civil action against the agency, and the district courts of the United States shall have jurisdiction in the matters under the provisions of this subsection.

(2)(A) In any suit brought under the provisions of subsection (g)(1)(A) of this section, the court may order the agency to amend the individual's record in accordance with his request or in such other way as the court may direct. In such a case the court shall determine the matter de novo.

(B) The court may assess against the United States reasonable attorney fees and other litigation costs reasonably incurred in any case under this paragraph in which the complainant has substantially prevailed.

(3)(A) In any suit brought under the provisions of subsection (g)(1)(B) of this section, the court may enjoin the agency from withholding the records and order the production to the complainant of any agency records improperly withheld from him. In such a case the court shall determine the matter de novo, and may examine the contents of any agency records in camera to determine whether the records or any portion thereof may be withheld under any of the exemptions set forth in subsection (k) of this section, and the burden is on the agency to sustain its action.

(B) The court may assess against the United States reasonable attorney fees and other litigation costs reasonably incurred in any case under this paragraph in which the complainant has substantially prevailed.

(4) In any suit brought under the provisions of subsection (g)(1)(C) or (D) of this section in which the court determines that the agency acted in a manner which was intentional or willful, the United States shall be liable to the individual in an amount equal to the sum of—

(A) actual damages sustained by the individual as a result of the refusal or failure, but in no case shall a person entitled to recovery receive less than the sum of $1,000; and

(B) the costs of the action together with reasonable attorney fees as determined by the court.

(5) An action to enforce any liability created under this section may be brought in the district court of the United States in the district in which the complainant resides, or has his principal place of business, or in which the agency records are situated, or in the District of Columbia, without regard to the amount in controversy, within two years from the date on which the cause of action arises, except that where an agency has materially and willfully misrepresented any information required under this section to be disclosed to an individual and the information so misrepresented is material to establishment of the liability of the agency to the individual under this section, the action may be brought at any time within two years after discovery by the individual of the misrepresentation. Nothing in this section shall be construed to authorize any civil action by reason of any injury sustained as the result of a disclosure of a record prior to September 27, 1975.

(h) Rights of legal guardians.—For the purposes of this section, the parent of any minor, or the legal guardian of any individual who has been declared to be incompetent due to physical or mental incapacity or age by a court of competent jurisdiction, may act on behalf of the individual.

(i)(1) Criminal penalties.—Any officer or employee of an agency, who by virtue of his employment or official position, has possession of, or access to, agency records which contain individually identifiable information the disclosure of which is prohibited by this section or by rules or regulations established thereunder, and who knowing that disclosure of the specific material is so prohibited, willfully discloses the material in any manner to any person or agency not entitled to receive it, shall be guilty of a misdemeanor and fined not more than $5,000.

(2) Any officer or employee of any agency who willfully maintains a system of records without meeting the notice requirements of subsection (e)(4) of this section shall be guilty of a misdemeanor and fined not more than $5,000.

(3) Any person who knowingly and willfully requests or obtains any record concerning an individual from an agency under false pretenses shall be guilty of a misdemeanor and fined not more than $5,000.

(j) General exemptions.—The head of any agency may promulgate rules, in accordance with the requirements (including general notice) of sections 553(b)(1), (2), and (3), (c), and (e) of this title, to exempt any system of records within the agency from any part of this section except subsections (b), (c)(1) and (2), (e)(4)(A) through (F), (e)(6), (7), (9), (10), and (11), and (i) if the system of records is—

(1) maintained by the Central Intelligence Agency; or

(2) maintained by an agency or component thereof which performs as its principal function any activity pertaining to the enforcement of criminal laws, including police efforts to prevent, control, or reduce crime or to apprehend criminals, and the activities of prosecutors, courts, correctional, probation, pardon, or parole authorities, and which consists of (A) information compiled for the purpose of identifying individual criminal offenders and alleged offenders and consisting only of identifying data and notations of arrests, the nature and disposition of criminal charges, sentencing, confinement, release, and parole and probation status; (B) information compiled for the purpose of a criminal investigation, including reports of informants and investigators, and associated with an identifiable individual; or (C) reports identifiable to an individual compiled at any stage of the process of enforcement of the criminal laws from arrest or indictment through release from supervision.

At the time rules are adopted under this subsection, the agency shall include in the statement required under section 553(c) of this title, the reasons why the system of records is to be exempted from a provision of this section.

(k) Specific exemptions.—The head of any agency may promulgate rules, in accordance with the requirements (including general notice) of sections 553(b)(1), (2), and (3), (c), and (e) of this title, to exempt any system of records within the agency from subsections (c)(3), (d), (e)(1), (e)(4)(G), (H), and (I) and (f) of this section if the system of records is—

(1) subject to the provisions of section 552(b)(1) of this title;

(2) investigatory material compiled for law enforcement purposes, other than material within the scope of subsection (j)(2) of this section: Provided, however, That if any individual is denied any right, privilege, or benefit that he would otherwise be entitled by

Federal law, or for which he would otherwise be eligible, as a result of the maintenance of such material, such material shall be provided to such individual, except to the extent that the disclosure of such material would reveal the identity of a source who furnished information to the Government under an express promise that the identity of the source would be held in confidence, or, prior to the effective date of this section, under an implied promise that the identity of the source would be held in confidence;

(3) maintained in connection with providing protective services to the President of the United States or other individuals pursuant to section 3056 of title 18;

(4) required by statute to be maintained and used solely as statistical records;

(5) investigatory material compiled solely for the purpose of determining suitability, eligibility, or qualifications for Federal civilian employment, military service, Federal contracts, or access to classified information, but only to the extent that the disclosure of such material would reveal the identity of a source who furnished information to the Government under an express promise that the identity of the source would be held in confidence, or, prior to the effective date of this section, under an implied promise that the identity of the source would be held in confidence;

(6) testing or examination material used solely to determine individual qualifications for appointment or promotion in the Federal service the disclosure of which would compromise the objectivity or fairness of the testing or examination process; or

(7) evaluation material used to determine potential for promotion in the armed services, but only to the extent that the disclosure of such material would reveal the identity of a source who furnished information to the Government under an express promise that the identity of the source would be held in confidence, or, prior to the effective date of this section, under an implied promise that the identity of the source would be held in confidence.

At the time rules are adopted under this subsection, the agency shall include in the statement required under section 553(c) of this title, the reasons why the system of records is to be exempted from a provision of this section.

(*l*)(1) Archival records.—Each agency record which is accepted by the Archivist of the United States for storage, processing, and servicing in accordance with section 3103 of title 44 shall, for the purposes of this section, be considered to be maintained by the agency which deposited the record and shall be subject to the provisions of this section. The Archivist of the United States shall not disclose the record except to the agency which maintains the record, or under rules established by that agency which are not inconsistent with the provisions of this section.

(2) Each agency record pertaining to an identifiable individual which was transferred to the National Archives of the United States as a record which has sufficient historical or other value to warrant its continued preservation by the United States Government, prior to the effective date of this section, shall, for the purposes of this section, be considered to be maintained by the National Archives and shall not be subject to the provisions of this section, except that a statement generally describing such records (modeled after the requirements relating to records subject to subsections (e)(4)(A) through (G) of this section) shall be published in the Federal Register.

(3) Each agency record pertaining to an identifiable individual which is transferred to the National Archives of the United States as a record which has sufficient historical or other value to warrant its continued preservation by the United States Government, on or after the effective date of this section, shall, for the purposes of this section, be considered to be maintained by the National Archives and shall be exempt from the requirements of this section except subsections (e)(4)(A) through (G) and (e)(9) of this section.

(m)(1) Government contractors.—When an agency provides by a contract for the operation by or on behalf of the agency of a system of records to accomplish an agency function, the agency shall, consistent with its authority, cause the requirements of this section to be applied to such system. For purposes of subsection (i) of this section any such contractor and any employee of such contractor, if such contract is agreed to on or after the effective date of this section, shall be considered to be an employee of an agency.

(2) A consumer reporting agency to which a record is disclosed under section 3711(e) of title 31 shall not be considered a contractor for the purposes of this section.

(n) Mailing lists.—An individual's name and address may not be sold or rented by an agency unless such action is specifically authorized by law. This provision shall not be construed to require the withholding of names and addresses otherwise permitted to be made public.

(o) Matching agreements.—

(1) No record which is contained in a system of records may be disclosed to a recipient agency or non-Federal agency for use in a computer matching program except pursuant to a written agreement between the source agency and the recipient agency or non-Federal agency specifying—

(A) the purpose and legal authority for conducting the program;

(B) the justification for the program and the anticipated results, including a specific estimate of any savings;

(C) a description of the records that will be matched, including each data element that will be used, the approximate number of records that will be matched, and the projected starting and completion dates of the matching program;

(D) procedures for providing individualized notice at the time of application, and notice periodically thereafter as directed by the Data Integrity Board of such agency (subject to guidance provided by the Director of the Office of Management and Budget pursuant to subsection (v)), to—

> (i) applicants for and recipients of financial assistance or payments under Federal benefit programs, and

> (ii) applicants for and holders of positions as Federal personnel,

that any information provided by such applicants, recipients, holders, and individuals may be subject to verification through matching programs;

(E) procedures for verifying information produced in such matching program as required by subsection (p);

(F) procedures for the retention and timely destruction of identifiable records created by a recipient agency or non-Federal agency in such matching program;

(G) procedures for ensuring the administrative, technical, and physical security of the records matched and the results of such programs;

(H) prohibitions on duplication and redisclosure of records provided by the source agency within or outside the recipient agency or the non-Federal agency, except where required by law or essential to the conduct of the matching program;

(I) procedures governing the use by a recipient agency or non-Federal agency of records provided in a matching program by a source agency, including procedures governing return of the records to the source agency or destruction of records used in such program;

(J) information on assessments that have been made on the accuracy of the records that will be used in such matching program; and

(K) that the Comptroller General may have access to all records of a recipient agency or a non-Federal agency that the Comptroller General deems necessary in order to monitor or verify compliance with the agreement.

(2)(A) A copy of each agreement entered into pursuant to paragraph (1) shall—

> (i) be transmitted to the Committee on Governmental Affairs of the Senate and the Committee on Government Operations of the House of Representatives; and

> (ii) be available upon request to the public.

(B) No such agreement shall be effective until 30 days after the date on which such a copy is transmitted pursuant to subparagraph (A)(i).

(C) Such an agreement shall remain in effect only for such period, not to exceed 18 months, as the Data Integrity Board of the agency determines is appropriate in light of the purposes, and length of time necessary for the conduct, of the matching program.

(D) Within 3 months prior to the expiration of such an agreement pursuant to subparagraph (C), the Data Integrity Board of the agency may, without additional review, renew the matching agreement for a current, ongoing matching program for not more than one additional year if—

> (i) such program will be conducted without any change; and

> (ii) each party to the agreement certifies to the Board in writing that the program has been conducted in compliance with the agreement.

(p) Verification and opportunity to contest findings.—

(1) In order to protect any individual whose records are used in a matching program, no recipient agency, non-Federal agency, or source agency may suspend, terminate, reduce, or make a final denial of any financial assistance or payment under a Federal benefit program to such individual, or take other adverse action against such individual, as a result of information produced by such matching program, until—

> (A)(i) the agency has independently verified the information; or

> > (ii) the Data Integrity Board of the agency, or in the case of a non-Federal agency the Data Integrity Board of the source agency, determines in accordance with guidance issued by the Director of the Office of Management and Budget that—

> > > (I) the information is limited to identification and amount of benefits paid by the source agency under a Federal benefit program; and

70

(II) there is a high degree of confidence that the information provided to the recipient agency is accurate;

(B) the individual receives a notice from the agency containing a statement of its findings and informing the individual of the opportunity to contest such findings; and

(C)(i) the expiration of any time period established for the program by statute or regulation for the individual to respond to that notice; or

(ii) in the case of a program for which no such period is established, the end of the 30–day period beginning on the date on which notice under subparagraph (B) is mailed or otherwise provided to the individual.

(2) Independent verification referred to in paragraph (1) requires investigation and confirmation of specific information relating to an individual that is used as a basis for an adverse action against the individual, including where applicable investigation and confirmation of—

(A) the amount of any asset or income involved;

(B) whether such individual actually has or had access to such asset or income for such individual's own use; and

(C) the period or periods when the individual actually had such asset or income.

(3) Notwithstanding paragraph (1), an agency may take any appropriate action otherwise prohibited by such paragraph if the agency determines that the public health or public safety may be adversely affected or significantly threatened during any notice period required by such paragraph.

(q) Sanctions.—

(1) Notwithstanding any other provision of law, no source agency may disclose any record which is contained in a system of records to a recipient agency or non-Federal agency for a matching program if such source agency has reason to believe that the requirements of subsection (p), or any matching agreement entered into pursuant to subsection (o), or both, are not being met by such recipient agency.

(2) No source agency may renew a matching agreement unless—

(A) the recipient agency or non-Federal agency has certified that it has complied with the provisions of that agreement; and

(B) the source agency has no reason to believe that the certification is inaccurate.

(r) Report on new systems and matching programs.—Each agency that proposes to establish or make a significant change in a system of records or a matching program shall provide adequate advance notice of any such proposal (in duplicate) to the Committee on Government Operations of the House of Representatives, the Committee on Governmental Affairs of the Senate, and the Office of Management and Budget in order to permit an evaluation of the probable or potential effect of such proposal on the privacy or other rights of individuals.

(s) Biennial report.—The President shall biennially submit to the Speaker of the House of Representatives and the President pro tempore of the Senate a report—

(1) describing the actions of the Director of the Office of Management and Budget pursuant to section 6 of the Privacy Act of 1974 during the preceding 2 years;

(2) describing the exercise of individual rights of access and amendment under this section during such years;

(3) identifying changes in or additions to systems of records;

(4) containing such other information concerning administration of this section as may be necessary or useful to the Congress in reviewing the effectiveness of this section in carrying out the purposes of the Privacy Act of 1974.

(t)(1) Effect of other laws.—No agency shall rely on any exemption contained in section 552 of this title to withhold from an individual any record which is otherwise accessible to such individual under the provisions of this section.

(2) No agency shall rely on any exemption in this section to withhold from an individual any record which is otherwise accessible to such individual under the provisions of section 552 of this title.

(u) Data Integrity Boards.—

(1) Every agency conducting or participating in a matching program shall establish a Data Integrity Board to oversee and coordinate among the various components of such agency the agency's implementation of this section.

(2) Each Data Integrity Board shall consist of senior officials designated by the head of the agency, and shall include any senior official designated by the head of the agency as responsible for implementation of this section, and the inspector general of the agency, if any. The inspector general shall not serve as chairman of the Data Integrity Board.

(3) Each Data Integrity Board—

(A) shall review, approve, and maintain all written agreements for receipt or disclosure of agency records for matching programs to ensure compliance with subsection (o), and all relevant statutes, regulations, and guidelines;

(B) shall review all matching programs in which the agency has participated during the year, either as a source agency or recipient agency, determine compliance with applicable laws, regulations, guidelines, and agency agreements, and assess the costs and benefits of such programs;

(C) shall review all recurring matching programs in which the agency has participated during the year, either as a source agency or recipient agency, for continued justification for such disclosures;

(D) shall compile an annual report, which shall be submitted to the head of the agency and the Office of Management and Budget and made available to the public on request, describing the matching activities of the agency, including—

(i) matching programs in which the agency has participated as a source agency or recipient agency;

(ii) matching agreements proposed under subsection (o) that were disapproved by the Board;

(iii) any changes in membership or structure of the Board in the preceding year;

(iv) the reasons for any waiver of the requirement in paragraph (4) of this section for completion and submission of a cost-benefit analysis prior to the approval of a matching program;

(v) any violations of matching agreements that have been alleged or identified and any corrective action taken; and

(vi) any other information required by the Director of the Office of Management and Budget to be included in such report;

(E) shall serve as a clearinghouse for receiving and providing information on the accuracy, completeness, and reliability of records used in matching programs;

(F) shall provide interpretation and guidance to agency components and personnel on the requirements of this section for matching programs;

(G) shall review agency recordkeeping and disposal policies and practices for matching programs to assure compliance with this section; and

(H) may review and report on any agency matching activities that are not matching programs.

(4)(A) Except as provided in subparagraphs (B) and (C), a Data Integrity Board shall not approve any written agreement for a matching program unless the agency has completed and submitted to such Board a cost-benefit analysis of the proposed program and such analysis demonstrates that the program is likely to be cost effective.[3]

(B) The Board may waive the requirements of subparagraph (A) of this paragraph if it determines in writing, in accordance with guidelines prescribed by the Director of the Office of Management and Budget, that a cost-benefit analysis is not required.

(C) A cost-benefit analysis shall not be required under subparagraph (A) prior to the initial approval of a written agreement for a matching program that is specifically required by statute. Any subsequent written agreement for such a program shall not be approved by the Data Integrity Board unless the agency has submitted a cost-benefit analysis of the program as conducted under the preceding approval of such agreement.

(5)(A) If a matching agreement is disapproved by a Data Integrity Board, any party to such agreement may appeal the disapproval to the Director of the Office of Management and Budget. Timely notice of the filing of such an appeal shall be provided by the Director of the Office of Management and Budget to the Committee on Governmental Affairs of the Senate and the Committee on Government Operations of the House of Representatives.

(B) The Director of the Office of Management and Budget may approve a matching agreement notwithstanding the disapproval of a Data Integrity Board if the Director determines that—

(i) the matching program will be consistent with all applicable legal, regulatory, and policy requirements;

(ii) there is adequate evidence that the matching agreement will be cost-effective; and

(iii) the matching program is in the public interest.

(C) The decision of the Director to approve a matching agreement shall not take effect until 30 days after it is reported to committees described in subparagraph (A).

(D) If the Data Integrity Board and the Director of the Office of Management and Budget disapprove a matching program proposed by the inspector general of an agency, the inspector general may report the disapproval to the head of the agency and to the Congress.

(6) In the reports required by paragraph (3)(D), agency matching activities that are not matching programs may be reported on an aggregate basis, if and to the extent necessary to protect ongoing law enforcement or counterintelligence investigations.

---

3. So in original. Probably should be "cost-effective".

(v) Office of Management and Budget responsibilities.—The Director of the Office of Management and Budget shall—

(1) develop and, after notice and opportunity for public comment, prescribe guidelines and regulations for the use of agencies in implementing the provisions of this section; and

(2) provide continuing assistance to and oversight of the implementation of this section by agencies.

GOVERNMENT IN THE SUNSHINE ACT

5 U.S.C. § 552b

§ 552b. Open meetings

(a) For purposes of this section—

(1) the term "agency" means any agency, as defined in section 552(e) of this title, headed by a collegial body composed of two or more individual members, a majority of whom are appointed to such position by the President with the advice and consent of the Senate, and any subdivision thereof authorized to act on behalf of the agency;

(2) the term "meeting" means the deliberations of at least the number of individual agency members required to take action on behalf of the agency where such deliberations determine or result in the joint conduct or disposition of official agency business, but does not include deliberations required or permitted by subsection (d) or (e); and

(3) the term "member" means an individual who belongs to a collegial body heading an agency.

(b) Members shall not jointly conduct or dispose of agency business other than in accordance with this section. Except as provided in subsection (c), every portion of every meeting of an agency shall be open to public observation.

(c) Except in a case where the agency finds that the public interest requires otherwise, the second sentence of subsection (b) shall not apply to any portion of an agency meeting, and the requirements of subsections (d) and (e) shall not apply to any information pertaining to such meeting otherwise required by this section to be disclosed to the public, where the agency properly determines that such portion or portions of its meeting or the disclosure of such information is likely to—

(1) disclose matters that are (A) specifically authorized under criteria established by an Executive order to be kept secret in the interests of national defense or foreign policy and (B) in fact properly classified pursuant to such Executive order;

(2) relate solely to the internal personnel rules and practices of an agency;

(3) disclose matters specifically exempted from disclosure by statute (other than section 552 of this title), provided that such statute (A) requires that the matters be withheld from the public in such a manner as to leave no discretion on the issue, or (B) establishes

particular criteria for withholding or refers to particular types of matters to be withheld;

(4) disclose trade secrets and commercial or financial information obtained from a person and privileged or confidential;

(5) involve accusing any person of a crime, or formally censuring any person;

(6) disclose information of a personal nature where disclosure would constitute a clearly unwarranted invasion of personal privacy;

(7) disclose investigatory records compiled for law enforcement purposes, or information which if written would be contained in such records, but only to the extent that the production of such records or information would (A) interfere with enforcement proceedings, (B) deprive a person of a right to a fair trial or an impartial adjudication, (C) constitute an unwarranted invasion of personal privacy, (D) disclose the identity of a confidential source and, in the case of a record compiled by a criminal law enforcement authority in the course of a criminal investigation, or by an agency conducting a lawful national security intelligence investigation, confidential information furnished only by the confidential source, (E) disclose investigative techniques and procedures, or (F) endanger the life or physical safety of law enforcement personnel;

(8) disclose information contained in or related to examination, operating, or condition reports prepared by, on behalf of, or for the use of an agency responsible for the regulation or supervision of financial institutions;

(9) disclose information the premature disclosure of which would—

    (A) in the case of an agency which regulates currencies, securities, commodities, or financial institutions, be likely to (i) lead to significant financial speculation in currencies, securities, or commodities, or (ii) significantly endanger the stability of any financial institution; or

    (B) in the case of any agency, be likely to significantly frustrate implementation of a proposed agency action, except that subparagraph (B) shall not apply in any instance where the agency has already disclosed to the public the content or nature of its proposed action, or where the agency is required by law to make such disclosure on its own initiative prior to taking final agency action on such proposal; or

(10) specifically concern the agency's issuance of a subpena, or the agency's participation in a civil action or proceeding, an action in a foreign court or international tribunal, or an arbitration, or the initiation, conduct, or disposition by the agency of a particular case of formal agency adjudication pursuant to the procedures in section

554 of this title or otherwise involving a determination on the record after opportunity for a hearing.

(d)(1) Action under subsection (c) shall be taken only when a majority of the entire membership of the agency (as defined in subsection (a)(1)) votes to take such action. A separate vote of the agency members shall be taken with respect to each agency meeting a portion or portions of which are proposed to be closed to the public pursuant to subsection (c), or with respect to any information which is proposed to be withheld under subsection (c). A single vote may be taken with respect to a series of meetings, a portion or portions of which are proposed to be closed to the public, or with respect to any information concerning such series of meetings, so long as each meeting in such series involves the same particular matters and is scheduled to be held no more than thirty days after the initial meeting in such series. The vote of each agency member participating in such vote shall be recorded and no proxies shall be allowed.

(2) Whenever any person whose interests may be directly affected by a portion of a meeting requests that the agency close such portion to the public for any of the reasons referred to in paragraph (5), (6), or (7) of subsection (c), the agency, upon request of any one of its members, shall vote by recorded vote whether to close such meeting.

(3) Within one day of any vote taken pursuant to paragraph (1) or (2), the agency shall make publicly available a written copy of such vote reflecting the vote of each member on the question. If a portion of a meeting is to be closed to the public, the agency shall, within one day of the vote taken pursuant to paragraph (1) or (2) of this subsection, make publicly available a full written explanation of its action closing the portion together with a list of all persons expected to attend the meeting and their affiliation.

(4) Any agency, a majority of whose meetings may properly be closed to the public pursuant to paragraph (4), (8), (9)(A), or (10) of subsection (c), or any combination thereof, may provide by regulation for the closing of such meetings or portions thereof in the event that a majority of the members of the agency votes by recorded vote at the beginning of such meeting, or portion thereof, to close the exempt portion or portions of the meeting, and a copy of such vote, reflecting the vote of each member on the question, is made available to the public. The provisions of paragraphs (1), (2), and (3) of this subsection and subsection (e) shall not apply to any portion of a meeting to which such regulations apply: Provided, That the agency shall, except to the extent that such information is exempt from disclosure under the provisions of subsection (c), provide the public with public announcement of the time, place, and subject matter of the meeting and of each portion thereof at the earliest practicable time.

(e)(1) In the case of each meeting, the agency shall make public announcement, at least one week before the meeting, of the time, place, and subject matter of the meeting, whether it is to be open or closed to the public, and the name and phone number of the official designated by the agency to respond to requests for information about the meeting. Such announcement shall be made unless a majority of the members of the agency determines by a recorded vote that agency business requires that such meeting be called at an earlier date, in which case the agency shall make public announcement of the time, place, and subject matter of such meeting, and whether open or closed to the public, at the earliest practicable time.

(2) The time or place of a meeting may be changed following the public announcement required by paragraph (1) only if the agency publicly announces such change at the earliest practicable time. The subject matter of a meeting, or the determination of the agency to open or close a meeting, or portion of a meeting, to the public, may be changed following the public announcement required by this subsection only if (A) a majority of the entire membership of the agency determines by a recorded vote that agency business so requires and that no earlier announcement of the change was possible, and (B) the agency publicly announces such change and the vote of each member upon such change at the earliest practicable time.

(3) Immediately following each public announcement required by this subsection, notice of the time, place, and subject matter of a meeting, whether the meeting is open or closed, any change in one of the preceding, and the name and phone number of the official designated by the agency to respond to requests for information about the meeting, shall also be submitted for publication in the Federal Register.

(f)(1) For every meeting closed pursuant to paragraphs (1) through (10) of subsection (c), the General Counsel or chief legal officer of the agency shall publicly certify that, in his or her opinion, the meeting may be closed to the public and shall state each relevant exemptive provision. A copy of such certification, together with a statement from the presiding officer of the meeting setting forth the time and place of the meeting, and the persons present, shall be retained by the agency. The agency shall maintain a complete transcript or electronic recording adequate to record fully the proceedings of each meeting, or portion of a meeting, closed to the public, except that in the case of a meeting, or portion of a meeting, closed to the public pursuant to paragraph (8), (9)(A), or (10) of subsection (c), the agency shall maintain either such a transcript or recording, or a set of minutes. Such minutes shall fully and clearly describe all matters discussed and shall provide a full and accurate summary of any actions taken, and the reasons therefor, including a description of each of the views expressed on any item and the record of any rollcall vote (reflecting the vote of each member on the question). All documents considered in connection with any action shall be identified in such minutes.

> (2) The agency shall make promptly available to the public, in a place easily accessible to the public, the transcript, electronic recording, or minutes (as required by paragraph (1)) of the discussion of any item on the agenda, or of any item of the testimony of any witness received at the meeting, except for such item or items of such discussion or testimony as the agency determines to contain information which may be withheld under subsection (c). Copies of such transcript, or minutes, or a transcription of such recording disclosing the identity of each speaker, shall be furnished to any person at the actual cost of duplication or transcription. The agency shall maintain a complete verbatim copy of the transcript, a complete copy of the minutes, or a complete electronic recording of each meeting, or portion of a meeting, closed to the public, for a period of at least two years after such meeting, or until one year after the conclusion of any agency proceeding with respect to which the meeting or portion was held, whichever occurs later.

(g) Each agency subject to the requirements of this section shall, within 180 days after the date of enactment of this section, following consultation with the Office of the Chairman of the Administrative Conference of the United States and published notice in the Federal Register of at least thirty days and opportunity for written comment by any person, promulgate regulations to implement the requirements of subsections (b) through (f) of this section. Any person may bring a proceeding in the United States District Court for the District of Columbia to require an agency to promulgate such regulations if such agency has not promulgated such regulations within the time period specified herein. Subject to any limitations of time provided by law, any person may bring a proceeding in the United States Court of Appeals for the District of Columbia to set aside agency regulations issued pursuant to this subsection that are not in accord with the requirements of subsections (b) through (f) of this section and to require the promulgation of regulations that are in accord with such subsections.

(h)(1) The district courts of the United States shall have jurisdiction to enforce the requirements of subsections (b) through (f) of this section by declaratory judgment, injunctive relief, or other relief as may be appropriate. Such actions may be brought by any person against an agency prior to, or within sixty days after, the meeting out of which the violation of this section arises, except that if public announcement of such meeting is not initially provided by the agency in accordance with the requirements of this section, such action may be instituted pursuant to this section at any time prior to sixty days after any public announcement of such meeting. Such actions may be brought in the district court of the United States for the district in which the agency meeting is held or in which the agency in question has its headquarters, or in the District Court for the District of Columbia. In such actions a defendant shall serve his answer within thirty days after the service of the complaint. The burden is on the defendant to sustain his action. In deciding such cases the court may examine in camera any portion of the transcript, electronic recording, or minutes of a meeting closed to the public, and may take such additional evidence as it deems necessary. The court, having due regard for orderly administration and the public interest, as well as the interests of the parties, may grant such equitable relief as it deems appropriate, including granting an injunction against future violations of this section or ordering the agency to make available to the public such portion of the transcript, recording, or minutes of a meeting as is not authorized to be withheld under subsection (c) of this section.

(2) Any Federal court otherwise authorized by law to review agency action may, at the application of any person properly participating in the proceeding pursuant to other applicable law, inquire into violations by the agency of the requirements of this section and afford such relief as it deems appropriate. Nothing in this section authorizes any Federal court having jurisdiction solely on the basis of paragraph (1) to set aside, enjoin, or invalidate any agency action (other than an action to close a meeting or to withhold information under this section) taken or discussed at any agency meeting out of which the violation of this section arose.

(i) The court may assess against any party reasonable attorney fees and other litigation costs reasonably incurred by any other party who substantially prevails in any action brought in accordance with the provisions of subsection (g) or (h) of this section, except that costs may be assessed against the plaintiff only where the court finds that the suit was initiated by the plaintiff primarily for frivolous or dilatory purposes. In the case of assessment of costs against an agency, the costs may be assessed by the court against the United States.

(j) Each agency subject to the requirements of this section shall annually report to the Congress regarding the following:

(1) The changes in the policies and procedures of the agency under this section that have occurred during the preceding 1-year period.

(2) A tabulation of the number of meetings held, the exemptions applied to close meetings, and the days of public notice provided to close meetings.

(3) A brief description of litigation or formal complaints concerning the implementation of this section by the agency.

(4) A brief explanation of any changes in law that have affected the responsibilities of the agency under this section.

(k) Nothing herein expands or limits the present rights of any person under section 552 of this title, except that the exemptions set forth in subsection (c) of this section shall govern in the case of any request made pursuant to section 552 to copy or inspect the transcripts, recordings, or minutes described in subsection (f) of this section. The requirements of chapter 33 of title 44, United States Code, shall not apply to the transcripts, recordings, and minutes described in subsection (f) of this section.

(*l*) This section does not constitute authority to withhold any information from Congress, and does not authorize the closing of any agency meeting or portion thereof required by any other provision of law to be open.

(m) Nothing in this section authorizes any agency to withhold from any individual any record, including transcripts, recordings, or minutes required by this section, which is otherwise accessible to such individual under section 552a of this title.

NEGOTIATED RULEMAKING ACT

TITLE 5. GOVERNMENT ORGANIZATION AND EMPLOYEES
PART I—THE AGENCIES GENERALLY
CHAPTER 5—ADMINISTRATIVE PROCEDURE
SUBCHAPTER III—NEGOTIATED RULEMAKING PROCEDURE

§ 561. Purpose

The purpose of this subchapter is to establish a framework for the conduct of negotiated rulemaking, consistent with section 553 of this title, to encourage agencies to use the process when it enhances the informal rulemaking process. Nothing in this subchapter should be construed as an attempt to limit innovation and experimentation with the negotiated rulemaking process or with other innovative rulemaking procedures otherwise authorized by law.

§ 562. Definitions

For the purposes of this subchapter, the term—

(1) "agency" has the same meaning as in section 551(1) of this title;

(2) "consensus" means unanimous concurrence among the interests represented on a negotiated rulemaking committee established under this subchapter, unless such committee—

(A) agrees to define such term to mean a general but not unanimous concurrence; or

(B) agrees upon another specified definition;

(3) "convener" means a person who impartially assists an agency in determining whether establishment of a negotiated rulemaking committee is feasible and appropriate in a particular rulemaking;

(4) "facilitator" means a person who impartially aids in the discussions and negotiations among the members of a negotiated rulemaking committee to develop a proposed rule;

(5) "interest" means, with respect to an issue or matter, multiple parties which have a similar point of view or which are likely to be affected in a similar manner;

(6) "negotiated rulemaking" means rulemaking through the use of a negotiated rulemaking committee;

(7) "negotiated rulemaking committee" or "committee" means an advisory committee established by an agency in accordance with this subchapter and the Federal Advisory Committee Act to consider and discuss issues for the purpose of reaching a consensus in the development of a proposed rule;

(8) "party" has the same meaning as in section 551(3) of this title;

(9) "person" has the same meaning as in section 551(2) of this title;

(10) "rule" has the same meaning as in section 551(4) of this title; and

(11) "rulemaking" means "rule making" as that term is defined in section 551(5) of this title.

§ 563. Determination of need for negotiated rulemaking committee

(a) Determination of need by the agency.—An agency may establish a negotiated rulemaking committee to negotiate and develop a proposed rule, if the head of the agency determines that the use of the negotiated rulemaking procedure is in the public interest. In making such a determination, the head of the agency shall consider whether—

(1) there is a need for a rule;

(2) there are a limited number of identifiable interests that will be significantly affected by the rule;

(3) there is a reasonable likelihood that a committee can be convened with a balanced representation of persons who—

    (A) can adequately represent the interests identified under paragraph (2); and

    (B) are willing to negotiate in good faith to reach a consensus on the proposed rule;

(4) there is a reasonable likelihood that a committee will reach a consensus on the proposed rule within a fixed period of time;

(5) the negotiated rulemaking procedure will not unreasonably delay the notice of proposed rulemaking and the issuance of the final rule;

(6) the agency has adequate resources and is willing to commit such resources, including technical assistance, to the committee; and

(7) the agency, to the maximum extent possible consistent with the legal obligations of the agency, will use the consensus of the committee with respect to the proposed rule as the basis for the rule proposed by the agency for notice and comment.

(b) Use of conveners.—(1) Purposes of conveners.—An agency may use the services of a convener to assist the agency in—

(A) identifying persons who will be significantly affected by a proposed rule, including residents of rural areas; and

(B) conducting discussions with such persons to identify the issues of concern to such persons, and to ascertain whether the establishment of a negotiated rulemaking committee is feasible and appropriate in the particular rulemaking.

(2) Duties of conveners.—The convener shall report findings and may make recommendations to the agency. Upon request of the agency, the convener shall ascertain the names of persons who are willing and qualified to represent interests that will be significantly affected by the proposed rule, including residents of rural areas. The report and any recommendations of the convener shall be made available to the public upon request.

§ 564. Publication of notice; applications for membership on committees

(a) Publication of notice.—If, after considering the report of a convener or conducting its own assessment, an agency decides to establish a negotiated rulemaking committee, the agency shall publish in the Federal Register and, as appropriate, in trade or other specialized publications, a notice which shall include—

(1) an announcement that the agency intends to establish a negotiated rulemaking committee to negotiate and develop a proposed rule;

(2) a description of the subject and scope of the rule to be developed, and the issues to be considered;

(3) a list of the interests which are likely to be significantly affected by the rule;

(4) a list of the persons proposed to represent such interests and the person or persons proposed to represent the agency;

(5) a proposed agenda and schedule for completing the work of the committee, including a target date for publication by the agency of a proposed rule for notice and comment;

(6) a description of administrative support for the committee to be provided by the agency, including technical assistance;

(7) a solicitation for comments on the proposal to establish the committee, and the proposed membership of the negotiated rulemaking committee; and

(8) an explanation of how a person may apply or nominate another person for membership on the committee, as provided under subsection (b).

(b) Applications for membership or committee.—Persons who will be significantly affected by a proposed rule and who believe that their interests will not be adequately represented by any person specified in a notice under subsection (a)(4) may apply for, or nominate another person for, membership on the negotiated rulemaking committee to represent such interests with respect to the proposed rule. Each application or nomination shall include—

(1) the name of the applicant or nominee and a description of the interests such person shall represent;

(2) evidence that the applicant or nominee is authorized to represent parties related to the interests the person proposes to represent;

(3) a written commitment that the applicant or nominee shall actively participate in good faith in the development of the rule under consideration; and

(4) the reasons that the persons specified in the notice under subsection (a)(4) do not adequately represent the interests of the person submitting the application or nomination.

(c) Period for submission of comments and applications.—The agency shall provide for a period of at least 30 calendar days for the submission of comments and applications under this section.

§ 565. Establishment of committee

(a) Establishment.—(1) Determination to establish committee.—If after considering comments and applications submitted under section 564, the agency determines that a negotiated rulemaking committee can adequately represent the interests that will be significantly affected by a proposed rule and that it is feasible and appropriate in the particular rulemaking, the agency may establish a negotiated rulemaking committee. In establishing and administering such a committee, the agency shall comply with the Federal Advisory Committee Act with respect to such committee, except as otherwise provided in this subchapter.

(2) Determination not to establish committee.—If after considering such comments and applications, the agency decides not to establish a negotiated rulemaking committee, the agency shall promptly publish notice of such decision and the reasons therefor in the Federal Register and, as appropriate, in trade or other specialized publications, a copy of which shall be sent to any person who applied for, or nominated another person for membership on the negotiating rulemaking committee to represent such interests with respect to the proposed rule.

(b) Membership.—The agency shall limit membership on a negotiated rulemaking committee to 25 members, unless the agency head determines that a greater number of members is necessary for the functioning of the committee or to achieve balanced membership. Each committee shall include at least one person representing the agency.

(c) Administrative support.—The agency shall provide appropriate administrative support to the negotiated rulemaking committee, including technical assistance.

§ 566. Conduct of committee activity

(a) Duties of committee.—Each negotiated rulemaking committee established under this subchapter shall consider the matter proposed by the agency for consideration and shall attempt to reach a consensus concerning a proposed rule with respect to such matter and any other matter the committee determines is relevant to the proposed rule.

(b) Representatives of agency on committee.—The person or persons representing the agency on a negotiated rulemaking committee shall participate in the deliberations and activities of the committee with the same rights and responsibilities as other members of the committee, and shall be authorized to fully represent the agency in the discussions and negotiations of the committee.

(c) Selecting facilitator.—Notwithstanding section 10(e) of the Federal Advisory Committee Act, an agency may nominate either a person from the Federal Government or a person from outside the Federal Government to serve as a facilitator for the negotiations of the committee, subject to the approval of the committee by consensus. If the committee does not approve the nominee of the agency for facilitator, the agency shall submit a substitute nomination. If a committee does not approve any nominee of the agency for facilitator, the committee shall select by consensus a person to serve as facilitator. A person designated to represent the agency in substantive issues may not serve as facilitator or otherwise chair the committee.

(d) Duties of facilitator.—A facilitator approved or selected by a negotiated rulemaking committee shall—

(1) chair the meetings of the committee in an impartial manner;

(2) impartially assist the members of the committee in conducting discussions and negotiations; and

(3) manage the keeping of minutes and records as required under section 10(b) and (c) of the Federal Advisory Committee Act, except that any personal notes and materials of the facilitator or of the members of a committee shall not be subject to section 552 of this title.

(e) Committee procedures.—A negotiated rulemaking committee established under this subchapter may adopt procedures for the operation of the committee. No provision of section 553 of this title shall apply to the procedures of a negotiated rulemaking committee.

(f) Report of committee.—If a committee reaches a consensus on a proposed rule, at the conclusion of negotiations the committee shall transmit to the agency that established the committee a report containing the proposed rule. If the committee does not reach a consensus on a proposed rule, the committee may transmit to the agency a report specifying any areas in which the committee reached a consensus. The committee may include in a report any other information, recommendations, or materials that the committee considers appropriate. Any committee member may include as an addendum to the report additional information, recommendations, or materials.

(g) Records of committee.—In addition to the report required by subsection (f), a committee shall submit to the agency the records required under section 10(b) and (c) of the Federal Advisory Committee Act.

§ 567. Termination of committee

A negotiated rulemaking committee shall terminate upon promulgation of the final rule under consideration, unless the committee's charter contains an earlier termination date or the agency, after consulting the committee, or the committee itself specifies an earlier termination date.

§ 568. Services, facilities, and payment of committee member expenses

(a) Services of conveners and facilitators. (1) In general.—An agency may employ or enter into contracts for the services of an individual or organization to serve as a convener or facilitator for a negotiated rulemaking committee under this subchapter, or may use the services of a Government employee to act as a convener or a facilitator for such a committee.

(2) Determination of conflicting interests.—An agency shall determine whether a person under consideration to serve as convener or facilitator of a committee under paragraph (1) has any financial or

other interest that would preclude such person from serving in an impartial and independent manner.

(b) Services and facilities of other entities.—For purposes of this subchapter, an agency may use the services and facilities of other Federal agencies and public and private agencies and instrumentalities with the consent of such agencies and instrumentalities, and with or without reimbursement to such agencies and instrumentalities, and may accept voluntary and uncompensated services without regard to the provisions of section 1342 of title 31. The Federal Mediation and Conciliation Service may provide services and facilities, with or without reimbursement, to assist agencies under this subchapter, including furnishing conveners, facilitators, and training in negotiated rulemaking.

(c) Expenses of committee members.—Members of a negotiated rulemaking committee shall be responsible for their own expenses of participation in such committee, except that an agency may, in accordance with section 7(d) of the Federal Advisory Committee Act, pay for a member's reasonable travel and per diem expenses, expenses to obtain technical assistance, and a reasonable rate of compensation, if—

(1) such member certifies a lack of adequate financial resources to participate in the committee; and

(2) the agency determines that such member's participation in the committee is necessary to assure an adequate representation of the member's interest.

(d) Status of member as federal employee.—A member's receipt of funds under this section or section 569 shall not conclusively determine for purposes of sections 202 through 209 of title 18 whether that member is an employee of the United States Government.

§ 569. Encouraging negotiated rulemaking

(a) The President shall designate an agency or designate or establish an interagency committee to facilitate and encourage agency use of negotiated rulemaking. An agency that is considering, planning, or conducting a negotiated rulemaking may consult with such agency or committee for information and assistance.

(b) To carry out the purposes of this subchapter, an agency planning or conducting a negotiated rulemaking may accept, hold, administer, and utilize gifts, devises, and bequests of property, both real and personal if that agency's acceptance and use of such gifts, devises, or bequests do not create a conflict of interest. Gifts and bequests of money and proceeds from sales of other property received as gifts, devises, or bequests shall be deposited in the Treasury and shall be disbursed upon the order of the head of such agency. Property accepted pursuant to this section, and the proceeds thereof, shall be used as nearly as possible in accordance with the terms of the gifts, devises, or bequests.

§ 570. Judicial review

Any agency action relating to establishing, assisting, or terminating a negotiated rulemaking committee under this subchapter shall not be subject to judicial review. Nothing in this section shall bar judicial review of a rule if such judicial review is otherwise provided by law. A rule which is the product of negotiated rulemaking and is subject to judicial review shall not be accorded any greater deference by a court than a rule which is the product of other rulemaking procedures.

ADMINISTRATIVE DISPUTE RESOLUTION ACT

TITLE 5. GOVERNMENT ORGANIZATION AND EMPLOYEES
PART I—THE AGENCIES GENERALLY
CHAPTER 5—ADMINISTRATIVE PROCEDURE
SUBCHAPTER IV—ALTERNATIVE MEANS OF DISPUTE RESOLUTION IN THE ADMINISTRATIVE PROCESS

§ 571. Definitions

For the purposes of this subchapter, the term—

(1) "agency" has the same meaning as in section 551(1) of this title;

(2) "administrative program" includes a Federal function which involves protection of the public interest and the determination of rights, privileges, and obligations of private persons through rule making, adjudication, licensing, or investigation, as those terms are used in subchapter II of this chapter;

(3) "alternative means of dispute resolution" means any procedure that is used to resolve issues in controversy, including, but not limited to, conciliation, facilitation, mediation, factfinding, minitrials, and arbitration, and use of ombuds, or any combination thereof;

(4) "award" means any decision by an arbitrator resolving the issues in controversy;

(5) "dispute resolution communication" means any oral or written communication prepared for the purposes of a dispute resolution proceeding, including any memoranda, notes or work product of the neutral, parties or nonparty participant; except that a written agreement to enter into a dispute resolution proceeding, or final

written agreement or arbitral award reached as a result of a dispute resolution proceeding, is not a dispute resolution communication;

(6) "dispute resolution proceeding" means any process in which an alternative means of dispute resolution is used to resolve an issue in controversy in which a neutral is appointed and specified parties participate;

(7) "in confidence" means, with respect to information, that the information is provided—

    (A) with the expressed intent of the source that it not be disclosed; or

    (B) under circumstances that would create the reasonable expectation on behalf of the source that the information will not be disclosed;

(8) "issue in controversy" means an issue which is material to a decision concerning an administrative program of an agency, and with which there is disagreement—

    (A) between an agency and persons who would be substantially affected by the decision; or

    (B) between persons who would be substantially affected by the decision;

(9) "neutral" means an individual who, with respect to an issue in controversy, functions specifically to aid the parties in resolving the controversy;

(10) "party" means—

    (A) for a proceeding with named parties, the same as in section 551(3) of this title; and

    (B) for a proceeding without named parties, a person who will be significantly affected by the decision in the proceeding and who participates in the proceeding;

(11) "person" has the same meaning as in section 551(2) of this title; and

(12) "roster" means a list of persons qualified to provide services as neutrals.

§ 572. General authority

(a) An agency may use a dispute resolution proceeding for the resolution of an issue in controversy that relates to an administrative program, if the parties agree to such proceeding.

(b) An agency shall consider not using a dispute resolution proceeding if—

(1) a definitive or authoritative resolution of the matter is required for precedential value, and such a proceeding is not likely to be accepted generally as an authoritative precedent;

(2) the matter involves or may bear upon significant questions of Government policy that require additional procedures before a final resolution may be made, and such a proceeding would not likely serve to develop a recommended policy for the agency;

(3) maintaining established policies is of special importance, so that variations among individual decisions are not increased and such a proceeding would not likely reach consistent results among individual decisions;

(4) the matter significantly affects persons or organizations who are not parties to the proceeding;

(5) a full public record of the proceeding is important, and a dispute resolution proceeding cannot provide such a record; and

(6) the agency must maintain continuing jurisdiction over the matter with authority to alter the disposition of the matter in the light of changed circumstances, and a dispute resolution proceeding would interfere with the agency's fulfilling that requirement.

(c) Alternative means of dispute resolution authorized under this subchapter are voluntary procedures which supplement rather than limit other available agency dispute resolution techniques.

§ 573. Neutrals

(a) A neutral may be a permanent or temporary officer or employee of the Federal Government or any other individual who is acceptable to the parties to a dispute resolution proceeding. A neutral shall have no official, financial, or personal conflict of interest with respect to the issues in controversy, unless such interest is fully disclosed in writing to all parties and all parties agree that the neutral may serve.

(b) A neutral who serves as a conciliator, facilitator, or mediator serves at the will of the parties.

(c) The President shall designate an agency or designate or establish an interagency committee to facilitate and encourage agency use of dispute resolution under this subchapter. Such agency or interagency committee, in consultation with other appropriate Federal agencies and professional organizations experienced in matters concerning dispute resolution, shall—

(1) encourage and facilitate agency use of alternative means of dispute resolution; and

(2) develop procedures that permit agencies to obtain the services of neutrals on an expedited basis.

(d) An agency may use the services of one or more employees of other agencies to serve as neutrals in dispute resolution proceedings. The agencies may enter into an interagency agreement that provides for the reimbursement by the user agency or the parties of the full or partial cost of the services of such an employee.

(e) Any agency may enter into a contract with any person for services as a neutral, or for training in connection with alternative means of dispute resolution. The parties in a dispute resolution proceeding shall agree on compensation for the neutral that is fair and reasonable to the Government.

§ 574. Confidentiality

(a) Except as provided in subsections (d) and (e), a neutral in a dispute resolution proceeding shall not voluntarily disclose or through discovery or compulsory process be required to disclose any dispute resolution communication or any communication provided in confidence to the neutral, unless—

(1) all parties to the dispute resolution proceeding and the neutral consent in writing, and, if the dispute resolution communication was provided by a nonparty participant, that participant also consents in writing;

(2) the dispute resolution communication has already been made public;

(3) the dispute resolution communication is required by statute to be made public, but a neutral should make such communication public only if no other person is reasonably available to disclose the communication; or

(4) a court determines that such testimony or disclosure is necessary to—

(A) prevent a manifest injustice;

(B) help establish a violation of law; or

(C) prevent harm to the public health or safety,

of sufficient magnitude in the particular case to outweigh the integrity of dispute resolution proceedings in general by reducing the confidence of parties in future cases that their communications will remain confidential.

(b) A party to a dispute resolution proceeding shall not voluntarily disclose or through discovery or compulsory process be required to disclose any dispute resolution communication, unless—

(1) the communication was prepared by the party seeking disclosure;

(2) all parties to the dispute resolution proceeding consent in writing;

(3) the dispute resolution communication has already been made public;

(4) the dispute resolution communication is required by statute to be made public;

(5) a court determines that such testimony or disclosure is necessary to—

(A) prevent a manifest injustice;

(B) help establish a violation of law; or

(C) prevent harm to the public health and safety,

of sufficient magnitude in the particular case to outweigh the integrity of dispute resolution proceedings in general by reducing the confidence of parties in future cases that their communications will remain confidential;

(6) the dispute resolution communication is relevant to determining the existence or meaning of an agreement or award that resulted from the dispute resolution proceeding or to the enforcement of such an agreement or award; or

(7) except for dispute resolution communications generated by the neutral, the dispute resolution communication was provided to or was available to all parties to the dispute resolution proceeding.

(c) Any dispute resolution communication that is disclosed in violation of subsection (a) or (b), shall not be admissible in any proceeding relating to the issues in controversy with respect to which the communication was made.

(d)(1) The parties may agree to alternative confidential procedures for disclosures by a neutral. Upon such agreement the parties shall inform the neutral before the commencement of the dispute resolution proceeding of any modifications to the provisions of subsection (a) that will govern the confidentiality of the dispute resolution proceeding. If the parties do not so inform the neutral, subsection (a) shall apply;

(2) To qualify for the exemption established under subsection (j), an alternative confidential procedure under this subsection may not provide for less disclosure than the confidential procedures otherwise provided under this section.

(e) If a demand for disclosure, by way of discovery request or other legal process, is made upon a neutral regarding a dispute resolution communication, the neutral shall make reasonable efforts to notify the parties and any affected nonparty participants of the demand. Any party or affected nonparty participant who receives such notice and within 15 calendar days does not offer to defend a refusal of the neutral to disclose the requested information shall have waived any objection to such disclosure.

(f) Nothing in this section shall prevent the discovery or admissibility of any evidence that is otherwise discoverable, merely because the evidence was presented in the course of a dispute resolution proceeding.

(g) Subsections (a) and (b) shall have no effect on the information and data that are necessary to document an agreement reached or order issued pursuant to a dispute resolution proceeding.

(h) Subsections (a) and (b) shall not prevent the gathering of information for research or educational purposes, in cooperation with other agencies, governmental entities, or dispute resolution programs, so long as the parties and the specific issues in controversy are not identifiable.

(i) Subsections (a) and (b) shall not prevent use of a dispute resolution communication to resolve a dispute between the neutral in a dispute resolution proceeding and a party to or participant in such proceeding, so long as such dispute resolution communication is disclosed only to the extent necessary to resolve such dispute.

(j) A dispute resolution communication which is between a neutral and a party and which may not be disclosed under this section shall also be exempt from disclosure under section 552(b)(3).

§ 575. Authorization of arbitration

(a)(1) Arbitration may be used as an alternative means of dispute resolution whenever all parties consent. Consent may be obtained either before or after an issue in controversy has arisen. A party may agree to—

> (A) submit only certain issues in controversy to arbitration; or

> (B) arbitration on the condition that the award must be within a range of possible outcomes.

(2) The arbitration agreement that sets forth the subject matter submitted to the arbitrator shall be in writing. Each such arbitration agreement shall specify a maximum award that may be issued by the arbitrator and may specify other conditions limiting the range of possible outcomes.

(3) An agency may not require any person to consent to arbitration as a condition of entering into a contract or obtaining a benefit.

(b) An officer or employee of an agency shall not offer to use arbitration for the resolution of issues in controversy unless such officer or employee—

> (1) would otherwise have authority to enter into a settlement concerning the matter; or

(2) is otherwise specifically authorized by the agency to consent to the use of arbitration.

(c) Prior to using binding arbitration under this subchapter, the head of an agency, in consultation with the Attorney General and after taking into account the factors in section 572(b), shall issue guidance on the appropriate use of binding arbitration and when an officer or employee of the agency has authority to settle an issue in controversy through binding arbitration.

§ 576. Enforcement of arbitration agreements

An agreement to arbitrate a matter to which this subchapter applies is enforceable pursuant to section 4 of title 9, and no action brought to enforce such an agreement shall be dismissed nor shall relief therein be denied on the grounds that it is against the United States or that the United States is an indispensable party.

§ 577. Arbitrators

(a) The parties to an arbitration proceeding shall be entitled to participate in the selection of the arbitrator.

(b) The arbitrator shall be a neutral who meets the criteria of section 573 of this title.

§ 578. Authority of the arbitrator

An arbitrator to whom a dispute is referred under this subchapter may—

(1) regulate the course of and conduct arbitral hearings;

(2) administer oaths and affirmations;

(3) compel the attendance of witnesses and production of evidence at the hearing under the provisions of section 7 of title 9 only to the extent the agency involved is otherwise authorized by law to do so; and

(4) make awards.

§ 579. Arbitration proceedings

(a) The arbitrator shall set a time and place for the hearing on the dispute and shall notify the parties not less than 5 days before the hearing.

(b) Any party wishing a record of the hearing shall—

(1) be responsible for the preparation of such record;

(2) notify the other parties and the arbitrator of the preparation of such record;

(3) furnish copies to all identified parties and the arbitrator; and

(4) pay all costs for such record, unless the parties agree otherwise or the arbitrator determines that the costs should be apportioned.

(c)(1) he parties to the arbitration are entitled to be heard, to present evidence material to the controversy, and to cross-examine witnesses appearing at the hearing.

(2) The arbitrator may, with the consent of the parties, conduct all or part of the hearing by telephone, television, computer, or other electronic means, if each party has an opportunity to participate.

(3) The hearing shall be conducted expeditiously and in an informal manner.

(4) The arbitrator may receive any oral or documentary evidence, except that irrelevant, immaterial, unduly repetitious, or privileged evidence may be excluded by the arbitrator.

(5) The arbitrator shall interpret and apply relevant statutory and regulatory requirements, legal precedents, and policy directives.

(d) No interested person shall make or knowingly cause to be made to the arbitrator an unauthorized ex parte communication relevant to the merits of the proceeding, unless the parties agree otherwise. If a communication is made in violation of this subsection, the arbitrator shall ensure that a memorandum of the communication is prepared and made a part of the record, and that an opportunity for rebuttal is allowed. Upon receipt of a communication made in violation of this subsection, the arbitrator may, to the extent consistent with the interests of justice and the policies underlying this subchapter, require the offending party to show cause why the claim of such party should not be resolved against such party as a result of the improper conduct.

(e) The arbitrator shall make the award within 30 days after the close of the hearing, or the date of the filing of any briefs authorized by the arbitrator, whichever date is later, unless—

(1) the parties agree to some other time limit; or

(2) the agency provides by rule for some other time limit.

§ 580. Arbitration awards

(a)(1) Unless the agency provides otherwise by rule, the award in an arbitration proceeding under this subchapter shall include a brief, informal discussion of the factual and legal basis for the award, but formal findings of fact or conclusions of law shall not be required.

(2) The prevailing parties shall file the award with all relevant agencies, along with proof of service on all parties.

(b) The award in an arbitration proceeding shall become final 30 days after it is served on all parties. Any agency that is a party to the proceeding may extend this 30–day period for an additional 30–day period by serving a notice of such extension on all other parties before the end of the first 30–day period.

(c) A final award is binding on the parties to the arbitration proceeding, and may be enforced pursuant to sections 9 through 13 of title 9. No action brought to enforce such an award shall be dismissed nor shall relief therein be denied on the grounds that it is against the United States or that the United States is an indispensable party.

(d) An award entered under this subchapter in an arbitration proceeding may not serve as an estoppel in any other proceeding for any issue that was resolved in the proceeding. Such an award also may not be used as precedent or otherwise be considered in any factually unrelated proceeding, whether conducted under this subchapter, by an agency, or in a court, or in any other arbitration proceeding.

§ 581. Judicial Review

(a) Notwithstanding any other provision of law, any person adversely affected or aggrieved by an award made in an arbitration proceeding conducted under this subchapter may bring an action for review of such award only pursuant to the provisions of sections 9 through 13 of title 9.

(b) A decision by an agency to use or not to use a dispute resolution proceeding under this subchapter shall be committed to the discretion of the agency and shall not be subject to judicial review, except that arbitration shall be subject to judicial review under section 10(b) of title 9.

§ 583. Support services

For the purposes of this subchapter, an agency may use (with or without reimbursement) the services and facilities of other Federal agencies, State, local, and tribal governments, public and private organizations and agencies, and individuals, with the consent of such agencies, organizations, and individuals. An agency may accept voluntary and uncompensated services for purposes of this subchapter without regard to the provisions of section 1342 of title 31.

REGULATORY FLEXIBILITY ACT

TITLE 5. GOVERNMENT ORGANIZATION AND EMPLOYEES
PART I—THE AGENCIES GENERALLY
CHAPTER 6—THE ANALYSIS OF REGULATORY FUNCTIONS

§ 601. Definitions

For purposes of this chapter—

(1) the term "agency" means an agency as defined in section 551(1) of this title;

(2) the term "rule" means any rule for which the agency publishes a general notice of proposed rulemaking pursuant to section 553(b) of this title, or any other law, including any rule of general applicability governing Federal grants to State and local governments for which the agency provides an opportunity for notice and public comment, except that the term "rule" does not include a rule of particular applicability relating to rates, wages, corporate or financial structures or reorganizations thereof, prices, facilities, appliances, services, or allowances therefor or to valuations, costs or accounting, or practices relating to such rates, wages, structures, prices, appliances, services, or allowances;

(3) the term "small business" has the same meaning as the term "small business concern" under section 3 of the Small Business Act, unless an agency, after consultation with the Office of Advocacy of the Small Business Administration and after opportunity for public comment, establishes one or more definitions of such term which are appropriate to the activities of the agency and publishes such definition(s) in the Federal Register;

(4) the term "small organization" means any not-for-profit enterprise which is independently owned and operated and is not dominant in its field, unless an agency establishes, after opportunity for public comment, one or more definitions of such term which are appropriate to the activities of the agency and publishes such definition(s) in the Federal Register;

(5) the term "small governmental jurisdiction" means governments of cities, counties, towns, townships, villages, school districts, or special districts, with a population of less than fifty thousand, unless an agency establishes, after opportunity for public comment, one or more definitions of such term which are appropriate to the activities of the agency and which are based on such factors as location in rural or sparsely populated areas or limited revenues due to the population of such jurisdiction, and publishes such definition(s) in the Federal Register; and

(6) the term "small entity" shall have the same meaning as the terms "small business", "small organization" and "small governmental jurisdiction" defined in paragraphs (3), (4) and (5) of this section; and

(7) the term "collection of information"—

(A) means the obtaining, causing to be obtained, soliciting, or requiring the disclosure to third parties or the public, of facts or opinions by or for an agency, regardless of form or format, calling for either—

(i) answers to identical questions posed to, or identical reporting or recordkeeping requirements imposed on, 10 or more persons, other than agencies, instrumentalities, or employees of the United States; or

(ii) answers to questions posed to agencies, instrumentalities or employees of the United States which are to be used for general statistical purposes; and

(B) shall not include a collection of information described under section 3518(c)(1) of title 44, United States Code; and

(8) Recordkeeping requirement. The term "recordkeeping requirement" means a requirement imposed by an agency on persons to maintain specified records.

§ 602. Regulatory agenda

(a) During the months of October and April of each year, each agency shall publish in the Federal Register a regulatory flexibility agenda which shall contain—

(1) a brief description of the subject area of any rule which the agency expects to propose or promulgate which is likely to have a

significant economic impact on a substantial number of small entities;

(2) a summary of the nature of any such rule under consideration for each subject area listed in the agenda pursuant to paragraph (1), the objectives and legal basis for the issuance of the rule, and an approximate schedule for completing action on any rule for which the agency has issued a general notice of proposed rulemaking, and

(3) the name and telephone number of an agency official knowledgeable concerning the items listed in paragraph (1).

(b) Each regulatory flexibility agenda shall be transmitted to the Chief Counsel for Advocacy of the Small Business Administration for comment, if any.

(c) Each agency shall endeavor to provide notice of each regulatory flexibility agenda to small entities or their representatives through direct notification or publication of the agenda in publications likely to be obtained by such small entities and shall invite comments upon each subject area on the agenda.

(d) Nothing in this section precludes an agency from considering or acting on any matter not included in a regulatory flexibility agenda, or requires an agency to consider or act on any matter listed in such agenda.

§ 603. Initial regulatory flexibility analysis

(a) Whenever an agency is required by section 553 of this title, or any other law, to publish general notice of proposed rulemaking for any proposed rule, or publishes a notice of proposed rulemaking for an interpretative rule involving the internal revenue laws of the United States, the agency shall prepare and make available for public comment an initial regulatory flexibility analysis. Such analysis shall describe the impact of the proposed rule on small entities. The initial regulatory flexibility analysis or a summary shall be published in the Federal Register at the time of the publication of general notice of proposed rulemaking for the rule. The agency shall transmit a copy of the initial regulatory flexibility analysis to the Chief Counsel for Advocacy of the Small Business Administration. In the case of an interpretative rule involving the internal revenue laws of the United States, this chapter [5 USC §§ 601 et seq.] applies to interpretative rules published in the Federal Register for codification in the Code of Federal Regulations, but only to the extent that such interpretative rules impose on small entities a collection of information requirement.

(b) Each initial regulatory flexibility analysis required under this section shall contain—

(1) a description of the reasons why action by the agency is being considered;

(2) a succinct statement of the objectives of, and legal basis for, the proposed rule;

(3) a description of and, where feasible, an estimate of the number of small entities to which the proposed rule will apply;

(4) a description of the projected reporting, recordkeeping and other compliance requirements of the proposed rule, including an estimate of the classes of small entities which will be subject to the requirement and the type of professional skills necessary for preparation of the report or record;

(5) an identification, to the extent practicable, of all relevant Federal rules which may duplicate, overlap or conflict with the proposed rule.

(c) Each initial regulatory flexibility analysis shall also contain a description of any significant alternatives to the proposed rule which accomplish the stated objectives of applicable statutes and which minimize any significant economic impact of the proposed rule on small entities. Consistent with the stated objectives of applicable statutes, the analysis shall discuss significant alternatives such as—

(1) the establishment of differing compliance or reporting requirements or timetables that take into account the resources available to small entities;

(2) the clarification, consolidation, or simplification of compliance and reporting requirements under the rule for such small entities;

(3) the use of performance rather than design standards; and

(4) an exemption from coverage of the rule, or any part thereof, for such small entities.

§ **604.** **Final regulatory flexibility analysis**

(a) When an agency promulgates a final rule under section 553 of this title, after being required by that section or any other law to publish a general notice of proposed rulemaking, or promulgates a final interpretative rule involving the internal revenue laws of the United States as described in section 603(a), the agency shall prepare a final regulatory flexibility analysis. Each final regulatory flexibility analysis shall contain—

(1) a succinct statement of the need for, and the objectives of, the rule;

(2) a summary of the issues raised by the public comments in response to the initial regulatory flexibility analysis, a summary of the assessment of the agency of such issues, and a statement of any changes made in the proposed rule as a result of such comments; and

(3) a description of and an estimate of the number of small entities to which the rule will apply or an explanation of why no such estimate is available;

(4) a description of the projected reporting, recordkeeping and other compliance requirements of the rule, including an estimate of the classes of small entities which will be subject to the requirement and the type of professional skills necessary for preparation of the report or record; and

(5) a description of the steps the agency has taken to minimize the significant economic impact on small entities consistent with the stated objectives of applicable statutes, including a statement on the factual, policy and legal reasons for selecting the alternative adopted in the final rule and why each one of the other significant alternatives to the rule considered by the agency which affect the impact on small entities was rejected.

(b) The agency shall make copies of the final regulatory flexibility analysis available to members of the public and shall publish in the Federal Register such analysis or a summary thereof.

§ 605. Avoidance of duplicative or unnecessary analyses

(a) Any Federal agency may perform the analyses required by sections 602, 603, and 604 of this title in conjunction with or as a part of any other agenda or analysis required by any other law if such other analysis satisfies the provisions of such sections.

(b) Sections 603 and 604 of this title shall not apply to any proposed or final rule if the head of the agency certifies that the rule will not, if promulgated, have a significant economic impact on a substantial number of small entities. If the head of the agency makes a certification under the preceding sentence, the agency shall publish such certification in the Federal Register, at the time of publication of general notice of proposed rulemaking for the rule or at the time of publication of the final rule, along with a statement providing the factual basis for such certification. The agency shall provide such certification and statement to the Chief Counsel for Advocacy of the Small Business Administration.

(c) In order to avoid duplicative action, an agency may consider a series of closely related rules as one rule for the purposes of sections 602, 603, 604 and 610 of this title.

§ 606. Effect on other law

The requirements of sections 603 and 604 of this title do not alter in any manner standards otherwise applicable by law to agency action.

§ 607.   Preparation of analyses

In complying with the provisions of sections 603 and 604 of this title, an agency may provide either a quantifiable or numerical description of the effects of a proposed rule or alternatives to the proposed rule, or more general descriptive statements if quantification is not practicable or reliable.

§ 608.   Procedure for waiver or delay of completion

(a) An agency head may waive or delay the completion of some or all of the requirements of section 603 of this title by publishing in the Federal Register, not later than the date of publication of the final rule, a written finding, with reasons therefor, that the final rule is being promulgated in response to an emergency that makes compliance or timely compliance with the provisions of section 603 of this title impracticable.

(b) Except as provided in section 605(b), an agency head may not waive the requirements of section 604 of this title. An agency head may delay the completion of the requirements of section 604 of this title for a period of not more than one hundred and eighty days after the date of publication in the Federal Register of a final rule by publishing in the Federal Register, not later than such date of publication, a written finding, with reasons therefor, that the final rule is being promulgated in response to an emergency that makes timely compliance with the provisions of section 604 of this title impracticable. If the agency has not prepared a final regulatory analysis pursuant to section 604 of this title within one hundred and eighty days from the date of publication of the final rule, such rule shall lapse and have no effect. Such rule shall not be repromulgated until a final regulatory flexibility analysis has been completed by the agency.

§ 609.   Procedures for gathering comments

(a) When any rule is promulgated which will have a significant economic impact on a substantial number of small entities, the head of the agency promulgating the rule or the official of the agency with statutory responsibility for the promulgation of the rule shall assure that small entities have been given an opportunity to participate in the rulemaking for the rule through techniques such as—

   (1) the inclusion in an advanced notice of proposed rulemaking, if issued, of a statement that the proposed rule may have a significant economic effect on a substantial number of small entities;

   (2) the publication of general notice of proposed rulemaking in publications likely to be obtained by small entities;

   (3) the direct notification of interested small entities;

(4) the conduct of open conferences or public hearings concerning the rule of small entities including soliciting and receiving comments over computer networks; and

(5) the adoption or modification of agency procedural rules to reduce the cost or complexity of participation in the rulemaking by small entities.

(b) Prior to publication of an initial regulatory flexibility analysis which a covered agency is required to conduct by this chapter [5 USC §§ 601 et seq.]—

(1) a covered agency shall notify the Chief Counsel for Advocacy of the Small Business Administration and provide the Chief Counsel with information on the potential impacts of the proposed rule on small entities and the type of small entities that might be affected;

(2) not later than 15 days after the date of receipt of the materials described in paragraph (1), the Chief Counsel shall identify individuals representative of affected small entities for the purpose of obtaining advice and recommendations from those individuals about the potential impacts of the proposed rule;

(3) the agency shall convene a review panel for such rule consisting of full time Federal employees of the office within the agency responsible for carrying out the proposed rule, the Office of Information and Regulatory Affairs within the Office of Management and Budget, and the Chief Counsel;

(4) the panel shall review an material the agency has prepared in connection with this chapter, including any draft proposed rule, collect advice and recommendations of each individual small entity representative identified by the agency after consultation with the Chief Counsel, on issues related to subsections 603(b), paragraphs (3), (4) and (5) and 603(c);

(5) not later than 60 days after the date a covered agency convenes a review panel pursuant to paragraph (3), the review panel shall report on the comments of the small entity representatives and its findings as to issues related to subsection 603(b), paragraphs (3), (4) and (5) and 603(c) provided that such report shall be made public as part of the rulemaking record; and

(6) where appropriate, the agency shall modify the proposed rule, the initial regulatory flexibility analysis or the decision on whether an initial regulatory flexibility analysis is required.

(c) An agency may in its discretion apply subsection (b) to rules that the agency intends to certify under subsection 605(b), but the agency believes may have a greater than de minimis impact on a substantial number of small entities.

(d) For purposes of this section, the term "covered agency" means the Environmental Protection Agency and the Occupational Safety and Health Administration of the Department of Labor.

(e) The Chief Counsel for Advocacy, in consultation with the individuals identified in subsection (b)(2), and with the Administrator of the Office of Information and Regulatory Affairs within the Office of Management and Budget, may waive the requirements of subsections (b)(3), (b)(4), and (b)(5) by including in the rulemaking record a written finding, with reasons therefor, that those requirements would not advance the effective participation of small entities in the rulemaking process. For purposes of this subsection, the factors to be considered in making such a finding are as follows:

(1) In developing a proposed rule, the extent to which the covered agency consulted with individuals representative of affected small entities with respect to the potential impacts of the rule and took such concerns into consideration.

(2) Special circumstances requiring prompt issuance of the rule.

(3) Whether the requirements of subsection (b) would provide the individuals identified in subsection (b)(2) with a competitive advantage relative to other small entities.

§ 610. Periodic review of rules

(a) Within one hundred and eighty days after the effective date of this chapter, each agency shall publish in the Federal Register a plan for the periodic review of the rules issued by the agency which have or will have a significant economic impact upon a substantial number of small entities. Such plan may be amended by the agency at any time by publishing the revision in the Federal Register. The purpose of the review shall be to determine whether such rules should be continued without change, or should be amended or rescinded, consistent with the stated objectives of applicable statutes, to minimize any significant economic impact of the rules upon a substantial number of such small entities. The plan shall provide for the review of all such agency rules existing on the effective date of this chapter within ten years of that date and for the review of such rules adopted after the effective date of this chapter within ten years of the publication of such rules as the final rule. If the head of the agency determines that completion of the review of existing rules is not feasible by the established date, he shall so certify in a statement published in the Federal Register and may extend the completion date by one year at a time for a total of not more than five years.

(b) In reviewing rules to minimize any significant economic impact of the rule on a substantial number of small entities in a manner consistent with the stated objectives of applicable statutes, the agency shall consider the following factors—

(1) the continued need for the rule;

(2) the nature of complaints or comments received concerning the rule from the public;

(3) the complexity of the rule;

(4) the extent to which the rule overlaps, duplicates or conflicts with other Federal rules, and, to the extent feasible, with State and local governmental rules; and

(5) the length of time since the rule has been evaluated or the degree to which technology, economic conditions, or other factors have changed in the area affected by the rule.

(c) Each year, each agency shall publish in the Federal Register a list of the rules which have a significant economic impact on a substantial number of small entities, which are to be reviewed pursuant to this section during the succeeding twelve months. The list shall include a brief description of each rule and the need for and legal basis of such rule and shall invite public comment upon the rule.

§ 611. Judicial review

(a)(1) For any rule subject to this chapter [5 USC §§ 601 et seq.], a small entity that is adversely affected or aggrieved by final agency action is entitled to judicial review of agency compliance with the requirements of sections 601, 604, 605(b), 608(b), and 610 in accordance with chapter 7 [5 USC §§ 701 et seq.]. Agency compliance with sections 607 and 609(a) shall be judicially reviewable in connection with judicial review of section 604.

(2) Each court having jurisdiction to review such rule for compliance with section 553, or under any other provision of law, shall have jurisdiction to review any claims of noncompliance with sections 601, 604, 605(b), 608(b), and 610 in accordance with chapter 7 [5 USC §§ 701 et seq.]. Agency compliance with sections 607 and 609(a) shall be judicially reviewable in connection with judicial review of section 604.

(3)(A) A small entity may seek such review during the period beginning on the date of final agency action and ending one year later, except that where a provision of law requires that an action challenging a final agency action be commenced before the expiration of one year, such lesser period shall apply to an action for judicial review under this section.

(B) In the case where an agency delays the issuance of a final regulatory flexibility analysis pursuant to section 608(b) of this chapter, an action for judicial review under this section shall be filed not later than—

(i) one year after the date the analysis is made available to the public, or

(ii) where a provision of law requires that an action challenging a final agency regulation be commenced before the expiration of the 1–year period, the number of days specified in such provision of law that is after the date the analysis is made available to the public.

(4) In granting any relief in an action under this section, the court shall order the agency to take corrective action consistent with this chapter and chapter 7 [5 USC §§ 601 et seq., 701 et seq.], including, but not limited to—

(A) remanding the rule to the agency, and

(B) deferring the enforcement of the rule against small entities unless the court finds that continued enforcement of the rule is in the public interest.

(5) Nothing in this subsection shall be construed to limit the authority of any court to stay the effective date of any rule or provision thereof under any other provision of law or to grant any other relief in addition to the requirements of this section.

(b) In an action for the judicial review of a rule, the regulatory flexibility analysis for such rule, including an analysis prepared or corrected pursuant to paragraph (a)(4), shall constitute part of the entire record of agency action in connection with such review.

(c) Compliance or noncompliance by an agency with the provisions of this chapter [5 USC §§ 601 et seq.] shall be subject to judicial review only in accordance with this section.

(d) Nothing in this section bars judicial review of any other impact statement or similar analysis required by any other law if judicial review of such statement or analysis is otherwise permitted by law.

§ 612. Reports and intervention rights

(a) The Chief Counsel for Advocacy of the Small Business Administration shall monitor agency compliance with this chapter [5 USC §§ 601 et seq.] and shall report at least annually thereon to the President and to the Committees on the Judiciary and Small Business of the Senate and House of Representatives.

(b) The Chief Counsel for Advocacy of the Small Business Administration is authorized to appear as amicus curiae in any action brought in a court of the United States to review a rule. In any such action, the Chief Counsel is authorized to present his or her views with respect to compliance with this chapter [5 USC §§ 601 et seq.], the adequacy of the rulemaking record with respect to small entities and the effect of the rule on small entities.

(c) A court of the United States shall grant the application of the Chief Counsel for Advocacy of the Small Business Administration to appear in any such action for the purposes described in subsection (b).

ASSESSMENT OF FEDERAL REGULATIONS AND POLICIES ON FAMILIES

Public Law No. 105–277, October 21, 1998, 112 Stat. 2681

Note to 5 U.S.C. § 601

§ 654. ASSESSMENT OF FEDERAL REGULATIONS AND POLICIES ON FAMILIES.

(a) PURPOSES.—The purposes of this section are to—

(1) require agencies to assess the impact of proposed agency actions on family well-being; and

(2) improve the management of executive branch agencies.

(b) DEFINITIONS.—In this section—

(1) the term "agency" has the meaning given the term "Executive agency" by section 105 of title 5, United States Code, except such term does not include the Government Accountability Office; and

(2) the term "family" means–

(A) a group of individuals related by blood, marriage, adoption, or other legal custody who live together as a single household; and

(B) any individual who is not a member of such group, but who is related by blood, marriage, or adoption to a member of such group, and over half of whose support in a calendar year is received from such group.

(c) FAMILY POLICYMAKING ASSESSMENT.—Before implementing policies and regulations that may affect family well-being, each agency shall assess such actions with respect to whether—

(1) the action strengthens or erodes the stability or safety of the family and, particularly, the marital commitment;

(2) the action strengthens or erodes the authority and rights of parents in the education, nurture, and supervision of their children;

(3) the action helps the family perform its functions, or substitutes governmental activity for the function;

(4) the action increases or decreases disposable income or poverty of families and children;

(5) the proposed benefits of the action justify the financial impact on the family;

(6) the action may be carried out by State or local government or by the family; and

110

(7) the action establishes an implicit or explicit policy concerning the relationship between the behavior and personal responsibility of youth, and the norms of society.

(d) GOVERNMENTWIDE FAMILY POLICY COORDINATION AND REVIEW.—

(1) CERTIFICATION AND RATIONALE.—With respect to each proposed policy or regulation that may affect family well-being, the head of each agency shall—

(A) submit a written certification to the Director of the Office of Management and Budget and to Congress that such policy or regulation has been assessed in accordance with this section; and

(B) provide an adequate rationale for implementation of each policy or regulation that may negatively affect family well-being.

(2) OFFICE OF MANAGEMENT AND BUDGET.—The Director of the Office of Management and Budget shall—

(A) ensure that policies and regulations proposed by agencies are implemented consistent with this section; and

(B) compile, index, and submit annually to the Congress the written certifications received pursuant to paragraph (1)(A).

(3) OFFICE OF POLICY DEVELOPMENT.—The Office of Policy Development shall—

(A) assess proposed policies and regulations in accordance with this section;

(B) provide evaluations of policies and regulations that may affect family well-being to the Director of the Office of Management and Budget; and

(C) advise the President on policy and regulatory actions that may be taken to strengthen the institutions of marriage and family in the United States.

(e) ASSESSMENTS UPON REQUEST BY MEMBERS OF CONGRESS.—Upon request by a Member of Congress relating to a proposed policy or regulation, an agency shall conduct an assessment in accordance with subsection (c), and shall provide a certification and rationale in accordance with subsection (d).

(f) JUDICIAL REVIEW.—This section is not intended to create any right or benefit, substantive or procedural, enforceable at law by a party against the United States, its agencies, its officers, or any person.

CONGRESSIONAL REVIEW OF AGENCY RULEMAKING

TITLE 5. GOVERNMENT ORGANIZATION AND EMPLOYEES
PART I—THE AGENCIES GENERALLY
CHAPTER 8—CONGRESSIONAL REVIEW OF AGENCY RULEMAKING

§ 801. Congressional review

(a)(1)(A) Before a rule can take effect, the Federal agency promulgating such rule shall submit to each House of the Congress and to the Comptroller General a report containing—

> (i) a copy of the rule;

> (ii) a concise general statement relating to the rule, including whether it is a major rule; and

> (iii) the proposed effective date of the rule.

(B) On the date of the submission of the report under subparagraph (A), the Federal agency promulgating the rule shall submit to the Comptroller General and make available to each House of Congress—

> (i) a complete copy of the cost-benefit analysis of the rule, if any;

> (ii) the agency's actions relevant to sections 603, 604, 605, 607, and 609;

> (iii) the agency's actions relevant to sections 202, 203, 204, and 205 of the Unfunded Mandates Reform Act of 1995; and

> (iv) any other relevant information or requirements under any other Act and any relevant Executive orders.

(C) Upon receipt of a report submitted under subparagraph (A), each House shall provide copies of the report to the chairman and ranking member of each standing committee with jurisdiction under the rules of the House of Representatives or the Senate to report a bill to amend the provision of law under which the rule is issued.

(2)(A) The Comptroller General shall provide a report on each major rule to the committees of jurisdiction in each House of the Congress by the end of 15 calendar days after the submission or publication date as provided in section 802(b)(2). The report of the Comptroller General shall include an assessment of the agency's compliance with procedural steps required by paragraph (1)(B).

(B) Federal agencies shall cooperate with the Comptroller General by providing information relevant to the Comptroller General's report under subparagraph (A).

(3) A major rule relating to a report submitted under paragraph (1) shall take effect on the latest of—

(A) the later of the date occurring 60 days after the date on which—

(i) the Congress receives the report submitted under paragraph (1); or

(ii) the rule is published in the Federal Register, if so published;

(B) if the Congress passes a joint resolution of disapproval described in section 802 relating to the rule, and the President signs a veto of such resolution, the earlier date—

(i) on which either House of Congress votes and fails to override the veto of the President; or

(ii) occurring 30 session days after the date on which the Congress received the veto and objections of the President; or

(C) the date the rule would have otherwise taken effect, if not for this section (unless a joint resolution of disapproval under section 802 is enacted).

(4) Except for a major rule, a rule shall take effect as otherwise provided by law after submission to Congress under paragraph (1).

(5) Notwithstanding paragraph (3), the effective date of a rule shall not be delayed by operation of this chapter beyond the date on which either House of Congress votes to reject a joint resolution of disapproval under section 802.

(b)(1) A rule shall not take effect (or continue), if the Congress enacts a joint resolution of disapproval, described under section 802, of the rule.

(2) A rule that does not take effect (or does not continue) under paragraph (1) may not be reissued in substantially the same form, and a new rule that is substantially the same as such a rule may not be issued, unless the reissued or new rule is specifically authorized by a law enacted after the date of the joint resolution disapproving the original rule.

(c)(1) Notwithstanding any other provision of this section (except subject to paragraph (3)), a rule that would not take effect by reason of subsection (a)(3) may take effect, if the President makes a determination under paragraph (2) and submits written notice of such determination to the Congress.

(2) Paragraph (1) applies to a determination made by the President by Executive order that the rule should take effect because such rule is—

(A) necessary because of an imminent threat to health or safety or other emergency;

(B) necessary for the enforcement of criminal laws;

(C) necessary for national security; or

(D) issued pursuant to any statute implementing an international trade agreement.

(3) An exercise by the President of the authority under this subsection shall have no effect on the procedures under section 802 or the effect of a joint resolution of disapproval under this section.

(d)(1) In addition to the opportunity for review otherwise provided under this chapter, in the case of any rule for which a report was submitted in accordance with subsection (a)(1)(A) during the period beginning on the date occurring—

(A) in the case of the Senate, 60 session days, or

(B) in the case of the House of Representatives, 60 legislative days,

before the date the Congress adjourns a session of Congress through the date on which the same or succeeding Congress first convenes its next session, section 802 shall apply to such rule in the succeeding session of Congress.

(2)(A) In applying section 802 for purposes of such additional review, a rule described under paragraph (1) shall be treated as though—

(i) such rule were published in the Federal Register (as a rule that shall take effect) on—

(I) in the case of the Senate, the 15th session day, or

(II) in the case of the House of Representatives, the 15th legislative day,

114

after the succeeding session of Congress first convenes; and

(ii) a report on such rule were submitted to Congress under subsection (a)(1) on such date.

(B) Nothing in this paragraph shall be construed to affect the requirement under subsection (a)(1) that a report shall be submitted to Congress before a rule can take effect.

(3) A rule described under paragraph (1) shall take effect as otherwise provided by law (including other subsections of this section).

(e)(1) For purposes of this subsection, section 802 shall also apply to any major rule promulgated between March 1, 1996, and the date of the enactment of this chapter.

(2) In applying section 802 for purposes of Congressional review, a rule described under paragraph (1) shall be treated as though—

(A) such rule were published in the Federal Register on the date of enactment of this chapter; and

(B) a report on such rule were submitted to Congress under subsection (a)(1) on such date.

(3) The effectiveness of a rule described under paragraph (1) shall be as otherwise provided by law, unless the rule is made of no force or effect under section 802.

(f) Any rule that takes effect and later is made of no force or effect by enactment of a joint resolution under section 802 shall be treated as though such rule had never taken effect.

(g) If the Congress does not enact a joint resolution of disapproval under section 802 respecting a rule, no court or agency may infer any intent of the Congress from any action or inaction of the Congress with regard to such rule, related statute, or joint resolution of disapproval.

§ 802. Congressional disapproval procedure

(a) For purposes of this section, the term "joint resolution" means only a joint resolution introduced in the period beginning on the date on which the report referred to in section 801(a)(1)(A) is received by Congress and ending 60 days thereafter (excluding days either House of Congress is adjourned for more than 3 days during a session of Congress), the matter after the resolving clause of which is as follows: "That Congress disapproves the rule submitted by the _____ relating to _____, and such rule shall have no force or effect." (The blank spaces being appropriately filled in).

(b)(1) A joint resolution described in subsection (a) shall be referred to the committees in each House of Congress with jurisdiction.

(2) For purposes of this section, the term "submission or publication date" means the later of the date on which—

(A) the Congress receives the report submitted under section 801(a)(1); or

(B) the rule is published in the Federal Register, if so published.

(c) In the Senate, if the committee to which is referred a joint resolution described in subsection (a) has not reported such joint resolution (or an identical joint resolution) at the end of 20 calendar days after the submission or publication date defined under subsection (b)(2), such committee may be discharged from further consideration of such joint resolution upon a petition supported in writing by 30 Members of the Senate, and such joint resolution shall be placed on the calendar.

(d)(1) In the Senate, when the committee to which a joint resolution is referred has reported, or when a committee is discharged (under subsection (c)) from further consideration of a joint resolution described in subsection (a), it is at any time thereafter in order (even though a previous motion to the same effect has been disagreed to) for a motion to proceed to the consideration of the joint resolution, and all points of order against the joint resolution (and against consideration of the joint resolution) are waived. The motion is not subject to amendment, or to a motion to postpone, or to a motion to proceed to the consideration of other business. A motion to reconsider the vote by which the motion is agreed to or disagreed to shall not be in order. If a motion to proceed to the consideration of the joint resolution is agreed to, the joint resolution shall remain the unfinished business of the Senate until disposed of.

(2) In the Senate, debate on the joint resolution, and on all debatable motions and appeals in connection therewith, shall be limited to not more than 10 hours, which shall be divided equally between those favoring and those opposing the joint resolution. A motion further to limit debate is in order and not debatable. An amendment to, or a motion to postpone, or a motion to proceed to the consideration of other business, or a motion to recommit the joint resolution is not in order.

(3) In the Senate, immediately following the conclusion of the debate on a joint resolution described in subsection (a), and a single quorum call at the conclusion of the debate if requested in accordance with the rules of the Senate, the vote on final passage of the joint resolution shall occur.

(4) Appeals from the decisions of the Chair relating to the application of the rules of the Senate to the procedure relating to a joint resolution described in subsection (a) shall be decided without debate.

(e) In the Senate the procedure specified in subsection (c) or (d) shall not apply to the consideration of a joint resolution respecting a rule—

(1) after the expiration of the 60 session days beginning with the applicable submission or publication date, or

(2) if the report under section 801(a)(1)(A) was submitted during the period referred to in section 801(d)(1), after the expiration of the 60 session days beginning on the 15th session day after the succeeding session of Congress first convenes.

(f) If, before the passage by one House of a joint resolution of that House described in subsection (a), that House receives from the other House a joint resolution described in subsection (a), then the following procedures shall apply:

(1) The joint resolution of the other House shall not be referred to a committee.

(2) With respect to a joint resolution described in subsection (a) of the House receiving the joint resolution—

(A) the procedure in that House shall be the same as if no joint resolution had been received from the other House; but

(B) the vote on final passage shall be on the joint resolution of the other House.

(g) This section is enacted by Congress—

(1) as an exercise of the rulemaking power of the Senate and House of Representatives, respectively, and as such it is deemed a part of the rules of each House, respectively, but applicable only with respect to the procedure to be followed in that House in the case of a joint resolution described in subsection (a), and it supersedes other rules only to the extent that it is inconsistent with such rules; and

(2) with full recognition of the constitutional right of either House to change the rules (so far as relating to the procedure of that House) at any time, in the same manner, and to the same extent as in the case of any other rule of that House.

§ 803. Special rule on statutory; regulatory; and judicial deadlines

(a) In the case of any deadline for, relating to, or involving any rule which does not take effect (or the effectiveness of which is terminated) because of enactment of a joint resolution under section 802, that deadline is extended until the date 1 year after the date of enactment of the joint resolution. Nothing in this subsection shall be construed to affect a deadline merely by reason of the postponement of a rule's effective date under section 801(a).

(b) The term "deadline" means any date certain for fulfilling any obligation or exercising any authority established by or under any Federal statute or regulation, or by or under any court order implementing any Federal statute or regulation.

§ 804. Definitions

For purposes of this chapter—

(1) The term "Federal agency" means any agency as that term is defined in section 551(1).

(2) The term "major rule" means any rule that the Administrator of the Office of Information and Regulatory Affairs of the Office of Management and Budget finds has resulted in or is likely to result in—

(A) an annual effect on the economy of $100,000,000 or more;

(B) a major increase in costs or prices for consumers, individual industries, Federal, State, or local government agencies, or geographic regions; or

(C) significant adverse effects on competition, employment, investment, productivity, innovation, or on the ability of United States-based enterprises to compete with foreign-based enterprises in domestic and export markets.

The term does not include any rule promulgated under the Telecommunications Act of 1996 and the amendments made by that Act.

(3) The term "rule" has the meaning given such term in section 551, except that such term does not include—

(A) any rule of particular applicability, including a rule that approves or prescribes for the future rates, wages, prices, services, or allowances therefor, corporate or financial structures, reorganizations, mergers, or acquisitions thereof, or accounting practices or disclosures bearing on any of the foregoing;

(B) any rule relating to agency management or personnel; or

(C) any rule of agency organization, procedure, or practice that does not substantially affect the rights or obligations of non-agency parties.

§ 805. Judicial review

No determination, finding, action, or omission under this chapter shall be subject to judicial review.

§ 806. Applicability

(a) This chapter shall apply notwithstanding any other provision of law.

(b) If any provision of this chapter or the application of any provision of this chapter to any person or circumstance, is held invalid, the application of such provision to other persons or circumstances, and the remainder of this chapter, shall not be affected thereby.

§ 807. Exemption for monetary policy

Nothing in this chapter shall apply to rules that concern monetary policy proposed or implemented by the Board of Governors of the Federal Reserve System or the Federal Open Market Committee.

§ 808. Effective date of certain rules

Notwithstanding section 801—

(1) any rule that establishes, modifies, opens, closes, or conducts a regulatory program for a commercial, recreational, or subsistence activity related to hunting, fishing, or camping, or

(2) any rule which an agency for good cause finds (and incorporates the finding and a brief statement of reasons therefor in the rule issued) that notice and public procedure thereon are impracticable, unnecessary, or contrary to the public interest,

shall take effect at such time as the Federal agency promulgating the rule determines.

LOBBYING DISCLOSURE ACT OF 1995

TITLE 2. THE CONGRESS
CHAPTER 26—DISCLOSURE OF LOBBYING ACTIVITIES

§ 1601. Findings

The Congress finds that—

(1) responsible representative Government requires public awareness of the efforts of paid lobbyists to influence the public decision-making process in both the legislative and executive branches of the Federal Government;

(2) existing lobbying disclosure statutes have been ineffective because of unclear statutory language, weak administrative and enforcement provisions, and an absence of clear guidance as to who is required to register and what they are required to disclose; and

(3) the effective public disclosure of the identity and extent of the efforts of paid lobbyists to influence Federal officials in the conduct of Government actions will increase public confidence in the integrity of Government.

§ 1602. Definitions

As used in this chapter:

(1) *Agency*. The term "agency" has the meaning given that term in section 551(1) of Title 5.

(2) *Client*. The term "client" means any person or entity that employs or retains another person for financial or other compensation to conduct lobbying activities on behalf of that person or entity.

A person or entity whose employees act as lobbyists on its own behalf is both a client and an employer of such employees. In the case of a coalition or association that employs or retains other persons to conduct lobbying activities, the client is the coalition or association and not its individual members.

(3) *Covered executive branch official.* The term "covered executive branch official" means—

(A) the President;

(B) the Vice President;

(C) any officer or employee, or any other individual functioning in the capacity of such an officer or employee, in the Executive Office of the President;

(D) any officer or employee serving in a position in level I, II, III, IV, or V of the Executive Schedule, as designated by statute or Executive order;

(E) any member of the uniformed services whose pay grade is at or above O–7 under section 201 of Title 37; and

(F) any officer or employee serving in a position of a confidential, policy-determining, policy-making, or policy-advocating character described in section 7511(b)(2)(B) of Title 5.

(4) *Covered legislative branch official.* The term "covered legislative branch official" means—

(A) a Member of Congress;

(B) an elected officer of either House of Congress;

(C) any employee of, or any other individual functioning in the capacity of an employee of—

(i) a Member of Congress;

(ii) a committee of either House of Congress;

(iii) the leadership staff of the House of Representatives or the leadership staff of the Senate;

(iv) a joint committee of Congress; and

(v) a working group or caucus organized to provide legislative services or other assistance to Members of Congress; and

(D) any other legislative branch employee serving in a position described under section 109(13) of the Ethics in Government Act of 1978 (5 U.S.C.A. App. 4).

(5) *Employee.* The term "employee" means any individual who is an officer, employee, partner, director, or proprietor of a person or entity, but does not include—

(A) independent contractors; or

(B) volunteers who receive no financial or other compensation from the person or entity for their services.

(6) *Foreign entity.* The term "foreign entity" means a foreign principal (as defined in section 1(b) of the Foreign Agents Registration Act of 1938) (22 U.S.C. 611(b)).

(7) *Lobbying activities.* The term "lobbying activities" means lobbying contacts and efforts in support of such contacts, including preparation and planning activities, research and other background work that is intended, at the time it is performed, for use in contacts, and coordination with the lobbying activities of others.

(8) *Lobbying contact.*

(A) Definition. The term "lobbying contact" means any oral or written communication (including an electronic communication) to a covered executive branch official or a covered legislative branch official that is made on behalf of a client with regard to—

(i) the formulation, modification, or adoption of Federal legislation (including legislative proposals);

(ii) the formulation, modification, or adoption of a Federal rule, regulation, Executive order, or any other program, policy, or position of the United States Government;

(iii) the administration or execution of a Federal program or policy (including the negotiation, award, or administration of a Federal contract, grant, loan, permit, or license); or

(iv) the nomination or confirmation of a person for a position subject to confirmation by the Senate.

(B) Exceptions. The term "lobbying contact" does not include a communication that is—

(i) made by a public official acting in the public official's official capacity;

(ii) made by a representative of a media organization if the purpose of the communication is gathering and disseminating news and information to the public;

(iii) made in a speech, article, publication or other material that is distributed and made available to the public, or through radio, television, cable television, or other medium of mass communication;

(iv) made on behalf of a government of a foreign country or a foreign political party and disclosed under the Foreign Agents Registration Act of 1938 (22 U.S.C. 611 et seq.);

(v) a request for a meeting, a request for the status of an action, or any other similar administrative request, if the request does not include an attempt to influence a covered executive branch official or a covered legislative branch official;

(vi) made in the course of participation in an advisory committee subject to the Federal Advisory Committee Act;

(vii) testimony given before a committee, subcommittee, or task force of the Congress, or submitted for inclusion in the public record of a hearing conducted by such committee, subcommittee, or task force;

(viii) information provided in writing in response to an oral or written request by a covered executive branch official or a covered legislative branch official for specific information;

(ix) required by subpoena, civil investigative demand, or otherwise compelled by statute, regulation, or other action of the Congress or an agency, including any communication compelled by a Federal contract, grant, loan, permit, or license;

(x) made in response to a notice in the Federal Register, Commerce Business Daily, or other similar publication soliciting communications from the public and directed to the agency official specifically designated in the notice to receive such communications;

(xi) not possible to report without disclosing information, the unauthorized disclosure of which is prohibited by law;

(xii) made to an official in an agency with regard to—

(I) a judicial proceeding or a criminal or civil law enforcement inquiry, investigation, or proceeding; or

(II) a filing or proceeding that the Government is specifically required by statute or regulation to maintain or conduct on a confidential basis,

if that agency is charged with responsibility for such proceeding, inquiry, investigation, or filing;

(xiii) made in compliance with written agency procedures regarding an adjudication conducted by the agency under section 554 of Title 5 or substantially similar provisions;

(xiv) a written comment filed in the course of a public proceeding or any other communication that is made on the record in a public proceeding;

(xv) a petition for agency action made in writing and required to be a matter of public record pursuant to established agency procedures;

(xvi) made on behalf of an individual with regard to that individual's benefits, employment, or other personal matters involving only that individual, except that this clause does not apply to any communication with—

(I) a covered executive branch official, or

(II) a covered legislative branch official (other than the individual's elected Members of Congress or employees who work under such Members' direct supervision),

with respect to the formulation, modification, or adoption of private legislation for the relief of that individual;

(xvii) a disclosure by an individual that is protected under the amendments made by the Whistleblower Protection Act of 1989 [5 U.S.C.A. § 1211 et seq.] under the Inspector General Act of 1978 [5 U.S.C.A. App. 3] or under another provision of law;

(xviii) made by—

(I) a church, its integrated auxiliary, or a convention or association of churches that is exempt from filing a Federal income tax return under paragraph 2(A)(i) of section 6033(a) of Title 26, or

(II) a religious order that is exempt from filing a Federal income tax return under paragraph (2)(A)(iii) of such section 6033(a); and

(xix) between—

(I) officials of a self-regulatory organization (as defined in section 3(a)(26) of the Securities Exchange Act [15 U.S.C.A. § 78c(a)(26)]) that is registered with or established by the Securities and Exchange Commission as required by that Act [15 U.S.C.A. § 78a et seq.] or a similar organization that is designated by or registered with the Commodities Future Trading Commission as provided under the Commodity Exchange Act [7 U.S.C.A. § 1 et seq.]; and

(II) the Securities and Exchange Commission or the Commodities Future Trading Commission, respectively;

relating to the regulatory responsibilities of such organization under that Act.

(9) *Lobbying firm.* The term "lobbying firm" means a person or entity that has 1 or more employees who are lobbyists on behalf of a

client other than that person or entity. The term also includes a self-employed individual who is a lobbyist.

(10) *Lobbyist.* The term "lobbyist" means any individual who is employed or retained by a client for financial or other compensation for services that include more than one lobbying contact, other than an individual whose lobbying activities constitute less than 20 percent of the time engaged in the services provided by such individual to that client over a six month period.

(11) *Media organization.* The term "media organization" means a person or entity engaged in disseminating information to the general public through a newspaper, magazine, other publication, radio, television, cable television, or other medium of mass communication.

(12) *Member of Congress.* The term "Member of Congress" means a Senator or a Representative in, or Delegate or Resident Commissioner to, the Congress.

(13) *Organization.* The term "organization" means a person or entity other than an individual.

(14) *Person or entity.* The term "person or entity" means any individual, corporation, company, foundation, association, labor organization, firm, partnership, society, joint stock company, group of organizations, or State or local government.

(15) *Public official.* The term "public official" means any elected official, appointed official, or employee of—

(A) a Federal, State, or local unit of government in the United States other than—

(i) a college or university;

(ii) a government-sponsored enterprise (as defined in section 622(8) of this title);

(iii) a public utility that provides gas, electricity, water, or communications;

(iv) a guaranty agency (as defined in section 1085(j) of Title 20), including any affiliate of such an agency; or

(v) an agency of any State functioning as a student loan secondary market pursuant to section 1085(d)(1)(F) of Title 20;

(B) a Government corporation (as defined in section 9101 of Title 31);

(C) an organization of State or local elected or appointed officials other than officials of an entity described in clause (i), (ii), (iii), (iv), or (v) of subparagraph (A);

(D) an Indian tribe (as defined in section 450b(e) of Title 25);

(E) a national or State political party or any organizational unit thereof; or

(F) a national, regional, or local unit of any foreign government, or a group of governments acting together as an international organization.

(16) *State*. The term "State" means each of the several States, the District of Columbia, and any commonwealth, territory, or possession of the United States.

§ 1603. Registration of lobbyists

(a) *Registration*.

(1) General rule. No later than 45 days after a lobbyist first makes a lobbying contact or is employed or retained to make a lobbying contact, whichever is earlier, such lobbyist (or, as provided under paragraph (2), the organization employing such lobbyist), shall register with the Secretary of the Senate and the Clerk of the House of Representatives.

(2) Employer filing. Any organization that has 1 or more employees who are lobbyists shall file a single registration under this section on behalf of such employees for each client on whose behalf the employees act as lobbyists.

(3) Exemption.

(A) General rule. Notwithstanding paragraphs (1) and (2), a person or entity whose—

(i) total income for matters related to lobbying activities on behalf of a particular client (in the case of a lobbying firm) does not exceed and is not expected to exceed $5,000; or

(ii) total expenses in connection with lobbying activities (in the case of an organization whose employees engage in lobbying activities on its own behalf) do not exceed or are not expected to exceed $20,000,

(as estimated under section 1604 of this title) in the semiannual period described in section 1604(a) of this title during which the registration would be made is not required to register under this subsection with respect to such client.

(B) Adjustment. The dollar amounts in subparagraph (A) shall be adjusted—

(i) on January 1, 1997, to reflect changes in the Consumer Price Index (as determined by the Secretary of Labor) since December 19, 1995; and

(ii) on January 1 of each fourth year occurring after January 1, 1997, to reflect changes in the Consumer Price Index (as determined by the Secretary of Labor) during the preceding 4–year period, rounded to the nearest $500.

(b) *Contents of registration.* Each registration under this section shall contain—

(1) the name, address, business telephone number, and principal place of business of the registrant, and a general description of its business or activities;

(2) the name, address, and principal place of business of the registrant's client, and a general description of its business or activities (if different from paragraph (1));

(3) the name, address, and principal place of business of any organization, other than the client, that—

(A) contributes more than $10,000 toward the lobbying activities of the registrant in a semiannual period described in section 1604(a) of this tile; and

(B) in whole or in major part plans, supervises, or controls such lobbying activities.

(4) the name, address, principal place of business, amount of any contribution of more than $10,000 to the lobbying activities of the registrant, and approximate percentage of equitable ownership in the client (if any) of any foreign entity that—

(A) holds at least 20 percent equitable ownership in the client or any organization identified under paragraph (3);

(B) directly or indirectly, in whole or in major part, plans, supervises, controls, directs, finances, or subsidizes the activities of the client or any organization identified under paragraph (3); or

(C) is an affiliate of the client or any organization identified under paragraph (3) and has a direct interest in the outcome of the lobbying activity;

(5) a statement of—

(A) the general issue areas in which the registrant expects to engage in lobbying activities on behalf of the client; and

(B) to the extent practicable, specific issues that have (as of the date of the registration) already been addressed or are likely to be addressed in lobbying activities; and

(6) the name of each employee of the registrant who has acted or whom the registrant expects to act as a lobbyist on behalf of the client and, if any such employee has served as a covered executive branch official or a covered legislative branch official in the 2 years before the date on which such employee first acted (after December

19, 1995) as a lobbyist on behalf of the client, the position in which such employee served.

(c) *Guidelines for registration.*

(1) Multiple clients. In the case of a registrant making lobbying contacts on behalf of more than 1 client, a separate registration under this section shall be filed for each such client.

(2) Multiple contacts. A registrant who makes more than 1 lobbying contact for the same client shall file a single registration covering all such lobbying contacts.

(d) *Termination of registration.* A registrant who after registration—

(1) is no longer employed or retained by a client to conduct lobbying activities, and

(2) does not anticipate any additional lobbying activities for such client,

may so notify the Secretary of the Senate and the Clerk of the House of Representatives and terminate its registration.

§ 1604. Reports by registered lobbyists

(a) *Semiannual report.* No later than 45 days after the end of the semiannual period beginning on the first day of each January and the first day of July of each year in which a registrant is registered under section 1603 of this title, each registrant shall file a report with the Secretary of the Senate and the Clerk of the House of Representatives on its lobbying activities during such semiannual period. A separate report shall be filed for each client of the registrant.

(b) *Contents of report.* Each semiannual report filed under subsection (a) of this section shall contain—

(1) the name of the registrant, the name of the client, and any changes or updates to the information provided in the initial registration;

(2) for each general issue area in which the registrant engaged in lobbying activities on behalf of the client during the semiannual filing period—

(A) a list of the specific issues upon which a lobbyist employed by the registrant engaged in lobbying activities, including, to the maximum extent practicable, a list of bill numbers and references to specific executive branch actions;

(B) a statement of the Houses of Congress and the Federal agencies contacted by lobbyists employed by the registrant on behalf of the client;

(C) a list of the employees of the registrant who acted as lobbyists on behalf of the client; and

(D) a description of the interest, if any, of any foreign entity identified under section 1603(b)(4) of this title in the specific issues listed under subparagraph (A);

(3) in the case of a lobbying firm, a good faith estimate of the total amount of all income from the client (including any payments to the registrant by any other person for lobbying activities on behalf of the client) during the semiannual period, other than income for matters that are unrelated to lobbying activities; and

(4) in the case of a registrant engaged in lobbying activities on its own behalf, a good faith estimate of the total expenses that the registrant and its employees incurred in connection with lobbying activities during the semiannual filing period.

(c) *Estimates of income or expenses.* For purposes of this section, estimates of income or expenses shall be made as follows:

(1) Estimates of amounts in excess of $10,000 shall be rounded to the nearest $20,000.

(2) In the event income or expenses do not exceed $10,000, the registrant shall include a statement that income or expenses totaled less than $10,000 for the reporting period.

§ 1605. Disclosure and enforcement

The Secretary of the Senate and the Clerk of the House of Representatives shall—

(1) provide guidance and assistance on the registration and reporting requirements of this chapter and develop common standards, rules, and procedures for compliance with this chapter;

(2) review, and, where necessary, verify and inquire to ensure the accuracy, completeness, and timeliness of registration and reports;

(3) develop filing, coding, and cross-indexing systems to carry out the purpose of this chapter, including—

(A) a publicly available list of all registered lobbyists, lobbying firms, and their clients; and

(B) computerized systems designed to minimize the burden of filing and maximize public access to materials filed under this chapter;

(4) make available for public inspection and copying at reasonable times the registrations and reports filed under this chapter;

(5) retain registrations for a period of at least 6 years after they are terminated and reports for a period of at least 6 years after they are filed;

(6) compile and summarize, with respect to each semiannual period, the information contained in registrations and reports filed with respect to such period in a clear and complete manner;

(7) notify any lobbyist or lobbying firm in writing that may be in noncompliance with this chapter; and

(8) notify the United States Attorney for the District of Columbia that a lobbyist or lobbying firm may be in noncompliance with this chapter, if the registrant has been notified in writing and has failed to provide an appropriate response within 60 days after notice was given under paragraph (7).

§ 1606. Penalties

Whoever knowingly fails to—

(1) remedy a defective filing within 60 days after notice of such a defect by the Secretary of the Senate or the Clerk of the House of Representatives; or

(2) comply with any other provision of this chapter;

shall, upon proof of such knowing violation by a preponderance of the evidence, be subject to a civil fine of not more than $50,000, depending on the extent and gravity of the violation.

§ 1607. Rules of construction

(a) *Constitutional rights*. Nothing in this chapter shall be construed to prohibit or interfere with—

(1) the right to petition the Government for the redress of grievances;

(2) the right to express a personal opinion; or

(3) the right of association,

protected by the first amendment to the Constitution.

(b) *Prohibition of activities*. Nothing in this chapter shall be construed to prohibit, or to authorize any court to prohibit, lobbying activities or lobbying contacts by any person or entity, regardless of whether such person or entity is in compliance with the requirements of this chapter.

(c) *Audit and investigations*. Nothing in this chapter shall be construed to grant general audit or investigative authority to the Secretary of the Senate or the Clerk of the House of Representatives.

§ 1608. Severability

If any provision of this chapter, or the application thereof, is held invalid, the validity of the remainder of this chapter and the application of such provision to other persons and circumstances shall not be affected thereby.

§ **1609.**   **Identification of clients and covered officials**

(a) *Oral lobbying contacts.* Any person or entity that makes an oral lobbying contact with a covered legislative branch official or a covered executive branch official shall, on the request of the official at the time of the lobbying contact—

> (1) state whether the person or entity is registered under this chapter and identify the client on whose behalf the lobbying contact is made; and

> (2) state whether such client is a foreign entity and identify any foreign entity required to be disclosed under section 1603(b)(4) of this title that has a direct interest in the outcome of the lobbying activity.

(b) *Written lobbying contacts.* Any person or entity registered under this chapter that makes a written lobbying contact (including an electronic communication) with a covered legislative branch official or a covered executive branch official shall—

> (1) if the client on whose behalf the lobbying contact was made is a foreign entity, identify such client, state that the client is considered a foreign entity under this chapter, and state whether the person making the lobbying contact is registered on behalf of that client under section 1603 of this title; and

> (2) identify any other foreign entity identified pursuant to section 1603(b)(4) of this title that has a direct interest in the outcome of the lobbying activity.

(c) *Identification as covered official.* Upon request by a person or entity making a lobbying contact, the individual who is contacted or the office employing that individual shall indicate whether or not the individual is a covered legislative branch official or a covered executive branch official.

§ **1610.**   **Estimates based on tax reporting system**

(a) *Entities covered by section 6033(b) of Title 26.* A person, other than a lobbying firm, that is required to report and does report lobbying expenditures pursuant to section 6033(b)(8) of Title 26 may—

> (1) make a good faith estimate (by category of dollar value) of applicable amounts that would be required to be disclosed under such section for the appropriate semiannual period to meet the requirements of sections 1603(a)(3) and 1604(b)(4) of this title; and

> (2) for all other purposes consider as lobbying contacts and lobbying activities only—

>> (A) lobbying contacts with covered legislative branch officials (as defined in section 1602(4) of this title) and lobbying activities in support of such contacts; and

(B) lobbying of Federal executive branch officials to the extent that such activities are influencing legislation as defined in section 4911(d) of Title 26.

(b) *Entities covered by section 162(e) of Title 26.* A person, other than a lobbying firm, who is required to account and does account for lobbying expenditures pursuant to section 162(e) of Title 26 may—

(1) make a good faith estimate (by category of dollar value) of applicable amounts that would not be deductible pursuant to such section for the appropriate semiannual period to meet the requirements of sections 1603(a)(3) and 1604(b)(4) of this title; and

(2) for all other purposes consider as lobbying contacts and lobbying activities only—

(A) lobbying contacts with covered legislative branch officials (as defined in section 1602(4) of this title) and lobbying activities in support of such contacts; and

(B) lobbying of Federal executive branch officials to the extent that amounts paid or costs incurred in connection with such activities are not deductible pursuant to section 162(e) of Title 26.

(c) *Disclosure of estimate.* Any registrant that elects to make estimates required by this chapter under the procedures authorized by subsection (a) or (b) of this section for reporting or threshold purposes shall—

(1) inform the Secretary of the Senate and the Clerk of the House of Representatives that the registrant has elected to make its estimates under such procedures; and

(2) make all such estimates, in a given calendar year, under such procedures.

(d) *Study.* Not later than March 31, 1997, the Comptroller General of the United States shall review reporting by registrants under subsections (a) and (b) of this section and report to the Congress—

(1) the differences between the definition of "lobbying activities" in section 1602(7) of this title and the definitions of "lobbying expenditures", "influencing legislation", and related terms in sections 162(e) and 4911 of Title 26, as each are implemented by regulations;

(2) the impact that any such differences may have on filing and reporting under this chapter pursuant to this subsection; and

(3) any changes to this chapter or to the appropriate sections of Title 26 that the Comptroller General may recommend to harmonize the definitions.

§ 1611. Exempt organizations

An organization described in section 501(c)(4) of Title 26 which engages in lobbying activities shall not be eligible for the receipt of Federal funds constituting an award, grant, or loan.

§ 1612. Sense of Senate that lobbying expenses should remain nondeductible

(a) *Findings*. The Senate finds that ordinary Americans generally are not allowed to deduct the costs of communicating with their elected representatives.

(b) *Sense of Senate*. It is the sense of the Senate that lobbying expenses should not be tax deductible.

FEDERAL ADVISORY COMMITTEE ACT

TITLE 5. GOVERNMENT ORGANIZATION AND EMPLOYEES
APPENDIX 2. FEDERAL ADVISORY COMMITTEE ACT

§ 1. Short title

This Act may be cited as the "Federal Advisory Committee Act".

§ 2. Findings and purpose

(a) The Congress finds that there are numerous committees, boards, commissions, councils, and similar groups which have been established

134

to advise officers and agencies in the executive branch of the Federal Government and that they are frequently a useful and beneficial means of furnishing expert advice, ideas, and diverse opinions to the Federal Government.

(b) The Congress further finds and declares that—

(1) the need for many existing advisory committees has not been adequately reviewed;

(2) new advisory committees should be established only when they are determined to be essential and their number should be kept to the minimum necessary;

(3) advisory committees should be terminated when they are no longer carrying out the purposes for which they were established;

(4) standards and uniform procedures should govern the establishment, operation, administration, and duration of advisory committees;

(5) the Congress and the public should be kept informed with respect to the number, purpose, membership, activities, and cost of advisory committees; and

(6) the function of advisory committees should be advisory only, and that all matters under their consideration should be determined, in accordance with law, by the official, agency, or officer involved.

§ 3. Definitions

For the purpose of this Act—

(1) The term "Administrator" means the Administrator of General Services.

(2) The term "advisory committee" means any committee, board, commission, council, conference, panel, task force, or other similar group, or any subcommittee or other subgroup thereof (hereafter in this paragraph referred to as "committee"), which is—

(A) established by statute or reorganization plan, or

(B) established or utilized by the President, or

(C) established or utilized by one or more agencies,

in the interest of obtaining advice or recommendations for the President or one or more agencies or officers of the Federal Government, except that such term excludes (i) any committee that is composed wholly of full-time, or permanent part-time, officers or employees of the Federal Government, and (ii) any committee that is created by the National Academy of Sciences or the National Academy of Public Administration.

(3) The term "agency" has the same meaning as in section 551(1) of Title 5.

(4) The term "Presidential advisory committee" means an advisory committee which advises the President.

§ 4. Applicability; restrictions

(a) The provisions of this Act or of any rule, order, or regulation promulgated under this Act shall apply to each advisory committee except to the extent that any Act of Congress establishing any such advisory committee specifically provides otherwise.

(b) Nothing in this Act shall be construed to apply to any advisory committee established or utilized by—

(1) the Central Intelligence Agency; or

(2) the Federal Reserve System.

(c) Nothing in this Act shall be construed to apply to any local civic group whose primary function is that of rendering a public service with respect to a Federal program, or any State or local committee, council, board, commission, or similar group established to advise or make recommendations to State or local officials or agencies.

§ 5. Responsibilities of Congressional committees; review; guidelines

(a) In the exercise of its legislative review function, each standing committee of the Senate and the House of Representatives shall make a continuing review of the activities of each advisory committee under its jurisdiction to determine whether such advisory committee should be abolished or merged with any other advisory committee, whether the responsibilities of such advisory committee should be revised, and whether such advisory committee performs a necessary function not already being performed. Each such standing committee shall take appropriate action to obtain the enactment of legislation necessary to carry out the purpose of this subsection.

(b) In considering legislation establishing, or authorizing the establishment of any advisory committee, each standing committee of the Senate and of the House of Representatives shall determine, and report such determination to the Senate or to the House of Representatives, as the case may be, whether the functions of the proposed advisory committee are being or could be performed by one or more agencies or by an advisory committee already in existence, or by enlarging the mandate of an existing advisory committee. Any such legislation shall—

(1) contain a clearly defined purpose for the advisory committee;

(2) require the membership of the advisory committee to be fairly balanced in terms of the points of view represented and the functions to be performed by the advisory committee;

(3) contain appropriate provisions to assure that the advice and recommendations of the advisory committee will not be inappropriately influenced by the appointing authority or by any special interest, but will instead be the result of the advisory committee's independent judgment;

(4) contain provisions dealing with authorization of appropriations, the date for submission of reports (if any), the duration of the advisory committee, and the publication of reports and other materials, to the extent that the standing committee determines the provisions of section 10 of this Act to be inadequate; and

(5) contain provisions which will assure that the advisory committee will have adequate staff (either supplied by an agency or employed by it), will be provided adequate quarters, and will have funds available to meet its other necessary expenses.

(c) To the extent they are applicable, the guidelines set out in subsection (b) of this section shall be followed by the President, agency heads, or other Federal officials in creating an advisory committee.

§ 6. Responsibilities of the President; report to Congress; annual report to Congress; exclusion

(a) The President may delegate responsibility for evaluating and taking action, where appropriate, with respect to all public recommendations made to him by Presidential advisory committees.

(b) Within one year after a Presidential advisory committee has submitted a public report to the President, the President or his delegate shall make a report to the Congress stating either his proposals for action or his reasons for inaction, with respect to the recommendations contained in the public report.

(c) The President shall, not later than December 31 of each year, make an annual report to the Congress on the activities, status, and changes in the composition of advisory committees in existence during the preceding fiscal year. The report shall contain the name of every advisory committee, the date of and authority for its creation, its termination date or the date it is to make a report, its functions, a reference to the reports it has submitted, a statement of whether it is an ad hoc or continuing body, the dates of its meetings, the names and occupations of its current members, and the total estimated annual cost to the United States to fund, service, supply, and maintain such committee. Such report shall include a list of those advisory committees abolished by the President, and in the case of advisory committees established by statute, a list of those advisory committees which the President recommends be abolished together with his reasons therefor. The President shall exclude from this report any information which, in his judgment, should be withheld for reasons of national security, and he shall include in such report a statement that such information is excluded.

§ 7. Responsibilities of the Administrator of General Services; Committee Management Secretariat, establishment; review; recommendations to President and Congress; agency cooperation; performance guidelines; uniform pay guidelines; travel expenses; expense recommendations

(a) The Administrator shall establish and maintain within the General Services Administration a Committee Management Secretariat, which shall be responsible for all matters relating to advisory committees.

(b) The Administrator shall, immediately after October 6, 1972, institute a comprehensive review of the activities and responsibilities of each advisory committee to determine—

(1) whether such committee is carrying out its purpose;

(2) whether, consistent with the provisions of applicable statutes, the responsibilities assigned to it should be revised;

(3) whether it should be merged with other advisory committees; or

(4) whether it should be abolished.

The Administrator may from time to time request such information as he deems necessary to carry out his functions under this subsection. Upon the completion of the Administrator's review he shall make recommendations to the President and to either the agency head or the Congress with respect to action he believes should be taken. Thereafter, the Administrator shall carry out a similar review annually. Agency heads shall cooperate with the Administrator in making the reviews required by this subsection.

(c) The Administrator shall prescribe administrative guidelines and management controls applicable to advisory committees, and, to the maximum extent feasible, provide advice, assistance, and guidance to advisory committees to improve their performance. In carrying out his functions under this subsection, the Administrator shall consider the recommendations of each agency head with respect to means of improving the performance of advisory committees whose duties are related to such agency.

(d)(1) The Administrator after study and consultation with the Director of the Office of Personnel Management, shall establish guidelines with respect to uniform fair rates of pay for comparable services of members, staffs, and consultants of advisory committees in a manner which gives appropriate recognition to the responsibilities and qualifications required and other relevant factors. Such regulations shall provide that—

(A) no member of any advisory committee or of the staff of any advisory committee shall receive compensation at a rate in excess of the rate specified for GS–18 of the General Schedule under section 5332 of title 5, United States Code;

(B) such members, while engaged in the performance of their duties away from their homes or regular places of business, may be allowed travel expenses, including per diem in lieu of subsistence, as authorized by section 5703 of title 5, United States Code, for persons employed intermittently in the Government service; and

(C) such members—

(i) who are blind or deaf or who otherwise qualify as handicapped individuals (within the meaning of section 501 of the Rehabilitation Act of 1973 (29 U.S.C. 794)), and

(ii) who do not otherwise qualify for assistance under section 3102 of Title 5, by reason of being an employee of an agency (within the meaning of section 3102(a)(1) of such Title 5), may be provided services pursuant to section 3102 of such Title 5 while in performance of their advisory committee duties.

(2) Nothing in this subsection shall prevent—

(A) an individual who (without regard to his service with an advisory committee) is a full-time employee of the United States, or

(B) an individual who immediately before his service with an advisory committee was such an employee, from receiving compensation at the rate at which he otherwise would be compensated (or was compensated) as a full-time employee of the United States.

(e) The Administrator shall include in budget recommendations a summary of the amounts he deems necessary for the expenses of advisory committees, including the expenses for publication of reports where appropriate.

§ 8. Responsibilities of agency heads; Advisory Committee Management Officer, designation

(a) Each agency head shall establish uniform administrative guidelines and management controls for advisory committees established by that agency, which shall be consistent with directives of the Administrator under section 7 and section 10. Each agency shall maintain systematic information on the nature, functions, and operations of each advisory committee within its jurisdiction.

(b) The head of each agency which has an advisory committee shall designate an Advisory Committee Management Officer who shall—

(1) exercise control and supervision over the establishment, procedures, and accomplishments of advisory committees established by that agency;

(2) assemble and maintain the reports, records, and other papers of any such committee during its existence; and

(3) carry out, on behalf of that agency, the provisions of section 552 of title 5, United States Code, with respect to such reports, records, and other papers.

§ 9. Establishment and purpose of advisory committees; publication in Federal Register; charter: filing, contents, copy

(a) No advisory committee shall be established unless such establishment is—

(1) specifically authorized by statute or by the President; or

(2) determined as a matter of formal record, by the head of the agency involved after consultation with the Administrator with timely notice published in the Federal Register, to be in the public interest in connection with the performance of duties imposed on that agency by law.

(b) Unless otherwise specifically provided by statute or Presidential directive, advisory committees shall be utilized solely for advisory functions. Determinations of action to be taken and policy to be expressed with respect to matters upon which an advisory committee reports or makes recommendations shall be made solely by the President or an officer of the Federal Government.

(c) No advisory committee shall meet or take any action until an advisory committee charter has been filed with (1) the Administrator, in the case of Presidential advisory committees, or (2) with the head of the agency to whom any advisory committee reports and with the standing committees of the Senate and of the House of Representatives having legislative jurisdiction of such agency. Such charter shall contain the following information:

(A) the committee's official designation;

(B) the committee's objectives and the scope of its activity;

(C) the period of time necessary for the committee to carry out its purposes;

(D) the agency or official to whom the committee reports;

(E) the agency responsible for providing the necessary support for the committee;

(F) a description of the duties for which the committee is responsible, and, if such duties are not solely advisory, a specification of the authority for such functions;

(G) the estimated annual operating costs in dollars and man-years for such committee;

(H) the estimated number and frequency of committee meetings;

(I) the committee's termination date, if less than two years from the date of the committee's establishment; and

(J) the date the charter is filed.

A copy of any such charter shall also be furnished to the Library of Congress.

§ **10.** **Advisory committee procedures; meetings; notice, publication in Federal Register; regulations; minutes; certification; annual report; Federal officer or employee, attendance**

(a)(1) Each advisory committee meeting shall be open to the public.

(2) Except when the President determines otherwise for reasons of national security, timely notice of each such meeting shall be published in the Federal Register, and the Administrator shall prescribe regulations to provide for other types of public notice to insure that all interested persons are notified of such meeting prior thereto.

(3) Interested persons shall be permitted to attend, appear before, or file statements with any advisory committee, subject to such reasonable rules or regulations as the Administrator may prescribe.

(b) Subject to section 552 of title 5, United States Code, the records, reports, transcripts, minutes, appendixes, working papers, drafts, studies, agenda, or other documents which were made available to or prepared for or by each advisory committee shall be available for public inspection and copying at a single location in the offices of the advisory committee or the agency to which the advisory committee reports until the advisory committee ceases to exist.

(c) Detailed minutes of each meeting of each advisory committee shall be kept and shall contain a record of the persons present, a complete and accurate description of matters discussed and conclusions reached, and copies of all reports received, issued, or approved by the advisory committee. The accuracy of all minutes shall be certified to by the chairman of the advisory committee.

(d) Subsections (a)(1) and (a)(3) of this section shall not apply to any portion of an advisory committee meeting where the President, or the head of the agency to which the advisory committee reports, determines that such portion of such meeting may be closed to the public in accordance with subsection (c) of section 552b of title 5, United States Code. Any such determination shall be in writing and shall contain the reasons for such determination. If such a determination is made, the advisory committee shall issue a report at least annually setting forth a summary of its activities and such related matters as would be informative to the public consistent with the policy of section 552(b) of title 5, United States Code.

(e) There shall be designated an officer or employee of the Federal Government to chair or attend each meeting of each advisory committee. The officer or employee so designated is authorized, whenever he determines it to be in the public interest, to adjourn any such meeting. No advisory committee shall conduct any meeting in the absence of that officer or employee.

(f) Advisory committees shall not hold any meetings except at the call of, or with the advance approval of, a designated officer or employee of the Federal Government, and in the case of advisory committees (other than Presidential advisory committees), with an agenda approved by such officer or employee.

§ 11. Availability of transcripts; "agency proceeding"

(a) Except where prohibited by contractual agreements entered into prior to the effective date of this Act, agencies and advisory committees shall make available to any person, at actual cost of duplication, copies of transcripts of agency proceedings or advisory committee meetings.

(b) As used in this section "agency proceeding" means any proceeding as defined in section 551(12) of title 5, United States Code.

§ 12. Fiscal and administrative provisions; recordkeeping; audit; agency support services

(a) Each agency shall keep records as will fully disclose the disposition of any funds which may be at the disposal of its advisory committees and the nature and extent of their activities. The General Services Administration, or such other agency as the President may designate, shall maintain financial records with respect to Presidential advisory committees. The Comptroller General of the United States, or any of his authorized representatives, shall have access, for the purpose of audit and examination, to any such records.

(b) Each agency shall be responsible for providing support services for each advisory committee established by or reporting to it unless the establishing authority provides otherwise. Where any such advisory committee reports to more than one agency, only one agency shall be responsible for support services at any one time. In the case of Presidential advisory committees, such services may be provided by the General Services Administration.

§ 13. Responsibilities of Library of Congress; reports and background papers; depository

Subject to section 552 of title 5, United States Code, the Administrator shall provide for the filing with the Library of Congress of at least eight copies of each report made by every advisory committee and, where appropriate, background papers prepared by consultants. The Librarian of Congress shall establish a depository for such reports and papers where they shall be available to public inspection and use.

§ 14. Termination of advisory committees; renewal; continuation

(a)(1) Each advisory committee which is in existence on the effective date of this Act shall terminate not later than the expiration of the two-year period following such effective date unless—

(A) in the case of an advisory committee established by the President or an officer of the Federal Government, such advisory committee is renewed by the President or that officer by appropriate action prior to the expiration of such two-year period; or

(B) in the case of an advisory committee established by an Act of Congress, its duration is otherwise provided for by law.

(2) Each advisory committee established after such effective date shall terminate not later than the expiration of the two-year period beginning on the date of its establishment unless—

(A) in the case of an advisory committee established by the President or an officer of the Federal Government such advisory committee is renewed by the President or such officer by appropriate action prior to the end of such period; or

(B) in the case of an advisory committee established by an Act of Congress, its duration is otherwise provided for by law.

(b)(1) Upon the renewal of any advisory committee, such advisory committee shall file a charter in accordance with section 9(c).

(2) Any advisory committee established by an Act of Congress shall file a charter in accordance with such section upon the expiration of each successive two-year period following the date of enactment of the Act establishing such advisory committee.

(3) No advisory committee required under this subsection to file a charter shall take any action (other than preparation and filing of such charter) prior to the date on which such charter is filed.

(c) Any advisory committee which is renewed by the President or any officer of the Federal Government may be continued only for successive two-year periods by appropriate action taken by the President or such officer prior to the date on which such advisory committee would otherwise terminate.

§ 15. Requirements relating to the National Academy of Sciences and the National Academy of Public Administration

(a) *In General.*—An agency may not use any advice or recommendation provided by the National Academy of Sciences or National Academy of Public Administration that was developed by use of a committee created by that academy under an agreement with an agency, unless—

(1) the committee was not subject to any actual management or control by an agency or an officer of the Federal Government;

(2) in the case of a committee created after the date of the enactment of the Federal Advisory Committee Act Amendments of 1997, the membership of the committee was appointed in accordance with the requirements described in subsection (b)(1); and

(3) in developing the advice or recommendation, the academy complied with—

(A) subsection (b)(2) through (6), in the case of any advice or recommendation provided by the National Academy of Sciences; or

(B) subsection (b)(2) and (5), in the case of any advice or recommendation provided by the National Academy of Public Administration.

(b) Requirements.—The requirements referred to in subsection (a) are as follows:

(1) The Academy shall determine and provide public notice of the names and brief biographies of individuals that the Academy appoints or intends to appoint to serve on the committee. The Academy shall determine and provide a reasonable opportunity for the public to comment on such appointments before they are made or, if the Academy determines such prior comment is not practicable, in the period immediately following the appointments. The Academy shall make its best efforts to ensure that (A) no individual appointed to serve on the committee has a conflict of interest that is relevant to the functions to be performed, unless such conflict is promptly and publicly disclosed and the Academy determines that the conflict is unavoidable, (B) the committee membership is fairly balanced as determined by the Academy to be appropriate for the functions to be performed, and (C) the final report of the Academy will be the result of the Academy's independent judgment. The Academy shall require that individuals that the Academy appoints or intends to appoint to serve on the committee inform the Academy of the individual's conflicts of interest that are relevant to the functions to be performed.

(2) The Academy shall determine and provide public notice of committee meetings that will be open to the public.

(3) The Academy shall ensure that meetings of the committee to gather data from individuals who are not officials, agents, or employees of the Academy are open to the public, unless the Academy determines that a meeting would disclose matters described in section 552(b) of title 5, United States Code. The Academy shall make available to the public, at reasonable charge if appropriate, written materials presented to the committee by individuals who are not officials, agents, or employees of the Academy, unless the Academy determines that making material available would disclose matters described in that section.

(4) The Academy shall make available to the public as soon as practicable, at reasonable charge if appropriate, a brief summary of any committee meeting that is not a data gathering meeting, unless the Academy determines that the summary would disclose matters described in section 552(b) of title 5, United States Code. The summary shall identify the committee members present, the topics discussed, materials made available to the committee, and such other matters that the Academy determines should be included.

(5) The Academy shall make available to the public its final report, at reasonable charge if appropriate, unless the Academy determines that the report would disclose matters described in section 552(b) of title 5, United States Code. If the Academy determines that the report would disclose matters described in that section, the Academy shall make public an abbreviated version of the report that does not disclose those matters.

(6) After publication of the final report, the Academy shall make publicly available the names of the principal reviewers who reviewed the report in draft form and who are not officials, agents, or employees of the Academy.

(c) Regulations.—The Administrator of General Services may issue regulations implementing this section.

UNFUNDED MANDATES REFORM ACT/REGULATORY ACCOUNTABILITY AND REFORM ACT

§ 658. Definitions

For purposes of this part:

(1) Agency. The term "agency" has the same meaning as defined in section 551(1) of Title 5, but does not include independent regulatory agencies.

(2) Amount. The term "amount", with respect to an authorization of appropriations for Federal financial assistance, means the amount

of budget authority for any Federal grant assistance program or any Federal program providing loan guarantees or direct loans.

(3) Direct costs. The term "direct costs"—

(A)(i) in the case of a Federal intergovernmental mandate, means the aggregate estimated amounts that all State, local, and tribal governments would be required to spend or would be prohibited from raising in revenues in order to comply with the Federal intergovernmental mandate; or

(ii) in the case of a provision referred to in paragraph (5)(A)(ii), means the amount of Federal financial assistance eliminated or reduced;

(B) in the case of a Federal private sector mandate, means the aggregate estimated amounts that the private sector will be required to spend in order to comply with the Federal private sector mandate;

(C) shall be determined on the assumption that—

(i) State, local, and tribal governments, and the private sector will take all reasonable steps necessary to mitigate the costs resulting from the Federal mandate, and will comply with applicable standards of practice and conduct established by recognized professional or trade associations; and

(ii) reasonable steps to mitigate the costs shall not include increases in State, local, or tribal taxes or fees; and

(D) shall not include—

(i) estimated amounts that the State, local, and tribal governments (in the case of a Federal intergovernmental mandate) or the private sector (in the case of a Federal private sector mandate) would spend—

(I) to comply with or carry out all applicable Federal, State, local, and tribal laws and regulations in effect at the time of the adoption of the Federal mandate for the same activity as is affected by that Federal mandate; or

(II) to comply with or carry out State, local, and tribal governmental programs, or private-sector business or other activities in effect at the time of the adoption of the Federal mandate for the same activity as is affected by that mandate; or

(ii) expenditures to the extent that such expenditures will be offset by any direct savings to the State, local, and tribal governments, or by the private sector, as a result of—

(I) compliance with the Federal mandate; or

(II) other changes in Federal law or regulation that are enacted or adopted in the same bill or joint resolution or proposed or final Federal regulation and that govern the same activity as is affected by the Federal mandate.

(4) Direct savings.   The term "direct savings", when used with respect to the result of compliance with the Federal mandate—

(A) in the case of a Federal intergovernmental mandate, means the aggregate estimated reduction in costs to any State, local, or tribal government as a result of compliance with the Federal intergovernmental mandate; and

(B) in the case of a Federal private sector mandate, means the aggregate estimated reduction in costs to the private sector as a result of compliance with the Federal private sector mandate.

(5) Federal intergovernmental mandate.   The term "Federal intergovernmental mandate" means—

(A) any provision in legislation, statute, or regulation that—

(i) would impose an enforceable duty upon State, local, or tribal governments, except—

(I) a condition of Federal assistance; or

(II) a duty arising from participation in a voluntary Federal program, except as provided in subparagraph (B); or

(ii) would reduce or eliminate the amount of authorization of appropriations for—

(I) Federal financial assistance that would be provided to State, local, or tribal governments for the purpose of complying with any such previously imposed duty unless such duty is reduced or eliminated by a corresponding amount; or

(II) the control of borders by the Federal Government; or reimbursement to State, local, or tribal governments for the net cost associated with illegal, deportable, and excludable aliens, including court-mandated expenses related to emergency health care, education or criminal justice; when such a reduction or elimination would result in increased net costs to State, local, or tribal governments in providing education or emergency health care to, or incarceration of, illegal aliens; except that this subclause shall not be in effect with respect to a State, local, or tribal government, to the extent that such government has not fully cooperated in the efforts of the Federal Government to locate, apprehend, and deport illegal aliens;

(B) any provision in legislation, statute, or regulation that relates to a then-existing Federal program under which $500,000,000 or more is provided annually to State, local, and tribal governments under entitlement authority, if the provision—

(i)(I) would increase the stringency of conditions of assistance to State, local, or tribal governments under the program; or

(II) would place caps upon, or otherwise decrease, the Federal Government's responsibility to provide funding to State, local, or tribal governments under the program; and

(ii) the State, local, or tribal governments that participate in the Federal program lack authority under that program to amend their financial or programmatic responsibilities to continue providing required services that are affected by the legislation, statute, or regulation.

(6) Federal mandate. The term "Federal mandate" means a Federal intergovernmental mandate or a Federal private sector mandate, as defined in paragraphs (5) and (7).

(7) Federal private sector mandate. The term "Federal private sector mandate" means any provision in legislation, statute, or regulation that—

(A) would impose an enforceable duty upon the private sector except—

(i) a condition of Federal assistance; or

(ii) a duty arising from participation in a voluntary Federal program; or

(B) would reduce or eliminate the amount of authorization of appropriations for Federal financial assistance that will be provided to the private sector for the purposes of ensuring compliance with such duty.

(8) Local government. The term "local government" has the same meaning as defined in section 6501(6) of Title 31.

(9) Private sector. The term "private sector" means all persons or entities in the United States, including individuals, partnerships, associations, corporations, and educational and nonprofit institutions, but shall not include State, local, or tribal governments.

(10) Regulation; rule. The term "regulation" or "rule" (except with respect to a rule of either House of the Congress) has the meaning of "rule" as defined in section 601(2) of Title 5.

(11) Small government. The term "small government" means any small governmental jurisdictions defined in section 601(5) of Title 5, and any tribal government.

(12) State. The term "State" has the same meaning as defined in section 6501(9) of Title 31.

(13) Tribal government. The term "tribal government" means any Indian tribe, band, nation, or other organized group or community, including any Alaska Native village or regional or village corporation as defined in or established pursuant to the Alaska Native Claims Settlement Act (85 Stat. 688; 43 U.S.C. 1601 et seq.) which is recognized as eligible for the special programs and services provided by the United States to Indians because of their special status as Indians.

CHAPTER 25—UNFUNDED MANDATES REFORM

§ 1501. Purposes

The purposes of this chapter are—

* * *

(7) to assist Federal agencies in their consideration of proposed regulations affecting State, local, and tribal governments, by—

(A) requiring that Federal agencies develop a process to enable the elected and other officials of State, local, and tribal governments to provide input when Federal agencies are developing regulations; and

(B) requiring that Federal agencies prepare and consider estimates of the budgetary impact of regulations containing Federal mandates upon State, local, and tribal governments and the private sector before adopting such regulations, and ensuring that small governments are given special consideration in that process; and

(8) to begin consideration of the effect of previously imposed Federal mandates, including the impact on State, local, and tribal governments of Federal court interpretations of Federal statutes and regulations that impose Federal intergovernmental mandates.

§ 1502. Definitions

For purposes of this chapter—

(1) except as provided in section 1555 of this title, the terms defined under section 658 of this title shall have the meanings as so defined; and

(2) the term "Director" means the Director of the Congressional Budget Office.

§ 1503. Exclusions

This chapter shall not apply to any provision in a bill, joint resolution, amendment, motion, or conference report before Congress and any provision in a proposed or final Federal regulation that—

(1) enforces constitutional rights of individuals;

(2) establishes or enforces any statutory rights that prohibit discrimination on the basis of race, color, religion, sex, national origin, age, handicap, or disability;

(3) requires compliance with accounting and auditing procedures with respect to grants or other money or property provided by the Federal Government;

(4) provides for emergency assistance or relief at the request of any State, local, or tribal government or any official of a State, local, or tribal government;

(5) is necessary for the national security or the ratification or implementation of international treaty obligations;

(6) the President designates as emergency legislation and that the Congress so designates in statute; or

(7) relates to the old-age, survivors, and disability insurance program under title II of the Social Security Act (including taxes imposed by sections 3101(a) and 3111(a) of the Internal Revenue Code of 1986 (relating to old-age, survivors, and disability insurance)).

CHAPTER 25—UNFUNDED MANDATES REFORM

SUBCHAPTER II—REGULATORY ACCOUNTABILITY AND REFORM

§ 1531. Regulatory process

Each agency shall, unless otherwise prohibited by law, assess the effects of Federal regulatory actions on State, local, and tribal governments, and the private sector (other than to the extent that such regulations incorporate requirements specifically set forth in law).

§ 1532. Statements to accompany significant regulatory actions

(a) In general. Unless otherwise prohibited by law, before promulgating any general notice of proposed rulemaking that is likely to result in promulgation of any rule that includes any Federal mandate that may result in the expenditure by State, local, and tribal governments, in the aggregate, or by the private sector, of $100,000,000 or more (adjusted annually for inflation) in any 1 year, and before promulgating any final rule for which a general notice of proposed rulemaking was published, the agency shall prepare a written statement containing—

(1) an identification of the provision of Federal law under which the rule is being promulgated;

(2) a qualitative and quantitative assessment of the anticipated costs and benefits of the Federal mandate, including the costs and benefits to State, local, and tribal governments or the private sector, as well as the effect of the Federal mandate on health, safety, and the natural environment and such an assessment shall include—

(A) an analysis of the extent to which such costs to State, local, and tribal governments may be paid with Federal financial assistance (or otherwise paid for by the Federal Government); and

(B) the extent to which there are available Federal resources to carry out the intergovernmental mandate;

(3) estimates by the agency, if and to the extent that the agency determines that accurate estimates are reasonably feasible, of—

(A) the future compliance costs of the Federal mandate; and

(B) any disproportionate budgetary effects of the Federal mandate upon any particular regions of the nation or particular State, local, or tribal governments, urban or rural or other types of communities, or particular segments of the private sector;

(4) estimates by the agency of the effect on the national economy, such as the effect on productivity, economic growth, full employment, creation of productive jobs, and international competitiveness of United States goods and services, if and to the extent that the agency in its sole discretion determines that accurate estimates are reasonably feasible and that such effect is relevant and material; and

(5)(A) a description of the extent of the agency's prior consultation with elected representatives (under section 1534 of this title) of the affected State, local, and tribal governments;

(B) a summary of the comments and concerns that were presented by State, local, or tribal governments either orally or in writing to the agency; and

(C) a summary of the agency's evaluation of those comments and concerns.

(b) Promulgation. In promulgating a general notice of proposed rulemaking or a final rule for which a statement under subsection (a) of this section is required, the agency shall include in the promulgation a summary of the information contained in the statement.

(c) Preparation in conjunction with other statement. Any agency may prepare any statement required under subsection (a) of this section in conjunction with or as a part of any other statement or analysis, provided that the statement or analysis satisfies the provisions of subsection (a) of this section.

§ 1533. Small government agency plan

(a) Effects on small governments. Before establishing any regulatory requirements that might significantly or uniquely affect small governments, agencies shall have developed a plan under which the agency shall—

(1) provide notice of the requirements to potentially affected small governments, if any;

(2) enable officials of affected small governments to provide meaningful and timely input in the development of regulatory proposals containing significant Federal intergovernmental mandates; and

(3) inform, educate, and advise small governments on compliance with the requirements.

(b) Authorization of appropriations. There are authorized to be appropriated to each agency to carry out the provisions of this section and for no other purpose, such sums as are necessary.

§ 1534. State, local, and tribal government input

(a) In general. Each agency shall, to the extent permitted in law, develop an effective process to permit elected officers of State, local, and tribal governments (or their designated employees with authority to act on their behalf) to provide meaningful and timely input in the development of regulatory proposals containing significant Federal intergovernmental mandates.

(b) Meetings between State, local, tribal and Federal officers. The Federal Advisory Committee Act (5 U.S.C. App.) shall not apply to actions in support of intergovernmental communications where—

(1) meetings are held exclusively between Federal officials and elected officers of State, local, and tribal governments (or their designated employees with authority to act on their behalf) acting in their official capacities; and

(2) such meetings are solely for the purposes of exchanging views, information, or advice relating to the management or implementation of Federal programs established pursuant to public law that explicitly or inherently share intergovernmental responsibilities or administration.

(c) Implementing guidelines.   No later than 6 months after March 22, 1995, the President shall issue guidelines and instructions to Federal agencies for appropriate implementation of subsections (a) and (b) of this section consistent with applicable laws and regulations.

§ 1535. Least burdensome option or explanation required

(a) In general.   Except as provided in subsection (b) of this section, before promulgating any rule for which a written statement is required under section 1532 of this title, the agency shall identify and consider a reasonable number of regulatory alternatives and from those alternatives select the least costly, most cost-effective or least burdensome alternative that achieves the objectives of the rule, for—

(1) State, local, and tribal governments, in the case of a rule containing a Federal intergovernmental mandate; and

(2) the private sector, in the case of a rule containing a Federal private sector mandate.

(b) Exception.   The provisions of subsection (a) of this section shall apply unless—

(1) the head of the affected agency publishes with the final rule an explanation of why the least costly, most cost-effective or least burdensome method of achieving the objectives of the rule was not adopted; or

(2) the provisions are inconsistent with law.

(c) OMB certification.   No later than 1 year after March 22, 1995, the Director of the Office of Management and Budget shall certify to Congress, with a written explanation, agency compliance with this section and include in that certification agencies and rulemakings that fail to adequately comply with this section.

§ 1536. Assistance to the Congressional Budget Office

The Director of the Office of Management and Budget shall—

(1) collect from agencies the statements prepared under section 1532 of this title; and

(2) periodically forward copies of such statements to the Director of the Congressional Budget Office on a reasonably timely basis after

promulgation of the general notice of proposed rulemaking or of the final rule for which the statement was prepared.

* * *

CHAPTER 25—UNFUNDED MANDATES REFORM

SUBCHAPTER IV—JUDICIAL REVIEW

§ 1571. Judicial review

(a) Agency statements on significant regulatory actions

(1) In general. Compliance or noncompliance by any agency with the provisions of sections 1532 and 1533(a)(1) and (2) of this title shall be subject to judicial review only in accordance with this section.

(2) Limited review of agency compliance or noncompliance

(A) Agency compliance or noncompliance with the provisions of sections 1532 and 1533(a)(1) and (2) of this title shall be subject to judicial review only under section 706(1) of Title 5, and only as provided under subparagraph (B).

(B) If an agency fails to prepare the written statement (including the preparation of the estimates, analyses, statements, or descriptions) under section 1532 of this title or the written plan under section 1533(a)(1) and (2) of this title, a court may compel the agency to prepare such written statement.

(3) Review of agency rules. In any judicial review under any other Federal law of an agency rule for which a written statement or plan is required under sections 1532 and 1533(a)(1) and (2) of this title, the inadequacy or failure to prepare such statement (including the inadequacy or failure to prepare any estimate, analysis, statement or description) or written plan shall not be used as a basis for staying, enjoining, invalidating or otherwise affecting such agency rule.

(4) Certain information as part of record. Any information generated under sections 1532 and 1533(a)(1) and (2) of this title that is part of the rulemaking record for judicial review under the provisions of any other Federal law may be considered as part of the record for judicial review conducted under such other provisions of Federal law.

(5) Application of other Federal law. For any petition under paragraph (2) the provisions of such other Federal law shall control all other matters, such as exhaustion of administrative remedies, the time for and manner of seeking review and venue, except that if such other Federal law does not provide a limitation on the time for filing a petition for judicial review that is less than 180 days, such

limitation shall be 180 days after a final rule is promulgated by the appropriate agency.

(6) Effective date.   This subsection shall take effect on October 1, 1995, and shall apply only to any agency rule for which a general notice of proposed rulemaking is promulgated on or after such date.

(b) Judicial review and rule of construction.   Except as provided in subsection (a) of this section—

(1) any estimate, analysis, statement, description or report prepared under this chapter, and any compliance or noncompliance with the provisions of this chapter, and any determination concerning the applicability of the provisions of this chapter shall not be subject to judicial review; and

(2) no provision of this chapter shall be construed to create any right or benefit, substantive or procedural, enforceable by any person in any administrative or judicial action.

NATIONAL ENVIRONMENTAL POLICY ACT

TITLE 42. THE PUBLIC HEALTH AND WELFARE
CHAPTER 55—NATIONAL ENVIRONMENTAL POLICY

§ 4321. Congressional declaration of purpose

The purposes of this chapter are: To declare a national policy which will encourage productive and enjoyable harmony between man and his environment; to promote efforts which will prevent or eliminate damage to the environment and biosphere and stimulate the health and welfare of man; to enrich the understanding of the ecological systems and natural resources important to the Nation; and to establish a Council on Environmental Quality.

SUBCHAPTER I—POLICIES AND GOALS

§ 4331. Congressional declaration of national environmental policy

(a) Creation and maintenance of conditions under which man and nature can exist in productive harmony. The Congress, recognizing the profound impact of man's activity on the interrelations of all components of the natural environment, particularly the profound influences of population growth, high-density urbanization, industrial expansion, resource exploitation, and new and expanding technological advances and recognizing further the critical importance of restoring and maintaining environmental quality to the overall welfare and development of man, declares that it is the continuing policy of the Federal Government, in cooperation with State and local governments, and other concerned public and private organizations, to use all practicable means and measures, including financial and technical assistance, in a manner calculated to foster and promote the general welfare, to create and maintain conditions under which man and nature can exist in productive harmony, and fulfill the social, economic, and other requirements of present and future generations of Americans.

(b) Continuing responsibility of Federal Government to use all practicable means to improve and coordinate Federal plans, functions, programs, and resources. In order to carry out the policy set forth in this chapter, it is the continuing responsibility of the Federal Government to use all practicable means, consistent with other essential considerations of national policy, to improve and coordinate Federal plans, functions, programs, and resources to the end that the Nation may—

(1) fulfill the responsibilities of each generation as trustee of the environment for succeeding generations;

(2) assure for all Americans safe, healthful, productive, and esthetically and culturally pleasing surroundings;

(3) attain the widest range of beneficial uses of the environment without degradation, risk to health or safety, or other undesirable and unintended consequences;

(4) preserve important historic, cultural, and natural aspects of our national heritage, and maintain, wherever possible, an environment which supports diversity and variety of individual choice;

(5) achieve a balance between population and resource use which will permit high standards of living and a wide sharing of life's amenities; and

(6) enhance the quality of renewable resources and approach the maximum attainable recycling of depletable resources.

(c) Responsibility of each person to contribute to preservation and enhancement of environment. The Congress recognizes that each person

should enjoy a healthful environment and that each person has a responsibility to contribute to the preservation and enhancement of the environment.

§ 4332. Cooperation of agencies; reports; availability of information; recommendations; international and national coordination of efforts

The Congress authorizes and directs that, to the fullest extent possible:

(1) the policies, regulations, and public laws of the United States shall be interpreted and administered in accordance with the policies set forth in this chapter, and (2) all agencies of the Federal Government shall—

(A) utilize a systematic, interdisciplinary approach which will insure the integrated use of the natural and social sciences and the environmental design arts in planning and in decisionmaking which may have an impact on man's environment;

(B) identify and develop methods and procedures, in consultation with the Council on Environmental Quality established by subchapter II of this chapter, which will insure that presently unquantified environmental amenities and values may be given appropriate consideration in decisionmaking along with economic and technical considerations;

(C) include in every recommendation or report on proposals for legislation and other major Federal actions significantly affecting the quality of the human environment, a detailed statement by the responsible official on—

(i) the environmental impact of the proposed action,

(ii) any adverse environmental effects which cannot be avoided should the proposal be implemented,

(iii) alternatives to the proposed action,

(iv) the relationship between local short-term uses of man's environment and the maintenance and enhancement of long-term productivity, and

(v) any irreversible and irretrievable commitments of resources which would be involved in the proposed action should it be implemented.

Prior to making any detailed statement, the responsible Federal official shall consult with and obtain the comments of any Federal agency which has jurisdiction by law or special expertise with respect to any environmental impact involved. Copies of such statement and the comments and views of the appropriate Federal, State, and local agencies, which are authorized to develop and enforce environmental standards, shall be made available to the President, the Council on Environmental Quality and to the public as provided by section 552 of Title 5, and shall accompany the proposal through the existing agency review processes;

(D) Any detailed statement required under subparagraph (C) after January 1, 1970, for any major Federal action funded under a program of grants to States shall not be deemed to be legally insufficient solely by reason of having been prepared by a State agency or official, if:

(i) the State agency or official has statewide jurisdiction and has the responsibility for such action,

(ii) the responsible Federal official furnishes guidance and participates in such preparation,

(iii) the responsible Federal official independently evaluates such statement prior to its approval and adoption, and

(iv) after January 1, 1976, the responsible Federal official provides early notification to, and solicits the views of, any other State or any Federal land management entity of any action or any alternative thereto which may have significant impacts upon such State or affected Federal land management entity and, if there is any disagreement on such impacts, prepares a written assessment of such impacts and views for incorporation into such detailed statement.

The procedures in this subparagraph shall not relieve the Federal official of his responsibilities for the scope, objectivity, and content of the entire statement or of any other responsibility under this chapter; and further, this subparagraph does not affect the legal sufficiency of statements prepared by State agencies with less than statewide jurisdiction.

(E) study, develop, and describe appropriate alternatives to recommended courses of action in any proposal which involves unresolved conflicts concerning alternative uses of available resources;

(F) recognize the worldwide and long-range character of environmental problems and, where consistent with the foreign policy of the United States, lend appropriate support to initiatives, resolutions, and programs designed to maximize international cooperation in anticipating and preventing a decline in the quality of mankind's world environment;

(G) make available to States, counties, municipalities, institutions, and individuals, advice and information useful in restoring, maintaining, and enhancing the quality of the environment;

(H) initiate and utilize ecological information in the planning and development of resource-oriented projects; and

(I) assist the Council on Environmental Quality established by subchapter II of this chapter.

§ 4333. Conformity of administrative procedures to national environmental policy

All agencies of the Federal Government shall review their present statutory authority, administrative regulations, and current policies and procedures for the purpose of determining whether there are any deficiencies or inconsistencies therein which prohibit full compliance with the purposes and provisions of this chapter and shall propose to the President not later than July 1, 1971, such measures as may be necessary to bring their authority and policies into conformity with the intent, purposes, and procedures set forth in this chapter.

§ 4334. Other statutory obligations of agencies

Nothing in section 4332 or 4333 of this title shall in any way affect the specific statutory obligations of any Federal agency (1) to comply with criteria or standards of environmental quality, (2) to coordinate or consult with any other Federal or State agency, or (3) to act, or refrain from acting contingent upon the recommendations or certification of any other Federal or State agency.

§ 4335. Efforts supplemental to existing authorizations

The policies and goals set forth in this chapter are supplementary to those set forth in existing authorizations of Federal agencies.

* * *

SUBCHAPTER II—COUNCIL ON ENVIRONMENTAL QUALITY

§ 4342. Establishment; membership; Chairman; appointments

There is created in the Executive Office of the President a Council on Environmental Quality (hereinafter referred to as the "Council"). The Council shall be composed of three members who shall be appointed by the President to serve at his pleasure, by and with the advice and consent of the Senate. The President shall designate one of the members of the Council to serve as Chairman. Each member shall be a person who, as a result of his training, experience, and attainments, is exceptionally well qualified to analyze and interpret environmental trends and information of all kinds; to appraise programs and activities of the Federal Government in the light of the policy set forth in subchapter I of this chapter; to be conscious of and responsive to the scientific, economic, social, esthetic, and cultural needs and interests of the Nation; and to formulate and recommend national policies to promote the improvement of the quality of the environment.

Note: Pub.L. 105–65, Title III, Oct. 27, 1997, 111 Stat. 1375, provided in part that: "notwithstanding section 202 of the National Environmental Policy Act of 1970, the Council shall consist of one member, appointed by the President, by and with the advice and consent of the Senate, serving as Chairman and exercising all powers, functions, and duties of the Council." This provision was contained in the act appropriating funds for that year for the Council on Environmental Quality, so its effect was limited to that appropriation year. However, the same provision has been included in the appropriation act for the Council every year subsequently. *See, e.g.,* Pub.L. 109–54, Title III, Aug. 2, 2005, 119 Stat. 543.

* * *

§ 4344. Duties and functions

It shall be the duty and function of the Council—

(1) to assist and advise the President in the preparation of the Environmental Quality Report required by section 4341 of this title;

(2) to gather timely and authoritative information concerning the conditions and trends in the quality of the environment both current and prospective, to analyze and interpret such information for the purpose of determining whether such conditions and trends are interfering, or are likely to interfere, with the achievement of the policy set forth in subchapter I of this chapter, and to compile and submit to the President studies relating to such conditions and trends;

(3) to review and appraise the various programs and activities of the Federal Government in the light of the policy set forth in subchapter I of this chapter for the purpose of determining the extent to which such programs and activities are contributing to the achievement of such policy, and to make recommendations to the President with respect thereto;

(4) to develop and recommend to the President national policies to foster and promote the improvement of environmental quality to meet the conservation, social, economic, health, and other requirements and goals of the Nation;

(5) to conduct investigations, studies, surveys, research, and analyses relating to ecological systems and environmental quality;

(6) to document and define changes in the natural environment, including the plant and animal systems, and to accumulate necessary data and other information for a continuing analysis of these changes or trends and an interpretation of their underlying causes;

(7) to report at least once each year to the President on the state and condition of the environment; and

(8) to make and furnish such studies, reports thereon, and recommendations with respect to matters of policy and legislation as the President may request.

* * *

SUBCHAPTER III—MISCELLANEOUS PROVISIONS

* * *

§ 4365. Science Advisory Board

(a) Establishment; requests for advice by Administrator of Environmental Protection Agency and Congressional committees. The Administrator of the Environmental Protection Agency shall establish a Science Advisory Board which shall provide such scientific advice as may be requested by the Administrator, the Committee on Environment and Public Works of the United States Senate, or the Committee on Science, Space, and Technology, on Energy and Commerce, or on Public Works and Transportation of the House of Representatives.

(b) Membership; Chairman; meetings; qualifications of members. Such Board shall be composed of at least nine members, one of whom shall be designated Chairman, and shall meet at such times and places as may be designated by the Chairman of the Board in consultation with the Administrator. Each member of the Board shall be qualified by education, training, and experience to evaluate scientific and technical information on matters referred to the Board under this section.

(c) Proposed environmental criteria document, standard, limitation, or regulation; functions respecting in conjunction with Administrator.

(1) The Administrator, at the time any proposed criteria document, standard, limitation, or regulation under the Clean Air Act [42 U.S.C.A. § 7401 et seq.], the Federal Water Pollution Control Act [33 U.S.C.A. § 1251 et seq.], the Resource, Conservation and Recovery Act of 1976 [42 U.S.C.A. § 6901 et seq.], the Noise Control Act [42 U.S.C.A. § 4901 et seq.], the Toxic Substances Control Act [15 U.S.C.A. § 2601 et seq.], or the Safe Drinking Water Act [42 U.S.C.A. § 300f et seq.], or under any other authority of the Administrator, is provided to any other Federal agency for formal review and comment, shall make available to the Board such proposed criteria document, standard, limitation, or regulation, together with relevant scientific and technical information in the possession of the Environmental Protection Agency on which the proposed action is based.

(2) The Board may make available to the Administrator, within the time specified by the Administrator, its advice and comments on the adequacy of the scientific and technical basis of the proposed criteria document, standard, limitation, or regulation, together with any pertinent information in the Board's possession.

(d) Utilization of technical and scientific capabilities of Federal agencies and national environmental laboratories for determining adequacy of scientific and technical basis of proposed criteria document, etc. In preparing such advice and comments, the Board shall avail itself of the technical and scientific capabilities of any Federal agency, including the Environmental Protection Agency and any national environmental laboratories.

(e) Member committees and investigative panels; establishment; chairmenship. The Board is authorized to constitute such member committees and investigative panels as the Administrator and the Board find necessary to carry out this section.   Each such member committee or investigative panel shall be chaired by a member of the Board.

(f) Appointment and compensation of secretary and other personnel; compensation of members.

(1) Upon the recommendation of the Board, the Administrator shall appoint a secretary, and such other employees as deemed necessary to exercise and fulfill the Board's powers and responsibilities.   The compensation of all employees appointed under this paragraph shall be fixed in accordance with chapter 51 and subchapter III of chapter 53 of Title 5.

(2) Members of the Board may be compensated at a rate to be fixed by the President but not in excess of the maximum rate of pay for grade GS–18, as provided in the General Schedule under section 5332 of Title 5.

(g) Consultation and coordination with Scientific Advisory Panel. In carrying out the functions assigned by this section, the Board shall consult and coordinate its activities with the Scientific Advisory Panel established by the Administrator pursuant to section 136w(d) of Title 7.

FEDERAL REGISTER ACT

TITLE 44. PUBLIC PRINTING AND DOCUMENTS
CHAPTER 15—FEDERAL REGISTER AND CODE OF FEDERAL REGULATIONS

§ 1501. Definitions

As used in this chapter, unless the context otherwise requires—

"document" means a Presidential proclamation or Executive order and an order, regulation, rule, certificate, code of fair competition, license, notice, or similar instrument, issued, prescribed, or promulgated by a Federal agency;

"Federal agency" or "agency" means the President of the United States, or an executive department, independent board, establishment, bureau, agency, institution, commission, or separate office of the administrative branch of the Government of the United States but not the legislative or judicial branches of the Government;

"person" means an individual, partnership, association, or corporation; and

"National Archives of the United States" has the same meaning as in section 2901(11) of this title.

§ 1502. Custody and printing of Federal documents; appointment of Director

The Archivist of the United States, acting through the Office of the Federal Register, is charged with the custody and, together with the Public Printer, with the prompt and uniform printing and distribution of the documents required or authorized to be published by section 1505 of this title. There shall be at the head of the Office a director, appointed by, and who shall act under the general direction of, the Archivist of the United States in carrying out this chapter and the regulations prescribed under it.

§ 1503. Filing documents with Office; notation of time; public inspection; transmission for printing

The original and two duplicate originals or certified copies of a document required or authorized to be published by section 1505 of this title shall be filed with the Office of the Federal Register, which shall be open for that purpose during all hours of the working days when the National Archives Building is open for official business. The Archivist of the United States shall cause to be noted on the original and duplicate originals or certified copies of each document the day and hour of filing. When the original is issued, prescribed, or promulgated outside the District of Columbia, and certified copies are filed before the filing of the original, the notation shall be of the day and hour of filing of the certified copies. Upon filing, at least one copy shall be immediately available for public inspection in the Office. The original shall be retained by the National Archives and Records Administration and shall be available for inspection under regulations prescribed by the Archivist, unless such original is disposed of in accordance with disposal schedules submitted by the Administrative Committee of the Federal Register and authorized by the Archivist pursuant to regulations issued under chapter 33 of this title; however, originals of proclamations of the President and Executive orders shall be permanently retained by the Administration as part of the National Archives of the United States. The Office shall transmit immediately to the Government Printing Office for printing, as provided by this chapter, one duplicate original or certified copy of each document required or authorized to be published by section 1505 of this title. Every Federal agency shall cause to be transmitted for filing the original and the duplicate originals or certified copies of all such documents issued, prescribed, or promulgated by the agency.

§ 1504. "Federal Register"; printing; contents; distribution; price

Documents required or authorized to be published by section 1505 of this title shall be printed and distributed immediately by the Government Printing Office in a serial publication designated the "Federal Register." The Public Printer shall make available the facilities of the

Government Printing Office for the prompt printing and distribution of the Federal Register in the manner and at the times required by this chapter and the regulations prescribed under it. The contents of the daily issues shall be indexed and shall comprise all documents, required or authorized to be published, filed with the Office of the Federal Register up to the time of the day immediately preceding the day of distribution fixed by regulations under this chapter. There shall be printed with each document a copy of the notation, required to be made by section 1503 of this title, of the day and hour when, upon filing with the Office, the document was made available for public inspection. Distribution shall be made by delivery or by deposit at a post office at a time in the morning of the day of distribution fixed by regulations prescribed under this chapter. The prices to be charged for the Federal Register may be fixed by the Administrative Committee of the Federal Register established by section 1506 of this title without reference to the restrictions placed upon and fixed for the sale of Government publications by sections 1705 and 1708 of this title.

§ **1505.** Documents to be published in Federal Register

(a) Proclamations and Executive Orders; documents having general applicability and legal effect; documents required to be published by Congress. There shall be published in the Federal Register—

> (1) Presidential proclamations and Executive orders, except those not having general applicability and legal effect or effective only against Federal agencies or persons in their capacity as officers, agents, or employees thereof;

> (2) documents or classes of documents that the President may determine from time to time have general applicability and legal effect; and

> (3) documents or classes of documents that may be required so to be published by Act of Congress.

For the purposes of this chapter every document or order which prescribes a penalty has general applicability and legal effect.

(b) Documents authorized to be published by regulations; comments and news items excluded. In addition to the foregoing there shall also be published in the Federal Register other documents or classes of documents authorized to be published by regulations prescribed under this chapter with the approval of the President, but comments or news items of any character may not be published in the Federal Register.

(c) Suspension of requirements for filing of documents; alternate systems for promulgating, filing, or publishing documents; preservation of originals. In the event of an attack or threatened attack upon the continental United States and a determination by the President that as a result of an attack or threatened attack—

(1) publication of the Federal Register or filing of documents with the Office of the Federal Register is impracticable, or

(2) under existing conditions publication in the Federal Register would not serve to give appropriate notice to the public of the contents of documents, the President may, without regard to any other provision of law, suspend all or part of the requirements of law or regulation for filing with the Office or publication in the Federal Register of documents or classes of documents.

The suspensions shall remain in effect until revoked by the President, or by concurrent resolution of the Congress. The President shall establish alternate systems for promulgating, filing, or publishing documents or classes of documents affected by such suspensions, including requirements relating to their effectiveness or validity, that may be considered under the then existing circumstances practicable to provide public notice of the issuance and of the contents of the documents. The alternate systems may, without limitation, provide for the use of regional or specialized publications or depositories for documents, or of the press, the radio, or similar mediums of general communication. Compliance with alternate systems of filing or publication shall have the same effect as filing with the Office or publication in the Federal Register under this chapter or other law or regulation. With respect to documents promulgated under alternate systems, each agency shall preserve the original and two duplicate originals or two certified copies for filing with the Office when the President determines that it is practicable.

§ 1506. Administrative Committee of the Federal Register; establishment and composition; powers and duties

The Administrative Committee of the Federal Register shall consist of the Archivist of the United States or Acting Archivist, who shall be chairman, an officer of the Department of Justice designated by the Attorney General, and the Public Printer or Acting Public Printer. The Director of the Federal Register shall act as secretary of the committee. The committee shall prescribe, with the approval of the President, regulations for carrying out this chapter. The regulations shall provide, among other things—

(1) the manner of certification of copies required to be certified under section 1503 of this title, which certification may be permitted to be based upon confirmed communications from outside the District of Columbia;

(2) the documents which shall be authorized under section 1505(b) of this title to be published in the Federal Register;

(3) the manner and form in which the Federal Register shall be printed, reprinted, compiled, indexed, bound, and distributed;

(4) the number of copies of the Federal Register, which shall be printed, reprinted, and compiled, the number which shall be distributed without charge to Members of Congress, officers and employees of the United States, or Federal agency, for official use, and the number which shall be available for distribution to the public; and

(5) the prices to be charged for individual copies of, and subscriptions to, the Federal Register and reprints and bound volumes of it.

§ 1507. Filing document as constructive notice; publication in Federal Register as presumption of validity; judicial notice; citation

A document required by section 1505(a) of this title to be published in the Federal Register is not valid as against a person who has not had actual knowledge of it until the duplicate originals or certified copies of the document have been filed with the Office of the Federal Register and a copy made available for public inspection as provided by section 1503 of this title. Unless otherwise specifically provided by statute, filing of a document, required or authorized to be published by section 1505 of this title, except in cases where notice by publication is insufficient in law, is sufficient to give notice of the contents of the document to a person subject to or affected by it. The publication in the Federal Register of a document creates a rebuttable presumption—

(1) that it was duly issued, prescribed, or promulgated;

(2) that it was filed with the Office of the Federal Register and made available for public inspection at the day and hour stated in the printed notation;

(3) that the copy contained in the Federal Register is a true copy of the original; and

(4) that all requirements of this chapter and the regulations prescribed under it relative to the document have been complied with.

The contents of the Federal Register shall be judicially noticed and without prejudice to any other mode of citation, may be cited by volume and page number.

§ 1508. Publication in Federal Register as notice of hearing

A notice of hearing or of opportunity to be heard, required or authorized to be given by an Act of Congress, or which may otherwise properly be given, shall be deemed to have been given to all persons residing within the States of the Union and the District of Columbia, except in cases where notice by publication is insufficient in law, when the notice is published in the Federal Register at such a time that the period between the publication and the date fixed in the notice for the hearing or for the termination of the opportunity to be heard is—

(1) not less than the time specifically prescribed for the publication of the notice by the appropriate Act of Congress; or

(2) not less than fifteen days when time for publication is not specifically prescribed by the Act, without prejudice, however, to the effectiveness of a notice of less than fifteen days where the shorter period is reasonable.

§ 1509. Costs of publication, etc.

(a) The cost of printing reprinting, wrapping, binding, and distributing the Federal Register and the Code of Federal Regulations, and, except as provided in subsection (b), other expenses incurred by the Government Printing Office in carrying out the duties placed upon it by this chapter shall be charged to the revolving fund provided in section 309. Reimbursements for such costs and expenses shall be made by the Federal agencies and credited, together with all receipts, as provided in section 309(b).

(b) The cost of printing, reprinting, wrapping, binding, and distributing all other publications of the Federal Register program, and other expenses incurred by the Government Printing Office in connection with such publications, shall be borne by the appropriations to the Government Printing Office and the appropriations are made available, and are authorized to be increased by additional sums necessary for the purposes, the increases to be based upon estimates submitted by the Public Printer.

§ 1510. Code of Federal Regulations

(a) The Administrative Committee of the Federal Register, with the approval of the President, may require, from time to time as it considers necessary, the preparation and publication in special or supplemental editions of the Federal Register of complete codifications of the documents of each agency of the Government having general applicability and legal effect, issued or promulgated by the agency by publication in the Federal Register or by filing with the Administrative Committee, and are relied upon by the agency as authority for, or are invoked or used by it in the discharge of, its activities or functions, and are in effect as to facts arising on or after dates specified by the Administrative Committee.

(b) A codification published under subsection (a) of this section shall be printed and bound in permanent form and shall be designated as the "Code of Federal Regulations." The Administrative Committee shall regulate the binding of the printed codifications into separate books with a view to practical usefulness and economical manufacture. Each book shall contain an explanation of its coverage and other aids to users that the Administrative Committee may require. A general index to the entire Code of Federal Regulations shall be separately printed and bound.

(c) The Administrative Committee shall regulate the supplementation and the collation and republication of the printed codifications with a view to keeping the Code of Federal Regulations as current as practicable. Each book shall be either supplemented or collated and republished at least once each calendar year.

(d) The Office of the Federal Register shall prepare and publish the codifications, supplements, collations, and indexes authorized by this section.

(e) The codified documents of the several agencies published in the supplemental edition of the Federal Register under this section, as amended by documents subsequently filed with the Office and published in the daily issues of the Federal Register, shall be prima facie evidence of the text of the documents and of the fact that they are in effect on and after the date of publication.

(f) The Administrative Committee shall prescribe, with the approval of the President, regulations for carrying out this section.

(g) This section does not require codification of the text of Presidential documents published and periodically compiled in supplements to Title 3 of the Code of Federal Regulations.

§ 1511. International agreements excluded from provisions of chapter

This chapter does not apply to treaties, conventions, protocols, and other international agreements, or proclamations thereof by the President.

PAPERWORK REDUCTION ACT

TITLE 44. PUBLIC PRINTING AND DOCUMENTS
CHAPTER 35—COORDINATION OF FEDERAL INFORMATION POLICY
SUBCHAPTER I—FEDERAL INFORMATION POLICY

§ 3501. Purposes

The purposes of this subchapter are to—

(1) minimize the paperwork burden for individuals, small businesses, educational and nonprofit institutions, Federal contractors, State, local and tribal governments, and other persons resulting from the collection of information by or for the Federal Government;

(2) ensure the greatest possible public benefit from and maximize the utility of information created, collected, maintained, used, shared and disseminated by or for the Federal Government;

(3) coordinate, integrate, and to the extent practicable and appropriate, make uniform Federal information resources management poli-

cies and practices as a means to improve the productivity, efficiency, and effectiveness of Government programs, including the reduction of information collection burdens on the public and the improvement of service delivery to the public;

(4) improve the quality and use of Federal information to strengthen decisionmaking, accountability, and openness in Government and society;

(5) minimize the cost to the Federal Government of the creation, collection, maintenance, use, dissemination, and disposition of information;

(6) strengthen the partnership between the Federal Government and State, local, and tribal governments by minimizing the burden and maximizing the utility of information created, collected, maintained, used, disseminated, and retained by or for the Federal Government;

(7) provide for the dissemination of public information on a timely basis, on equitable terms, and in a manner that promotes the utility of the information to the public and makes effective use of information technology;

(8) ensure that the creation, collection, maintenance, use, dissemination, and disposition of information by or for the Federal Government is consistent with applicable laws, including laws relating to—

(A) privacy and confidentiality, including section 552a of title 5;

(B) security of information, including section 11332 of title 40; and

(C) access to information, including section 552 of title 5;

(9) ensure the integrity, quality, and utility of the Federal statistical system;

(10) ensure that information technology is acquired, used, and managed to improve performance of agency missions, including the reduction of information collection burdens on the public; and

(11) improve the responsibility and accountability of the Office of Management and Budget and all other Federal agencies to Congress and to the public for implementing the information collection review process, information resources management, and related policies and guidelines established under this subchapter.

§ 3502. Definitions

As used in this subchapter—

(1) the term "agency" means any executive department, military department, Government corporation, Government controlled corporation, or other establishment in the executive branch of the Gov-

ernment (including the Executive Office of the President), or any independent regulatory agency, but does not include—

(A) the General Accounting Office;

(B) Federal Election Commission;

(C) the governments of the District of Columbia and of the territories and possessions of the United States, and their various subdivisions; or

(D) Government-owned contractor-operated facilities, including laboratories engaged in national defense research and production activities;

(2) the term "burden" means time, effort, or financial resources expended by persons to generate, maintain, or provide information to or for a Federal agency, including the resources expended for—

(A) reviewing instructions;

(B) acquiring, installing, and utilizing technology and systems;

(C) adjusting the existing ways to comply with any previously applicable instructions and requirements;

(D) searching data sources;

(E) completing and reviewing the collection of information; and

(F) transmitting, or otherwise disclosing the information;

(3) the term "collection of information"—

(A) means the obtaining, causing to be obtained, soliciting, or requiring the disclosure to third parties or the public, of facts or opinions by or for an agency, regardless of form or format, calling for either—

(i) answers to identical questions posed to, or identical reporting or recordkeeping requirements imposed on, ten or more persons, other than agencies, instrumentalities, or employees of the United States; or

(ii) answers to questions posed to agencies, instrumentalities, or employees of the United States which are to be used for general statistical purposes; and

(B) shall not include a collection of information described under section 3518(c)(1);

(4) the term "Director" means the Director of the Office of Management and Budget;

(5) the term "independent regulatory agency" means the Board of Governors of the Federal Reserve System, the Commodity Futures Trading Commission, the Consumer Product Safety Commission, the Federal Communications Commission, the Federal Deposit Insurance Corporation, the Federal Energy Regulatory Commission,

the Federal Housing Finance Board, the Federal Maritime Commission, the Federal Trade Commission, the Interstate Commerce Commission, the Mine Enforcement Safety and Health Review Commission, the National Labor Relations Board, the Nuclear Regulatory Commission, the Occupational Safety and Health Review Commission, the Postal Regulatory Commission, the Securities and Exchange Commission, and any other similar agency designated by statute as a Federal independent regulatory agency or commission;

(6) the term "information resources" means information and related resources, such as personnel, equipment, funds, and information technology;

(7) the term "information resources management" means the process of managing information resources to accomplish agency missions and to improve agency performance, including through the reduction of information collection burdens on the public;

(8) the term "information system" means a discrete set of information resources organized for the collection, processing, maintenance, use, sharing, dissemination, or disposition of information;

(9) the term "information technology" has the meaning given that term in section 11101 of Title 40 but does not include national security systems as defined in section 11103 of title 40;

(10) the term "person" means an individual, partnership, association, corporation, business trust, or legal representative, an organized group of individuals, a State, territorial, tribal, or local government or branch thereof, or a political subdivision of a State, territory, tribal, or local government or a branch of a political subdivision;

(11) the term "practical utility" means the ability of an agency to use information, particularly the capability to process such information in a timely and useful fashion;

(12) the term "public information" means any information, regardless of form or format, that an agency discloses, disseminates, or makes available to the public;

(13) the term "recordkeeping requirement" means a requirement imposed by or for an agency on persons to maintain specified records, including a requirement to—

(A) retain such records;

(B) notify third parties, the Federal Government, or the public of the existence of such records;

(C) disclose such records to third parties, the Federal Government, or the public; or

(D) report to third parties, the Federal Government, or the public regarding such records; and

(14) the term "penalty" includes the imposition by an agency or court of a fine or other punishment; a judgment for monetary damages or equitable relief; or the revocation, suspension, reduction, or denial of a license, privilege, right, grant, or benefit.

§ 3503. Office of Information and Regulatory Affairs

(a) There is established in the Office of Management and Budget an office to be known as the Office of Information and Regulatory Affairs.

(b) There shall be at the head of the Office an Administrator who shall be appointed by the President, by and with the advice and consent of the Senate. The Director shall delegate to the Administrator the authority to administer all functions under this subchapter, except that any such delegation shall not relieve the Director of responsibility for the administration of such functions. The Administrator shall serve as principal adviser to the Director on Federal information resources management policy.

§ 3504. Authority and functions of Director

(a)(1) The Director shall oversee the use of information resources to improve the efficiency and effectiveness of governmental operations to serve agency missions, including burden reduction and service delivery to the public. In performing such oversight, the Director shall—

(A) develop, coordinate and oversee the implementation of Federal information resources management policies, principles, standards, and guidelines; and

(B) provide direction and oversee—

(i) the review and approval of the collection of information and the reduction of the information collection burden;

(ii) agency dissemination of and public access to information;

(iii) statistical activities;

(iv) records management activities;

(v) privacy, confidentiality, security, disclosure, and sharing of information; and

(vi) the acquisition and use of information technology, including alternative information technologies that provide for electronic submission, maintenance, or disclosure of information as a substitute for paper and for the use and acceptance of electronic signatures.

(2) The authority of the Director under this subchapter shall be exercised consistent with applicable law.

(b) With respect to general information resources management policy, the Director shall—

(1) develop and oversee the implementation of uniform information resources management policies, principles, standards, and guidelines;

(2) foster greater sharing, dissemination, and access to public information, including through—

(A) the use of the Government Information Locator Service; and

(B) the development and utilization of common standards for information collection, storage, processing and communication, including standards for security, interconnectivity and interoperability;

(3) initiate and review proposals for changes in legislation, regulations, and agency procedures to improve information resources management practices;

(4) oversee the development and implementation of best practices in information resources management, including training; and

(5) oversee agency integration of program and management functions with information resources management functions.

(c) With respect to the collection of information and the control of paperwork, the Director shall—

(1) review and approve proposed agency collections of information;

(2) coordinate the review of the collection of information associated with Federal procurement and acquisition by the Office of Information and Regulatory Affairs with the Office of Federal Procurement Policy, with particular emphasis on applying information technology to improve the efficiency and effectiveness of Federal procurement, acquisition and payment, and to reduce information collection burdens on the public;

(3) minimize the Federal information collection burden, with particular emphasis on those individuals and entities most adversely affected;

(4) maximize the practical utility of and public benefit from information collected by or for the Federal Government;

(5) establish and oversee standards and guidelines by which agencies are to estimate the burden to comply with a proposed collection of information;

(6) publish in the Federal Register and make available on the Internet (in consultation with the Small Business Administration) on an annual basis a list of the compliance assistance resources available to small businesses, with the first such publication occur-

ring not later than 1 year after the date of enactment of the Small Business Paperwork Relief Act of 2002.

(d) With respect to information dissemination, the Director shall develop and oversee the implementation of policies, principles, standards, and guidelines to—

(1) apply to Federal agency dissemination of public information, regardless of the form or format in which such information is disseminated; and

(2) promote public access to public information and fulfill the purposes of this subchapter, including through the effective use of information technology.

(e) With respect to statistical policy and coordination, the Director shall—

(1) coordinate the activities of the Federal statistical system to ensure—

(A) the efficiency and effectiveness of the system; and

(B) the integrity, objectivity, impartiality, utility, and confidentiality of information collected for statistical purposes;

(2) ensure that budget proposals of agencies are consistent with system-wide priorities for maintaining and improving the quality of Federal statistics and prepare an annual report on statistical program funding;

(3) develop and oversee the implementation of Governmentwide policies, principles, standards, and guidelines concerning—

(A) statistical collection procedures and methods;

(B) statistical data classification;

(C) statistical information presentation and dissemination;

(D) timely release of statistical data; and

(E) such statistical data sources as may be required for the administration of Federal programs;

(4) evaluate statistical program performance and agency compliance with Governmentwide policies, principles, standards and guidelines;

(5) promote the sharing of information collected for statistical purposes consistent with privacy rights and confidentiality pledges;

(6) coordinate the participation of the United States in international statistical activities, including the development of comparable statistics;

(7) appoint a chief statistician who is a trained and experienced professional statistician to carry out the functions described under this subsection;

(8) establish an Interagency Council on Statistical Policy to advise and assist the Director in carrying out the functions under this subsection that shall—

(A) be headed by the chief statistician; and

(B) consist of—

(i) the heads of the major statistical programs; and

(ii) representatives of other statistical agencies under rotating membership; and

(9) provide opportunities for training in statistical policy functions to employees of the Federal Government under which—

(A) each trainee shall be selected at the discretion of the Director based on agency requests and shall serve under the chief statistician for at least 6 months and not more than 1 year; and

(B) all costs of the training shall be paid by the agency requesting training.

(f) With respect to records management, the Director shall—

(1) provide advice and assistance to the Archivist of the United States and the Administrator of General Services to promote coordination in the administration of chapters 29, 31, and 33 of this title with the information resources management policies, principles, standards, and guidelines established under this subchapter;

(2) review compliance by agencies with—

(A) the requirements of chapters 29, 31, and 33 of this title; and

(B) regulations promulgated by the Archivist of the United States and the Administrator of General Services; and

(3) oversee the application of records management policies, principles, standards, and guidelines, including requirements for archiving information maintained in electronic format, in the planning and design of information systems.

(g) With respect to privacy and security, the Director shall—

(1) develop and oversee the implementation of policies, principles, standards, and guidelines on privacy, confidentiality, security, disclosure and sharing of information collected or maintained by or for agencies;

(2) oversee and coordinate compliance with sections 552 and 552a of title 5, sections 20 and 21 of the National Institute of Standards and Technology Act (15 U.S.C. 278g–3 and 278g–4), section 11331 of title 40 and subchapter II of this title, and related information management laws; and

(3) [Repealed. Pub. L. 107–296, Title X, § 1005(c)(1)(C), Nov. 25, 2002, 116 Stat. 2272.].

(h) With respect to Federal information technology, the Director shall—

(1) in consultation with the Director of the National Institute of Standards and Technology and the Administrator of General Services—

(A) develop and oversee the implementation of policies, principles, standards, and guidelines for information technology functions and activities of the Federal Government, including periodic evaluations of major information systems; and

(B) oversee the development and implementation of standards under section 11331 of title 40;

(2) monitor the effectiveness of, and compliance with, directives issued under subtitle III of title 40 and directives issued under section 322 of title 40;

(3) coordinate the development and review by the Office of Information and Regulatory Affairs of policy associated with Federal procurement and acquisition of information technology with the Office of Federal Procurement Policy;

(4) ensure, through the review of agency budget proposals, information resources management plans and other means—

(A) agency integration of information resources management plans, program plans and budgets for acquisition and use of information technology; and

(B) the efficiency and effectiveness of inter-agency information technology initiatives to improve agency performance and the accomplishment of agency missions; and

(5) promote the use of information technology by the Federal Government to improve the productivity, efficiency, and effectiveness of Federal programs, including through dissemination of public information and the reduction of information collection burdens on the public.

§ 3505. Assignment of tasks and deadlines

(a) In carrying out the functions under this subchapter, the Director shall—

(1) in consultation with agency heads, set an annual Government-wide goal for the reduction of information collection burdens by at least 10 percent during each of fiscal years 1996 and 1997 and 5 percent during each of fiscal years 1998, 1999, 2000, and 2001, and set annual agency goals to—

(A) reduce information collection burdens imposed on the public that—

(i) represent the maximum practicable opportunity in each agency; and

(ii) are consistent with improving agency management of the process for the review of collections of information established under section 3506(c); and

(B) improve information resources management in ways that increase the productivity, efficiency and effectiveness of Federal programs, including service delivery to the public;

(2) with selected agencies and non-Federal entities on a voluntary basis, conduct pilot projects to test alternative policies, practices, regulations, and procedures to fulfill the purposes of this subchapter, particularly with regard to minimizing the Federal information collection burden; and

(3) in consultation with the Administrator of General Services, the Director of the National Institute of Standards and Technology, the Archivist of the United States, and the Director of the Office of Personnel Management, develop and maintain a Governmentwide strategic plan for information resources management, that shall include—

(A) a description of the objectives and the means by which the Federal Government shall apply information resources to improve agency and program performance;

(B) plans for—

(i) reducing information burdens on the public, including reducing such burdens through the elimination of duplication and meeting shared data needs with shared resources;

(ii) enhancing public access to and dissemination of, information, using electronic and other formats; and

(iii) meeting the information technology needs of the Federal Government in accordance with the purposes of this subchapter; and

(C) a description of progress in applying information resources management to improve agency performance and the accomplishment of missions.

(b) For purposes of any pilot project conducted under subsection (a)(2), the Director may, after consultation with the agency head, waive the application of any administrative directive issued by an agency with which the project is conducted, including any directive requiring a collection of information, after giving timely notice to the public and the Congress regarding the need for such waiver.

(c)[1] Inventory of major information systems.—

---

1. So in original. Two subsecs. (c) were added.

(1) The head of each agency shall develop and maintain an inventory of major information systems (including major national security systems) operated by or under the control of such agency.

(2) The identification of information systems in an inventory under this subsection shall include an identification of the interfaces between each such system and all other systems or networks, including those not operated by or under the control of the agency.

(3) Such inventory shall be—

    (A) updated at least annually;

    (B) made available to the Comptroller General; and

    (C) used to support information resources management, including—

        (i) preparation and maintenance of the inventory of information resources under section 3506(b)(4);

        (ii) information technology planning, budgeting, acquisition, and management under section 3506(h), subtitle III of title 40, and related laws and guidance;

        (iii) monitoring, testing, and evaluation of information security controls under subchapter II;

        (iv) preparation of the index of major information systems required under section 552(g) of title 5, United States Code; and

        (v) preparation of information system inventories required for records management under chapters 21, 29, 31, and 33.

(4) The Director shall issue guidance for and oversee the implementation of the requirements of this subsection.

(c)[2] Inventory of information systems.—

(1) The head of each agency shall develop and maintain an inventory of the information systems (including national security systems) operated by or under the control of such agency;

(2) The identification of information systems in an inventory under this subsection shall include an identification of the interfaces between each such system and all other systems or networks, including those not operated by or under the control of the agency;

(3) Such inventory shall be—

    (A) updated at least annually;

    (B) made available to the Comptroller General; and

    (C) used to support information resources management, including—

---

2. So in original. Two subsecs. (c) were added.

(i) preparation and maintenance of the inventory of information resources under section 3506(b)(4);

(ii) information technology planning, budgeting, acquisition, and management under section 3506(h), subtitle III of title 40, and related laws and guidance;

(iii) monitoring, testing, and evaluation of information security controls under subchapter II;

(iv) preparation of the index of major information systems required under section 552(g) of title 5, United States Code; and

(v) preparation of information system inventories required for records management under chapters 21, 29, 31, and 33.

(4) The Director shall issue guidance for and oversee the implementation of the requirements of this subsection.

§ 3506. Federal agency responsibilities

(a)(1) The head of each agency shall be responsible for—

(A) carrying out the agency's information resources management activities to improve agency productivity, efficiency, and effectiveness; and

(B) complying with the requirements of this subchapter and related policies established by the Director.

(2)(A) Except as provided under subparagraph (B), the head of each agency shall designate a Chief Information Officer who shall report directly to such agency head to carry out the responsibilities of the agency under this subchapter.

(B) The Secretary of the Department of Defense and the Secretary of each military department may each designate Chief Information Officers who shall report directly to such Secretary to carry out the responsibilities of the department under this subchapter. If more than one Chief Information Officer is designated, the respective duties of the Chief Information Officers shall be clearly delineated.

(3) The Chief Information Officer designated under paragraph (2) shall head an office responsible for ensuring agency compliance with and prompt, efficient, and effective implementation of the information policies and information resources management responsibilities established under this subchapter, including the reduction of information collection burdens on the public. The Chief Information Officer and employees of such office shall be selected with special attention to the professional qualifications required to administer the functions described under this subchapter.

(4) Each agency program official shall be responsible and accountable for information resources assigned to and supporting the programs under such official. In consultation with the Chief Information Officer designated under paragraph (2) and the agency Chief Financial Officer (or comparable official), each agency program official shall define program information needs and develop strategies, systems, and capabilities to meet those needs.

(b) With respect to general information resources management, each agency shall—

(1) manage information resources to—

(A) reduce information collection burdens on the public;

(B) increase program efficiency and effectiveness; and

(C) improve the integrity, quality, and utility of information to all users within and outside the agency, including capabilities for ensuring dissemination of public information, public access to government information, and protections for privacy and security;

(2) in accordance with guidance by the Director, develop and maintain a strategic information resources management plan that shall describe how information resources management activities help accomplish agency missions;

(3) develop and maintain an ongoing process to—

(A) ensure that information resources management operations and decisions are integrated with organizational planning, budget, financial management, human resources management, and program decisions;

(B) in cooperation with the agency Chief Financial Officer (or comparable official), develop a full and accurate accounting of information technology expenditures, related expenses, and results; and

(C) establish goals for improving information resources management's contribution to program productivity, efficiency, and effectiveness, methods for measuring progress towards those goals, and clear roles and responsibilities for achieving those goals;

(4) in consultation with the Director, the Administrator of General Services, and the Archivist of the United States, maintain a current and complete inventory of the agency's information resources, including directories necessary to fulfill the requirements of section 3511 of this subchapter; and

(5) in consultation with the Director and the Director of the Office of Personnel Management, conduct formal training programs to

educate agency program and management officials about information resources management.

(c) With respect to the collection of information and the control of paperwork, each agency shall—

(1) establish a process within the office headed by the Chief Information Officer designated under subsection (a), that is sufficiently independent of program responsibility to evaluate fairly whether proposed collections of information should be approved under this subchapter, to—

(A) review each collection of information before submission to the Director for review under this subchapter, including—

(i) an evaluation of the need for the collection of information;

(ii) a functional description of the information to be collected;

(iii) a plan for the collection of the information;

(iv) a specific, objectively supported estimate of burden;

(v) a test of the collection of information through a pilot program, if appropriate; and

(vi) a plan for the efficient and effective management and use of the information to be collected, including necessary resources;

(B) ensure that each information collection—

(i) is inventoried, displays a control number and, if appropriate, an expiration date;

(ii) indicates the collection is in accordance with the clearance requirements of section 3507; and

(iii) informs the person receiving the collection of information of—

(I) the reasons the information is being collected;

(II) the way such information is to be used;

(III) an estimate, to the extent practicable, of the burden of the collection;

(IV) whether responses to the collection of information are voluntary, required to obtain a benefit, or mandatory; and

(V) the fact that an agency may not conduct or sponsor, and a person is not required to respond to, a collection of information unless it displays a valid control number; and

(C) assess the information collection burden of proposed legislation affecting the agency;

(2)(A) except as provided under subparagraph (B) or section 3507(j), provide 60–day notice in the Federal Register, and otherwise consult with members of the public and affected agencies concerning each proposed collection of information, to solicit comment to—

(i) evaluate whether the proposed collection of information is necessary for the proper performance of the functions of the agency, including whether the information shall have practical utility;

(ii) evaluate the accuracy of the agency's estimate of the burden of the proposed collection of information;

(iii) enhance the quality, utility, and clarity of the information to be collected; and

(iv) minimize the burden of the collection of information on those who are to respond, including through the use of automated collection techniques or other forms of information technology; and

(B) for any proposed collection of information contained in a proposed rule (to be reviewed by the Director under section 3507(d)), provide notice and comment through the notice of proposed rulemaking for the proposed rule and such notice shall have the same purposes specified under subparagraph (A)(i) through (iv);

(3) certify (and provide a record supporting such certification, including public comments received by the agency) that each collection of information submitted to the Director for review under section 3507—

(A) is necessary for the proper performance of the functions of the agency, including that the information has practical utility;

(B) is not unnecessarily duplicative of information otherwise reasonably accessible to the agency;

(C) reduces to the extent practicable and appropriate the burden on persons who shall provide information to or for the agency, including with respect to small entities, as defined under section 601(6) of title 5, the use of such techniques as—

(i) establishing differing compliance or reporting requirements or timetables that take into account the resources available to those who are to respond;

(ii) the clarification, consolidation, or simplification of compliance and reporting requirements; or

(iii) an exemption from coverage of the collection of information, or any part thereof;

(D) is written using plain, coherent, and unambiguous terminology and is understandable to those who are to respond;

(E) is to be implemented in ways consistent and compatible, to the maximum extent practicable, with the existing reporting and recordkeeping practices of those who are to respond;

(F) indicates for each recordkeeping requirement the length of time persons are required to maintain the records specified;

(G) contains the statement required under paragraph (1)(B)(iii);

(H) has been developed by an office that has planned and allocated resources for the efficient and effective management and use of the information to be collected, including the processing of the information in a manner which shall enhance, where appropriate, the utility of the information to agencies and the public;

(I) uses effective and efficient statistical survey methodology appropriate to the purpose for which the information is to be collected; and

(J) to the maximum extent practicable, uses information technology to reduce burden and improve data quality, agency efficiency and responsiveness to the public; and

(4) in addition to the requirements of this chapter regarding the reduction of information collection burdens for small business concerns (as defined in section 3 of the Small Business Act 15 U.S.C. 632)), make efforts to further reduce the information collection burden for small business concerns with fewer than 25 employees.

(d) With respect to information dissemination, each agency shall—

(1) ensure that the public has timely and equitable access to the agency's public information, including ensuring such access through—

(A) encouraging a diversity of public and private sources for information based on government public information;

(B) in cases in which the agency provides public information maintained in electronic format, providing timely and equitable access to the underlying data (in whole or in part); and

(C) agency dissemination of public information in an efficient, effective, and economical manner;

(2) regularly solicit and consider public input on the agency's information dissemination activities;

(3) provide adequate notice when initiating, substantially modifying, or terminating significant information dissemination products; and

187

(4) not, except where specifically authorized by statute—

(A) establish an exclusive, restricted, or other distribution arrangement that interferes with timely and equitable availability of public information to the public;

(B) restrict or regulate the use, resale, or redissemination of public information by the public;

(C) charge fees or royalties for resale or redissemination of public information; or

(D) establish user fees for public information that exceed the cost of dissemination.

(e) With respect to statistical policy and coordination, each agency shall—

(1) ensure the relevance, accuracy, timeliness, integrity, and objectivity of information collected or created for statistical purposes;

(2) inform respondents fully and accurately about the sponsors, purposes, and uses of statistical surveys and studies;

(3) protect respondents' privacy and ensure that disclosure policies fully honor pledges of confidentiality;

(4) observe Federal standards and practices for data collection, analysis, documentation, sharing, and dissemination of information;

(5) ensure the timely publication of the results of statistical surveys and studies, including information about the quality and limitations of the surveys and studies; and

(6) make data available to statistical agencies and readily accessible to the public.

(f) With respect to records management, each agency shall implement and enforce applicable policies and procedures, including requirements for archiving information maintained in electronic format, particularly in the planning, design and operation of information systems.

(g) With respect to privacy and security, each agency shall—

(1) implement and enforce applicable policies, procedures, standards, and guidelines on privacy, confidentiality, security, disclosure and sharing of information collected or maintained by or for the agency; and

(2) assume responsibility and accountability for compliance with and coordinated management of sections 552 and 552a of title 5, subchapter II of this chapter, and related information management laws.

(3) [Repealed. Pub.L. 107–296, Title X § 1005(c)(3)(C), Nov. 25, 2002, 116 Stat. 2273.]

(h) With respect to Federal information technology, each agency shall—

(1) implement and enforce applicable Governmentwide and agency information technology management policies, principles, standards, and guidelines;

(2) assume responsibility and accountability for information technology investments;

(3) promote the use of information technology by the agency to improve the productivity, efficiency, and effectiveness of agency programs, including the reduction of information collection burdens on the public and improved dissemination of public information;

(4) propose changes in legislation, regulations, and agency procedures to improve information technology practices, including changes that improve the ability of the agency to use technology to reduce burden; and

(5) assume responsibility for maximizing the value and assessing and managing the risks of major information systems initiatives through a process that is—

(A) integrated with budget, financial, and program management decisions; and

(B) used to select, control, and evaluate the results of major information systems initiatives.

(i)(1) In addition to the requirements described in subsection (c), each agency shall, with respect to the collection of information and the control of paperwork, establish 1 point of contact in the agency to act as a liaison between the agency and small business concerns (as defined in section 3 of the Small Business Act 15 U.S.C. 632)).

(2) Each point of contact described under paragraph (1) shall be established not later than 1 year after the date of enactment of the Small Business Paperwork Relief Act of 2002.

§ **3507.** Public information collection activities; submission to Director; approval and delegation

(a) An agency shall not conduct or sponsor the collection of information unless in advance of the adoption or revision of the collection of information—

(1) the agency has—

(A) conducted the review established under section 3506(c)(1);

(B) evaluated the public comments received under section 3506(c)(2);

(C) submitted to the Director the certification required under section 3506(c)(3), the proposed collection of information, copies of pertinent statutory authority, regulations, and other related materials as the Director may specify; and

(D) published a notice in the Federal Register—

(i) stating that the agency has made such submission; and

(ii) setting forth—

(I) a title for the collection of information;

(II) a summary of the collection of information;

(III) a brief description of the need for the information and the proposed use of the information;

(IV) a description of the likely respondents and proposed frequency of response to the collection of information;

(V) an estimate of the burden that shall result from the collection of information; and

(VI) notice that comments may be submitted to the agency and Director;

(2) the Director has approved the proposed collection of information or approval has been inferred, under the provisions of this section; and

(3) the agency has obtained from the Director a control number to be displayed upon the collection of information.

(b) The Director shall provide at least 30 days for public comment prior to making a decision under subsection (c), (d), or (h), except as provided under subsection (j).

(c)(1) For any proposed collection of information not contained in a proposed rule, the Director shall notify the agency involved of the decision to approve or disapprove the proposed collection of information.

(2) The Director shall provide the notification under paragraph (1),within 60 days after receipt or publication of the notice under subsection (a)(1)(D), whichever is later.

(3) If the Director does not notify the agency of a denial or approval within the 60–day period described under paragraph (2)—

(A) the approval may be inferred;

(B) a control number shall be assigned without further delay; and

(C) the agency may collect the information for not more than 1 year.

(d)(1) For any proposed collection of information contained in a proposed rule—

(A) as soon as practicable, but no later than the date of publication of a notice of proposed rulemaking in the Federal Register, each agency shall forward to the Director a copy of any proposed rule which contains a collection of information and any information requested by the Director necessary to make the determination required under this subsection; and

(B) within 60 days after the notice of proposed rulemaking is published in the Federal Register, the Director may file public comments pursuant to the standards set forth in section 3508 on the collection of information contained in the proposed rule;

(2) When a final rule is published in the Federal Register, the agency shall explain—

(A) how any collection of information contained in the final rule responds to the comments, if any, filed by the Director or the public; or

(B) the reasons such comments were rejected.

(3) If the Director has received notice and failed to comment on an agency rule within 60 days after the notice of proposed rulemaking, the Director may not disapprove any collection of information specifically contained in an agency rule.

(4) No provision in this section shall be construed to prevent the Director, in the Director's discretion—

(A) from disapproving any collection of information which was not specifically required by an agency rule;

(B) from disapproving any collection of information contained in an agency rule, if the agency failed to comply with the requirements of paragraph (1) of this subsection;

(C) from disapproving any collection of information contained in a final agency rule, if the Director finds within 60 days after the publication of the final rule that the agency's response to the Director's comments filed under paragraph (2) of this subsection was unreasonable; or

(D) from disapproving any collection of information contained in a final rule, if—

(i) the Director determines that the agency has substantially modified in the final rule the collection of information contained in the proposed rule; and

(ii) the agency has not given the Director the information required under paragraph (1) with respect to the modified collection of information, at least 60 days before the issuance of the final rule.

(5) This subsection shall apply only when an agency publishes a notice of proposed rulemaking and requests public comments.

(6) The decision by the Director to approve or not act upon a collection of information contained in an agency rule shall not be subject to judicial review.

(e)(1) Any decision by the Director under subsection (c), (d), (h), or (j) to disapprove a collection of information, or to instruct the agency to make substantive or material change to a collection of information, shall be publicly available and include an explanation of the reasons for such decision.

(2) Any written communication between the Administrator of the Office of Information and Regulatory Affairs, or any employee of the Office of Information and Regulatory Affairs, and an agency or person not employed by the Federal Government concerning a proposed collection of information shall be made available to the public.

(3) This subsection shall not require the disclosure of—

(A) any information which is protected at all times by procedures established for information which has been specifically authorized under criteria established by an Executive order or an Act of Congress to be kept secret in the interest of national defense or foreign policy; or

(B) any communication relating to a collection of information which is not approved under this subchapter, the disclosure of which could lead to retaliation or discrimination against the communicator.

(f)(1) An independent regulatory agency which is administered by 2 or more members of a commission, board, or similar body, may by majority vote void—

(A) any disapproval by the Director, in whole or in part, of a proposed collection of information of that agency; or

(B) an exercise of authority under subsection (d) of section 3507 concerning that agency.

(2) The agency shall certify each vote to void such disapproval or exercise to the Director, and explain the reasons for such vote. The Director shall without further delay assign a control number to such collection of information, and such vote to void the disapproval or exercise shall be valid for a period of 3 years.

(g) The Director may not approve a collection of information for a period in excess of 3 years.

(h)(1) If an agency decides to seek extension of the Director's approval granted for a currently approved collection of information, the agency shall—

(A) conduct the review established under section 3506(c), including the seeking of comment from the public on the continued need for, and burden imposed by the collection of information; and

(B) after having made a reasonable effort to seek public comment, but no later than 60 days before the expiration date of the control number assigned by the Director for the currently approved collection of information, submit the collection of information for review and approval under this section, which shall include an explanation of how the agency has used the information that it has collected.

(2) If under the provisions of this section, the Director disapproves a collection of information contained in an existing rule, or recommends or instructs the agency to make a substantive or material change to a collection of information contained in an existing rule, the Director shall—

(A) publish an explanation thereof in the Federal Register; and

(B) instruct the agency to undertake a rulemaking within a reasonable time limited to consideration of changes to the collection of information contained in the rule and thereafter to submit the collection of information for approval or disapproval under this subchapter.

(3) An agency may not make a substantive or material modification to a collection of information after such collection has been approved by the Director, unless the modification has been submitted to the Director for review and approval under this subchapter.

(i)(1) If the Director finds that a senior official of an agency designated under section 3506(a) is sufficiently independent of program responsibility to evaluate fairly whether proposed collections of information should be approved and has sufficient resources to carry out this responsibility effectively, the Director may, by rule in accordance with the notice and comment provisions of chapter 5 of title 5, United States Code, delegate to such official the authority to approve proposed collections of information in specific program areas, for specific purposes, or for all agency purposes.

(2) A delegation by the Director under this section shall not preclude the Director from reviewing individual collections of information if the Director determines that circumstances warrant such a review. The Director shall retain authority to revoke such delegations, both in general and with regard to any specific matter. In acting for the Director, any official to whom approval authority has been delegated under this section shall comply fully with the rules and regulations promulgated by the Director.

(j)(1) The agency head may request the Director to authorize a collection of information, if an agency head determines that—

(A) a collection of information—

(i) is needed prior to the expiration of time periods established under this subchapter; and

(ii) is essential to the mission of the agency; and

(B) the agency cannot reasonably comply with the provisions of this subchapter because—

(i) public harm is reasonably likely to result if normal clearance procedures are followed;

(ii) an unanticipated event has occurred; or

(iii) the use of normal clearance procedures is reasonably likely to prevent or disrupt the collection of information or is reasonably likely to cause a statutory or court ordered deadline to be missed.

(2) The Director shall approve or disapprove any such authorization request within the time requested by the agency head and, if approved, shall assign the collection of information a control number. Any collection of information conducted under this subsection may be conducted without compliance with the provisions of this subchapter for a maximum of 180 days after the date on which the Director received the request to authorize such collection.

§ 3508. Determination of necessity for information; hearing

Before approving a proposed collection of information, the Director shall determine whether the collection of information by the agency is necessary for the proper performance of the functions of the agency, including whether the information shall have practical utility. Before making a determination the Director may give the agency and other interested persons an opportunity to be heard or to submit statements in writing. To the extent, if any, that the Director determines that the collection of information by an agency is unnecessary for any reason, the agency may not engage in the collection of information.

§ 3509. Designation of central collection agency

The Director may designate a central collection agency to obtain information for two or more agencies if the Director determines that the needs of such agencies for information will be adequately served by a single collection agency, and such sharing of data is not inconsistent with applicable law. In such cases the Director shall prescribe (with reference to the collection of information) the duties and functions of the collection agency so designated and of the agencies for which it is to act as agent (including reimbursement for costs). While the designation is in effect, an agency covered by the designation may not obtain for itself information for the agency which is the duty of the collection agency to obtain. The Director may modify the designation from time to time as circumstances require. The authority to designate under this section is subject to the provisions of section 3507(f) of this subchapter.

§ 3510. Cooperation of agencies in making information available

(a) The Director may direct an agency to make available to another agency, or an agency may make available to another agency, information obtained by a collection of information if the disclosure is not inconsistent with applicable law.

(b)(1) If information obtained by an agency is released by that agency to another agency, all the provisions of law (including penalties) that relate to the unlawful disclosure of information apply to the officers and employees of the agency to which information is released to the same extent and in the same manner as the provisions apply to the officers and employees of the agency which originally obtained the information.

(2) The officers and employees of the agency to which the information is released, in addition, shall be subject to the same provisions of law, including penalties, relating to the unlawful disclosure of information as if the information had been collected directly by that agency.

§ 3511. Establishment and operation of Government Information Locator Service

(a) In order to assist agencies and the public in locating information and to promote information sharing and equitable access by the public, the Director shall—

(1) cause to be established and maintained a distributed agency-based electronic Government Information Locator Service (hereafter in this section referred to as the 'Service'), which shall identify the major information systems, holdings, and component of, and to support the establishment and operation of the Service;

(2) require each agency to establish and maintain an agency information locator service as a component of, and to support the establishment and operation of the Service;

(3) in cooperation with the Archivist of the United States, the Administrator of General Services, the Public Printer, and the Librarian of Congress, establish an interagency committee to advise the Secretary of Commerce on the development of technical standards for the Service to ensure compatibility, promote information sharing, and uniform access by the public;

(4) consider public access and other user needs in the establishment and operation of the Service;

195

(5) ensure the security and integrity of the Service, including measures to ensure that only information which is intended to be disclosed to the public is disclosed through the Service; and

(6) periodically review the development and effectiveness of the Service and make recommendations for improvement, including other mechanisms for improving public access to Federal agency public information.

(b) This section shall not apply to operational files as defined by the Central Intelligence Agency Information Act (50 U.S.C. 431 et seq.).

§ 3512. Public protection

(a) Notwithstanding any other provision of law, no person shall be subject to any penalty for failing to comply with a collection of information that is subject to this subchapter if—

(1) the collection of information does not display a valid control number assigned by the Director in accordance with this subchapter; or

(2) the agency fails to inform the person who is to respond to the collection of information that such person is not required to respond to the collection of information unless it displays a valid control number.

(b) The protection provided by this section may be raised in the form of a complete defense, bar, or otherwise at any time during the agency administrative process or judicial action applicable thereto.

§ 3513. Director review of agency activities; reporting; agency response

(a) In consultation with the Administrator of General Services, the Archivist of the United States, the Director of the National Institute of Standards and Technology, and the Director of the Office of Personnel Management, the Director shall periodically review selected agency information resources management activities to ascertain the efficiency and effectiveness of such activities to improve agency performance and the accomplishment of agency missions.

(b) Each agency having an activity reviewed under subsection (a) shall, within 60 days after receipt of a report on the review, provide a written plan to the Director describing steps (including milestones) to—

(1) be taken to address information resources management problems identified in the report; and

(2) improve agency performance and the accomplishment of agency missions.

§ 3514. Responsiveness to Congress

(a) (1) The Director shall—

(A) keep the Congress and congressional committees fully and currently informed of the major activities under this subchapter; and

(B) submit a report on such activities to the President of the Senate and the Speaker of the House of Representatives annually and at such other times as the Director determines necessary.

(2) The Director shall include in any such report a description of the extent to which agencies have—

(A) reduced information collection burdens on the public, including—

(i) a summary of accomplishments and planned initiatives to reduce collection of information burdens;

(ii) a list of all violations of this subchapter and of any rules, guidelines, policies, and procedures issued pursuant to this subchapter;

(iii) a list of any increase in the collection of information burden, including the authority for each such collection; and

(iv) a list of agencies that in the preceding year did not reduce information collection burdens in accordance with section 3505(a)(1), a list of the programs and statutory responsibilities of those agencies that precluded that reduction, and recommendations to assist those agencies to reduce information collection burdens in accordance with that section;

(B) improved the quality and utility of statistical information;

(C) improved public access to Government information; and

(D) improved program performance and the accomplishment of agency missions through information resources management.

(b) The preparation of any report required by this section shall be based on performance results reported by the agencies and shall not increase the collection of information burden on persons outside the Federal Government.

§ 3515. Administrative powers

Upon the request of the Director, each agency (other than an independent regulatory agency) shall, to the extent practicable, make its services, personnel, and facilities available to the Director for the performance of functions under this subchapter.

§ 3516. Rules and regulations

The Director shall promulgate rules, regulations, or procedures necessary to exercise the authority provided by this subchapter.

§ 3517. Consultation with other agencies and the public

(a) In developing information resources management policies, plans, rules, regulations, procedures, and guidelines and in reviewing collections of information, the Director shall provide interested agencies and persons early and meaningful opportunity to comment.

(b) Any person may request the Director to review any collection of information conducted by or for an agency to determine, if, under this subchapter, a person shall maintain, provide, or disclose the information to or for the agency. Unless the request is frivolous, the Director shall, in coordination with the agency responsible for the collection of information—

> (1) respond to the request within 60 days after receiving the request, unless such period is extended by the Director to a specified date and the person making the request is given notice of such extension; and

> (2) take appropriate remedial action, if necessary.

§ 3518. Effect on existing laws and regulations

(a) Except as otherwise provided in this subchapter, the authority of an agency under any other law to prescribe policies, rules, regulations, and procedures for Federal information resources management activities is subject to the authority of the Director under this subchapter.

(b) Nothing in this subchapter shall be deemed to affect or reduce the authority of the Secretary of Commerce or the Director of the Office of Management and Budget pursuant to Reorganization Plan No. 1 of 1977 (as amended) and Executive order, relating to telecommunications and information policy, procurement and management of telecommunications and information systems, spectrum use, and related matters.

(c) (1) Except as provided in paragraph (2), this subchapter shall not apply to the collection of information—

> (A) during the conduct of a Federal criminal investigation or prosecution, or during the disposition of a particular criminal matter;

> (B) during the conduct of—

>> (i) a civil action to which the United States or any official or agency thereof is a party; or

>> (ii) an administrative action or investigation involving an agency against specific individuals or entities;

(C) by compulsory process pursuant to the Antitrust Civil Process Act and section 13 of the Federal Trade Commission Improvements Act of 1980; or

(D) during the conduct of intelligence activities as defined in section 3.4(e) of Executive Order No. 12333, issued December 4, 1981, or successor orders, or during the conduct of cryptologic activities that are communications security activities.

(2) This subchapter applies to the collection of information during the conduct of general investigations (other than information collected in an antitrust investigation to the extent provided in subparagraph (C) of paragraph (1)) undertaken with reference to a category of individuals or entities such as a class of licensees or an entire industry.

(d) Nothing in this subchapter shall be interpreted as increasing or decreasing the authority conferred by sections 11331 and 11332 of title 40 on the Secretary of Commerce or the Director of the Office of Management and Budget.

(e) Nothing in this subchapter shall be interpreted as increasing or decreasing the authority of the President, the Office of Management and Budget or the Director thereof, under the laws of the United States, with respect to the substantive policies and programs of departments, agencies and offices, including the substantive authority of any Federal agency to enforce the civil rights laws.

§ 3519. Access to information

Under the conditions and procedures prescribed in section 716 of title 31, the Director and personnel in the Office of Information and Regulatory Affairs shall furnish such information as the Comptroller General may require for the discharge of the responsibilities of the Comptroller General. For the purpose of obtaining such information, the Comptroller General or representatives thereof shall have access to all books, documents, papers and records, regardless of form or format, of the Office.

§ 3520. Establishment of task force on information collection and dissemination

(a) There is established a task force to study the feasibility of streamlining requirements with respect to small business concerns regarding collection of information and strengthening dissemination of information (in this section referred to as the "task force").

(b)(1) The Director shall determine—

(A) subject to the minimum requirements under paragraph (2), the number of representatives to be designated under each subparagraph of that paragraph; and

(B) the agencies to be represented under paragraph (2)(K).

(2) After all determinations are made under paragraph (1), the members of the task force shall be designated by the head of each applicable department or agency, and include—

(A) 1 representative of the Director, who shall convene and chair the task force;

(B) not less than 2 representatives of the Department of Labor, including 1 representative of the Bureau of Labor Statistics and 1 representative of the Occupational Safety and Health Administration;

(C) not less than 1 representative of the Environmental Protection Agency;

(D) not less than 1 representative of the Department of Transportation;

(E) not less than 1 representative of the Office of Advocacy of the Small Business Administration;

(F) not less than 1 representative of the Internal Revenue Service;

(G) not less than 2 representatives of the Department of Health and Human Services, including 1 representative of the Centers for Medicare and Medicaid Services;

(H) not less than 1 representative of the Department of Agriculture;

(I) not less than 1 representative of the Department of the Interior;

(J) not less than 1 representative of the General Services Administration; and

(K) not less than 1 representative of each of 2 agencies not represented by representatives described under subparagraphs (A) through (J).

(c) The task force shall—

(1) identify ways to integrate the collection of information across Federal agencies and programs and examine the feasibility and desirability of requiring each agency to consolidate requirements regarding collections of information with respect to small business concerns within and across agencies, without negatively impacting the effectiveness of underlying laws and regulations regarding such collections of information, in order that each small business concern may submit all information required by the agency—

(A) to 1 point of contact in the agency;

(B) in a single format, such as a single electronic reporting system, with respect to the agency; and

(C) with synchronized reporting for information submissions having the same frequency, such as synchronized quarterly, semiannual, and annual reporting dates;

(2) examine the feasibility and benefits to small businesses of publishing a list by the Director of the collections of information applicable to small business concerns (as defined in section 3 of the Small Business Act (15 U.S.C. 632)), organized—

(A) by North American Industry Classification System code;

(B) by industrial sector description; or

(C) in another manner by which small business concerns can more easily identify requirements with which those small business concerns are expected to comply;

(3) examine the savings, including cost savings, and develop recommendations for implementing—

(A) systems for electronic submissions of information to the Federal Government; and

(B) interactive reporting systems, including components that provide immediate feedback to assure that data being submitted—

(i) meet requirements of format; and

(ii) are within the range of acceptable options for each data field;

(4) make recommendations to improve the electronic dissemination of information collected under Federal requirements;

(5) recommend a plan for the development of an interactive Governmentwide system, available through the Internet, to allow each small business to—

(A) better understand which Federal requirements regarding collection of information (and, when possible, which other Federal regulatory requirements) apply to that particular business; and

(B) more easily comply with those Federal requirements; and

(6) in carrying out this section, consider opportunities for the coordination—

(A) of Federal and State reporting requirements; and

(B) among the points of contact described under section 3506(i), such as to enable agencies to provide small business concerns with contacts for information collection requirements for other agencies.

(d) The task force shall—

  (1) by publication in the Federal Register, provide notice and an opportunity for public comment on each report in draft form; and

  (2) make provision in each report for the inclusion of—

    (A) any additional or dissenting views of task force members; and

    (B) a summary of significant public comments.

(e) Not later than 1 year after the date of enactment of the Small Business Paperwork Relief Act of 2002, the task force shall submit a report of its findings under subsection (c)(1), (2), and (3) to—

  (1) the Director;

  (2) the chairpersons and ranking minority members of—

    (A) the Committee on Governmental Affairs and the Committee on Small Business and Entrepreneurship of the Senate; and

    (B) the Committee on Government Reform and the Committee on Small Business of the House of Representatives; and

  (3) the Small Business and Agriculture Regulatory Enforcement Ombudsman designated under section 30(b) of the Small Business Act (15 U.S.C. 657(b)).

(f) Not later than 2 years after the date of enactment of the Small Business Paperwork Relief Act of 2002, the task force shall submit a report of its findings under subsection (c)(4) and (5) to—

  (1) the Director;

  (2) the chairpersons and ranking minority members of—

    (A) the Committee on Governmental Affairs and the Committee on Small Business and Entrepreneurship of the Senate; and

    (B) the Committee on Government Reform and the Committee on Small Business of the House of Representatives; and

  (3) the Small Business and Agriculture Regulatory Enforcement Ombudsman designated under section 30(b) of the Small Business Act (15 U.S.C. 657(b)).

(g) The task force shall terminate after completion of its work.

(h) In this section, the term "small business concern" has the meaning given under section 3 of the Small Business Act (15 U.S.C. 632).

INFORMATION QUALITY ACT OF 2000

Section 515 of Treasury and General Government Appropriations Act for Fiscal Year 2001 (Public Law 106–554, Dec. 21, 2000, 114 Stat. 2763)
Note to 44 U.S.C. § 3516

(a) IN GENERAL.—The Director of the Office of Management and Budget shall, by not later than September 30, 2001, and with public and Federal agency involvement, issue guidelines under sections 3504(d)(1) and 3516 of title 44, United States Code, that provide policy and procedural guidance to Federal agencies for ensuring and maximizing the quality, objectivity, utility, and integrity of information (including statistical information) disseminated by Federal agencies in fulfillment of the purposes and provisions of chapter 35 of title 44, United States Code, commonly referred to as the Paperwork Reduction Act.

(b) CONTENT OF GUIDELINES.—The guidelines under subsection (a) shall—

(1) apply to the sharing by Federal agencies of, and access to, information disseminated by Federal agencies; and

(2) require that each Federal agency to which the guidelines apply—

(A) issue guidelines ensuring and maximizing the quality, objectivity, utility, and integrity of information (including statistical information) disseminated by the agency, by not later than 1 year after the date of issuance of the guidelines under subsection (a);

(B) establish administrative mechanisms allowing affected persons to seek and obtain correction of information maintained and disseminated by the agency that does not comply with the guidelines issued under subsection (a); and

(C) report periodically to the Director—

(i) the number and nature of complaints received by the agency regarding the accuracy of information disseminated by the agency; and

(ii) how such complaints were handled by the agency.

OFFICE OF MANAGEMENT AND BUDGET
Guidelines for Ensuring and Maximizing the Quality, Objectivity, Utility, and Integrity of Information Disseminated by Federal Agencies

67 Fed. Reg. 8452 (2002)

I. OMB Responsibilities

Section 515 of the Treasury and General Government Appropriations Act for FY2001 (Public Law 106–554) directs the Office of Management and Budget to issue government-wide guidelines that provide policy and procedural guidance to Federal agencies for ensuring and maximizing the quality, objectivity, utility, and integrity of information, including statistical information, disseminated by Federal agencies.

II. Agency Responsibilities

Section 515 directs agencies subject to the Paperwork Reduction Act (44 U.S.C. 3502(1)) to—

1. Issue their own information quality guidelines ensuring and maximizing the quality, objectivity, utility, and integrity of information, including statistical information, disseminated by the agency no later than one year after the date of issuance of the OMB guidelines;

2. Establish administrative mechanisms allowing affected persons to seek and obtain correction of information maintained and disseminated by the agency that does not comply with these OMB guidelines; and

3. Report to the Director of OMB the number and nature of complaints received by the agency regarding agency compliance with these OMB guidelines concerning the quality, objectivity, utility, and integrity of information and how such complaints were resolved.

III. Guidelines for Ensuring and Maximizing the Quality, Objectivity, Utility, and Integrity of Information Disseminated by Federal Agencies

1. Overall, agencies shall adopt a basic standard of quality (including objectivity, utility, and integrity) as a performance goal and should take appropriate steps to incorporate information quality criteria into agency information dissemination practices. Quality is to be ensured and established at levels appropriate to the nature and timeliness of the information to be disseminated. Agencies shall adopt specific standards of quality that are appropriate for the various categories of information they disseminate.

2. As a matter of good and effective agency information resources management, agencies shall develop a process for reviewing the quality (including the objectivity, utility, and integrity) of information before it is disseminated. Agencies shall treat information quality as integral to every step of an agency's development of information, including creation, collection, maintenance, and dissemination. This process shall enable the agency to substantiate the quality of the information it has disseminated through documentation or other means appropriate to the information.

3. To facilitate public review, agencies shall establish administrative mechanisms allowing affected persons to seek and obtain, where appropriate, timely correction of information maintained and disseminated by the agency that does not comply with OMB or agency guidelines. These administrative mechanisms shall be flexible, appropriate to the nature

and timeliness of the disseminated information, and incorporated into agency information resources management and administrative practices.

>   i. Agencies shall specify appropriate time periods for agency decisions on whether and how to correct the information, and agencies shall notify the affected persons of the corrections made.

>   ii. If the person who requested the correction does not agree with the agency's decision (including the corrective action, if any), the person may file for reconsideration within the agency. The agency shall establish an administrative appeal process to review the agency's initial decision, and specify appropriate time limits in which to resolve such requests for reconsideration.

4. The agency's pre-dissemination review, under paragraph III.2, shall apply to information that the agency first disseminates on or after October 1, 2002. The agency's administrative mechanisms, under paragraph III.3., shall apply to information that the agency disseminates on or after October 1, 2002, regardless of when the agency first disseminated the information.

IV. Agency Reporting Requirements

1. Agencies must designate the Chief Information Officer or another official to be responsible for agency compliance with these guidelines.

2. The agency shall respond to complaints in a manner appropriate to the nature and extent of the complaint. Examples of appropriate responses include personal contacts via letter or telephone, form letters, press releases or mass mailings that correct a widely disseminated error or address a frequently raised complaint.

3. Each agency must prepare a draft report, no later than April 1, 2002, providing the agency's information quality guidelines and explaining how such guidelines will ensure and maximize the quality, objectivity, utility, and integrity of information, including statistical information, disseminated by the agency. This report must also detail the administrative mechanisms developed by that agency to allow affected persons to seek and obtain appropriate correction of information maintained and disseminated by the agency that does not comply with the OMB or the agency guidelines.

4. The agency must publish a notice of availability of this draft report in the Federal Register, and post this report on the agency's website, to provide an opportunity for public comment.

5. Upon consideration of public comment and after appropriate revision, the agency must submit this draft report to OMB for review regarding consistency with these OMB guidelines no later than July 1, 2002. Upon completion of that OMB review and completion of this report, agencies must publish notice of the availability of this report in

its final form in the Federal Register, and post this report on the agency's web site no later than October 1, 2002.

6. On an annual fiscal-year basis, each agency must submit a report to the Director of OMB providing information (both quantitative and qualitative, where appropriate) on the number and nature of complaints received by the agency regarding agency compliance with these OMB guidelines and how such complaints were resolved. Agencies must submit these reports no later than January 1 of each following year, with the first report due January 1, 2004.

V. *Definitions*

1. "Quality" is an encompassing term comprising utility, objectivity, and integrity. Therefore, the guidelines sometimes refer to these four statutory terms, collectively, as "quality."

2. "Utility" refers to the usefulness of the information to its intended users, including the public. In assessing the usefulness of information that the agency disseminates to the public, the agency needs to consider the uses of the information not only from the perspective of the agency but also from the perspective of the public. As a result, when transparency of information is relevant for assessing the information's usefulness from the public's perspective, the agency must take care to ensure that transparency has been addressed in its review of the information.

3. "Objectivity" involves two distinct elements, presentation and substance

    a. "Objectivity" includes whether disseminated information is being presented in an accurate, clear, complete, and unbiased manner. This involves whether the information is presented within a proper context. Sometimes, in disseminating certain types of information to the public, other information must also be disseminated in order to ensure an accurate, clear, complete, and unbiased presentation. Also, the agency needs to identify the sources of the disseminated information (to the extent possible, consistent with confidentiality protections) and, in a scientific, financial, or statistical context, the supporting data and models, so that the public can assess for itself whether there may be some reason to question the objectivity of the sources. Where appropriate, data should have full, accurate, transparent documentation, and error sources affecting data quality should be identified and disclosed to users.

    b. In addition, "objectivity" involves a focus on ensuring accurate, reliable, and unbiased information. In a scientific, financial, or statistical context, the original and supporting data shall be generated, and the analytic results shall be developed, using sound statistical and research methods.

        i. If data and analytic results have been subjected to formal, independent, external peer review, the information may generally be presumed to be of acceptable objectivity. However, this presumption is rebuttable based on a persuasive showing by the petitioner in a particular instance. If agency-sponsored peer review is employed to help satisfy the objectivity standard, the review process employed shall meet the general criteria for competent and credible peer review recommended by OMB–OIRA to the President's Management Council (9/20/01) (http://www.whitehouse.gov/omb/inforeg/oira_review-process.html),

namely, "that (a) peer reviewers be selected primarily on the basis of necessary technical expertise, (b) peer reviewers be expected to disclose to agencies prior technical/policy positions they may have taken on the issues at hand, (c) peer reviewers be expected to disclose to agencies their sources of personal and institutional funding (private or public sector), and (d) peer reviews be conducted in an open and rigorous manner."

ii. If an agency is responsible for disseminating influential scientific, financial, or statistical information, agency guidelines shall include a high degree of transparency about data and methods to facilitate the reproducibility of such information by qualified third parties.

A. With regard to original and supporting data related thereto, agency guidelines shall not require that all disseminated data be subjected to a reproducibility requirement. Agencies may identify, in consultation with the relevant scientific and technical communities, those particular types of data that can practicable be subjected to a reproducibility requirement, given ethical, feasibility, or confidentiality constraints. It is understood that reproducibility of data is an indication of transparency about research design and methods and thus a replication exercise (i.e., a new experiment, test, or sample) shall not be required prior to each dissemination.

B. With regard to analytic results related thereto, agency guidelines shall generally require sufficient transparency about data and methods that an independent reanalysis could be undertaken by a qualified member of the public. These transparency standards apply to agency analysis of data from a single study as well as to analyses that combine information from multiple studies.

i. Making the data and methods publicly available will assist in determining whether analytic results are reproducible. However, the objectivity standard does not override other compelling interests such as privacy, trade secrets, intellectual property, and other confidentiality protections.

207

ii. In situations where public access to data and methods will not occur due to other compelling interests, agencies shall apply especially rigorous robustness checks to analytic results and document what checks were undertaken. Agency guidelines shall, however, in all cases, require a disclosure of the specific data sources that have been used and the specific quantitative methods and assumptions that have been employed. Each agency is authorized to define the type of robustness checks, and the level of detail for documentation thereof, in ways appropriate for it given the nature and multiplicity of issues for which the agency is responsible.

C. With regard to analysis of risks to human health, safety and the environment maintained or disseminated by the agencies, agencies shall either adopt or adapt the quality principles applied by Congress to risk information used and disseminated pursuant to the Safe Drinking Water Act Amendments of 1996 (42 U.S.C. 300g–1(b)(3)(A) & (B)). Agencies responsible for dissemination of vital health and medical information shall interpret the reproducibility and peer-review standards in a manner appropriate to assuring the timely flow of vital information from agencies to medical providers, patients, health agencies, and the public. Information quality standards may be waived temporarily by agencies under urgent situations (e.g., imminent threats to public health or homeland security) in accordance with the latitude specified in agency-specific guidelines.

4. "Integrity" refers to the security of information—protection of the information from unauthorized access or revision, to ensure that the information is not compromised through corruption or falsification.

5. "Information" means any communication or representation of knowledge such as facts or data, in any medium or form, including textual, numerical, graphic, cartographic, narrative, or audiovisual forms. This definition includes information that an agency disseminates from a web page, but does not include the provision of hyperlinks to information that others disseminate. This definition does not include opinions, where the agency's presentation makes it clear that what is being offered is someone's opinion rather than fact or the agency's views.

6. "Government information" means information created, collected, processed, disseminated, or disposed of by or for the Federal Government.

7. "Information dissemination product" means any books, paper, map, machine-readable material, audiovisual production, or other documentary material, regardless of physical form or characteristic, an agency

disseminates to the public. This definition includes any electronic document, CD–ROM, or web page.

8. "Dissemination" means agency initiated or sponsored distribution of information to the public (see 5 CFR 1320.3(d) (definition of "Conduct or Sponsor")). Dissemination does not include distribution limited to government employees or agency contractors or grantees; intra-or interagency use or sharing of government information; and responses to requests for agency records under the Freedom of Information Act, the Privacy Act, the Federal Advisory Committee Act or other similar law. This definition also does not include distribution limited to correspondence with individuals or persons, press releases, archival records, public filings, subpoenas or adjudicative processes.

9. "Influential", when used in the phrase "influential scientific, financial, or statistical information", means that the agency can reasonably determine that dissemination of the information will have or does have a clear and substantial impact on important public policies or important private sector decisions. Each agency is authorized to define "influential" in ways appropriate for it given the nature and multiplicity of issues for which the agency is responsible.

10. "Reproducibility" means that the information is capable of being substantially reproduced, subject to an acceptable degree of imprecision. For information judged to have more (less) important impacts, the degree of imprecision that is tolerated is reduced (increased). If agencies apply the reproducibility test to specific types of original or supporting data, the associated guidelines shall provide relevant definitions of reproducibility (e.g., standards for replication of laboratory data). With respect to analytic results, "capable of being substantially reproduced" means that independent analysis of the original or supporting data using identical methods would generate similar analytic results, subject to an acceptable degree of imprecision or error.

EQUAL ACCESS TO JUSTICE ACT

TITLE 5. GOVERNMENT ORGANIZATION AND EMPLOYEES
PART I—THE AGENCIES GENERALLY
CHAPTER 5—ADMINISTRATIVE PROCEDURE
SUBCHAPTER I—GENERAL PROVISIONS

Sec.
504. Costs and fees of parties

TITLE 28. JUDICIARY AND JUDICIAL PROCEDURE
PART VI—PARTICULAR PROCEEDINGS
CHAPTER 161—UNITED STATES AS PARTY GENERALLY

2412. Costs and fees

§ 504. Costs and fees of parties

(a)(1) An agency that conducts an adversary adjudication shall award, to a prevailing party other than the United States, fees and other expenses incurred by that party in connection with that proceeding, unless the adjudicative officer of the agency finds that the position of the agency was substantially justified or that special circumstances make an award unjust. Whether or not the position of the agency was substantially justified shall be determined on the basis of the administrative record, as a whole, which is made in the adversary adjudication for which fees and other expenses are sought.

(2) A party seeking an award of fees and other expenses shall, within thirty days of a final disposition in the adversary adjudication, submit to the agency an application which shows that the party is a prevailing party and is eligible to receive an award under this section, and the amount sought, including an itemized statement from any attorney, agent, or expert witness representing or appearing in behalf of the party stating the actual time expended and the rate at which fees and other expenses were computed. The party shall also allege that the position of the agency was not substantially justified. When the United States appeals the underlying merits of an adversary adjudication, no decision on an application for fees and other expenses in connection with that adversary adjudication shall be made under this section until a final and unreviewable decision is rendered by the court on the appeal or until the underlying merits of the case have been finally determined pursuant to the appeal.

(3) The adjudicative officer of the agency may reduce the amount to be awarded, or deny an award, to the extent that the party during the course of the proceedings engaged in conduct which unduly and

210

unreasonably protracted the final resolution of the matter in controversy. The decision of the adjudicative officer of the agency under this section shall be made a part of the record containing the final decision of the agency and shall include written findings and conclusions and the reason or basis therefor. The decision of the agency on the application for fees and other expenses shall be the final administrative decision under this section.

(4) If, in an adversary adjudication arising from an agency action to enforce a party's compliance with a statutory or regulatory requirement, the demand by the agency is substantially in excess of the decision of the adjudicative officer and is unreasonable when compared with such decision, under the facts and circumstances of the case, the adjudicative officer shall award to the party the fees and other expenses related to defending against the excessive demand, unless the party has committed a willful violation of law or otherwise acted in bad faith, or special circumstances make an award unjust. Fees and expenses awarded under this paragraph shall be paid only as a consequence of appropriations provided in advance.

(b)(1) For the purposes of this section—

(A) "fees and other expenses" includes the reasonable expenses of expert witnesses, the reasonable cost of any study, analysis, engineering report, test, or project which is found by the agency to be necessary for the preparation of the party's case, and reasonable attorney or agent fees (The amount of fees awarded under this section shall be based upon prevailing market rates for the kind and quality of the services furnished, except that

(i) no expert witness shall be compensated at a rate in excess of the highest rate of compensation for expert witnesses paid by the agency involved, and

(ii) attorney or agent fees shall not be awarded in excess of $125 per hour unless the agency determines by regulation that an increase in the cost of living or a special factor, such as the limited availability of qualified attorneys or agents for the proceedings involved, justifies a higher fee.);

(B) "party" means a party, as defined in section 551(3) of this title, who is (i) an individual whose net worth did not exceed $2,000,000 at the time the adversary adjudication was initiated, or (ii) any owner of an unincorporated business, or any partnership, corporation, association, unit of local government, or organization, the net worth of which did not exceed $7,000,000 at the time the adversary adjudication was initiated, and which had not more than 500 employees at the time the adversary adjudication was initiated; except that an organization described in section 501(c)(3) of the Internal Revenue Code of 1986 (26 U.S.C. 501(c)(3)) exempt from taxation under section

501(a) of such Code, or a cooperative association as defined in section 15(a) of the Agricultural Marketing Act (12 U.S.C. 1141j(a)), may be a party regardless of the net worth of such organization or cooperative association or for purposes of subsection (a)(4), a small entity as defined in section 601;

(C) "adversary adjudication" means (i) an adjudication under section 554 of this title in which the position of the United States is represented by counsel or otherwise, but excludes an adjudication for the purpose of establishing or fixing a rate or for the purpose of granting or renewing a license, (ii) any appeal of a decision made pursuant to section 6 of the Contract Disputes Act of 1978 (41 U.S.C. 605) before an agency board of contract appeals as provided in section 8 of that Act (41 U.S.C. 607), (iii) any hearing conducted under chapter 38 of title 31, and (iv) the Religious Freedom Restoration Act of 1993;

(D) "adjudicative officer" means the deciding official, without regard to whether the official is designated as an administrative law judge, a hearing officer or examiner, or otherwise, who presided at the adversary adjudication;

(E) "position of the agency" means, in addition to the position taken by the agency in the adversary adjudication, the action or failure to act by the agency upon which the adversary adjudication is based; except that fees and other expenses may not be awarded to a party for any portion of the adversary adjudication in which the party has unreasonably protracted the proceedings; and

(F) "demand" means the express demand of the agency which led to the adversary adjudication, but does not include a recitation by the agency of the maximum statutory penalty (i) in the administrative complaint, or (ii) elsewhere when accompanied by an express demand for a lesser amount.

(2) Except as otherwise provided in paragraph (1), the definitions provided in section 551 of this title apply to this section.

(c)(1) After consultation with the Chairman of the Administrative Conference of the United States, each agency shall by rule establish uniform procedures for the submission and consideration of applications for an award of fees and other expenses. If a court reviews the underlying decision of the adversary adjudication, an award for fees and other expenses may be made only pursuant to section 2412(d)(3) of title 28, United States Code.

(2) If a party other than the United States is dissatisfied with a determination of fees and other expenses made under subsection (a), that party may, within 30 days after the determination is made, appeal the determination to the court of the United States having

jurisdiction to review the merits of the underlying decision of the agency adversary adjudication. The court's determination on any appeal heard under this paragraph shall be based solely on the factual record made before the agency. The court may modify the determination of fees and other expenses only if the court finds that the failure to make an award of fees and other expenses, or the calculation of the amount of the award, was unsupported by substantial evidence.

(d) Fees and other expenses awarded under this subsection shall be paid by any agency over which the party prevails from any funds made available to the agency by appropriation or otherwise.

(e) The Chairman of the Administrative Conference of the United States, after consultation with the Chief Counsel for Advocacy of the Small Business Administration, shall report annually to the Congress on the amount of fees and other expenses awarded during the preceding fiscal year pursuant to this section. The report shall describe the number, nature, and amount of the awards, the claims involved in the controversy, and any other relevant information which may aid the Congress in evaluating the scope and impact of such awards. Each agency shall provide the Chairman with such information as is necessary for the Chairman to comply with the requirements of this subsection.

(f) No award may be made under this section for costs, fees, or other expenses which may be awarded under section 7430 of the Internal Revenue Code of 1986.

TITLE 28. JUDICIARY AND JUDICIAL PROCEDURE
PART VI—PARTICULAR PROCEEDINGS
CHAPTER 161—UNITED STATES AS PARTY GENERALLY

§ 2412. Costs and fees

(a)(1) Except as otherwise specifically provided by statute, a judgment for costs, as enumerated in section 1920 of this title, but not including the fees and expenses of attorneys, may be awarded to the prevailing party in any civil action brought by or against the United States or any agency or any official of the United States acting in his or her official capacity in any court having jurisdiction of such action. A judgment for costs when taxed against the United States shall, in an amount established by statute, court rule, or order, be limited to reimbursing in whole or in part the prevailing party for the costs incurred by such party in the litigation.

(2) A judgment for costs, when awarded in favor of the United States in an action brought by the United States, may include an amount equal to the filing fee prescribed under section 1914(a) of

this title. The preceding sentence shall not be construed as requiring the United States to pay any filing fee.

(b) Unless expressly prohibited by statute, a court may award reasonable fees and expenses of attorneys, in addition to the costs which may be awarded pursuant to subsection (a), to the prevailing party in any civil action brought by or against the United States or any agency or any official of the United States acting in his or her official capacity in any court having jurisdiction of such action. The United States shall be liable for such fees and expenses to the same extent that any other party would be liable under the common law or under the terms of any statute which specifically provides for such an award.

(c)(1) Any judgment against the United States or any agency and any official of the United States acting in his or her official capacity for costs pursuant to subsection (a) shall be paid as provided in sections 2414 and 2517 of this title and shall be in addition to any relief provided in the judgment.

(2) Any judgment against the United States or any agency and any official of the United States acting in his or her official capacity for fees and expenses of attorneys pursuant to subsection (b) shall be paid as provided in sections 2414 and 2517 of this title, except that if the basis for the award is a finding that the United States acted in bad faith, then the award shall be paid by any agency found to have acted in bad faith and shall be in addition to any relief provided in the judgment.

(d)(1)(A) Except as otherwise specifically provided by statute, a court shall award to a prevailing party other than the United States fees and other expenses, in addition to any costs awarded pursuant to subsection (a), incurred by that party in any civil action (other than cases sounding in tort), including proceedings for judicial review of agency action, brought by or against the United States in any court having jurisdiction of that action, unless the court finds that the position of the United States was substantially justified or that special circumstances make an award unjust.

(B) A party seeking an award of fees and other expenses shall, within thirty days of final judgment in the action, submit to the court an application for fees and other expenses which shows that the party is a prevailing party and is eligible to receive an award under this subsection, and the amount sought, including an itemized statement from any attorney or expert witness representing or appearing in behalf of the party stating the actual time expended and the rate at which fees and other expenses were computed. The party shall also allege that the position of the United States was not substantially justified. Whether or not the position of the United States was substantially justified shall be determined on the basis of the record (including the record with respect to the action or failure to act by the agency upon which the civil action is based) which is made in the civil action for which fees and other expenses are sought.

(C) The court, in its discretion, may reduce the amount to be awarded pursuant to this subsection, or deny an award, to the extent that the prevailing party during the course of the proceedings engaged in conduct which unduly and unreasonably protracted the final resolution of the matter in controversy.

(D) If, in a civil action brought by the United States or a proceeding for judicial review of an adversary adjudication described in section 504(a)(4) of title 5, the demand by the United States is substantially in excess of the judgment finally obtained by the United States and is unreasonable when compared with such judgment, under the facts and circumstances of the case, the court shall award to the party the fees and other expenses related to defending against the excessive demand, unless the party has committed a willful violation of law or otherwise acted in bad faith, or special circumstances make an award unjust. Fees and expenses awarded under this subparagraph shall be paid only as a consequence of appropriations provided in advance.

(2) For the purposes of this subsection—

(A) "fees and other expenses" includes the reasonable expenses of expert witnesses, the reasonable cost of any study, analysis, engineering report, test, or project which is found by the court to be necessary for the preparation of the party's case, and reasonable attorney fees (The amount of fees awarded under this subsection shall be based upon prevailing market rates for the kind and quality of the services furnished, except that (i) no expert witness shall be compensated at a rate in excess of the highest rate of compensation for expert witnesses paid by the United States; and (ii) attorney fees shall not be awarded in excess of $125 per hour unless the court determines that an increase in the cost of living or a special factor, such as the limited availability of qualified attorneys for the proceedings involved, justifies a higher fee.);

(B) "party" means (i) an individual whose net worth did not exceed $2,000,000 at the time the civil action was filed, or (ii) any owner of an unincorporated business, or any partnership, corporation, association, unit of local government, or organization, the net worth of which did not exceed $7,000,000 at the time the civil action was filed, and which had not more than 500 employees at the time the civil action was filed; except that an organization described in section 501(c)(3) of the Internal Revenue Code of 1986 (26 U.S.C. 501(c)(3)) exempt from taxation under section 501(a) of such Code, or a cooperative association as defined in section 15(a) of the Agricultural Marketing Act (12 U.S.C. 1141j(a)), may be a party regardless of the net worth of such organization or cooperative association or for purposes of subsection (d)(1)(D), a small entity as defined in section 601 of Title 5;

(C) "United States" includes any agency and any official of the United States acting in his or her official capacity;

(D) "position of the United States" means, in addition to the position taken by the United States in the civil action, the action or failure to act by the agency upon which the civil action is based; except that fees and expenses may not be awarded to a party for any portion of the litigation in which the party has unreasonably protracted the proceedings;

(E) "civil action brought by or against the United States" includes an appeal by a party, other than the United States, from a decision of a contracting officer rendered pursuant to a disputes clause in a contract with the Government or pursuant to the Contract Disputes Act of 1978;

(F) "court" includes the United States Court of Federal Claims and the United States Court of Appeals for Veterans Claims;

(G) "final judgment" means a judgment that is final and not appealable, and includes an order of settlement;

(H) "prevailing party", in the case of eminent domain proceedings, means a party who obtains a final judgment (other than by settlement), exclusive of interest, the amount of which is at least as close to the highest valuation of the property involved that is attested to at trial on behalf of the property owner as it is to the highest valuation of the property involved that is attested to at trial on behalf of the Government; and

(I) "demand" means the express demand of the United States which led to the adversary adjudication, but shall not include a recitation of the maximum statutory penalty (i) in the complaint, or (ii) elsewhere when accompanied by an express demand for a lesser amount.

(3) In awarding fees and other expenses under this subsection to a prevailing party in any action for judicial review of an adversary adjudication, as defined in subsection (b)(1)(C) of section 504 of title 5, United States Code, or an adversary adjudication subject to the Contract Disputes Act of 1978, the court shall include in that award fees and other expenses to the same extent authorized in subsection (a) of such section, unless the court finds that during such adversary

adjudication the position of the United States was substantially justified, or that special circumstances make an award unjust.

(4) Fees and other expenses awarded under this subsection to a party shall be paid by any agency over which the party prevails from any funds made available to the agency by appropriation or otherwise.

(e) The provisions of this section shall not apply to any costs, fees, and other expenses in connection with any proceeding to which section 7430 of the Internal Revenue Code of 1986 applies (determined without regard to subsections (b) and (f) of such section). Nothing in the preceding sentence shall prevent the awarding under subsection (a) of section 2412 of title 28, United States Code, of costs enumerated in section 1920 of such title (as in effect on October 1, 1981).

(f) If the United States appeals an award of costs or fees and other expenses made against the United States under this section and the award is affirmed in whole or in part, interest shall be paid on the amount of the award as affirmed. Such interest shall be computed at the rate determined under section 1961(a) of this title, and shall run from the date of the award through the day before the date of the mandate of affirmance.

FEDERAL TRADE COMMISSION ACT

TITLE 15. COMMERCE AND TRADE
CHAPTER 2—FEDERAL TRADE COMMISSION; PROMOTION OF EXPORT TRADE AND PREVENTION OF UNFAIR METHODS OF COMPETITION
SUBCHAPTER I—FEDERAL TRADE COMMISSION

§ 41. Federal Trade Commission established; membership; vacancies; seal

A commission is created and established, to be known as the Federal Trade Commission (hereinafter referred to as the Commission), which shall be composed of five Commissioners, who shall be appointed by the President, by and with the advice and consent of the Senate. Not more than three of the Commissioners shall be members of the same political party. The first Commissioners appointed shall continue in office for terms of three, four, five, six, and seven years, respectively, from September 26, 1914, the term of each to be designated by the President, but their successors shall be appointed for terms of seven years, except that any person chosen to fill a vacancy shall be appointed only for the unexpired term of the Commissioner whom he shall succeed: Provided, however, That upon the expiration of his term of office a Commissioner shall continue to serve until his successor shall have been appointed and shall have qualified. The President shall choose a chairman from the Commission's membership. No Commissioner shall engage in any other business, vocation, or employment. Any Commissioner may be removed by the President for inefficiency, neglect of duty, or malfeasance in office. A vacancy in the Commission shall not impair the right of the remaining Commissioners to exercise all the powers of the Commission.

The Commission shall have an official seal, which shall be judicially noticed.

* * *

§ 44. Definitions

The words defined in this section shall have the following meaning when found in this subchapter, to wit:

"Commerce" means commerce among the several States or with foreign nations, or in any Territory of the United States or in the District of Columbia, or between any such Territory and another, or between any such Territory and any State or foreign nation, or between the District of Columbia and any State or Territory or foreign nation.

"Corporation" shall be deemed to include any company, trust, so-called Massachusetts trust, or association, incorporated or unincorporated, which is organized to carry on business for its own profit or that of its members, and has shares of capital or capital stock or certificates of interest, and any company, trust, so-called Massachusetts trust, or association, incorporated or unincorporated, without shares of capital or capital stock or certificates of interest, except partnerships, which is organized to carry on business for its own profit or that of its members.

"Documentary evidence" includes all documents, papers, correspondence, books of account, and financial and corporate records.

"Acts to regulate commerce" means subtitle IV of Title 49 and the Communications Act of 1934 [47 U.S.C. § 151 et seq.] and all Acts amendatory thereof and supplementary thereto.

"Antitrust Acts" means the Act entitled "An Act to protect trade and commerce against unlawful restraints and monopolies", approved July 2, 1890; also sections 73 to 76, of an Act entitled "An Act to reduce taxation, to provide revenue for the Government, and for other purposes", approved August 27, 1894; also the Act entitled "An Act to amend sections 73 and 76 of the Act of August 27, 1894, entitled 'An Act to reduce taxation, to provide revenue for the Government, and for other purposes' ", approved February 12, 1913; and also the Act entitled "An Act of supplement existing laws against unlawful restraints and monopolies, and for other purposes", approved October 15, 1914.

"Banks" means the types of banks and other financial institutions referred to in section 57a(f)(2) of this title.

"Foreign law enforcement agency" means—

(1) any agency or judicial authority of a foreign government, including a foreign state, a political subdivision of a foreign state, or a multinational organization constituted by and comprised of foreign states, that is vested with law enforcement or investigative authority in civil, criminal, or administrative matters; and

(2) any multinational organization, to the extent that it is acting on behalf of an entity described in paragraph (1).

§ 45. Unfair methods of competition unlawful; prevention by Commission

(a) Declaration of unlawfulness; power to prohibit unfair practices; inapplicability to foreign trade.

(1) Unfair methods of competition in or affecting commerce, and unfair or deceptive acts or practices in or affecting commerce, are declared unlawful.

(2) The Commission is empowered and directed to prevent persons, partnerships, or corporations, except banks, savings and loan institutions described in section 57a(f)(3) of this title, Federal credit unions described in section 57a(f)(4) of this title, common carriers subject to the Acts to regulate commerce, air carriers and foreign air carriers subject to the Federal Aviation Act of 1958, and persons, partnerships, or corporations insofar as they are subject to the Packers and Stockyards Act, 1921, as amended [7 U.S.C. § 181 et seq.], except as provided in section 406(b) of said Act [7 U.S.C. § 227(a)], from using unfair methods of competition in or affecting commerce and unfair or deceptive acts or practices in or affecting commerce.

(3) This subsection shall not apply to unfair methods of competition involving commerce with foreign nations (other than import commerce) unless—

(A) such methods of competition have a direct, substantial, and reasonably foreseeable effect—

(i) on commerce which is not commerce with foreign nations, or on import commerce with foreign nations; or

(ii) on export commerce with foreign nations, of a person engaged in such commerce in the United States; and

(B) such effect gives rise to a claim under the provisions of this subsection, other than this paragraph.

If this subsection applies to such methods of competition only because of the operation of subparagraph (A)(ii), this subsection shall apply to such conduct only for injury to export business in the United States.

(4)(A) For purposes of subsection (a) of this section, the term "unfair or deceptive acts or practices" includes such acts or practices involving foreign commerce that—

(i) cause or are likely to cause reasonably foreseeable injury within the United States; or

(ii) involve material conduct occurring within the United States.

(B) All remedies available to the Commission with respect to unfair and deceptive acts or practices shall be available for acts and practices described in this paragraph, including restitution to domestic or foreign victims.

(b) Proceeding by Commission; modifying and setting aside orders. Whenever the Commission shall have reason to believe that any such person, partnership, or corporation has been or is using any unfair method of competition or unfair or deceptive act or practice in or affecting commerce, and if it shall appear to the Commission that a proceeding by it in respect thereof would be to the interest of the public, it shall issue and serve upon such person, partnership, or corporation a complaint stating its charges in that respect and containing a notice of a hearing upon a day and at a place therein fixed at least thirty days after the service of said complaint. The person, partnership, or corporation so complained of shall have the right to appear at the place and time so fixed and show cause why an order should not be entered by the Commission requiring such person, partnership, or corporation to cease and desist from the violation of the law so charged in said complaint. Any person, partnership, or corporation may make application, and upon good cause shown may be allowed by the Commission to intervene and appear in said proceeding by counsel or in person. The testimony in any such proceeding shall be reduced to writing and filed in the office of the Commission. If upon such hearing the Commission shall be of the opinion that the method of competition or the act or practice in question is prohibited by this subchapter, it shall make a report in writing in which it shall state its findings as to the facts and shall issue and cause to be served on such person, partnership, or corporation an order requiring such person, partnership, or corporation to cease and desist from using such method of competition or such act or practice. Until the expiration of the time allowed for filing a petition for review, if no such petition has been duly filed within such time, or, if a petition for review has been filed within such time then until the record in the proceeding has been filed in a court of appeals of the United States, as

hereinafter provided, the Commission may at any time, upon such notice and in such manner as it shall deem proper, modify or set aside, in whole or in part, any report or any order made or issued by it under this section. After the expiration of the time allowed for filing a petition for review, if no such petition has been duly filed within such time, the Commission may at any time, after notice and opportunity for hearing, reopen and alter, modify, or set aside, in whole or in part, any report or order made or issued by it under this section, whenever in the opinion of the Commission conditions of fact or of law have so changed as to require such action or if the public interest shall so require, except that (1) the said person, partnership, or corporation may, within sixty days after service upon him or it of said report or order entered after such a reopening, obtain a review thereof in the appropriate court of appeals of the United States, in the manner provided in subsection (c) of this section; and (2) in the case of an order, the Commission shall reopen any such order to consider whether such order (including any affirmative relief provision contained in such order) should be altered, modified, or set aside, in whole or in part, if the person, partnership, or corporation involved files a request with the Commission which makes a satisfactory showing that changed conditions of law or fact require such order to be altered, modified, or set aside, in whole or in part. The Commission shall determine whether to alter, modify, or set aside any order of the Commission in response to a request made by a person, partnership, or corporation under paragraph (2) not later than 120 days after the date of the filing of such request.

(c) Review of order; rehearing. Any person, partnership, or corporation required by an order of the Commission to cease and desist from using any method of competition or act or practice may obtain a review of such order in the court of appeals of the United States, within any circuit where the method of competition or the act or practice in question was used or where such person, partnership, or corporation resides or carries on business, by filing in the court, within sixty days from the date of the service of such order, a written petition praying that the order of the Commission be set aside. A copy of such petition shall be forthwith transmitted by the clerk of the court to the Commission, and thereupon the Commission shall file in the court the record in the proceeding, as provided in section 2112 of Title 28. Upon such filing of the petition the court shall have jurisdiction of the proceeding and of the question determined therein concurrently with the Commission until the filing of the record and shall have power to make and enter a decree affirming, modifying, or setting aside the order of the Commission, and enforcing the same to the extent that such order is affirmed and to issue such writs as are ancillary to its jurisdiction or are necessary in its judgment to prevent injury to the public or to competitors pendente lite. The findings of the Commission as to the facts, if supported by evidence, shall be conclusive. To the extent that the order of the Commission is

affirmed, the court shall thereupon issue its own order commanding obedience to the terms of such order of the Commission. If either party shall apply to the court for leave to adduce additional evidence, and shall show to the satisfaction of the court that such additional evidence is material and that there were reasonable grounds for the failure to adduce such evidence in the proceeding before the Commission, the court may order such additional evidence to be taken before the Commission and to be adduced upon the hearing in such manner and upon such terms and conditions as to the court may seem proper. The Commission may modify its findings as to the facts, or make new findings, by reason of the additional evidence so taken, and it shall file such modified or new findings, which, if supported by evidence, shall be conclusive, and its recommendation, if any, for the modification or setting aside of its original order, with the return of such additional evidence. The judgment and decree of the court shall be final, except that the same shall be subject to review by the Supreme Court upon certiorari, as provided in section 347 of Title 28.

(d) Jurisdiction of court. Upon the filing of the record with it the jurisdiction of the court of appeals of the United States to affirm, enforce, modify, or set aside orders of the Commission shall be exclusive.

(e) Exemption from liability. No order of the Commission or judgment of court to enforce the same shall in anywise relieve or absolve any person, partnership, or corporation from any liability under the Antitrust Acts.

(f) Service of complaints, orders and other processes; return. Complaints, orders, and other processes of the Commission under this section may be served by anyone duly authorized by the Commission, either (a) by delivering a copy thereof to the person to be served, or to a member of the partnership to be served, or the president, secretary, or other executive officer or a director of the corporation to be served; or (b) by leaving a copy thereof at the residence or the principal office or place of business of such person, partnership, or corporation; or (c) by mailing a copy thereof by registered mail or by certified mail addressed to such person, partnership, or corporation at his or its residence or principal office or place of business. The verified return by the person so serving said complaint, order, or other process setting forth the manner of said service shall be proof of the same, and the return post office receipt for said complaint, order, or other process mailed by registered mail or by certified mail as aforesaid shall be proof of the service of the same.

(g) Finality of order. An order of the Commission to cease and desist shall become final—

> (1) Upon the expiration of the time allowed for filing a petition for review, if no such petition has been duly filed within such time; but the Commission may thereafter modify or set aside its order to the extent provided in the last sentence of subsection (b) of this section.

(2) Except as to any order provision subject to paragraph (4), upon the sixtieth day after such order is served, if a petition for review has been duly filed; except that any such order may be stayed, in whole or in part and subject to such conditions as may be appropriate, by—

(A) the Commission;

(B) an appropriate court of appeals of the United States, if (i) a petition for review of such order is pending in such court, and (ii) an application for such a stay was previously submitted to the Commission and the Commission, within the 30-day period beginning on the date the application was received by the Commission, either denied the application or did not grant or deny the application; or

(C) the Supreme Court, if an applicable petition for certiorari is pending.

(3) For purposes of subsection (m)(1)(B) of this section and of section 57b(a)(2) of this title, if a petition for review of the order of the Commission has been filed—

(A) upon the expiration of the time allowed for filing a petition for certiorari, if the order of the Commission has been affirmed or the petition for review has been dismissed by the court of appeals and no petition for certiorari has been duly filed;

(B) upon the denial of a petition for certiorari, if the order of the Commission has been affirmed or the petition for review has been dismissed by the court of appeals; or

(C) upon the expiration of 30 days from the date of issuance of a mandate of the Supreme Court directing that the order of the Commission be affirmed or the petition for review be dismissed.

(4) In the case of an order provision requiring a person, partnership, or corporation to divest itself of stock, other share capital, or assets, if a petition for review of such order of the Commission has been filed—

(A) upon the expiration of the time allowed for filing a petition for certiorari, if the order of the Commission has been affirmed or the petition for review has been dismissed by the court of appeals and no petition for certiorari has been duly filed;

(B) upon the denial of a petition for certiorari, if the order of the Commission has been affirmed or the petition for review has been dismissed by the court of appeals; or

(C) upon the expiration of 30 days from the date of issuance of a mandate of the Supreme Court directing that the order of the Commission be affirmed or the petition for review be dismissed.

(h) Modification or setting aside of order by Supreme Court. If the Supreme Court directs that the order of the Commission be modified or set aside, the order of the Commission rendered in accordance with the mandate of the Supreme Court shall become final upon the expiration of thirty days from the time it was rendered, unless within such thirty days either party has instituted proceedings to have such order corrected to accord with the mandate, in which event the order of the Commission shall become final when so corrected.

(i) Modification or setting aside of order by Court of Appeals. If the order of the Commission is modified or set aside by the court of appeals, and if (1) the time allowed for filing a petition for certiorari has expired and no such petition has been duly filed, or (2) the petition for certiorari has been denied, or (3) the decision of the court has been affirmed by the Supreme Court, then the order of the Commission rendered in accordance with the mandate of the court of appeals shall become final on the expiration of thirty days from the time such order of the Commission was rendered, unless within such thirty days either party has instituted proceedings to have such order corrected so that it will accord with the mandate, in which event the order of the Commission shall become final when so corrected.

(j) Rehearing upon order or remand. If the Supreme Court orders a rehearing; or if the case is remanded by the court of appeals to the Commission for a rehearing, and if (1) the time allowed for filing a petition for certiorari has expired, and no such petition has been duly filed, or (2) the petition for certiorari has been denied, or (3) the decision of the court has been affirmed by the Supreme Court, then the order of the Commission rendered upon such rehearing shall become final in the same manner as though no prior order of the Commission had been rendered.

(k) "Mandate" defined. As used in this section the term "mandate", in case a mandate has been recalled prior to the expiration of thirty days from the date of issuance thereof, means the final mandate.

(l) Penalty for violation of order; injunctions and other appropriate equitable relief. Any person, partnership, or corporation who violates an order of the Commission after it has become final, and while such order is in effect, shall forfeit and pay to the United States a civil penalty of not more than $10,000 for each violation, which shall accrue to the United States and may be recovered in a civil action brought by the Attorney General of the United States. Each separate violation of such an order shall be a separate offense, except that in the case of a violation through continuing failure to obey or neglect to obey a final order of the Commission, each day of continuance of such failure or neglect shall be deemed a separate offense. In such actions, the United States district courts are empowered to grant mandatory injunctions and such other

and further equitable relief as they deem appropriate in the enforcement of such final orders of the Commission.

(m) Civil actions for recovery of penalties for knowing violations of rules and cease and desist orders respecting unfair or deceptive acts or practices; jurisdiction; maximum amount of penalties; continuing violations; de novo determinations; compromise or settlement procedure.

(1)(A) The Commission may commence a civil action to recover a civil penalty in a district court of the United States against any person, partnership, or corporation which violates any rule under this chapter respecting unfair or deceptive acts or practices (other than an interpretive rule or a rule violation of which the Commission has provided is not an unfair or deceptive act or practice in violation of subsection (a)(1) of this section) with actual knowledge or knowledge fairly implied on the basis of objective circumstances that such act is unfair or deceptive and is prohibited by such rule. In such action, such person, partnership, or corporation shall be liable for a civil penalty of not more than $10,000 for each violation.

(B) If the Commission determines in a proceeding under subsection (b) of this section that any act or practice is unfair or deceptive, and issues a final cease and desist order, other than a consent order, with respect to such act or practice, then the Commission may commence a civil action to obtain a civil penalty in a district court of the United States against any person, partnership, or corporation which engages in such act or practice—

(1) after such cease and desist order becomes final (whether or not such person, partnership, or corporation was subject to such cease and desist order), and

(2) with actual knowledge that such act or practice is unfair or deceptive and is unlawful under subsection (a)(1) of this section.

In such action, such person, partnership, or corporation shall be liable for a civil penalty of not more than $10,000 for each violation.

(C) In the case of a violation through continuing failure to comply with a rule or with subsection (a)(1) of this section, each day of continuance of such failure shall be treated as a separate violation, for purposes of subparagraphs (A) and (B). In determining the amount of such a civil penalty, the court shall take into account the degree of culpability, any history of prior such conduct, ability to pay, effect on ability to continue to do business, and such other matters as justice may require.

(2) If the cease and desist order establishing that the act or practice is unfair or deceptive was not issued against the defendant in a civil

penalty action under paragraph (1)(B) the issues of fact in such action against such defendant shall be tried de novo. Upon request of any party to such an action against such defendant, the court shall also review the determination of law made by the Commission in the proceeding under subsection (b) of this section that the act or practice which was the subject of such proceeding constituted an unfair or deceptive act or practice in violation of subsection (a) of this section.

(3) The Commission may compromise or settle any action for a civil penalty if such compromise or settlement is accompanied by a public statement of its reasons and is approved by the court.

(n) Standard of proof; public policy considerations. The Commission shall have no authority under this section or section 57a of this title to declare unlawful an act or practice on the grounds that such act or practice is unfair unless the act or practice causes or is likely to cause substantial injury to consumers which is not reasonably avoidable by consumers themselves and not outweighed by countervailing benefits to consumers or to competition. In determining whether an act or practice is unfair, the Commission may consider established public policies as evidence to be considered with all other evidence. Such public policy considerations may not serve as a primary basis for such determination.

§ 46. Additional powers of Commission

The Commission shall also have power—

(a) Investigation of persons, partnerships, or corporations. To gather and compile information concerning, and to investigate from time to time the organization, business, conduct, practices, and management of any person, partnership, or corporation engaged in or whose business affects commerce, excepting banks, savings and loan institutions described in section 57a(f)(3) of this title, Federal credit unions described in section 57a(f)(4) of this title, and common carriers subject to the Act to regulate commerce, and its relation to other persons, partnerships, and corporations.

(b) Reports of persons, partnerships, and corporations. To require, by general or special orders, persons, partnerships, and corporations, engaged in or whose business affects commerce, excepting banks, savings and loan institutions described in section 57a(f)(3) of this title, Federal credit unions described in section 57a(f)(4) of this title, and common carriers subject to the Act to regulate commerce, or any class of them, or any of them, respectively, to file with the Commission in such form as the Commission may prescribe annual or special, or both annual and special, reports or answers in writing to specific questions, furnishing to the Commission such information as it may require as to the organization, business, conduct, practices, management, and relation to other corporations, partnerships, and individuals of the respective persons,

partnerships, and corporations filing such reports or answers in writing. Such reports and answers shall be made under oath, or otherwise, as the Commission may prescribe, and shall be filed with the Commission within such reasonable period as the Commission may prescribe, unless additional time be granted in any case by the Commission.

(c) Investigation of compliance with antitrust decrees. Whenever a final decree has been entered against any defendant corporation in any suit brought by the United States to prevent and restrain any violation of the antitrust Acts, to make investigation, upon its own initiative, of the manner in which the decree has been or is being carried out, and upon the application of the Attorney General it shall be its duty to make such investigation. It shall transmit to the Attorney General a report embodying its findings and recommendations as a result of any such investigation, and the report shall be made public in the discretion of the Commission.

(d) Investigations of violations of antitrust statutes. Upon the direction of the President or either House of Congress to investigate and report the facts relating to any alleged violations of the antitrust Acts by any corporation.

(e) Readjustment of business of corporations violating antitrust statutes. Upon the application of the Attorney General to investigate and make recommendations for the readjustment of the business of any corporation alleged to be violating the antitrust Acts in order that the corporation may thereafter maintain its organization, management, and conduct of business in accordance with law.

(f) Publication of information; reports. To make public from time to time such portions of the information obtained by it hereunder as are in the public interest; and to make annual and special reports to the Congress and to submit therewith recommendations for additional legislation; and to provide for the publication of its reports and decisions in such form and manner as may be best adapted for public information and use: Provided, That the Commission shall not have any authority to make public any trade secret or any commercial or financial information which is obtained from any person and which is privileged or confidential, except that the Commission may disclose such information to officers and employees of appropriate Federal law enforcement agencies or to any officer or employee of any State law enforcement agency upon the prior certification of an officer of any such Federal or State law enforcement agency that such information (1) will be maintained in confidence and will be used only for official law enforcement purposes, and (2) to any officer or employee of any foreign law enforcement agency under the same circumstances that making material available to foreign law enforcement agencies is permitted under section 57b–2(b) of this title.

(g) Classification of corporations; regulations. From time to time to classify corporations and (except as provided in section 57a(a)(2) of this title) to make rules and regulations for the purpose of carrying out the provisions of this subchapter.

(h) Investigations of foreign trade conditions; reports. To investigate, from time to time, trade conditions in and with foreign countries where associations, combinations, or practices of manufacturers, merchants, or traders, or other conditions, may affect the foreign trade of the United States, and to report to Congress thereon, with such recommendations as it deems advisable.

(i) Investigations of foreign antitrust law violations. With respect to the International Antitrust Enforcement Assistance Act of 1994 [15 U.S.C. § 6201 et seq.], to conduct investigations of possible violations of foreign antitrust laws (as defined in section 12 of such Act [15 U.S.C. § 6211]).

(j) Investigative assistance for foreign law enforcement agencies.

(1) In general. Upon a written request from a foreign law enforcement agency to provide assistance in accordance with this subsection, if the requesting agency states that it is investigating, or engaging in enforcement proceedings against, possible violations of laws prohibiting fraudulent or deceptive commercial practices, or other practices substantially similar to practices prohibited by any provision of the laws administered by the Commission, other than Federal antitrust laws (as defined in section 6211(5) of this title, to provide the assistance described in paragraph (2) without requiring that the conduct identified in the request constitute a violation of the laws of the United States.

(2) Type of assistance. In providing assistance to a foreign law enforcement agency under this subsection, the Commission may—

(A) conduct such investigation as the Commission deems necessary to collect information and evidence pertinent to the request for assistance, using all investigative powers authorized by this subchapter; and

(B) when the request is from an agency acting to investigate or pursue the enforcement of civil laws, or when the Attorney General refers a request to the Commission from an agency acting to investigate or pursue the enforcement of criminal laws, seek and accept appointment by a United States district court of Commission attorneys to provide assistance to foreign and international tribunals and to litigants before such tribunals on behalf of a foreign law enforcement agency pursuant to section 1782 of Title 28.

(3) Criteria for determination. In deciding whether to provide such assistance, the Commission shall consider all relevant factors, including—

(A) whether the requesting agency has agreed to provide or will provide reciprocal assistance to the Commission;

(B) whether compliance with the request would prejudice the public interest of the United States; and

(C) whether the requesting agency's investigation or enforcement proceeding concerns acts or practices that cause or are likely to cause injury to a significant number of persons.

(4) International agreements. If a foreign law enforcement agency has set forth a legal basis for requiring execution of an international agreement as a condition for reciprocal assistance, or as a condition for provision of materials or information to the Commission, the Commission, with prior approval and ongoing oversight of the Secretary of State, and with final approval of the agreement by the Secretary of State, may negotiate and conclude an international agreement, in the name of either the United States or the Commission, for the purpose of obtaining such assistance, materials, or information. The Commission may undertake in such an international agreement to—

(A) provide assistance using the powers set forth in this subsection;

(B) disclose materials and information in accordance with subsection (f) of this section and section 57b–2(b) of this title; and

(C) engage in further cooperation, and protect materials and information received from disclosure, as authorized by this subchapter.

(5) Additional authority. The authority provided by this subsection is in addition to, and not in lieu of, any other authority vested in the Commission or any other officer of the United States.

(6) Limitation. The authority granted by this subsection shall not authorize the Commission to take any action or exercise any power with respect to a bank, a savings and loan institution described in section 57a(f)(3) of this title, a Federal credit union described in section 57a(f)(4) of this title, or a common carrier subject to the Act to regulate commerce, except in accordance with the undesignated proviso following the last designated subsection of this section.

(7) Assistance to certain countries. The Commission may not provide investigative assistance under this subsection to a foreign law enforcement agency from a foreign state that the Secretary of State has determined, in accordance with section 2405(j) of the Appendix to Title 50, has repeatedly provided support for acts of international terrorism, unless and until such determination is rescinded pursuant to section 2405(j)(4) of the Appendix to Title 50.

(k) *Referral of evidence for criminal proceedings.*

(1) In general. Whenever the Commission obtains evidence that any person, partnership, or corporation, either domestic or foreign, has engaged in conduct that may constitute a violation of Federal criminal law, to transmit such evidence to the Attorney General, who may institute criminal proceedings under appropriate statutes.

Nothing in this paragraph affects any other authority of the Commission to disclose information.

(2) International information. The Commission shall endeavor to ensure, with respect to memoranda of understanding and international agreements it may conclude, that material it has obtained from foreign law enforcement agencies acting to investigate or pursue the enforcement of foreign criminal laws may be used for the purpose of investigation, prosecution, or prevention of violations of United States criminal laws.

(l) Expenditures for cooperative arrangements. To expend appropriated funds for—

(1) operating expenses and other costs of bilateral and multilateral cooperative law enforcement groups conducting activities of interest to the Commission and in which the Commission participates; and

(2) expenses for consultations and meetings hosted by the Commission with foreign government agency officials, members of their delegations, appropriate representatives and staff to exchange views concerning developments relating to the Commission's mission, development and implementation of cooperation agreements, and provision of technical assistance for the development of foreign consumer protection or competition regimes, such expenses to include necessary administrative and logistic expenses and the expenses of Commission staff and foreign invitees in attendance at such consultations and meetings including—

(A) such incidental expenses as meals taken in the course of such attendance;

(B) any travel and transportation to or from such meetings; and

(C) any other related lodging or subsistence.

Provided, That the exception of "banks, savings and loan institutions described in section 57a(f)(3) of this title, Federal credit unions described in section 57a(f)(3) of this title, and common carriers subject to the Act to regulate commerce" from the Commission's powers defined in clauses (a), (b), and (j) of this section, shall not be construed to limit the Commission's authority to gather and compile information, to investigate, or to require reports or answers from, any person, partnership, or corporation to the extent that such action is necessary to the investigation of any person, partnership, or corporation, group of persons, partnerships, or corporations, or industry which is not engaged or is engaged only incidentally in banking, in business as a savings and loan institution, in business as a Federal credit union, or in business as a common carrier subject to the Act to regulate commerce.

The Commission shall establish a plan designed to substantially reduce burdens imposed upon small businesses as a result of requirements established by the Commission under clause (b) relating to the filing of quarterly financial reports. Such plan shall (1) be established after consultation with small businesses and persons who use the information contained in such quarterly financial reports; (2) provide for a reduction of the number of small businesses required to file such quarterly financial reports; and (3) make revisions in the forms used for such quarterly financial reports for the purpose of reducing the complexity of such forms. The Commission, not later than December 31, 1980, shall submit such plan to the Committee on Commerce, Science, and Transportation of the Senate and to the Committee on Energy and Commerce of the House of Representatives. Such plan shall take effect not later than October 31, 1981.

No officer or employee of the Commission or any Commissioner may publish or disclose information to the public, or to any Federal agency, whereby any line-of-business data furnished by a particular establishment or individual can be identified. No one other than designated sworn officers and employees of the Commission may examine the line-of-business reports from individual firms, and information provided in the line-of-business program administered by the Commission shall be used only for statistical purposes. Information for carrying out specific law enforcement responsibilities of the Commission shall be obtained under practices and procedures in effect on May 28, 1980, or as changed by law.

Nothing in this section (other than the provisions of clause (c) and clause (d)) shall apply to the business of insurance, except that the Commission shall have authority to conduct studies and prepare reports relating to the business of insurance. The Commission may exercise such authority only upon receiving a request which is agreed to by a majority of the members of the Committee on Commerce, Science, and Transportation of the Senate or the Committee on Energy and Commerce of the House of Representatives. The authority to conduct any such study shall expire at the end of the Congress during which the request for such study was made.

* * *

§ 49. Documentary evidence; depositions; witnesses

For the purposes of this subchapter the Commission, or its duly authorized agent or agents, shall at all reasonable times have access to, for the purpose of examination, and the right to copy any documentary evidence of any person, partnership, or corporation being investigated or proceeded against; and the Commission shall have power to require by subpoena the attendance and testimony of witnesses and the production of all such documentary evidence relating to any matter under investigation. Any member of the Commission may sign subpoenas, and members and examiners of the Commission may administer oaths and affirmations, examine witnesses, and receive evidence.

Such attendance of witnesses, and the production of such documentary evidence, may be required from any place in the United States, at any designated place of hearing. And in case of disobedience to a subpoena the Commission may invoke the aid of any court of the United States in requiring the attendance and testimony of witnesses and the production of documentary evidence.

Any of the district courts of the United States within the jurisdiction of which such inquiry is carried on may, in case of contumacy or refusal to obey a subpoena issued to any person, partnership, or corporation issue an order requiring such person, partnership, or corporation to appear before the Commission, or to produce documentary evidence if so ordered, or to give evidence touching the matter in question; and any failure to obey such order of the court may be punished by such court as a contempt thereof.

Upon the application of the Attorney General of the United States, at the request of the Commission, the district courts of the United States shall have jurisdiction to issue writs of mandamus commanding any person, partnership, or corporation to comply with the provisions of this subchapter or any order of the Commission made in pursuance thereof.

The Commission may order testimony to be taken by deposition in any proceeding or investigation pending under this subchapter at any stage of such proceeding or investigation. Such depositions may be taken before any person designated by the Commission and having power to administer oaths. Such testimony shall be reduced to writing by the person taking the deposition, or under his direction, and shall then be subscribed by the deponent. Any person may be compelled to appear and depose and to produce documentary evidence in the same manner as witnesses may be compelled to appear and testify and produce documentary evidence before the Commission as hereinbefore provided.

Witnesses summoned before the Commission shall be paid the same fees and mileage that are paid witnesses in the courts of the United States, and witnesses whose depositions are taken and the persons taking the same shall severally be entitled to the same fees as are paid for like services in the courts of the United States.

§ 50. Offenses and penalties

Any person who shall neglect or refuse to attend and testify, or to answer any lawful inquiry or to produce any documentary evidence, if in his power to do so, in obedience to an order of a district court of the United States directing compliance with the subpoena or lawful requirement of the Commission, shall be guilty of an offense and upon conviction thereof by a court of competent jurisdiction shall be punished by a fine of not less than $1,000 nor more than $5,000, or by imprisonment for not more than one year, or by both such fine and imprisonment.

Any person who shall willfully make, or cause to be made, any false entry or statement of fact in any report required to be made under this subchapter, or who shall willfully make, or cause to be made, any false entry in any account, record, or memorandum kept by any person, partnership, or corporation subject to this subchapter, or who shall willfully neglect or fail to make, or to cause to be made, full, true, and correct entries in such accounts, records, or memoranda of all facts and transactions appertaining to the business of such person, partnership, or corporation or who shall willfully remove out of the jurisdiction of the United States, or willfully mutilate, alter, or by any other means falsify any documentary evidence of such person, partnership, or corporation or who shall willfully refuse to submit to the Commission or to any of its authorized agents, for the purpose of inspection and taking copies, any documentary evidence of such person, partnership, or corporation in his possession or within his control, shall be deemed guilty of an offense against the United States, and shall be subject, upon conviction in any court of the United States of competent jurisdiction, to a fine of not less than $1,000 nor more than $5,000, or to imprisonment for a term of not more than three years, or to both such fine and imprisonment.

If any persons, partnership, or corporation required by this subchapter to file any annual or special report shall fail so to do within the time fixed by the Commission for filling the same, and such failure shall continue for thirty days after notice of such default, the corporation shall forfeit to the United States the sum of $100 for each and every day of the continuance of such failure, which forfeiture shall be payable into the Treasury of the United States, and shall be recoverable in a civil suit in the name of the United States brought in the case of a corporation or partnership in the district where the corporation or partnership has its principal office or in any district in which it shall do business, and in the case of any person in the district where such person resides or has his principal place of business. It shall be the duty of the various United States attorneys, under the direction of the Attorney General of the United States, to prosecute for the recovery of forfeitures. The costs and expenses of such prosecution shall be paid out of the appropriation for the expenses of the courts of the United States.

Any officer or employee of the Commission who shall make public any information obtained by the Commission without its authority, unless directed by a court, shall be deemed guilty of a misdemeanor, and, upon conviction thereof, shall be punished by a fine not exceeding $5,000, or by imprisonment not exceeding one year, or by fine and imprisonment, in the discretion of the court.

* * *

§ 52. Dissemination of false advertisements

(a) *Unlawfulness.* It shall be unlawful for any person, partnership, or corporation to disseminate, or cause to be disseminated, any false advertisement—

(1) By United States mails, or in or having an effect upon commerce, by any means, for the purpose of inducing, or which is likely to induce, directly or indirectly the purchase of food, drugs, devices, services, or cosmetics; or

(2) By any means, for the purpose of inducing, or which is likely to induce, directly or indirectly, the purchase in or having an effect upon commerce of food, drugs, devices, services, or cosmetics.

(b) Unfair or deceptive act or practice. The dissemination or the causing to be disseminated of any false advertisement within the provisions of subsection (a) of this section shall be an unfair or deceptive act or practice in or affecting commerce within the meaning of section 45 of this title.

§ 53. False advertisements; injunctions and restraining orders

(a) Power of Commission; jurisdiction of courts. Whenever the Commission has reason to believe—

(1) that any person, partnership, or corporation is engaged in, or is about to engage in, the dissemination or the causing of the dissemination of any advertisement in violation of section 52 of this title, and

(2) that the enjoining thereof pending the issuance of a complaint by the Commission under section 45 of this title, and until such complaint is dismissed by the Commission or set aside by the court on review, or the order of the Commission to cease and desist made thereon has become final within the meaning of section 45 of this title, would be to the interest of the public, the Commission by any of its attorneys designated by it for such purpose may bring suit in a district court of the United States or in the United States court of any Territory, to enjoin the dissemination or the causing of the dissemination of such advertisement. Upon proper showing a temporary injunction or restraining order shall be granted without bond. Any suit may be brought where such person, partnership, or corporation resides or transacts business, or wherever venue is proper under section 1391 of Title 28. In addition, the court may, if the court determines that the interests of justice require that any other person, partnership, or corporation should be a party in such suit, cause such other person, partnership, or corporation to be added as a party without regard to whether venue is otherwise proper in the district in which the suit is brought. In any suit under this section, process may be served on any person, partnership, or corporation wherever it may be found.

(b) Temporary restraining orders; preliminary injunctions. Whenever the Commission has reason to believe—

(1) that any person, partnership, or corporation is violating, or is about to violate, any provision of law enforced by the Federal Trade Commission, and

(2) that the enjoining thereof pending the issuance of a complaint by the Commission and until such complaint is dismissed by the Commission or set aside by the court on review, or until the order of the Commission made thereon has become final, would be in the interest of the public—

The Commission by any of its attorneys designated by it for such purpose may bring suit in a district court of the United States to enjoin any such act or practice. Upon a proper showing that, weighing the equities and considering the Commission's likelihood of ultimate success, such action would be in the public interest, and after notice to the defendant, a temporary restraining order or a preliminary injunction may be granted without bond: Provided, however, That if a complaint is not filed within such period (not exceeding 20 days) as may be specified by the court after issuance of the temporary restraining order or preliminary injunction, the order or injunction shall be dissolved by the court and be of no further force and effect: Provided further, That in proper cases the Commission may seek, and after proper proof, the court may issue, a permanent injunction. Any suit may be brought where such person, partnership, or corporation resides or transacts business, or wherever venue is proper under section 1391 of Title 28. In addition, the court may, if the court determines that the interests of justice require that any other person, partnership, or corporation should be a party in such suit, cause such other person, partnership, or corporation to be added as a party without regard to whether venue is otherwise proper in the district in which the suit is brought. In any suit under this section, process may be served on any person, partnership, or corporation wherever it may be found.

(c) *Service of process; proof of service.* Any process of the Commission under this section may be served by any person duly authorized by the Commission—

(1) by delivering a copy of such process to the person to be served, to a member of the partnership to be served, or to the president, secretary, or other executive officer or a director of the corporation to be served;

(2) by leaving a copy of such process at the residence or the principal office or place of business of such person, partnership, or corporation; or

(3) by mailing a copy of such process by registered mail or certified mail addressed to such person, partnership, or corporation at his, or her, or its residence, principal office, or principal place or business. The verified return by the person serving such process setting forth the manner of such service shall be proof of the same.

(d) Exception of periodical publications. Whenever it appears to the satisfaction of the court in the case of a newspaper, magazine, periodical, or other publication, published at regular intervals—

(1) that restraining the dissemination of a false advertisement in any particular issue of such publication would delay the delivery of such issue after the regular time therefor, and

(2) that such delay would be due to the method by which the manufacture and distribution of such publication is customarily conducted by the publisher in accordance with sound business practice, and not to any method or device adopted for the evasion of this section or to prevent or delay the issuance of an injunction or restraining order with respect to such false advertisement or any other advertisement, the court shall exclude such issue from the operation of the restraining order or injunction.

§ 54. False advertisements; penalties

(a) Imposition of penalties. Any person, partnership, or corporation who violates any provision of section 52(a) of this title shall, if the use of the commodity advertised may be injurious to health because of results from such use under the conditions prescribed in the advertisement thereof, or under such conditions as are customary or usual, or if such violation is with intent to defraud or mislead, be guilty of a misdemeanor, and upon conviction shall be punished by a fine of not more than $5,000 or by imprisonment for not more than six months, or by both such fine and imprisonment; except that if the conviction is for a violation committed after a first conviction of such person, partnership, or corporation, for any violation of such section, punishment shall be by a fine of not more than $10,000 or by imprisonment for not more than one year, or by both such fine and imprisonment: Provided, That for the purposes of this section meats and meat food products duly inspected, marked, and labeled in accordance with rules and regulations issued under the Meat Inspection Act, shall be conclusively presumed not injurious to health at the time the same leave official "establishments."

(b) Exception of advertising medium or agency. No publisher, radio-broadcast licensee, or agency or medium for the dissemination of advertising, except the manufacturer, packer, distributor, or seller of the commodity to which the false advertisement relates, shall be liable under this section by reason of the dissemination by him of any false advertisement, unless he has refused, on the request of the Commission, to furnish the Commission the name and post-office address of the manufacturer, packer, distributor, seller, or advertising agency, residing in the United States, who caused him to disseminate such advertisement. No advertising agency shall be liable under this section by reason of the causing by it of the dissemination of any false advertisement, unless it has refused, on the request of the Commission, to furnish the Commis-

sion the name and post-office address of the manufacturer, packer, distributor, or seller, residing in the United States, who caused it to cause the dissemination of such advertisement.

§ 55. Additional definitions

For the purposes of sections 52 to 54 of this title—

(a) False advertisement.

(1) The term "false advertisement" means an advertisement, other than labeling, which is misleading in a material respect; and in determining whether any advertisement is misleading, there shall be taken into account (among other things) not only representations made or suggested by statement, word, design, device, sound, or any combination thereof, but also the extent to which the advertisement fails to reveal facts material in the light of such representations or material with respect to consequences which may result from the use of the commodity to which the advertisement relates under the conditions prescribed in said advertisement, or under such conditions as are customary or usual. No advertisement of a drug shall be deemed to be false if it is disseminated only to members of the medical profession, contains no false representation of a material fact, and includes, or is accompanied in each instance by truthful disclosure of, the formula showing quantitatively each ingredient of such drug.

(2) In the case of oleomargarine or margarine an advertisement shall be deemed misleading in a material respect if in such advertisement representations are made or suggested by statement, word, grade designation, design, device, symbol, sound, or any combination thereof, that such oleomargarine or margarine is a dairy product, except that nothing contained herein shall prevent a truthful, accurate, and full statement in any such advertisement of all the ingredients contained in such oleomargarine or margarine.

(b) Food. The term "food" means (1) articles used for food or drink for man or other animals, (2) chewing gum, and (3) articles used for components of any such article.

(c) Drug. The term "drug" means (1) articles recognized in the official United States Pharmacopoeia, official Homeopathic Pharmacopoeia of the United States, or official National Formulary, or any supplement to any of them; and (2) articles intended for use in the diagnosis, cure, mitigation, treatment, or prevention of disease in man or other animals; and (3) articles (other than food) intended to affect the structure or any function of the body of man or other animals; and (4) articles intended for use as a component of any article specified in clauses (1), (2), or (3); but does not include devices or their components, parts, or accessories.

(d) Device. The term "device" (except when used in subsection (a) of this section) means an instrument, apparatus, implement, machine, contrivance, implant, in vitro reagent, or other similar or related article, including any component, part, or accessory, which is—

(1) recognized in the official National Formulary, or the United States Pharmacopeia, or any supplement to them,

(2) intended for use in the diagnosis of disease or other conditions, or in the cure, mitigation, treatment, or prevention of disease, in man or other animals, or

(3) intended to affect the structure or any function of the body of man or other animals, and which does not achieve any of its principal intended purposes through chemical action within or on the body of man or other animals and which is not depended upon being metabolized for the achievement of any of its principal intended purposes.

(e) Cosmetic. The term "cosmetic" means (1) articles to be rubbed, poured, sprinkled, or sprayed on, introduced into, or otherwise applied to the human body or any part thereof intended for cleansing, beautifying, promoting attractiveness, or altering the appearance, and (2) articles intended for use as a component of any such article; except that such term shall not include soap.

(f) Oleomargarine or margarine. For the purposes of this section and section 347 of Title 21, the term "oleomargarine" or "margarine" includes—

(1) all substances, mixtures, and compounds known as oleomargarine or margarine;

(2) all substances, mixtures, and compounds which have a consistence similar to that of butter and which contain any edible oils or fats other than milk fat if made in imitation or semblance of butter.

* * *

§ 57a. Unfair or deceptive acts or practices rulemaking proceedings

(a) Authority of Commission to prescribe rules and general statements of policy.

(1) Except as provided in subsection (h) of this section, the Commission may prescribe—

(A) interpretive rules and general statements of policy with respect to unfair or deceptive acts or practices in or affecting commerce (within the meaning of section 45(a)(1) of this title), and

(B) rules which define with specificity acts or practices which are unfair or deceptive acts or practices in or affecting commerce (within the meaning of section 45(a)(1) of this title), except that the Commission shall not develop or promulgate any trade rule or regulation with regard to the regulation of the development and utilization of the standards and certification activities pursuant to this section. Rules under this subparagraph may include requirements prescribed for the purpose of preventing such acts or practices.

(2) The Commission shall have no authority under this subchapter, other than its authority under this section, to prescribe any rule with respect to unfair or deceptive acts or practices in or affecting commerce (within the meaning of section 45(a)(1) of this title). The preceding sentence shall not affect any authority of the Commission to prescribe rules (including interpretive rules), and general statements of policy, with respect to unfair methods of competition in or affecting commerce.

(b) Procedures applicable.

(1) When prescribing a rule under subsection (a)(1)(B) of this section, the Commission shall proceed in accordance with section 553 of Title 5 (without regard to any reference in such section to sections 556 and 557 of such title), and shall also (A) publish a notice of proposed rulemaking stating with particularity the text of the rule, including any alternatives, which the Commission proposes to promulgate, and the reason for the proposed rule; (B) allow interested persons to submit written data, views, and arguments, and make all such submissions publicly available; (C) provide an opportunity for an informal hearing in accordance with subsection (c) of this section; and (D) promulgate, if appropriate, a final rule based on the matter in the rulemaking record (as defined in subsection (e)(1)(B) of this section), together with a statement of basis and purpose.

(2)(A) Prior to the publication of any notice of proposed rulemaking pursuant to paragraph (1)(A), the Commission shall publish an advance notice of proposed rulemaking in the Federal Register. Such advance notice shall—

> (i) contain a brief description of the area of inquiry under consideration, the objectives which the Commission seeks to achieve, and possible regulatory alternatives under consideration by the Commission; and

> (ii) invite the response of interested parties with respect to such proposed rulemaking, including any suggestions or alternative methods for achieving such objectives.

(B) The Commission shall submit such advance notice of proposed rulemaking to the Committee on Commerce, Science, and

Transportation of the Senate and to the Committee on Energy and Commerce of the House of Representatives. The Commission may use such additional mechanisms as the Commission considers useful to obtain suggestions regarding the content of the area of inquiry before the publication of a general notice of proposed rulemaking under paragraph (1)(A).

(C) The Commission shall, 30 days before the publication of a notice of proposed rulemaking pursuant to paragraph (1)(A), submit such notice to the Committee on Commerce, Science, and Transportation of the Senate and to the Committee on Energy and Commerce of the House of Representatives.

(3) The Commission shall issue a notice of proposed rulemaking pursuant to paragraph (1)(A) only where it has reason to believe that the unfair or deceptive acts or practices which are the subject of the proposed rulemaking are prevalent. The Commission shall make a determination that unfair or deceptive acts or practices are prevalent under this paragraph only if—

(A) it has issued cease and desist orders regarding such acts or practices, or

(B) any other information available to the Commission indicates a widespread pattern of unfair or deceptive acts or practices.

(c) Informal hearing procedure. The Commission shall conduct any informal hearings required by subsection (b)(1)(C) of this section in accordance with the following procedure:

(1)(A) The Commission shall provide for the conduct of proceedings under this subsection by hearing officers who shall perform their functions in accordance with the requirements of this subsection.

(B) The officer who presides over the rulemaking proceedings shall be responsible to a chief presiding officer who shall not be responsible to any other officer or employee of the Commission. The officer who presides over the rulemaking proceeding shall make a recommended decision based upon the findings and conclusions of such officer as to all relevant and material evidence, except that such recommended decision may be made by another officer if the officer who presided over the proceeding is no longer available to the Commission.

(C) Except as required for the disposition of ex parte matters as authorized by law, no presiding officer shall consult any person or party with respect to any fact in issue unless such officer gives notice and opportunity for all parties to participate.

(2) Subject to paragraph (3) of this subsection, an interested person is entitled—

(A) to present his position orally or by documentary submissions (or both), and

(B) if the Commission determines that there are disputed issues of material fact it is necessary to resolve, to present such rebuttal submissions and to conduct (or have conducted under paragraph (3)(B)) such cross-examination of persons as the Commission determines (i) to be appropriate, and (ii) to be required for a full and true disclosure with respect to such issues.

(3) The Commission may prescribe such rules and make such rulings concerning proceedings in such hearings as may tend to avoid unnecessary costs or delay. Such rules or rulings may include (A) imposition of reasonable time limits on each interested person's oral presentations, and (B) requirements that any cross-examination to which a person may be entitled under paragraph (2) be conducted by the Commission on behalf of that person in such manner as the Commission determines (i) to be appropriate, and (ii) to be required for a full and true disclosure with respect to disputed issues of material fact.

(4)(A) Except as provided in subparagraph (B), if a group of persons each of whom under paragraphs (2) and (3) would be entitled to conduct (or have conducted) cross-examination and who are determined by the Commission to have the same or similar interests in the proceeding cannot agree upon a single representative of such interests for purposes of cross-examination, the Commission may make rules and rulings

(i) limiting the representation of such interest, for such purposes, and

(ii) governing the manner in which such cross-examination shall be limited.

(B) When any person who is a member of a group with respect to which the Commission has made a determination under subparagraph (A) is unable to agree upon group representation with the other members of the group, then such person shall not be denied under the authority of subparagraph (A) the opportunity to conduct (or have conducted) cross-examination as to issues affecting his particular interests if

(i) he satisfies the Commission that he has made a reasonable and good faith effort to reach agreement upon group representation with the other members of the group and

(ii) the Commission determines that there are substantial and relevant issues which are not adequately presented by the group representative.

(5) A verbatim transcript shall be taken of any oral presentation, and cross-examination, in an informal hearing to which this subsection applies. Such transcript shall be available to the public.

(d) Statement of basis and purpose accompanying rule; "Commission" defined; judicial review of amendment or repeal of rule; violation of rule.

(1) The Commission's statement of basis and purpose to accompany a rule promulgated under subsection (a)(1)(B) of this section shall include (A) a statement as to the prevalence of the acts or practices treated by the rule; (B) a statement as to the manner and context in which such acts or practices are unfair or deceptive; and (C) a statement as to the economic effect of the rule, taking into account the effect on small business and consumers.

(2)(A) The term "Commission" as used in this subsection and subsections (b) and (c) of this section includes any person authorized to act in behalf of the Commission in any part of the rulemaking proceeding.

(B) A substantive amendment to, or repeal of, a rule promulgated under subsection (a)(1)(B) of this section shall be prescribed, and subject to judicial review, in the same manner as a rule prescribed under such subsection. An exemption under subsection (g) of this section shall not be treated as an amendment or repeal of a rule.

(3) When any rule under subsection (a)(1)(B) of this section takes effect a subsequent violation thereof shall constitute an unfair or deceptive act or practice in violation of section 45(a)(1) of this title, unless the Commission otherwise expressly provides in such rule.

(e) Judicial review; petition; jurisdiction and venue; rulemaking record; additional submissions and presentations; scope of review and relief; review by Supreme Court; additional remedies.

(1)(A) Not later than 60 days after a rule is promulgated under subsection (a)(1)(B) of this section by the Commission, any interested person (including a consumer or consumer organization) may file a petition, in the United States Court of Appeals for the District of Columbia circuit or for the circuit in which such person resides or has his principal place of business, for judicial review of such rule. Copies of the petition shall be forthwith transmitted by the clerk of the court to the Commission or other officer designated by it for that purpose. The provisions of section 2112 of Title 28 shall apply to the filing of the rulemaking record of proceedings on which the Commission based its rule and to the transfer of proceedings in the courts of appeals.

(B) For purpose of this section, the term "rulemaking record" means the rule, its statement of basis and purpose, the transcript required by subsection (c)(5) of this section, any written submissions, and any other information which the Commission considers relevant to such rule.

(2) If the petitioner or the Commission applies to the court for leave to make additional oral submissions or written presentations and shows to the satisfaction of the court that such submissions and presentations would be material and that there were reasonable grounds for the submissions and failure to make such submissions and presentations in the proceeding before the Commission, the court may order the Commission to provide additional opportunity to make such submissions and presentations. The Commission may modify or set aside its rule or make a new rule by reason of the additional submissions and presentations and shall file such modified or new rule, and the rule's statement of basis of purpose, with the return of such submissions and presentations. The court shall thereafter review such new or modified rule.

(3) Upon the filing of the petition under paragraph (1) of this subsection, the court shall have jurisdiction to review the rule in accordance with chapter 7 of Title 5 and to grant appropriate relief, including interim relief, as provided in such chapter. The court shall hold unlawful and set aside the rule on any ground specified in subparagraphs (A), (B), (C), or (D) of section 706(2) of Title 5 (taking due account of the rule of prejudicial error), or if—

(A) the court finds that the Commission's action is not supported by substantial evidence in the rulemaking record (as defined in paragraph (1) (B) of this subsection) taken as a whole, or

(B) the court finds that—

(i) a Commission determination under subsection (c) of this section that the petitioner is not entitled to conduct cross-examination or make rebuttal submissions, or

(ii) a Commission rule or ruling under subsection (c) of this section limiting the petitioner's cross-examination or rebuttal submissions, has precluded disclosure of disputed material facts which was necessary for fair determination by the Commission of the rulemaking proceeding taken as a whole. The term "evidence", as used in this paragraph, means any matter in the rulemaking record.

(4) The judgment of the court affirming or setting aside, in whole or in part, any such rule shall be final, subject to review by the Supreme Court of the United States upon certiorari or certification, as provided in section 1254 of Title 28.

(5)(A) Remedies under the preceding paragraphs of this subsection are in addition to and not in lieu of any other remedies provided by law.

(B) The United States Courts of Appeal shall have exclusive jurisdiction of any action to obtain judicial review (other than in an enforcement proceeding) of a rule prescribed under subsection (a)(1)(B) of this section, if any district court of the United States would have had jurisdiction of such action but for this subparagraph. Any such action shall be brought in the United States Court of Appeals for the District of Columbia circuit, or for any circuit which includes a judicial district in which the action could have been brought but for this subparagraph.

(C) A determination, rule, or ruling of the Commission described in paragraph (3)(B)(i) or (ii) may be reviewed only in a proceeding under this subsection and only in accordance with paragraph (3)(B). Section 706(2)(E) of Title 5 shall not apply to any rule promulgated under subsection (a)(1)(B) of this section. The contents and adequacy of any statement required by subsection (b)(1)(D) of this section shall not be subject to judicial review in any respect.

(f) Unfair or deceptive acts or practices by banks, savings and loan institutions, or Federal credit unions; promulgation of regulations by Board of Governors of Federal Reserve System, Federal Home Loan Bank Board, and National Credit Union Administration Board; agency enforcement and compliance proceedings; violations; power of other Federal agencies unaffected; reporting requirements.

(1) In order to prevent unfair or deceptive acts or practices in or affecting commerce (including acts or practices which are unfair or deceptive to consumers) by banks or savings and loan institutions described in paragraph (3), each agency specified in paragraph (2) or (3) of this subsection shall establish a separate division of consumer affairs which shall receive and take appropriate action upon complaints with respect to such acts or practices by banks or savings and loan institutions described in paragraph (3) subject to its jurisdiction. The Board of Governors of the Federal Reserve System (with respect to banks) and the Federal Home Loan Bank Board (with respect to savings and loan institutions described in paragraph (3)) and the National Credit Union Administration Board (with respect to Federal credit unions described in paragraph (4)) shall prescribe regulations to carry out the purposes of this section, including regulations defining with specificity such unfair or deceptive acts or practices, and containing requirements prescribed for the purpose of preventing such acts or practices. Whenever the Commission prescribes a rule under subsection (a)(1)(B) of this section, then within 60 days after such rule takes effect each such Board shall promulgate substantially similar regulations prohibiting acts or practices of banks or savings and loan institutions described in paragraph (3), or Federal credit unions described in paragraph (4), as the case may be, which are substantially similar to those

prohibited by rules of the Commission and which impose substantially similar requirements, unless (A) any such Board finds that such acts or practices of banks or savings and loan institutions described in paragraph (3), or Federal credit unions described in paragraph (4), as the case may be, are not unfair or deceptive, or (B) the Board of Governors of the Federal Reserve System finds that implementation of similar regulations with respect to banks, savings and loan institutions or Federal credit unions would seriously conflict with essential monetary and payments systems policies of such Board, and publishes any such finding, and the reasons therefor, in the Federal Register.

(2) Enforcement.—Compliance with regulations prescribed under this subsection shall be enforced under section 1818 of Title 12, in the case of—

> (A) national banks and Federal branches and Federal agencies of foreign banks, by the division of consumer affairs established by the Office of the Comptroller of the Currency;

> (B) member banks of the Federal Reserve System (other than national banks, branches and agencies of foreign banks (other than Federal branches, Federal agencies, and insured State branches of foreign banks), commercial lending companies owned or controlled by foreign banks, and organizations operating under section 25 or 25(a) of the Federal Reserve Act [12 U.S.C. §§ 601 et seq., 611 et seq.], by the division of consumer affairs established by the Board of Governors of the Federal Reserve System; and

> (C) banks insured by the Federal Deposit Insurance Corporation (other banks referred to in subparagraph (A) or (B)) and insured State branches of foreign banks, by the division of consumer affairs established by the Board of Directors of the Federal Deposit Insurance Corporation.

(3) Compliance with regulations prescribed under this subsection shall be enforced under section 1818 of Title 12 with respect to savings associations as defined in section 1813 of Title 12.

(4) Compliance with regulations prescribed under this subsection shall be enforced with respect to Federal credit unions under sections 120 and 206 of the Federal Credit Union Act (12 U.S.C. 1766 and 1786).

(5) For the purpose of the exercise by any agency referred to in paragraph (2) of its powers under any Act referred to in that paragraph, a violation of any regulation prescribed under this subsection shall be deemed to be a violation of a requirement imposed under that Act. In addition to its powers under any provision of law specifically referred to in paragraph (2), each of the agencies re-

ferred to in that paragraph may exercise, for the purpose of enforcing compliance with any regulation prescribed under this subsection, any other authority conferred on it by law.

(6) The authority of the Board of Governors of the Federal Reserve System to issue regulations under this subsection does not impair the authority of any other agency designated in this subsection to make rules respecting its own procedures in enforcing compliance with regulations prescribed under this subsection.

(7) Each agency exercising authority under this subsection shall transmit to the Congress each year a detailed report on its activities under this paragraph during the preceding calendar year.

The terms used in this paragraph that are not defined in this chapter or otherwise defined in section 1813(s) of Title 12 shall have the meaning given to them in section 3101 of Title 12.

(g) Exemptions and stays from application of rules; procedures.

(1) Any person to whom a rule under subsection (a)(1)(B) of this section applies may petition the Commission for an exemption from such rule.

(2) If, on its own motion or on the basis of a petition under paragraph (1), the Commission finds that the application of a rule prescribed under subsection (a)(1)(B) of this section to any person or class or persons is not necessary to prevent the unfair or deceptive act or practice to which the rule relates, the Commission may exempt such person or class from all or part of such rule. Section 553 of Title 5 shall apply to action under this paragraph.

(3) Neither the pendency of a proceeding under this subsection respecting an exemption from a rule, nor the pendency of judicial proceedings to review the Commission's action or failure to act under this subsection, shall stay the applicability of such rule under subsection (a)(1)(B) of this section.

(h) Restriction on rulemaking authority of Commission respecting children's advertising proceedings. The Commission shall not have any authority to promulgate any rule in the children's advertising proceeding pending on May 28, 1980, or in any substantially similar proceeding on the basis of a determination by the Commission that such advertising constitutes an unfair act or practice in or affecting commerce.

(i) Meetings with outside parties.

(1) For purposes of this subsection, the term "outside party" means any person other than (A) a Commissioner; (B) an officer or employee of the Commission; or (C) any person who has entered into a contract or any other agreement or arrangement with the Commission to provide any goods or services (including consulting services) to the Commission.

(2) Not later than 60 days after May 28, 1980, the Commission shall publish a proposed rule, and not later than 180 days after May 28, 1980, the Commission shall promulgate a final rule, which shall authorize the Commission or any Commissioner to meet with any outside party concerning any rulemaking proceeding of the Commission. Such rule shall provide that—

(A) notice of any such meeting shall be included in any weekly calendar prepared by the Commission; and

(B) a verbatim record or a summary of any such meeting, or of any communication relating to any such meeting, shall be kept, made available to the public, and included in the rulemaking record.

(j) Communications by investigative personnel with staff of Commission concerning matters outside rulemaking record prohibited. Not later than 60 days after May 28, 1980, the Commission shall publish a proposed rule, and not later than 180 days after May 28, 1980, the Commission shall promulgate a final rule, which shall prohibit any officer, employee, or agent of the Commission with any investigative responsibility or other responsibility relating to any rulemaking proceeding within any operating bureau of the Commission, from communicating or causing to be communicated to any Commissioner or to the personal staff of any Commissioner any fact which is relevant to the merits of such proceeding and which is not on the rulemaking record of such proceeding, unless such communication is made available to the public and is included in the rulemaking record. The provisions of this subsection shall not apply to any communication to the extent such communication is required for the disposition of ex parte matters as authorized by law.

§ 57b. Civil actions for violations of rules and cease and desist orders respecting unfair or deceptive acts or practices

(a) Suits by Commission against persons, partnerships, or corporations; jurisdiction; relief for dishonest or fraudulent acts.

(1) If any person, partnership, or corporation violates any rule under this chapter respecting unfair or deceptive acts or practices (other than an interpretive rule, or a rule violation of which the Commission has provided is not an unfair or deceptive act or practice in violation of section 45(a) of this title), then the Commission may commence a civil action against such person, partnership, or corporation for relief under subsection (b) of this section in a United States district court or in any court of competent jurisdiction of a State.

(2) If any person, partnership, or corporation engages in any unfair or deceptive act or practice (within the meaning of section 45(a)(1) of this title) with respect to which the Commission has issued a final

cease and desist order which is applicable to such person, partnership, or corporation, then the Commission may commence a civil action against such person, partnership, or corporation in a United States district court or in any court of competent jurisdiction of a State. If the Commission satisfies the court that the act or practice to which the cease and desist order relates is one which a reasonable man would have known under the circumstances was dishonest or fraudulent, the court may grant relief under subsection (b) of this section.

(b) Nature of relief available. The court in an action under subsection (a) of this section shall have jurisdiction to grant such relief as the court finds necessary to redress injury to consumers or other persons, partnerships, and corporations resulting from the rule violation or the unfair or deceptive act or practice, as the case may be. Such relief may include, but shall not be limited to, rescission or reformation of contracts, the refund of money or return of property, the payment of damages, and public notification respecting the rule violation or the unfair or deceptive act or practice, as the case may be; except that nothing in this subsection is intended to authorize the imposition of any exemplary or punitive damages.

(c) Conclusiveness of findings of Commission in cease and desist proceedings; notice of judicial proceedings to injured persons, etc.

(1) If

(A) a cease and desist order issued under section 45(b) of this title has become final under section 45(g) of this title with respect to any person's, partnership's, or corporation's rule violation or unfair or deceptive act or practice, and

(B) an action under this section is brought with respect to such person's partnership's, or corporation's rule violation or act or practice, then the findings of the Commission as to the material facts in the proceeding under section 45(b) of this title with respect to such person's, partnership's, or corporation's rule violation or act or practice, shall be conclusive unless

(i) the terms of such cease and desist order expressly provide that the Commission's findings shall not be conclusive, or

(ii) the order became final by reason of section 45(g)(1) of this title, in which case such finding shall be conclusive if supported by evidence.

(2) The court shall cause notice of an action under this section to be given in a manner which is reasonably calculated, under all of the circumstances, to apprise the persons, partnerships, and corporations allegedly injured by the defendant's rule violation or act or

practice of the pendency of such action. Such notice may, in the discretion of the court, be given by publication.

(d) Time for bringing of actions.   No action may be brought by the Commission under this section more than 3 years after the rule violation to which an action under subsection (a)(1) of this section relates, or the unfair or deceptive act or practice to which an action under subsection (a)(2) of this section relates; except that if a cease and desist order with respect to any person's, partnership's, or corporation's rule violation or unfair or deceptive act or practice has become final and such order was issued in a proceeding under section 45(b) of this title which was commenced not later than 3 years after the rule violation or act or practice occurred, a civil action may be commenced under this section against such person, partnership, or corporation at any time before the expiration of one year after such order becomes final.

(e) Availability of additional Federal or State remedies; other authority of Commission unaffected.   Remedies provided in this section are in addition to, and not in lieu of, any other remedy or right of action provided by State or Federal law.   Nothing in this section shall be construed to affect any authority of the Commission under any other provision of law.

§ 57b–1.   Civil investigative demands

(a) Definitions.   For purposes of this section:

(1) The terms "civil investigative demand" and "demand" mean any demand issued by the Commission under subsection (c)(1) of this section.

(2) The term "Commission investigation" means any inquiry conducted by a Commission investigator for the purpose of ascertaining whether any person is or has been engaged in any unfair or deceptive acts or practices in or affecting commerce (within the meaning of section 45(a)(1) of this title) or in any antitrust violations.

(3) The term "Commission investigator" means any attorney or investigator employed by the Commission who is charged with the duty of enforcing or carrying into effect any provisions relating to unfair or deceptive acts or practices in or affecting commerce (within the meaning of section 45(a)(1) of this title) or any provisions relating to antitrust violations.

(4) The term "custodian" means the custodian or any deputy custodian designated under section 57b–2(b)(2)(A) of this title.

(5) The term "documentary material" includes the original or any copy of any book, record, report, memorandum, paper, communication, tabulation, chart, or other document.

(6) The term "person" means any natural person, partnership, corporation, association, or other legal entity, including any person acting under color or authority of State law.

(7) The term "violation" means any act or omission constituting an unfair or deceptive act or practice in or affecting commerce (within the meaning of section 45(a)(1) of this title) or any antitrust violation.

(8) The term "antitrust violation" means—

> (A) any unfair method of competition (within the meaning of section 45(a)(1) of this title);

> (B) any violation of the Clayton Act or of any other Federal statute that prohibits, or makes available to the Commission a civil remedy with respect to, any restraint upon or monopolization of interstate or foreign trade or commerce;

> (C) with respect to the International Antitrust Enforcement Assistance Act of 1994 [15 U.S.C. § 6201 et seq.], any violation of any of the foreign antitrust laws (as defined in section 12 of such Act [15 U.S.C. § 6211]) with respect to which a request is made under section 3 of such Act [15 U.S.C. § 6202]; or

> (D) any activity in preparation for a merger, acquisition, joint venture, or similar transaction, which if consummated, may result in any such unfair method of competition or in any such violation.

(b) Actions conducted by Commission respecting unfair or deceptive acts or practices in or affecting commerce. For the purpose of investigations performed pursuant to this section with respect to unfair or deceptive acts or practices in or affecting commerce (within the meaning of section 45(a)(1) of this title), all actions of the Commission taken under section 46 and section 49 of this title shall be conducted pursuant to subsection (c) of this section.

(c) Issuance of demand; contents; service; verified return; sworn certificates; answers; taking of oral testimony.

> (1) Whenever the Commission has reason to believe that any person may be in possession, custody, or control of any documentary material or tangible things, or may have any information, relevant to unfair or deceptive acts or practices in or affecting commerce (within the meaning of section 45(a)(1) of this title), or to antitrust violations, the Commission may, before the institution of any proceedings under this subchapter, issue in writing, and cause to be served upon such person, a civil investigative demand requiring such person to produce such documentary material for inspection and copying or reproduction, to submit such tangible things, to file written reports or answers to questions, to give oral testimony

concerning documentary material or other information, or to furnish any combination of such material, answers, or testimony.

(2) Each civil investigative demand shall state the nature of the conduct constituting the alleged violation which is under investigation and the provision of law applicable to such violation.

(3) Each civil investigative demand for the production of documentary material shall—

> (A) describe each class of documentary material to be produced under the demand with such definiteness and certainty as to permit such material to be fairly identified;

> (B) prescribe a return date or dates which will provide a reasonable period of time within which the material so demanded may be assembled and made available for inspection and copying or reproduction; and

> (C) identify the custodian to whom such material shall be made available.

(4) Each civil investigative demand for the submission of tangible things shall—

> (A) describe each class of tangible things to be submitted under the demand with such definiteness and certainty as to permit such things to be fairly identified;

> (B) prescribe a return date or dates which will provide a reasonable period of time within which the things so demanded may be assembled and submitted; and

> (C) identify the custodian to whom such things shall be submitted.

(5) Each civil investigative demand for written reports or answers to questions shall—

> (A) propound with definiteness and certainty the reports to be produced or the questions to be answered;

> (B) prescribe a date or dates at which time written reports or answers to questions shall be submitted; and

> (C) identify the custodian to whom such reports or answers shall be submitted.

(6) Each civil investigative demand for the giving of oral testimony shall—

> (A) prescribe a date, time, and place at which oral testimony shall be commenced; and

> (B) identify a Commission investigator who shall conduct the investigation and the custodian to whom the transcript of such investigation shall be submitted.

(7)(A) Any civil investigative demand may be served by any Commission investigator at any place within the territorial jurisdiction of any court of the United States.

(B) Any such demand or any enforcement petition filed under this section may be served upon any person who is not found within the territorial jurisdiction of any court of the United States, in such manner as the Federal Rules of Civil Procedure prescribe for service in a foreign nation.

(C) To the extent that the courts of the United States have authority to assert jurisdiction over such person consistent with due process, the United States District Court for the District of Columbia shall have the same jurisdiction to take any action respecting compliance with this section by such person that such district court would have if such person were personally within the jurisdiction of such district court.

(8) Service of any civil investigative demand or any enforcement petition filed under this section may be made upon a partnership, corporation, association, or other legal entity by—

(A) delivering a duly executed copy of such demand or petition to any partner, executive officer, managing agent, or general agent of such partnership, corporation, association, or other legal entity, or to any agent of such partnership, corporation, association, or other legal entity authorized by appointment or by law to receive service of process on behalf of such partnership, corporation, association, or other legal entity;

(B) delivering a duly executed copy of such demand or petition to the principal office or place of business of the partnership, corporation, association, or other legal entity to be served; or

(C) depositing a duly executed copy in the United States mails, by registered or certified mail, return receipt requested, duly addressed to such partnership, corporation, association, or other legal entity at its principal office or place of business.

(9) Service of any civil investigative demand or of any enforcement petition filed under this section may be made upon any natural person by—

(A) delivering a duly executed copy of such demand or petition to the person to served; or

(B) depositing a duly executed copy in the United States mails by registered or certified mail, return receipt requested, duly addressed to such person at his residence or principal office or place of business.

(10) A verified return by the individual serving any civil investigative demand or any enforcement petition filed under this section

setting forth the manner of such service shall be proof of such service. In the case of service by registered or certified mail, such return shall be accompanied by the return post office receipt of delivery of such demand or enforcement petition.

(11) The production of documentary material in response to a civil investigative demand shall be made under a sworn certificate, in such form as the demand designates, by the person, if a natural person, to whom the demand is directed or, if not a natural person, by any person having knowledge of the facts and circumstances relating to such production, to the effect that all of the documentary material required by the demand and in the possession, custody, or control of the person to whom the demand is directed has been produced and made available to the custodian.

(12) The submission of tangible things in response to a civil investigative demand shall be made under a sworn certificate, in such form as the demand designates, by the person to whom the demand is directed or, if not a natural person, by any person having knowledge of the facts and circumstances relating to such production, to the effect that all of the tangible things required by the demand and in the possession, custody, or control of the person to whom the demand is directed have been submitted to the custodian.

(13) Each reporting requirement or question in a civil investigative demand shall be answered separately and fully in writing under oath, unless it is objected to, in which event the reasons for the objection shall be stated in lieu of an answer, and it shall be submitted under a sworn certificate, in such form as the demand designates, by the person, if a natural person, to whom the demand is directed or, if not a natural person, by any person responsible for answering each reporting requirement or question, to the effect that all information required by the demand and in the possession, custody, control, or knowledge of the person to whom the demand is directed has been submitted.

(14)(A) Any Commission investigator before whom oral testimony is to be taken shall put the witness on oath or affirmation and shall personally, or by any individual acting under his direction and in his presence, record the testimony of the witness. The testimony shall be taken stenographically and transcribed. After the testimony is fully transcribed, the Commission investigator before whom the testimony is taken shall promptly transmit a copy of the transcript of the testimony to the custodian.

(B) Any Commission investigator before whom oral testimony is to be taken shall exclude from the place where the testimony is to be taken all other persons except the person giving the testimony, his attorney, the officer before whom the testimony is to be taken, and any stenographer taking such testimony.

(C) The oral testimony of any person taken pursuant to a civil investigative demand shall be taken in the judicial district of the United States in which such person resides, is found, or transacts business, or in such other place as may be agreed upon by the Commission investigator before whom the oral testimony of such person is to be taken and such person.

(D)(i) Any person compelled to appear under a civil investigative demand for oral testimony pursuant to this section may be accompanied, represented, and advised by an attorney. The attorney may advise such person, in confidence, either upon the request of such person or upon the initiative of the attorney, with respect to any question asked of such person.

(ii) Such person or attorney may object on the record to any question, in whole or in part, and shall briefly state for the record the reason for the objection. An objection may properly be made, received, and entered upon the record when it is claimed that such person is entitled to refuse to answer the question on grounds of any constitutional or other legal right or privilege, including the privilege against self-incrimination. Such person shall not otherwise object to or refuse to answer any question, and shall not himself or through his attorney otherwise interrupt the oral examination. If such person refuses to answer any question, the Commission may petition the district court of the United States pursuant to this section for an order compelling such person to answer such question.

(iii) If such person refuses to answer any question on grounds of the privilege against self-incrimination, the testimony of such person may be compelled in accordance with the provisions of section 6004 of Title 18.

(E)(i) After the testimony of any witness is fully transcribed, the Commission investigator shall afford the witness (who may be accompanied by an attorney) a reasonable opportunity to examine the transcript. The transcript shall be read to or by the witness, unless such examination and reading are waived by the witness. Any changes in form or substance which the witness desires to make shall be entered and identified upon the transcript by the Commission investigator with a statement of the reasons given by the witness for making such changes. The transcript shall then be signed by the witness, unless the witness in writing waives the signing, is ill, cannot be found, or refuses to sign.

(ii) If the transcript is not signed by the witness during the 30-day period following the date upon which the witness is first afforded a reasonable opportunity to examine it, the

Commission investigator shall sign the transcript and state on the record the fact of the waiver, illness, absence of the witness, or the refusal to sign, together with any reasons given for the failure to sign.

(F) The Commission investigator shall certify on the transcript that the witness was duly sworn by him and that the transcript is a true record of the testimony given by the witness, and the Commission investigator shall promptly deliver the transcript or send it by registered or certified mail to the custodian.

(G) The Commission investigator shall furnish a copy of the transcript (upon payment of reasonable charges for the transcript) to the witness only, except that the Commission may for good cause limit such witness to inspection of the official transcript of his testimony.

(H) Any witness appearing for the taking of oral testimony pursuant to a civil investigative demand shall be entitled to the same fees and mileage which are paid to witnesses in the district courts of the United States.

(d) Procedures for demand material. Materials received as a result of a civil investigative demand shall be subject to the procedures established in section 57b-2 of this title.

(e) Petition for enforcement. Whenever any person fails to comply with any civil investigative demand duly served upon him under this section, or whenever satisfactory copying or reproduction of material requested pursuant to the demand cannot be accomplished and such person refuses to surrender such material, the Commission, through such officers or attorneys as it may designate, may file, in the district court of the United States for any judicial district in which such person resides, is found, or transacts business, and serve upon such person, a petition for an order of such court for the enforcement of this section. All process of any court to which application may be made as provided in this subsection may be served in any judicial district.

(f) Petition for order modifying or setting aside demand.

(1) Not later than 20 days after the service of any civil investigative demand upon any person under subsection (c) of this section, or at any time before the return date specified in the demand, whichever period is shorter, or within such period exceeding 20 days after service or in excess of such return date as may be prescribed in writing, subsequent to service, by any Commission investigator named in the demand, such person may file with the Commission a petition for an order by the Commission modifying or setting aside the demand.

(2) The time permitted for compliance with the demand in whole or in part, as deemed proper and ordered by the Commission, shall not

run during the pendency of such petition at the Commission, except that such person shall comply with any portions of the demand not sought to be modified or set aside. Such petition shall specify each ground upon which the petitioner relies in seeking such relief, and may be based upon any failure of the demand to comply with the provisions of this section, or upon any constitutional or other legal right or privilege of such person.

(g) Custodial control of documentary material, tangible things, reports, etc. At any time during which any custodian is in custody or control of any documentary material, tangible things, reports, answers to questions, or transcripts of oral testimony given by any person in compliance with any civil investigative demand, such person may file, in the district court of the United States for the judicial district within which the office of such custodian is situated, and serve upon such custodian, a petition for an order of such court requiring the performance by such custodian of any duty imposed upon him by this section or section 57b-2 of this title.

(h) Jurisdiction of court. Whenever any petition is filed in any district court of the United States under this section, such court shall have jurisdiction to hear and determine the matter so presented, and to enter such order or orders as may be required to carry into effect the provisions of this section. Any final order so entered shall be subject to appeal pursuant to section 1291 of Title 28. Any disobedience of any final order entered under this section by any court shall be punished as a contempt of such court.

(i) Commission authority to issue subpoenas or make demand for information. Notwithstanding any other provision of law, the Commission shall have no authority to issue a subpoena or make a demand for information, under authority of this subchapter or any other provision of law, unless such subpoena or demand for information is signed by a Commissioner acting pursuant to a Commission resolution. The Commission shall not delegate the power conferred by this section to sign subpoenas or demands for information to any other person.

(j) Applicability of this section. The provisions of this section shall not—

   (1) apply to any proceeding under section 45(b) of this title, any proceeding under section 11(b) of the Clayton Act (15 U.S.C. 21(b)), or any adjudicative proceeding under any other provision of law; or

   (2) apply to or affect the jurisdiction, duties, or powers of any agency of the Federal Government, other than the Commission, regardless of whether such jurisdiction, duties, or powers are derived in whole or in part, by reference to this subchapter.

§ 57b–2. Confidentiality

(a) Definitions. For purposes of this section:

257

(1) The term "material" means documentary material, tangible things, written reports or answers to questions, and transcripts of oral testimony.

(2) The term "Federal agency" has the meaning given it in section 552(e) of Title 5.

(b) Procedures respecting documents, tangible things or transcripts of oral testimony received pursuant to compulsory process or investigation.

(1) With respect to any document, tangible thing, or transcript of oral testimony received by the Commission pursuant to compulsory process in an investigation, a purpose of which is to determine whether any person may have violated any provision of the laws administered by the Commission, the procedures established in paragraph (2) through paragraph (7) shall apply.

(2)(A) The Commission shall designate a duly authorized agent to serve as custodian of documentary material, tangible things, or written reports or answers to questions, and transcripts of oral testimony, and such additional duly authorized agents as the Commission shall determine from time to time to be necessary to serve as deputies to the custodian.

(B) Any person upon whom any demand for the production of documentary material has been duly served shall make such material available for inspection and copying or reproduction to the custodian designated in such demand at the principal place of business of such person (or at such other place as such custodian and such person thereafter may agree and prescribe in writing or as the court may direct pursuant to section 57b–1(h) of this title) on the return date specified in such demand (or on such later date as such custodian may prescribe in writing). Such person may upon written agreement between such person and the custodian substitute copies for originals of all or any part of such material.

(3)(A) The custodian to whom any documentary material, tangible things, written reports or answers to questions, and transcripts of oral testimony are delivered shall take physical possession of such material, reports or answers, and transcripts, and shall be responsible for the use made of such material, reports or answers, and transcripts, and for the return of material, pursuant to the requirements of this section.

(B) The custodian may prepare such copies of the documentary material, written reports or answers to questions, and transcripts of oral testimony, and may make tangible things available, as may be required for official use by any duly authorized officer or employee of the Commission under regulations which shall be promulgated by the Commission. Notwithstanding subparagraph (C), such material, things, and transcripts may be used by any such officer or employee in connection with the taking of oral testimony under this section.

(C) Except as otherwise provided in this section, while in the possession of the custodian, no documentary material, tangible things, reports or answers to questions, and transcripts of oral testimony shall be available for examination by any individual other than a duly authorized officer or employee of the Commission without the consent of the person who produced the material, things, or transcripts. Nothing in this section is intended to prevent disclosure to either House of the Congress or to any committee or subcommittee of the Congress, except that the Commission immediately shall notify the owner or provider of any such information of a request for information designated as confidential by the owner or provider.

(D) While in the possession of the custodian and under such reasonable terms and conditions as the Commission shall prescribe—

(i) documentary material, tangible things, or written reports shall be available for examination by the person who produced the material, or by any duly authorized representative of such person; and

(ii) answers to questions in writing and transcripts of oral testimony shall be available for examination by the person who produced the testimony or by his attorney.

(4) Whenever the Commission has instituted a proceeding against a person, partnership, or corporation, the custodian may deliver to any officer or employee of the Commission documentary material, tangible things, written reports or answers to questions, and transcripts of oral testimony for official use in connection with such proceeding. Upon the completion of the proceeding, the officer or employee shall return to the custodian any such material so delivered which has not been received into the record of the proceeding.

(5) if any documentary material, tangible things, written reports or answers to questions, and transcripts of oral testimony have been produced in the course of any investigation by any person pursuant to compulsory process and—

(A) any proceeding arising out of the investigation has been completed; or

(B) no proceeding in which the material may be used has been commenced within a reasonable time after completion of the examination and analysis of all such material and other information assembled in the course of the investigation;

then the custodian shall, upon written request of the person who produced the material, return to the person any such material which has not been received into the record of any such proceeding (other than copies of such material made by the custodian pursuant to paragraph (3)(B)).

(6) The custodian of any documentary material, written reports or answers to questions, and transcripts of oral testimony may deliver to any officers or employees of appropriate Federal law enforcement agencies, in response to a written request, copies of such material for use in connection with an investigation or proceeding under the jurisdiction of any such agency.   The custodian of any tangible things may make such things available for inspection to such persons on the same basis.   Such materials shall not be made available to any such agency until the custodian receives certification of any officer of such agency that such information will be maintained in confidence and will be used only for official law enforcement purposes.   Such documentary material, results of inspections of tangible things, written reports or answers to questions, and transcripts of oral testimony may be used by any officer or employee of such agency only in such manner and subject to such conditions as apply to the Commission under this section.   The custodian may make such materials available to any State law enforcement agency upon the prior certification of any officer of such agency that such information will be maintained in confidence and will be used only for official law enforcement purposes. The custodian may make such material available to any foreign law enforcement agency upon the prior certification of an appropriate official of any such foreign law enforcement agency, either by a prior agreement or memorandum of understanding with the Commission or by other written certification, that such material will be maintained in confidence and will be used only for official law enforcement purposes, if—

(A) the foreign law enforcement agency has set forth a bona fide legal basis for its authority to maintain the material in confidence;

(B) the materials are to be used for purposes of investigating, or engaging in enforcement proceedings related to, possible violations of—

(i) foreign laws prohibiting fraudulent or deceptive commercial practices, or other practices substantially similar to practices prohibited by any law administered by the Commission;

(ii) a law administered by the Commission, if disclosure of the material would further a Commission investigation or enforcement proceeding; or

(iii) with the approval of the Attorney General, other foreign criminal laws, if such foreign criminal laws are offenses defined in or covered by a criminal mutual legal assistance treaty in force between the government of the United States and the foreign law enforcement agency's government;

(C) the appropriate Federal banking agency (as defined in section 1813(q) of Title 12) or, in the case of a Federal credit union, the National Credit Union Administration, has given its prior approval if the materials to be provided under subparagraph (B) are requested by the foreign law enforcement agency for the purpose of investigating, or engaging in enforcement proceedings based on, possible violations of law by a bank, a savings and loan institution described in section 57a(f)(3) of this title, or a Federal credit union described in section 57a(f)(4) of this title; and

(D) the foreign law enforcement agency is not from a foreign state that the Secretary of State has determined, in accordance with section 2405(j) of the Appendix to Title 50, has repeatedly provided support for acts of international terrorism, unless and until such determination is rescinded pursuant to section 2405(j)(4) of the Appendix to Title 50.

Nothing in the preceding sentence authorizes the disclosure of material obtained in connection with the administration of the Federal antitrust laws or foreign antitrust laws (as defined in paragraphs (5) and (7), respectively, of section 6211 of this title to any officer or employee of a foreign law enforcement agency.

(7) In the event of the death, disability, or separation from service in the Commission of the custodian of any documentary material, tangible things, written reports or answers to questions, and transcripts of oral testimony produced under any demand issued under this subchapter, or the official relief of the custodian from responsibility for the custody and control of such material, the Commission promptly shall—

(A) designate under paragraph (2)(A) another duly authorized agent to serve as custodian of such material; and

(B) transmit in writing to the person who produced the material or testimony notice as to the identity and address of the successor so designated. Any successor designated under paragraph (2)(A) as a result of the requirements of this paragraph shall have (with regard to the material involved) all duties and responsibilities imposed by this section upon his predecessor in office with regard to such material, except that he shall not be held responsible for any default or dereliction which occurred before his designation.

(c) Information considered confidential.

(1) All information reported to or otherwise obtained by the Commission which is not subject to the requirements of subsection (b) of this section shall be considered confidential when so marked by the person supplying the information and shall not be disclosed, except in accordance with the procedures established in paragraph (2) and paragraph (3).

(2) If the Commission determines that a document marked confidential by the person supplying it may be disclosed because it is not a trade secret or commercial or financial information which is obtained from any person and which is privileged or confidential, within the meaning of section 46(f) of this title, then the Commission shall notify such person in writing that the Commission intends to disclose the document at a date not less than 10 days after the date of receipt of notification.

(3) Any person receiving such notification may, if he believes disclosure of the document would cause disclosure of a trade secret, or commercial or financial information which is obtained from any person and which is privileged or confidential, within the meaning of section 46(f) of this title, before the date set for release of the document, bring an action in the district court of the United States for the district within which the documents are located or in the United States District Court for the District of Columbia to restrain disclosure of the document. Any person receiving such notification may file with the appropriate district court or court of appeals of the United States, as appropriate, an application for a stay of disclosure. The documents shall not be disclosed until the court has ruled on the application for a stay.

(d) Particular disclosures allowed.

(1) The provisions of subsection (c) of this section shall not be construed to prohibit—

(A) the disclosure of information to either House of the Congress or to any committee or subcommittee of the Congress, except that the Commission immediately shall notify the owner or provider of any such information of a request for information designated as confidential by the owner or provider;

(B) the disclosure of the results of any investigation or study carried out or prepared by the Commission, except that no information shall be identified nor shall information be disclosed in such a manner as to disclose a trade secret of any person supplying the trade secret, or to disclose any commercial or financial information which is obtained from any person and which is privileged or confidential;

(C) the disclosure of relevant and material information in Commission adjudicative proceedings or in judicial proceedings to which the Commission is a party; or

(D) the disclosure to a Federal agency of disaggregated information obtained in accordance with section 3512 of Title 44, except that the recipient agency shall use such disaggregated information for economic, statistical, or policymaking purposes only, and shall not disclose such information in an individually identifiable form.

(2) Any disclosure of relevant and material information in Commission adjudicative proceedings or in judicial proceedings to which the Commission is a party shall be governed by the rules of the Commission for adjudicative proceedings or by court rules or orders, except that the rules of the Commission shall not be amended in a manner inconsistent with the purposes of this section.

(e) Effect on other statutory provisions limiting disclosure. Nothing in this section shall supersede any statutory provision which expressly prohibits or limits particular disclosures by the Commission, or which authorizes disclosures to any other Federal agency.

(f) Exemption from disclosure.

(1) In general. Any material which is received by the Commission in any investigation, a purpose of which is to determine whether any person may have violated any provision of the laws administered by the Commission, and which is provided pursuant to any compulsory process under this subchapter or which is provided voluntarily in place of such compulsory process shall not be required to be disclosed under section 552 of Title 5, or any other provision of law, except as provided in paragraph (2)(B) of this section.

(2) Material obtained from a foreign source.

(A) In general. Except as provided in subparagraph (B) of this paragraph, the Commission shall not be required to disclose under section 552 of Title 5, or any other provision of law—

(i) any material obtained from a foreign law enforcement agency or other foreign government agency, if the foreign law enforcement agency or other foreign government agency has requested confidential treatment, or has precluded such disclosure under other use limitations, as a condition of providing the material;

(ii) any material reflecting a consumer complaint obtained from any other foreign source, if that foreign source supplying the material has requested confidential treatment as a condition of providing the material; or

(iii) any material reflecting a consumer complaint submitted to a Commission reporting mechanism sponsored in part by foreign law enforcement agencies or other foreign government agencies.

(B) Savings provision. Nothing in this subsection shall authorize the Commission to withhold information from the Congress or prevent the Commission from complying with an order of a court of the United States in an action commenced by the United States or the Commission.

* * *

§ 57b-3. Rulemaking process

(a) Definitions. For purposes of this section:

(1) The term "rule" means any rule promulgated by the Commission under section 46 or section 57a of this title, except that such term does not include interpretive rules, rules involving Commission management or personnel, general statements of policy, or rules relating to Commission organization, procedure, or practice. Such term does not include any amendment to a rule unless the Commission—

(A) estimates that such amendment will have an annual effect on the national economy of $100,000,000 or more;

(B) estimates that such amendment will cause a substantial change in the cost or price of goods or services which are used extensively by particular industries, which are supplied extensively in particular geographic regions, or which are acquired in significant quantities by the Federal Government, or by State or local governments; or

(C) otherwise determines that such amendment will have a significant impact upon persons subject to regulation under such amendment and upon consumers.

(2) The term "rulemaking" means any Commission process for formulating or amending a rule.

(b) Notice of proposed rulemaking; regulatory analysis; contents; issuance.

(1) In any case in which the Commission publishes notice of a proposed rulemaking, the Commission shall issue a preliminary regulatory analysis relating to the proposed rule involved. Each preliminary regulatory analysis shall contain—

(A) a concise statement of the need for, and the objectives of, the proposed rule;

(B) a description of any reasonable alternatives to the proposed rule which may accomplish the stated objective of the rule in a manner consistent with applicable law; and

(C) for the proposed rule, and for each of the alternatives described in the analysis, a preliminary analysis of the projected benefits and any adverse economic effects and any other effects, and of the effectiveness of the proposed rule and each alternative in meeting the stated objectives of the proposed rule.

(2) In any case in which the Commission promulgates a final rule, the Commission shall issue a final regulatory analysis relating to the final rule. Each final regulatory analysis shall contain—

(A) a concise statement of the need for, and the objectives of, the final rule;

(B) a description of any alternatives to the final rule which were considered by the Commission;

(C) an analysis of the projected benefits and any adverse economic effects and any other effects of the final rule;

(D) an explanation of the reasons for the determination of the Commission that the final rule will attain its objectives in a manner consistent with applicable law and the reasons the particular alternative was chosen; and

(E) a summary of any significant issues raised by the comments submitted during the public comment period in response to the preliminary regulatory analysis, and a summary of the assessment by the Commission of such issues.

(3)(A) In order to avoid duplication or waste, the Commission is authorized to—

(i) consider a series of closely related rules as one rule for purposes of this subsection; and

(ii) whenever appropriate, incorporate any data or analysis contained in a regulatory analysis issued under this subsection in the statement of basis and purpose to accompany any rule promulgated under section 57a(a)(1)(B) of this title, and incorporate by reference in any preliminary or final regulatory analysis information contained in a notice of proposed rulemaking or a statement of basis and purpose.

(B) The Commission shall include, in each notice of proposed rulemaking and in each publication of a final rule, a statement of the manner in which the public may obtain copies of the preliminary and final regulatory analyses. The Commission may charge a reasonable fee for the copying and mailing of regulatory analyses. The regulatory analyses shall be furnished without charge or at a reduced charge if the Commission determines that waiver or reduction of the fee is in the public interests because furnishing the information primarily benefits the general public.

(4) The Commission is authorized to delay the completion of any of the requirements established in this subsection by publishing in the Federal Register, not later than the date of publication of the final rule involved, a finding that the final rule is being promulgated in response to an emergency which makes timely compliance with the provisions of this subsection impracticable. Such publication shall include a statement of the reasons for such finding.

(5) The requirements of this subsection shall not be construed to alter in any manner the substantive standards applicable to any action by the Commission, or the procedural standards otherwise applicable to such action.

(c) Judicial review.

(1) The contents and adequacy of any regulatory analysis prepared or issued by the Commission under this section, including the adequacy of any procedure involved in such preparation or issuance, shall not be subject to any judicial review in any court, except that a court, upon review of a rule pursuant to section 57a(e) of this title, may set aside such rule if the Commission has failed entirely to prepare a regulatory analysis.

(2) Except as specified in paragraph (1), no Commission action may be invalidated, remanded, or otherwise affected by any court on account of any failure to comply with the requirements of this section.

(3) The provisions of this subsection do not alter the substantive or procedural standards otherwise applicable to judicial review of any action by the Commission.

(d) Regulatory agenda; contents; publication dates in Federal Register.

(1) The Commission shall publish at least semiannually a regulatory agenda. Each regulatory agenda shall contain a list of rules which the Commission intends to propose or promulgate during the 12-month period following the publication of the agenda. On the first Monday in October of each year, the Commission shall publish in the Federal Register a schedule showing the dates during the current fiscal year on which the semiannual regulatory agenda of the Commission will be published.

(2) For each rule listed in a regulatory agenda, the Commission shall—

(A) describe the rule;

(B) state the objectives of and the legal basis for the rule; and

(C) specify any dates established or anticipated by the Commission for taking action, including dates for advance notice of proposed rulemaking, notices of proposed rulemaking, and final action by the Commission.

(3) Each regulatory agenda shall state the name, office address, and office telephone number of the Commission officer or employee responsible for responding to any inquiry relating to each rule listed.

(4) The Commission shall not propose or promulgate a rule which was not listed on a regulatory agenda unless the Commission publishes with the rule an explanation of the reasons the rule was omitted from such agenda.

ETHICS IN GOVERNMENT ACT

18 U.S.C. § 207

§ 207. Restrictions on former officers, employees, and elected officials of the executive and legislative branches

(a) Restrictions on all officers and employees of the executive branch and certain other agencies.—

(1) Permanent restrictions on representation on particular matters.—Any person who is an officer or employee (including any special Government employee) of the executive branch of the United States (including any independent agency of the United States), or of the District of Columbia, and who, after the termination of his or her service or employment with the United States or the District of Columbia, knowingly makes, with the intent to influence, any communication to or appearance before any officer or employee of any department, agency, court, or court-martial of the United States or the District of Columbia, on behalf of any other person (except the United States or the District of Columbia) in connection with a particular matter—

(A) in which the United States or the District of Columbia is a party or has a direct and substantial interest,

(B) in which the person participated personally and substantially as such officer or employee, and

(C) which involved a specific party or specific parties at the time of such participation,

shall be punished as provided in section 216 of this title.

(2) Two-year restrictions concerning particular matters under official responsibility.—Any person subject to the restrictions contained in paragraph (1) who, within 2 years after the termination of his or her service or employment with the United States or the District of Columbia, knowingly makes, with the intent to influence, any communication to or appearance before any officer or employee of any department, agency, court, or court-martial of the United States or the District of Columbia, on behalf of any other person (except the United States or the District of Columbia), in connection with a particular matter—

(A) in which the United States or the District of Columbia is a party or has a direct and substantial interest,

(B) which such person knows or reasonably should know was actually pending under his or her official responsibility as such officer or employee within a period of 1 year before the termination of his or her service or employment with the United States or the District of Columbia, and

(C) which involved a specific party or specific parties at the time it was so pending,

shall be punished as provided in section 216 of this title.

(3) Clarification of restrictions.—The restrictions contained in paragraphs (1) and (2) shall apply—

(A) in the case of an officer or employee of the executive branch of the United States (including any independent agency), only with respect to communications to or appearances before any officer or employee of any department, agency, court, or court-martial of the United States on behalf of any other person (except the United States), and only with respect to a matter in which the United States is a party or has a direct and substantial interest; and

(B) in the case of an officer or employee of the District of Columbia, only with respect to communications to or appearances before any officer or employee of any department, agency, or court of the District of Columbia on behalf of any other person (except the District of Columbia), and only with respect to a matter in which the District of Columbia is a party or has a direct and substantial interest.

(b) One-year restrictions on aiding or advising.—

(1) In general.—Any person who is a former officer or employee of the executive branch of the United States (including any independent agency) and is subject to the restrictions contained in subsection (a)(1), or any person who is a former officer or employee of the legislative branch or a former Member of Congress, who personally and substantially participated in any ongoing trade or treaty negotiation on behalf of the United States within the 1-year period preceding the date on which his or her service or employment with the United States terminated, and who had access to information concerning such trade or treaty negotiation which is exempt from disclosure under section 552 of title 5, which is so designated by the appropriate department or agency, and which the person knew or should have known was so designated, shall not, on the basis of that information, knowingly represent, aid, or advise any other person (except the United States) concerning such ongoing trade or treaty negotiation for a period of 1 year after his or her service or employment with the United States terminates. Any person who violates this subsection shall be punished as provided in section 216 of this title.

(2) Definition.—For purposes of this paragraph—

(A) the term "trade negotiation" means negotiations which the President determines to undertake to enter into a trade agreement pursuant to section 1102 of the Omnibus Trade and Competitiveness Act of 1988, and does not include any action taken before that determination is made; and

(B) the term "treaty" means an international agreement made by the President that requires the advice and consent of the Senate.

(c) One-year restrictions on certain senior personnel of the executive branch and independent agencies.—

(1) Restrictions.—In addition to the restrictions set forth in subsections (a) and (b), any person who is an officer or employee (including any special Government employee) of the executive branch of the United States (including an independent agency), who is referred to in paragraph (2), and who, within 1 year after the termination of his or her service or employment as such officer or employee, knowingly makes, with the intent to influence, any communication to or appearance before any officer or employee of the department or agency in which such person served within 1 year before such termination, on behalf of any other person (except the United States), in connection with any matter on which such person seeks official action by any officer or employee of such department or agency, shall be punished as provided in section 216 of this title.

(2) Persons to whom restrictions apply.—

(A) Paragraph (1) shall apply to a person (other than a person subject to the restrictions of subsection (d))—

(i) employed at a rate of pay specified in or fixed according to subchapter II of chapter 53 of title 5,

(ii) employed in a position which is not referred to in clause (i) and for which that person is paid at a rate of basic pay which is equal to or greater than 86.5 percent of the rate of basic pay for level II of the Executive Schedule, or, for a period of 2 years following the enactment of the National Defense Authorization Act for Fiscal Year 2004, a person who, on the day prior to the enactment of that Act, was employed in a position which is not referred to in clause (i) and for which the rate of basic pay, exclusive of any locality-based pay adjustment under section 5304 or section 5304a of title 5, was equal to or greater than the rate of basic pay payable for level 5 of the Senior Executive Service on the day prior to the enactment of that Act,

(iii) appointed by the President to a position under section 105(a)(2)(B) of title 3 or by the Vice President to a position under section 106(a)(1)(B) of title 3,

(iv) employed in a position which is held by an active duty commissioned officer of the uniformed services who is serving in a grade or rank for which the pay grade (as specified in section 201 of title 37) is pay grade O-7 or above; or

(v) assigned from a private sector organization to an agency under chapter 37 of title 5.

(B) Paragraph (1) shall not apply to a special Government employee who serves less than 60 days in the 1-year period before his or her service or employment as such employee terminates.

(C) At the request of a department or agency, the Director of the Office of Government Ethics may waive the restrictions contained in paragraph (1) with respect to any position, or category of positions, referred to in clause (ii) or (iv) of subparagraph (A), in such department or agency if the Director determines that—

(i) the imposition of the restrictions with respect to such position or positions would create an undue hardship on the department or agency in obtaining qualified personnel to fill such position or positions, and

(ii) granting the waiver would not create the potential for use of undue influence or unfair advantage.

(d) Restrictions on very senior personnel of the executive branch and independent agencies.—

(1) Restrictions.—In addition to the restrictions set forth in subsections (a) and (b), any person who—

(A) serves in the position of Vice President of the United States,

(B) is employed in a position in the executive branch of the United States (including any independent agency) at a rate of pay payable for level I of the Executive Schedule or employed in a position in the Executive Office of the President at a rate of pay payable for level II of the Executive Schedule, or

(C) is appointed by the President to a position under section 105(a)(2)(A) of title 3 or by the Vice President to a position under section 106(a)(1)(A) of title 3, and who, within 1 year after the termination of that person's service in that position, knowingly makes, with the intent to influence, any communication to or appearance before any person described in paragraph (2), on behalf of any other person (except the United States), in connection with any matter on which such person seeks official action by any officer or employee of the executive branch of the United States, shall be punished as provided in section 216 of this title.

(2) Persons who may not be contacted.—The persons referred to in paragraph (1) with respect to appearances or communications by a person in a position described in subparagraph (A), (B), or (C) of paragraph (1) are—

    (A) any officer or employee of any department or agency in which such person served in such position within a period of 1 year before such person's service or employment with the United States Government terminated, and

    (B) any person appointed to a position in the executive branch which is listed in sections 5312, 5313, 5314, 5315, or 5316 of title 5.

(e) Restrictions on Members of Congress and officers and employees of the legislative branch.—

    (1) Members of Congress and elected officers.—

        (A) Any person who is a Member of Congress or an elected officer of either House of Congress and who, within 1 year after that person leaves office, knowingly makes, with the intent to influence, any communication to or appearance before any of the persons described in subparagraph (B) or (C), on behalf of any other person (except the United States) in connection with any matter on which such former Member of Congress or elected officer seeks action by a Member, officer, or employee of either House of Congress, in his or her official capacity, shall be punished as provided in section 216 of this title.

        (B) The persons referred to in subparagraph (A) with respect to appearances or communications by a former Member of Congress are any Member, officer, or employee of either House of Congress, and any employee of any other legislative office of the Congress.

        (C) The persons referred to in subparagraph (A) with respect to appearances or communications by a former elected officer are any Member, officer, or employee of the House of Congress in which the elected officer served.

    (2) Personal staff.—

        (A) Any person who is an employee of a Senator or an employee of a Member of the House of Representatives and who, within 1 year after the termination of that employment, knowingly makes, with the intent to influence, any communication to or appearance before any of the persons described in subparagraph (B), on behalf of any other person (except the United States) in connection with any matter on which such former employee seeks action by a Member, officer, or employee of either House of Congress, in his or her official capacity, shall be punished as provided in section 216 of this title.

(B) The persons referred to in subparagraph (A) with respect to appearances or communications by a person who is a former employee are the following:

(i) the Senator or Member of the House of Representatives for whom that person was an employee; and

(ii) any employee of that Senator or Member of the House of Representatives.

(3) Committee staff.—Any person who is an employee of a committee of Congress and who, within 1 year after the termination of that person's employment on such committee, knowingly makes, with the intent to influence, any communication to or appearance before any person who is a Member or an employee of that committee or who was a Member of the committee in the year immediately prior to the termination of such person's employment by the committee, on behalf of any other person (except the United States) in connection with any matter on which such former employee seeks action by a Member, officer, or employee of either House of Congress, in his or her official capacity, shall be punished as provided in section 216 of this title.

(4) Leadership staff.—

(A) Any person who is an employee on the leadership staff of the House of Representatives or an employee on the leadership staff of the Senate and who, within 1 year after the termination of that person's employment on such staff, knowingly makes, with the intent to influence, any communication to or appearance before any of the persons described in subparagraph (B), on behalf of any other person (except the United States) in connection with any matter on which such former employee seeks action by a Member, officer, or employee of either House of Congress, in his or her official capacity, shall be punished as provided in section 216 of this title.

(B) The persons referred to in subparagraph (A) with respect to appearances or communications by a former employee are the following:

(i) in the case of a former employee on the leadership staff of the House of Representatives, those persons are any Member of the leadership of the House of Representatives and any employee on the leadership staff of the House of Representatives; and

(ii) in the case of a former employee on the leadership staff of the Senate, those persons are any Member of the leadership of the Senate and any employee on the leadership staff of the Senate.

(5) Other legislative offices.—

(A) Any person who is an employee of any other legislative office of the Congress and who, within 1 year after the termination of that persons's employment in such office, knowingly makes, with the intent to influence, any communication to or appearance before any of the persons described in subparagraph (B), on behalf of any other person (except the United States) in connection with any matter on which such former employee seeks action by any officer or employee of such office, in his or her official capacity, shall be punished as provided in section 216 of this title.

(B) The persons referred to in subparagraph (A) with respect to appearances or communications by a former employee are the employees and officers of the former legislative office of the Congress of the former employee.

(6) Limitation on restrictions.—

(A) The restrictions contained in paragraphs (2), (3), and (4) apply only to acts by a former employee who, for at least 60 days, in the aggregate, during the 1-year period before that former employee's service as such employee terminated, was paid a rate of basic pay equal to or greater than an amount which is 75 percent of the basic rate of pay payable for a Member of the House of Congress in which such employee was employed.

(B) The restrictions contained in paragraph (5) apply only to acts by a former employee who, for at least 60 days, in the aggregate, during the 1-year period before that former employee's service as such employee terminated, was employed in a position for which the rate of basic pay, exclusive of any locality-based pay adjustment under section 5302 of title 5 (or any comparable adjustment pursuant to interim authority of the President), is equal to or greater than the basic rate of pay payable for level V of the Executive Schedule.

(7) Definitions.—As used in this subsection—

(A) the term "committee of Congress" includes standing committees, joint committees, and select committees;

(B) a person is an employee of a House of Congress if that person is an employee of the Senate or an employee of the House of Representatives;

(C) the term "employee of the House of Representatives" means an employee of a Member of the House of Representatives, an employee of a committee of the House of Representatives, an employee of a joint committee of the Congress whose pay is disbursed by the Clerk of the House of Representatives, and an employee on the leadership staff of the House of Representatives;

(D) the term "employee of the Senate" means an employee of a Senator, an employee of a committee of the Senate, an employee of a joint committee of the Congress whose pay is disbursed by the Secretary of the Senate, and an employee on the leadership staff of the Senate;

(E) a person is an employee of a Member of the House of Representatives if that person is an employee of a Member of the House of Representatives under the clerk hire allowance;

(F) a person is an employee of a Senator if that person is an employee in a position in the office of a Senator;

(G) the term "employee of any other legislative office of the Congress" means an officer or employee of the Architect of the Capitol, the United States Botanic Garden, the Government Accountability Office, the Government Printing Office, the Library of Congress, the Office of Technology Assessment, the Congressional Budget Office, the Copyright Royalty Tribunal, the United States Capitol Police, and any other agency, entity, or office in the legislative branch not covered by paragraph (1), (2), (3), or (4) of this subsection;

(H) the term "employee on the leadership staff of the House of Representatives" means an employee of the office of a Member of the leadership of the House of Representatives described in subparagraph (L), and any elected minority employee of the House of Representatives;

(I) the term "employee on the leadership staff of the Senate" means an employee of the office of a Member of the leadership of the Senate described in subparagraph (M);

(J) the term "Member of Congress" means a Senator or a Member of the House of Representatives;

(K) the term "Member of the House of Representatives" means a Representative in, or a Delegate or Resident Commissioner to, the Congress;

(L) the term "Member of the leadership of the House of Representatives" means the Speaker, majority leader, minority leader, majority whip, minority whip, chief deputy majority whip, chief deputy minority whip, chairman of the Democratic Steering Committee, chairman and vice chairman of the Democratic Caucus, chairman, vice chairman, and secretary of the Republican Conference, chairman of the Republican Research Committee, and chairman of the Republican Policy Committee, of the House of Representatives (or any similar position created on or after the effective date set forth in section 102(a) of the Ethics Reform Act of 1989);

(M) the term "Member of the leadership of the Senate" means the Vice President, and the President pro tempore, Deputy President pro tempore, majority leader, minority leader, majority whip, minority whip, chairman and secretary of the Conference of the Majority, chairman and secretary of the Conference of the Minority, chairman and co-chairman of the Majority Policy Committee, and chairman of the Minority Policy Committee, of the Senate (or any similar position created on or after the effective date set forth in section 102(a) of the Ethics Reform Act of 1989).

(f) Restrictions relating to foreign entities.—

(1) Restrictions.—Any person who is subject to the restrictions contained in subsection (c), (d), or (e) and who knowingly, within 1 year after leaving the position, office, or employment referred to in such subsection—

(A) represents a foreign entity before any officer or employee of any department or agency of the United States with the intent to influence a decision of such officer or employee in carrying out his or her official duties, or

(B) aids or advises a foreign entity with the intent to influence a decision of any officer or employee of any department or agency of the United States, in carrying out his or her official duties, shall be punished as provided in section 216 of this title.

(2) Special rule for Trade Representative.—With respect to a person who is the United States Trade Representative or Deputy United States Trade Representative, the restrictions described in paragraph (1) shall apply to representing, aiding, or advising foreign entities at any time after the termination of that person's service as the United States Trade Representative.

(3) Definition.—For purposes of this subsection, the term "foreign entity" means the government of a foreign country as defined in section 1(e) of the Foreign Agents Registration Act of 1938, as amended, or a foreign political party as defined in section 1(f) of that Act.

(g) Special rules for detailees.—For purposes of this section, a person who is detailed from one department, agency, or other entity to another department, agency, or other entity shall, during the period such person is detailed, be deemed to be an officer or employee of both departments, agencies, or such entities.

(h) Designations of separate statutory agencies and bureaus.—

(1) Designations.—For purposes of subsection (c) and except as provided in paragraph (2), whenever the Director of the Office of Government Ethics determines that an agency or bureau within a department or agency in the executive branch exercises functions which are distinct and separate from the remaining functions of the department or agency and that there exists no potential for use of undue influence or unfair advantage based on past Government service, the Director shall by rule designate such agency or bureau as a separate department or agency. On an annual basis the Director of the Office of Government Ethics shall review the designations and determinations made under this subparagraph and, in consultation with the department or agency concerned, make such additions and deletions as are necessary. Departments and agencies shall cooperate to the fullest extent with the Director of the Office of Government Ethics in the exercise of his or her responsibilities under this paragraph.

(2) Inapplicability of designations.—No agency or bureau within the Executive Office of the President may be designated under paragraph (1) as a separate department or agency. No designation under paragraph (1) shall apply to persons referred to in subsection (c)(2)(A)(i) or (iii).

(i) Definitions.—For purposes of this section—

(1) the term "officer or employee", when used to describe the person to whom a communication is made or before whom an appearance is made, with the intent to influence, shall include—

(A) in subsections (a), (c), and (d), the President and the Vice President; and

(B) in subsection (f), the President, the Vice President, and Members of Congress;

(2) the term "participated" means an action taken as an officer or employee through decision, approval, disapproval, recommendation, the rendering of advice, investigation, or other such action; and

(3) the term "particular matter" includes any investigation, application, request for a ruling or determination, rulemaking, contract, controversy, claim, charge, accusation, arrest, or judicial or other proceeding.

(j) Exceptions.—

(1) Official government duties.—The restrictions contained in this section shall not apply to acts done in carrying out official duties on behalf of the United States or the District of Columbia or as an elected official of a State or local government.

(2) State and local governments and institutions, hospitals, and organizations.—The restrictions contained in subsections (c), (d),

and (e) shall not apply to acts done in carrying out official duties as an employee of—

> (A) an agency or instrumentality of a State or local government if the appearance, communication, or representation is on behalf of such government, or

> (B) an accredited, degree-granting institution of higher education, as defined in section 101 of the Higher Education Act of 1965, or a hospital or medical research organization, exempted and defined under section 501(c)(3) of the Internal Revenue Code of 1986, if the appearance, communication, or representation is on behalf of such institution, hospital, or organization.

(3) International organizations.—The restrictions contained in this section shall not apply to an appearance or communication on behalf of, or advice or aid to, an international organization in which the United States participates, if the Secretary of State certifies in advance that such activity is in the interests of the United States.

(4) Special knowledge.—The restrictions contained in subsections (c), (d), and (e) shall not prevent an individual from making or providing a statement, which is based on the individual's own special knowledge in the particular area that is the subject of the statement, if no compensation is thereby received.

(5) Exception for scientific or technological information—The restrictions contained in subsections (a), (c), and (d) shall not apply with respect to the making of communications solely for the purpose of furnishing scientific or technological information, if such communications are made under procedures acceptable to the department or agency concerned or if the head of the department or agency concerned with the particular matter, in consultation with the Director of the Office of Government Ethics, makes a certification, published in the Federal Register, that the former officer or employee has outstanding qualifications in a scientific, technological, or other technical discipline, and is acting with respect to a particular matter which requires such qualifications, and that the national interest would be served by the participation of the former officer or employee. For purposes of this paragraph, the term "officer or employee" includes the Vice President.

(6) Exception for testimony.—Nothing in this section shall prevent an individual from giving testimony under oath, or from making statements required to be made under penalty of perjury. Notwithstanding the preceding sentence—

> (A) a former officer or employee of the executive branch of the United States (including any independent agency) who is subject to the restrictions contained in subsection (a)(1) with respect to a particular matter may not, except pursuant to court

order, serve as an expert witness for any other person (except the United States) in that matter; and

(B) a former officer or employee of the District of Columbia who is subject to the restrictions contained in subsection (a)(1) with respect to a particular matter may not, except pursuant to court order, serve as an expert witness for any other person (except the District of Columbia) in that matter.

(k)(1)(A) The President may grant a waiver of a restriction imposed by this section to any officer or employee described in paragraph (2) if the President determines and certifies in writing that it is in the public interest to grant the waiver and that the services of the officer or employee are critically needed for the benefit of the Federal Government. Not more than 25 officers and employees currently employed by the Federal Government at any one time may have been granted waivers under this paragraph.

(B)(i) A waiver granted under this paragraph to any person shall apply only with respect to activities engaged in by that person after that person's Federal Government employment is terminated and only to that person's employment at a Government-owned, contractor operated entity with which the person served as an officer or employee immediately before the person's Federal Government employment began.

(ii) Notwithstanding clause (i), a waiver granted under this paragraph to any person who was an officer or employee of Lawrence Livermore National Laboratory, Los Alamos National Laboratory, or Sandia National Laboratory immediately before the person's Federal Government employment began shall apply to that person's employment by any such national laboratory after the person's employment by the Federal Government is terminated.

(2) Waivers under paragraph (1) may be granted only to civilian officers and employees of the executive branch, other than officers and employees in the Executive Office of the President.

(3) A certification under paragraph (1) shall take effect upon its publication in the Federal Register and shall identify—

(A) the officer or employee covered by the waiver by name and by position, and

(B) the reasons for granting the waiver. A copy of the certification shall also be provided to the Director of the Office of Government Ethics.

(4) The President may not delegate the authority provided by this subsection.

(5)(A) Each person granted a waiver under this subsection shall prepare reports, in accordance with subparagraph (B), stating whether the person has engaged in activities otherwise prohibited by this section for each six-month period described in subparagraph (B), and if so, what those activities were.

(B) A report under subparagraph (A) shall cover each six-month period beginning on the date of the termination of the person's Federal Government employment (with respect to which the waiver under this subsection was granted) and ending two years after that date. Such report shall be filed with the President and the Director of the Office of Government Ethics not later than 60 days after the end of the six-month period covered by the report. All reports filed with the Director under this paragraph shall be made available for public inspection and copying.

(C) If a person fails to file any report in accordance with subparagraphs (A) and (B), the President shall revoke the waiver and shall notify the person of the revocation. The revocation shall take effect upon the person's receipt of the notification and shall remain in effect until the report is filed.

(D) Any person who is granted a waiver under this subsection shall be ineligible for appointment in the civil service unless all reports required of such person by subparagraphs (A) and (B) have been filed.

(E) As used in this subsection, the term "civil service" has the meaning given that term in section 2101 of title 5.

(*l*) Contract advice by former details.—Whoever, being an employee of a private sector organization assigned to an agency under chapter 37 of title 5, within one year after the end of that assignment, knowingly represents or aids, counsels, or assists in representing any other person (except the United States) in connection with any contract with that agency shall be punished as provided in section 216 of this title.

NATIONAL LABOR RELATIONS ACT

TITLE 29. LABOR
CHAPTER 7—LABOR–MANAGEMENT RELATIONS
SUBCHAPTER II—NATIONAL LABOR RELATIONS

§ 151. Findings and declaration of policy

The denial by some employers of the right of employees to organize and the refusal by some employers to accept the procedure of collective bargaining lead to strikes and other forms of industrial strife or unrest, which have the intent or the necessary effect of burdening or obstructing commerce by (a) impairing the efficiency, safety, or operation of the instrumentalities of commerce; (b) occurring in the current of commerce; (c) materially affecting, restraining, or controlling the flow of raw materials or manufactured or processed goods from or into the channels of commerce, or the prices of such materials or goods in commerce; or (d) causing diminution of employment and wages in such volume as substantially to impair or disrupt the market for goods flowing from or into the channels of commerce.

The inequality of bargaining power between employees who do not possess full freedom of association or actual liberty of contract, and employers who are organized in the corporate or other forms of ownership association substantially burdens and affects the flow of commerce, and tends to aggravate recurrent business depressions, by depressing wage rates and the purchasing power of wage earners in industry and by preventing the stabilization of competitive wage rates and working conditions within and between industries.

Experience has proved that protection by law of the right of employees to organize and bargain collectively safeguards commerce from injury, impairment, or interruption, and promotes the flow of commerce by removing certain recognized sources of industrial strife and unrest, by encouraging practices fundamental to the friendly adjustment of industrial disputes arising out of differences as to wages, hours, or other working conditions, and by restoring equality of bargaining power between employers and employees.

Experience has further demonstrated that certain practices by some labor organizations, their officers, and members have the intent or the necessary effect of burdening or obstructing commerce by preventing the free flow of goods in such commerce through strikes and other forms of industrial unrest or through concerted activities which impair the interest of the public in the free flow of such commerce. The elimination of such practices is a necessary condition to the assurance of the rights herein guaranteed.

It is hereby declared to be the policy of the United States to eliminate the causes of certain substantial obstructions to the free flow of commerce and to mitigate and eliminate these obstructions when they have occurred by encouraging the practice and procedure of collective bargaining and by protecting the exercise by workers of full freedom of association, self-organization, and designation of representatives of their own choosing, for the purpose of negotiating the terms and conditions of their employment or other mutual aid or protection.

§ 152. Definitions

When used in this subchapter—

(1) The term "person" includes one or more individuals, labor organizations, partnerships, associations, corporations, legal representatives, trustees, trustees in cases under Title 11, or receivers.

(2) The term "employer" includes any person acting as an agent of an employer, directly or indirectly, but shall not include the United States or any wholly owned Government corporation, or any Federal Reserve Bank, or any State or political subdivision thereof, or any person subject to the Railway Labor Act [45 U.S.C. § 151 *et seq.*], as amended from time to time, or any labor organization (other than when acting as an employer), or anyone acting in the capacity of officer or agent of such labor organization.

(3) The term "employee" shall include any employee, and shall not be limited to the employees of a particular employer, unless this subchapter explicitly states otherwise, and shall include any individual whose work has ceased as a consequence of, or in connection

with, any current labor dispute or because of any unfair labor practice, and who has not obtained any other regular and substantially equivalent employment, but shall not include any individual employed as an agricultural laborer, or in the domestic service of any family or person at his home, or any individual employed by his parent or spouse, or any individual having the status of an independent contractor, or any individual employed as a supervisor, or any individual employed by an employer subject to the Railway Labor Act, as amended from time to time, or by any other person who is not an employer as herein defined.

(4) The term "representatives" includes any individual or labor organization.

(5) The term "labor organization" means any organization of any kind, or any agency or employee representation committee or plan, in which employees participate and which exists for the purpose, in whole or in part, of dealing with employers concerning grievances, labor disputes, wages, rates of pay, hours of employment, or conditions of work.

(6) The term "commerce" means trade, traffic, commerce, transportation, or communication among the several States, or between the District of Columbia or any Territory of the United States and any State or other Territory, or between any foreign country and any State, Territory, or the District of Columbia, or within the District of Columbia or any Territory, or between points in the same State but through any other State or any Territory or the District of Columbia or any foreign country.

(7) The term "affecting commerce" means in commerce, or burdening or obstructing commerce or the free flow of commerce, or having led or tending to lead to a labor dispute burdening or obstructing commerce or the free flow of commerce.

(8) The term "unfair labor practice" means any unfair labor practice listed in section 158 of this title.

(9) The term "labor dispute" includes any controversy concerning terms, tenure or conditions of employment, or concerning the association or representation of persons in negotiating, fixing, maintaining, changing, or seeking to arrange terms or conditions of employment, regardless of whether the disputants stand in the proximate relation of employer and employee.

(10) The term "National Labor Relations Board" means the National Labor Relations Board provided for in section 153 of this title.

(11) The term "supervisor" means any individual having authority, in the interest of the employer, to hire, transfer, suspend, lay off, recall, promote, discharge, assign, reward, or discipline other employees, or responsibly to direct them, or to adjust their grievances,

or effectively to recommend such action, if in connection with the foregoing the exercise of such authority is not of a merely routine or clerical nature, but requires the use of independent judgment.

(12) The term "professional employee" means—

(a) any employee engaged in work (i) predominantly intellectual and varied in character as opposed to routine mental, manual, mechanical, or physical work; (ii) involving the consistent exercise of discretion and judgment in its performance; (iii) of such a character that the output produced or the result accomplished cannot be standardized in relation to a given period of time; (iv) requiring knowledge of an advanced type in a field of science or learning customarily acquired by a prolonged course of specialized intellectual instruction and study in an institution of higher learning or a hospital, as distinguished from a general academic education or from an apprenticeship or from training in the performance of routine mental, manual, or physical processes; or

(b) any employee, who (i) has completed the courses of specialized intellectual instruction and study described in clause (iv) of paragraph (a), and (ii) is performing related work under the supervision of a professional person to qualify himself to become a professional employee as defined in paragraph (a).

(13) In determining whether any person is acting as an "agent" of another person so as to make such other person responsible for his acts, the question of whether the specific acts performed were actually authorized or subsequently ratified shall not be controlling.

(14) The term "health care institution" shall include any hospital, convalescent hospital, health maintenance organization, health clinic, nursing home, extended care facility, or other institution devoted to the care of sick, infirm, or aged person.

§ 153. National Labor Relations Board

(a) Creation, composition, appointment, and tenure; Chairman; removal of members. The National Labor Relations Board (hereinafter called the "Board") created by this subchapter prior to its amendment by the Labor Management Relations Act, 1947 [29 U.S.C. § 141 *et seq.*], is continued as an agency of the United States, except that the Board shall consist of five instead of three members, appointed by the President by and with the advice and consent of the Senate. Of the two additional members so provided for, one shall be appointed for a term of five years and the other for a term of two years. Their successors, and the successors of the other members, shall be appointed for terms of five years each, excepting that any individual chosen to fill a vacancy shall be appointed only for the unexpired term of the member whom he shall succeed. The President shall designate one member to serve as Chair-

man of the Board. Any member of the Board may be removed by the President, upon notice and hearing, for neglect of duty or malfeasance in office, but for no other cause.

(b) Delegation of powers to members and regional directors; review and stay of actions of regional directors; quorum; seal. The Board is authorized to delegate to any group of three or more members any or all of the powers which it may itself exercise. The Board is also authorized to delegate to its regional directors its powers under section 159 of this title to determine the unit appropriate for the purpose of collective bargaining, to investigate and provide for hearings, and determine whether a question of representation exists, and to direct an election or take a secret ballot under subsection (c) or (e) of section 159 of this title and certify the results thereof, except that upon the filing of a request therefor with the Board by any interested person, the Board may review any action of a regional director delegated to him under this paragraph, but such a review shall not, unless specifically ordered by the Board, operate as a stay of any action taken by the regional director. A vacancy in the Board shall not impair the right of the remaining members to exercise all of the powers of the Board, and three members of the Board shall, at all times, constitute a quorum of the Board, except that two members shall constitute a quorum of any group designated pursuant to the first sentence hereof. The Board shall have an official seal which shall be judicially noticed.

(c) Annual reports to Congress and the President. The Board shall at the close of each fiscal year make a report in writing to Congress and to the President summarizing significant case activities and operations for that fiscal year.

(d) General Counsel; appointment and tenure; powers and duties; vacancy. There shall be a General Counsel of the Board who shall be appointed by the President, by and with the advice and consent of the Senate, for a term of four years. The General Counsel of the Board shall exercise general supervision over all attorneys employed by the Board (other than administrative law judges and legal assistants to Board members) and over the officers and employees in the regional offices. He shall have final authority, on behalf of the Board, in respect of the investigation of charges and issuance of complaints under section 160 of this title, and in respect of the prosecution of such complaints before the Board, and shall have such other duties as the Board may prescribe or as may be provided by law. In case of a vacancy in the office of the General Counsel the President is authorized to designate the officer or employee who shall act as General Counsel during such vacancy, but no person or persons so designated shall so act (1) for more than forty days when the Congress is in session unless a nomination to fill such vacancy shall have been submitted to the Senate, or (2) after the adjournment sine die of the session of the Senate in which such nomination was submitted.

§ 154. National Labor Relations Board; eligibility for reappointment; officers and employees; payment of expenses

(a) Each member of the Board and the General Counsel of the Board shall be eligible for reappointment, and shall not engage in any other business, vocation, or employment. The Board shall appoint an executive secretary, and such attorneys, examiners, and regional directors, and such other employees as it may from time to time find necessary for the proper performance of its duties. The Board may not employ any attorneys for the purpose of reviewing transcripts of hearings or preparing drafts of opinions except that any attorney employed for assignment as a legal assistant to any Board member may for such Board member review such transcripts and prepare such drafts. No administrative law judge's report shall be reviewed, either before or after its publication, by any person other than a member of the Board or his legal assistant, and no administrative law judge shall advise or consult with the Board with respect to exceptions taken to his findings, rulings, or recommendations. The Board may establish or utilize such regional, local, or other agencies, and utilize such voluntary and uncompensated services, as may from time to time be needed. Attorneys appointed under this section may, at the direction of the Board, appear for and represent the Board in any case in court. Nothing in this subchapter shall be construed to authorize the Board to appoint individuals for the purpose of conciliation or mediation, or for economic analysis.

(b) All of the expenses of the Board, including all necessary traveling and subsistence expenses outside the District of Columbia incurred by the members or employees of the Board under its orders, shall be allowed and paid on the presentation of itemized vouchers therefor approved by the Board or by any individual it designates for that purpose.

§ 155. National Labor Relations Board; principal office, conducting inquiries throughout country; participation in decisions or inquiries conducted by member

The principal office of the Board shall be in the District of Columbia, but it may meet and exercise any or all of its powers at any other place. The Board may, by one or more of its members or by such agents or agencies as it may designate, prosecute any inquiry necessary to its functions in any part of the United States. A member who participates in such an inquiry shall not be disqualified from subsequently participating in a decision of the Board in the same case.

§ 156. Rules and regulations

The Board shall have authority from time to time to make, amend, and rescind, in the manner prescribed by subchapter II of chapter 5 of Title

5, such rules and regulations as may be necessary to carry out the provisions of this subchapter.

§ 157. Right of employees as to organization, collective bargaining, etc.

Employees shall have the right to self-organization, to form, join, or assist labor organizations, to bargain collectively through representatives of their own choosing, and to engage in other concerted activities for the purpose of collective bargaining or other mutual aid or protection, and shall also have the right to refrain from any or all of such activities except to the extent that such right may be affected by an agreement requiring membership in a labor organization as a condition of employment as authorized in section 158(a)(3) of this title.

§ 158. Unfair labor practices

(a) Unfair labor practices for an employer. It shall be an unfair labor practice for an employer—

(1) to interfere with, restrain, or coerce employees in the exercise of the rights guaranteed in section 157 of this title;

(2) to dominate or interfere with the formation or administration of any labor organization or contribute financial or other support to it: Provided, That subject to rules and regulations made and published by the Board pursuant to section 156 of this title, an employer shall not be prohibited from permitting employees to confer with him during working hours without loss of time or pay;

(3) by discrimination in regard to hire or tenure of employment or any term or condition of employment to encourage or discourage membership in any labor organization: Provided, That nothing in this subchapter, or in any other statute of the United States, shall preclude an employer from making an agreement with a labor organization (not established, maintained, or assisted by any action defined in this subsection as an unfair labor practice) to require as a condition of employment membership therein on or after the thirtieth day following the beginning of such employment or the effective date of such agreement, whichever is the later, (i) if such labor organization is the representative of the employees as provided in section 159(a) of this title, in the appropriate collective-bargaining unit covered by such agreement when made, and (ii) unless following an election held as provided in section 159(e) of this title within one year preceding the effective date of such agreement, the Board shall have certified that at least a majority of the employees eligible to vote in such election have voted to rescind the authority of such labor organization to make such an agreement: Provided further, That no employer shall justify any discrimination against an employee for nonmembership in a labor organization (A) if he has

reasonable grounds for believing that such membership was not available to the employee on the same terms and conditions generally applicable to other members, or (B) if he has reasonable grounds for believing that membership was denied or terminated for reasons other than the failure of the employee to tender the periodic dues and the initiation fees uniformly required as a condition of acquiring or retaining membership;

(4) to discharge or otherwise discriminate against an employee because he has filed charges or given testimony under this subchapter;

(5) to refuse to bargain collectively with the representatives of his employees, subject to the provisions of section 159(a) of this title.

(b) Unfair labor practices by labor organization. It shall be an unfair labor practice for a labor organization or its agents—

(1) to restrain or coerce (A) employees in the exercise of the rights guaranteed in section 157 of this title: Provided, That this paragraph shall not impair the right of a labor organization to prescribe its own rules with respect to the acquisition or retention of membership therein; or (B) an employer in the selection of his representatives for the purposes of collective bargaining or the adjustment of grievances;

(2) to cause or attempt to cause an employer to discriminate against an employee in violation of subsection (a)(3) of this section or to discriminate against an employee with respect to whom membership in such organization has been denied or terminated on some ground other than his failure to tender the periodic dues and the initiation fees uniformly required as a condition of acquiring or retaining membership;

(3) to refuse to bargain collectively with an employer, provided it is the representative of his employees subject to the provisions of section 159(a) of this title;

(4)(i) to engage in, or to induce or encourage any individual employed by any person engaged in commerce or in an industry affecting commerce to engage in, a strike or a refusal in the course of his employment to use, manufacture, process, transport, or otherwise handle or work on any goods, articles, materials, or commodities or to perform any services; or (ii) to threaten, coerce, or restrain any person engaged in commerce or in an industry affecting commerce, where in either case an object thereof is—

(A) forcing or requiring any employer or self-employed person to join any labor or employer organization or to enter into any agreement which is prohibited by subsection (e) of this section;

(B) forcing or requiring any person to cease using, selling, handling, transporting, or otherwise dealing in the products of any other producer, processor, or manufacturer, or to cease doing business with any other person, or forcing or requiring any other employer to recognize or bargain with a labor organization as the representative of his employees unless such labor organization has been certified as the representative of such employees under the provisions of section 159 of this title: Provided, That nothing contained in this clause (B) shall be construed to make unlawful, where not otherwise unlawful, any primary strike or primary picketing;

(C) forcing or requiring any employer to recognize or bargain with a particular labor organization as the representative of his employees if another labor organization has been certified as the representative of such employees under the provisions of section 159 of this title;

(D) forcing or requiring any employer to assign particular work to employees in a particular labor organization or in a particular trade, craft, or class rather than to employees in another labor organization or in another trade, craft, or class, unless such employer is failing to conform to an order or certification of the Board determining the bargaining representative for employees performing such work: Provided, That nothing contained in this subsection shall be construed to make unlawful a refusal by any person to enter upon the premises of any employer (other than his own employer), if the employees of such employer are engaged in a strike ratified or approved by a representative of such employees whom such employer is required to recognize under this subchapter: Provided further, That for the purposes of this paragraph (4) only, nothing contained in such paragraph shall be construed to prohibit publicity, other than picketing, for the purpose of truthfully advising the public, including consumers and members of a labor organization, that a product or products are produced by an employer with whom the labor organization has a primary dispute and are distributed by another employer, as long as such publicity does not have an effect of inducing any individual employed by any person other than the primary employer in the course of his employment to refuse to pick up, deliver, or transport any goods, or not to perform any services, at the establishment of the employer engaged in such distribution;

(5) to require of employees covered by an agreement authorized under subsection (a)(3) of this section the payment, as a condition

precedent to becoming a member of such organization, of a fee in an amount which the Board finds excessive or discriminatory under all the circumstances. In making such a finding, the Board shall consider, among other relevant factors, the practices and customs of labor organizations in the particular industry, and the wages currently paid to the employees affected;

(6) to cause or attempt to cause an employer to pay or deliver or agree to pay or deliver any money or other thing of value, in the nature of an exaction, for services which are not performed or not to be performed; and

(7) to picket or cause to be picketed, or threaten to picket or cause to be picketed, any employer where an object thereof is forcing or requiring an employer to recognize or bargain with a labor organization as the representative of his employees, or forcing or requiring the employees of an employer to accept or select such labor organization as their collective bargaining representative, unless such labor organization is currently certified as the representative of such employees:

(A) where the employer has lawfully recognized in accordance with this subchapter any other labor organization and a question concerning representation may not appropriately be raised under section 159(c) of this title,

(B) where within the preceding twelve months a valid election under section 159(c) of this title has been conducted, or

(C) where such picketing has been conducted without a petition under section 159(c) of this title being filed within a reasonable period of time not to exceed thirty days from the commencement of such picketing: Provided, That when such a petition has been filed the Board shall forthwith, without regard to the provisions of section 159(c)(1) of this title or the absence of a showing of a substantial interest on the part of the labor organization, direct an election in such unit as the Board finds to be appropriate and shall certify the results thereof: Provided further, That nothing in this subparagraph (C) shall be construed to prohibit any picketing or other publicity for the purpose of truthfully advising the public (including consumers) that an employer does not employ members of, or have a contract with, a labor organization, unless an effect of such picketing is to induce any individual employed by any other person in the course of his employment, not to pick up, deliver or transport any goods or not to perform any services. Nothing in this paragraph (7) shall be construed to permit any act which would otherwise be an unfair labor practice under this subsection.

(c) Expression of views without threat of reprisal or force or promise of benefit. The expressing of any views, argument, or opinion, or the dissemination thereof, whether in written, printed, graphic, or visual form, shall not constitute or be evidence of an unfair labor practice under any of the provisions of this subchapter, if such expression contains no threat of reprisal or force or promise of benefit.

(d) Obligation to bargain collectively. For the purposes of this section, to bargain collectively is the performance of the mutual obligation of the employer and the representative of the employees to meet at reasonable times and confer in good faith with respect to wages, hours, and other terms and conditions of employment, or the negotiation of an agreement, or any question arising thereunder, and the execution of a written contract incorporating any agreement reached if requested by either party, but such obligation does not compel either party to agree to a proposal or require the making of a concession: Provided, That where there is in effect a collective-bargaining contract covering employees in an industry affecting commerce, the duty to bargain collectively shall also mean that no party to such contract shall terminate or modify such contract, unless the party desiring such termination or modification—

(1) serves a written notice upon the other party to the contract of the proposed termination or modification sixty days prior to the expiration date thereof, or in the event such contract contains no expiration date, sixty days prior to the time it is proposed to make such termination or modification;

(2) offers to meet and confer with the other party for the purpose of negotiating a new contract or a contract containing the proposed modifications;

(3) notifies the Federal Mediation and Conciliation Service within thirty days after such notice of the existence of a dispute, and simultaneously therewith notifies any State or Territorial agency established to mediate and conciliate disputes within the State or Territory where the dispute occurred, provided no agreement has been reached by that time; and

(4) continues in full force and effect, without resorting to strike or lock-out, all the terms and conditions of the existing contract for a period of sixty days after such notice is given or until the expiration date of such contract, whichever occurs later: The duties imposed upon employers, employees, and labor organizations by paragraphs (2) to (4) of this subsection shall become inapplicable upon an intervening certification of the Board, under which the labor organization or individual, which is a party to the contract, has been superseded as or ceased to be the representative of the employees subject to the provisions of section 159(a) of this title, and the duties so imposed shall not be construed as requiring either party to discuss or agree to any modification of the terms and conditions

contained in a contract for a fixed period, if such modification is to become effective before such terms and conditions can be reopened under the provisions of the contract. Any employee who engages in a strike within any notice period specified in this subsection, or who engages in any strike within the appropriate period specified in subsection (g) of this section, shall lose his status as an employee of the employer engaged in the particular labor dispute, for the purposes of sections 158, 159 and 160 of this title, but such loss of status for such employee shall terminate if and when he is reemployed by such employer. Whenever the collective bargaining involves employees of a health care institution, the provisions of this subsection shall be modified as follows:

(A) The notice of paragraph (1) of this subsection shall be ninety days; the notice of paragraph (3) of this subsection shall be sixty days; and the contract period of paragraph (4) of this subsection shall be ninety days.

(B) Where the bargaining is for an initial agreement following certification or recognition, at least thirty days' notice of the existence of a dispute shall be given by the labor organization to the agencies set forth in paragraph (3) of this subsection.

(C) After notice is given to the Federal Mediation and Conciliation Service under either clause (A) or (B) of this sentence, the Service shall promptly communicate with the parties and use its best efforts, by mediation and conciliation, to bring them to agreement. The parties shall participate fully and promptly in such meetings as may be undertaken by the Service for the purpose of aiding in a settlement of the dispute.

(e) *Enforceability of contract or agreement to boycott any other employer; exception.* It shall be an unfair labor practice for any labor organization and any employer to enter into any contract or agreement, express or implied, whereby such employer ceases or refrains or agrees to cease or refrain from handling, using, selling, transporting or otherwise dealing in any of the products of any other employer, or to cease doing business with any other person, and any contract or agreement entered into heretofore or hereafter containing such an agreement shall be to such extent unenforcible and void: Provided, That nothing in this subsection shall apply to an agreement between a labor organization and an employer in the construction industry relating to the contracting or subcontracting of work to be done at the site of the construction, alteration, painting, or repair of a building, structure, or other work: Provided further, That for the purposes of this subsection and subsection (b)(4)(B) of this section the terms "any employer", "any person engaged in commerce or an industry affecting commerce", and "any person" when used in relation to the terms "any other producer, processor, or manufacturer", "any other employer", or "any other person" shall not include persons in the relation of a jobber, manufacturer, contractor, or subcontractor working on the goods or premises of the jobber or manufacturer or performing parts of an integrated process of production in the apparel and clothing industry: Provided further, That nothing in this subchapter shall prohibit the enforcement of any agreement which is within the foregoing exception.

(f) Agreement covering employees in the building and construction industry. It shall not be an unfair labor practice under subsections (a) and (b) of this section for an employer engaged primarily in the building and construction industry to make an agreement covering employees engaged (or who, upon their employment, will be engaged) in the building and construction industry with a labor organization of which building and construction employees are members (not established, maintained, or assisted by any action defined in subsection (a) of this section as an unfair labor practice) because (1) the majority status of such labor organization has not been established under the provisions of section 159 of this title prior to the making of such agreement, or (2) such agreement requires as a condition of employment, membership in such labor organization after the seventh day following the beginning of such employment or the effective date of the agreement, whichever is later, or (3) such agreement requires the employer to notify such labor organization of opportunities for employment with such employer, or gives such labor organization an opportunity to refer qualified applicants for such employment, or (4) such agreement specifies minimum training or experience qualifications for employment or provides for priority in opportunities for employment based upon length of service with such employer, in the industry or in the particular geographical area: Provided, That nothing in this subsection shall set aside the final proviso to subsection (a)(3) of this section: Provided further, That any agreement which would be invalid, but for clause (1) of this subsection, shall not be a bar to a petition filed pursuant to section 159(c) or 159(e) of this title.

(g) Notification of intention to strike or picket at any health care institution. A labor organization before engaging in any strike, picketing, or other concerted refusal to work at any health care institution shall, not less than ten days prior to such action, notify the institution in writing and the Federal Mediation and Conciliation Service of that intention, except that in the case of bargaining for an initial agreement following certification or recognition the notice required by this subsection shall not be given until the expiration of the period specified in clause (B) of the last sentence of subsection (d) of this section. The notice shall state the date and time that such action will commence. The notice, once given, may be extended by the written agreement of both parties.

§ 159. Representatives and elections

(a) Exclusive representatives; employees' adjustment of grievances directly with employer. Representatives designated or selected for the purposes

of collective bargaining by the majority of the employees in a unit appropriate for such purposes, shall be the exclusive representatives of all the employees in such unit for the purposes of collective bargaining in respect to rates of pay, wages, hours of employment, or other conditions of employment: *Provided,* That any individual employee or a group of employees shall have the right at any time to present grievances to their employer and to have such grievances adjusted, without the intervention of the bargaining representative, as long as the adjustment is not inconsistent with the terms of a collective-bargaining contract or agreement then in effect: *Provided further,* That the bargaining representative has been given opportunity to be present at such adjustment.

(b) Determination of bargaining unit by Board. The Board shall decide in each case whether, in order to assure to employees the fullest freedom in exercising the rights guaranteed by this subchapter, the unit appropriate for the purposes of collective bargaining shall be the employer unit, craft unit, plant unit, or subdivision thereof: *Provided,* That the Board shall not (1) decide that any unit is appropriate for such purposes if such unit includes both professional employees and employees who are not professional employees unless a majority of such professional employees vote for inclusion in such unit; or (2) decide that any craft unit is inappropriate for such purposes on the ground that a different unit has been established by a prior Board determination, unless a majority of the employees in the proposed craft unit vote against separate representation or (3) decide that any unit is appropriate for such purposes if it includes, together with other employees, any individual employed as a guard to enforce against employees and other persons rules to protect property of the employer or to protect the safety of persons on the employer's premises; but no labor organization shall be certified as the representative of employees in a bargaining unit of guards if such organization admits to membership, or is affiliated directly or indirectly with an organization which admits to membership, employees other than guards.

(c) Hearings on questions affecting commerce; rules and regulations.

(1) Whenever a petition shall have been filed, in accordance with such regulations as may be prescribed by the Board—

(A) by an employee or group of employees or any individual or labor organization acting in their behalf alleging that a substantial number of employees (i) wish to be represented for collective bargaining and that their employer declines to recognize their representative as the representative defined in subsection (a) of this section, or (ii) assert that the individual or labor organization, which has been certified or is being currently recognized by their employer as the bargaining representative, is no longer a representative as defined in subsection (a) of this section; or

(B) by an employer, alleging that one or more individuals or labor organizations have presented to him a claim to be recognized as the representative defined in subsection (a) of this section; the Board shall investigate such petition and if it has reasonable cause to believe that a question of representation affecting commerce exists shall provide for an appropriate hearing upon due notice. Such hearing may be conducted by an officer or employee of the regional office, who shall not make any recommendations with respect thereto. If the Board finds upon the record of such hearing that such a question of representation exists, it shall direct an election by secret ballot and shall certify the results thereof.

(2) In determining whether or not a question of representation affecting commerce exists, the same regulations and rules of decision shall apply irrespective of the identity of the persons filing the petition or the kind of relief sought and in no case shall the Board deny a labor organization a place on the ballot by reason of an order with respect to such labor organization or its predecessor not issued in conformity with section 160(c) of this title.

(3) No election shall be directed in any bargaining unit or any subdivision within which in the preceding twelve-month period, a valid election shall have been held. Employees engaged in an economic strike who are not entitled to reinstatement shall be eligible to vote under such regulations as the Board shall find are consistent with the purposes and provisions of this subchapter in any election conducted within twelve months after the commencement of the strike. In any election where none of the choices on the ballot receives a majority, a run-off shall be conducted, the ballot providing for a selection between the two choices receiving the largest and second largest number of valid votes cast in the election.

(4) Nothing in this section shall be construed to prohibit the waiving of hearings by stipulation for the purpose of a consent election in conformity with regulations and rules of decision of the Board.

(5) In determining whether a unit is appropriate for the purposes specified in subsection (b) of this section the extent to which the employees have organized shall not be controlling.

(d) Petition for enforcement or review; transcript. Whenever an order of the Board made pursuant to section 160(c) of this title is based in whole or in part upon facts certified following an investigation pursuant to subsection (c) of this section and there is a petition for the enforcement or review of such order, such certification and the record of such investigation shall be included in the transcript of the entire record required to be filed under subsection (e) or (f) of section 160 of this title, and thereupon the decree of the court enforcing, modifying, or setting aside in whole or in part the order of the Board shall be made and

entered upon the pleadings, testimony, and proceedings set forth in such transcript.

(e) Secret ballot; limitation of elections.

(1) Upon the filing with the Board, by 30 per centum or more of the employees in a bargaining unit covered by an agreement between their employer and a labor organization made pursuant to section 158(a)(3) of this title, of a petition alleging they desire that such authority be rescinded, the Board shall take a secret ballot of the employees in such unit and certify the results thereof to such labor organization and to the employer.

(2) No election shall be conducted pursuant to this subsection in any bargaining unit or any subdivision within which, in the preceding twelve-month period, a valid election shall have been held.

§ 160.   Prevention of unfair labor practices

(a) Powers of Board generally. The Board is empowered, as hereinafter provided, to prevent any person from engaging in any unfair labor practice (listed in section 158 of this title) affecting commerce. This power shall not be affected by any other means of adjustment or prevention that has been or may be established by agreement, law, or otherwise: Provided, That the Board is empowered by agreement with any agency of any State or Territory to cede to such agency jurisdiction over any cases in any industry (other than mining, manufacturing, communications, and transportation except where predominantly local in character) even though such cases may involve labor disputes affecting commerce, unless the provision of the State or Territorial statute applicable to the determination of such cases by such agency is inconsistent with the corresponding provision of this subchapter or has received a construction inconsistent therewith.

(b) Complaint and notice of hearing; answer; court rules of evidence inapplicable. Whenever it is charged that any person has engaged in or is engaging in any such unfair labor practice, the Board, or any agent or agency designated by the Board for such purposes, shall have power to issue and cause to be served upon such person a complaint stating the charges in that respect, and containing a notice of hearing before the Board or a member thereof, or before a designated agent or agency, at a place therein fixed, not less than five days after the serving of said complaint: Provided, That no complaint shall issue based upon any unfair labor practice occurring more than six months prior to the filing of the charge with the Board and the service of a copy thereof upon the person against whom such charge is made, unless the person aggrieved thereby was prevented from filing such charge by reason of service in the armed forces, in which event the six-month period shall be computed from the day of his discharge. Any such complaint may be amended by the member, agent, or agency conducting the hearing or the Board in its

discretion at any time prior to the issuance of an order based thereon. The person so complained of shall have the right to file an answer to the original or amended complaint and to appear in person or otherwise and give testimony at the place and time fixed in the complaint. In the discretion of the member, agent, or agency conducting the hearing or the Board, any other person may be allowed to intervene in the said proceeding and to present testimony. Any such proceeding shall, so far as practicable, be conducted in accordance with the rules of evidence applicable in the district courts of the United States under the rules of civil procedure for the district courts of the United States, adopted by the Supreme Court of the United States pursuant to section 2072 of Title 28.

(c) Reduction of testimony to writing; findings and orders of Board. The testimony taken by such member, agent, or agency or the Board shall be reduced to writing and filed with the Board. Thereafter, in its discretion, the Board upon notice may take further testimony or hear argument. If upon the preponderance of the testimony taken the Board shall be of the opinion that any person named in the complaint has engaged in or is engaging in any such unfair labor practice, then the Board shall state its findings of fact and shall issue and cause to be served on such person an order requiring such person to cease and desist from such unfair labor practice, and to take such affirmative action including reinstatement of employees with or without back pay, as will effectuate the policies of this subchapter: Provided, That where an order directs reinstatement of an employee, back pay may be required of the employer or labor organization, as the case may be, responsible for the discrimination suffered by him: And provided further, That in determining whether a complaint shall issue alleging a violation of subsection (a)(1) or (a)(2) of section 158 of this title, and in deciding such cases, the same regulations and rules of decision shall apply irrespective of whether or not the labor organization affected is affiliated with a labor organization national or international in scope. Such order may further require such person to make reports from time to time showing the extent to which it has complied with the order. If upon the preponderance of the testimony taken the Board shall not be of the opinion that the person named in the complaint has engaged in or is engaging in any such unfair labor practice, then the Board shall state its findings of fact and shall issue an order dismissing the said complaint. No order of the Board shall require the reinstatement of any individual as an employee who has been suspended or discharged, or the payment to him of any back pay, if such individual was suspended or discharged for cause. In case the evidence is presented before a member of the Board, or before an administrative law judge or judges thereof, such member, or such judge or judges as the case may be, shall issue and cause to be served on the parties to the proceeding a proposed report, together with a recommended order, which shall be filed with the Board, and if no exceptions are filed within twenty

days after service thereof upon such parties, or within such further period as the Board may authorize, such recommended order shall become the order of the Board and become effective as therein prescribed.

(d) Modification of findings or orders prior to filing record in court. Until the record in a case shall have been filed in a court, as hereinafter provided, the Board may at any time upon reasonable notice and in such manner as it shall deem proper, modify or set aside, in whole or in part, any finding or order made or issued by it.

(e) Petition to court for enforcement of order; proceedings; review of judgment. The Board shall have power to petition any court of appeals of the United States, or if all the courts of appeals to which application may be made are in vacation, any district court of the United States, within any circuit or district, respectively, wherein the unfair labor practice in question occurred or wherein such person resides or transacts business, for the enforcement of such order and for appropriate temporary relief or restraining order, and shall file in the court the record in the proceedings, as provided in section 2112 of Title 28. Upon the filing of such petition, the court shall cause notice thereof to be served upon such person, and thereupon shall have jurisdiction of the proceeding and of the question determined therein, and shall have power to grant such temporary relief or restraining order as it deems just and proper, and to make and enter a decree enforcing, modifying and enforcing as so modified, or setting aside in whole or in part the order of the Board. No objection that has not been urged before the Board, its member, agent, or agency, shall be considered by the court, unless the failure or neglect to urge such objection shall be excused because of extraordinary circumstances. The findings of the Board with respect to questions of fact if supported by substantial evidence on the record considered as a whole shall be conclusive. If either party shall apply to the court for leave to adduce additional evidence and shall show to the satisfaction of the court that such additional evidence is material and that there were reasonable grounds for the failure to adduce such evidence in the hearing before the Board, its member, agent, or agency, the court may order such additional evidence to be taken before the Board, its member, agent, or agency, and to be made a part of the record. The Board may modify its findings as to the facts, or make new findings by reason of additional evidence so taken and filed, and it shall file such modified or new findings, which findings with respect to questions of fact if supported by substantial evidence on the record considered as a whole shall be conclusive, and shall file its recommendations, if any, for the modification or setting aside of its original order. Upon the filing of the record with it the jurisdiction of the court shall be exclusive and its judgment and decree shall be final, except that the same shall be subject to review by the appropriate United States court of appeals if application was made to the district court as hereinabove provided, and by the Supreme Court of the

United States upon writ of certiorari or certification as provided in section 1254 of Title 28.

(f) Review of final order of Board on petition to court. Any person aggrieved by a final order of the Board granting or denying in whole or in part the relief sought may obtain a review of such order in any United States court of appeals in the circuit wherein the unfair labor practice in question was alleged to have been engaged in or wherein such person resides or transacts business, or in the United States Court of Appeals for the District of Columbia, by filing in such a court a written petition praying that the order of the Board be modified or set aside. A copy of such petition shall be forthwith transmitted by the clerk of the court to the Board, and thereupon the aggrieved party shall file in the court the record in the proceeding, certified by the Board, as provided in section 2112 of Title 28. Upon the filing of such petition, the court shall proceed in the same manner as in the case of an application by the Board under subsection (e) of this section, and shall have the same jurisdiction to grant to the Board such temporary relief or restraining order as it deems just and proper, and in like manner to make and enter a decree enforcing, modifying, and enforcing as so modified, or setting aside in whole or in part the order of the Board; the findings of the Board with respect to questions of fact if supported by substantial evidence on the record considered as a whole shall in like manner be conclusive.

(g) Institution of court proceedings as stay of Board's order. The commencement of proceedings under subsection (e) or (f) of this section shall not, unless specifically ordered by the court, operate as a stay of the Board's order.

(h) Jurisdiction of courts unaffected by limitations prescribed in chapter 6 of this title. When granting appropriate temporary relief or a restraining order, or making and entering a decree enforcing, modifying, and enforcing as so modified or setting aside in whole or in part an order of the Board, as provided in this section, the jurisdiction of courts sitting in equity shall not be limited by chapter 6 of this title.

(i) Repealed.

(j) Injunctions. The Board shall have power, upon issuance of a complaint as provided in subsection (b) of this section charging that any person has engaged in or is engaging in an unfair labor practice, to petition any United States district court, within any district wherein the unfair labor practice in question is alleged to have occurred or wherein such person resides or transacts business, for appropriate temporary relief or restraining order. Upon the filing of any such petition the court shall cause notice thereof to be served upon such person, and thereupon shall have jurisdiction to grant to the Board such temporary relief or restraining order as it deems just and proper.

(k) Hearings on jurisdictional strikes. Whenever it is charged that any person has engaged in an unfair labor practice within the meaning of

paragraph (4)(D) of section 158(b) of this title, the Board is empowered and directed to hear and determine the dispute out of which such unfair labor practice shall have arisen, unless, within ten days after notice that such charge has been filed, the parties to such dispute submit to the Board satisfactory evidence that they have adjusted, or agreed upon methods for the voluntary adjustment of, the dispute. Upon compliance by the parties to the dispute with the decision of the Board or upon such voluntary adjustment of the dispute, such charge shall be dismissed.

(*l*) *Boycotts and strikes to force recognition of uncertified labor organizations; injunctions; notice; service of process.* Whenever it is charged that any person has engaged in an unfair labor practice within the meaning of paragraph (4)(A), (B), or (C) of section 158(b) of this title, or section 158(e) of this title or section 158(b)(7) of this title, the preliminary investigation of such charge shall be made forthwith and given priority over all other cases except cases of like character in the office where it is filed or to which it is referred. If, after such investigation, the officer or regional attorney to whom the matter may be referred has reasonable cause to believe such charge is true and that a complaint should issue, he shall, on behalf of the Board, petition any United States district court within any district where the unfair labor practice in question has occurred, is alleged to have occurred, or wherein such person resides or transacts business, for appropriate injunctive relief pending the final adjudication of the Board with respect to such matter. Upon the filing of any such petition the district court shall have jurisdiction to grant such injunctive relief or temporary restraining order as it deems just and proper, notwithstanding any other provision of law: Provided further, That no temporary restraining order shall be issued without notice unless a petition alleges that substantial and irreparable injury to the charging party will be unavoidable and such temporary restraining order shall be effective for no longer than five days and will become void at the expiration of such period: Provided further, That such officer or regional attorney shall not apply for any restraining order under section 158(b)(7) of this title if a charge against the employer under section 158(a)(2) of this title has been filed and after the preliminary investigation, he has reasonable cause to believe that such charge is true and that a complaint should issue. Upon filing of any such petition the courts shall cause notice thereof to be served upon any person involved in the charge and such person, including the charging party, shall be given an opportunity to appear by counsel and present any relevant testimony: Provided further, That for the purposes of this subsection district courts shall be deemed to have jurisdiction of a labor organization (1) in the district in which such organization maintains its principal office, or (2) in any district in which its duly authorized officers or agents are engaged in promoting or protecting the interests of employee members. The service of legal process upon such officer or agent shall constitute service upon the labor organization and make such organization a party to the suit.

In situations where such relief is appropriate the procedure specified herein shall apply to charges with respect to section 158(b)(4)(D) of this title.

(m) Priority of cases. Whenever it is charged that any person has engaged in an unfair labor practice within the meaning of subsection (a)(3) or (b)(2) of section 158 of this title, such charge shall be given priority over all other cases except cases of like character in the office where it is filed or to which it is referred and cases given priority under subsection (*l*) of this section.

§ 161. Investigatory powers of Board

For the purpose of all hearings and investigations, which, in the opinion of the Board, are necessary and proper for the exercise of the powers vested in it by sections 159 and 160 of this title—

(1) Documentary evidence; summoning witnesses and taking testimony. The Board, or its duly authorized agents or agencies, shall at all reasonable times have access to, for the purpose of examination, and the right to copy any evidence of any person being investigated or proceeded against that relates to any matter under investigation or in question. The Board, or any member thereof, shall upon application of any party to such proceedings, forthwith issue to such party subpenas requiring the attendance and testimony of witnesses or the production of any evidence in such proceeding or investigation requested in such application. Within five days after the service of a subpena on any person requiring the production of any evidence in his possession or under his control, such person may petition the Board to revoke, and the Board shall revoke, such subpena if in its opinion the evidence whose production is required does not relate to any matter under investigation, or any matter in question in such proceedings, or if in its opinion such subpena does not describe with sufficient particularity the evidence whose production is required. Any member of the Board, or any agent or agency designated by the Board for such purposes, may administer oaths and affirmations, examine witnesses, and receive evidence. Such attendance of witnesses and the production of such evidence may be required from any place in the United States or any Territory or possession thereof, at any designated place of hearing.

(2) Court aid in compelling production of evidence and attendance of witnesses. In case of contumacy or refusal to obey a subpena issued to any person, any district court of the United States or the United States courts of any Territory or possession, within the jurisdiction of which the inquiry is carried on or within the jurisdiction of which said person guilty of contumacy or refusal to obey is found or resides or transacts business, upon application by the Board shall have jurisdiction to issue to such person an order requiring such person

to appear before the Board, its member, agent, or agency, there to produce evidence if so ordered, or there to give testimony touching the matter under investigation or in question; and any failure to obey such order of the court may be punished by said court as a contempt thereof.

(3) Repealed.

(4) Process, service and return; fees of witnesses. Complaints, orders, and other process and papers of the Board, its member, agent, or agency, may be served either personally or by registered or certified mail or by telegraph or by leaving a copy thereof at the principal office or place of business of the person required to be served. The verified return by the individual so serving the same setting forth the manner of such service shall be proof of the same, and the return post office receipt or telegraph receipt therefor when registered or certified and mailed or when telegraphed as aforesaid shall be proof of service of the same. Witnesses summoned before the Board, its member, agent, or agency, shall be paid the same fees and mileage that are paid witnesses in the courts of the United States, and witnesses whose depositions are taken and the persons taking the same shall severally be entitled to the same fees as are paid for like services in the courts of the United States.

(5) Process, where served. All process of any court to which application may be made under this subchapter may be served in the judicial district wherein the defendant or other person required to be served resides or may be found.

(6) Information and assistance from departments. The several departments and agencies of the Government, when directed by the President, shall furnish the Board, upon its request, all records, papers, and information in their possession relating to any matter before the Board.

§ 162. Offenses and penalties

Any person who shall willfully resist, prevent, impede, or interfere with any member of the Board or any of its agents or agencies in the performance of duties pursuant to this subchapter shall be punished by a fine of not more than $5,000 or by imprisonment for not more than one year, or both.

OCCUPATIONAL SAFETY & HEALTH ACT

TITLE 29. LABOR
CHAPTER 15—OCCUPATIONAL SAFETY AND HEALTH

§ 651. Congressional statement of findings and declaration of purpose and policy

(a) The Congress finds that personal injuries and illnesses arising out of work situations impose a substantial burden upon, and are a hindrance to, interstate commerce in terms of lost production, wage loss, medical expenses, and disability compensation payments.

(b) The Congress declares it to be its purpose and policy, through the exercise of its powers to regulate commerce among the several States and with foreign nations and to provide for the general welfare, to assure so far as possible every working man and woman in the Nation safe and healthful working conditions and to preserve our human resources—

> (1) by encouraging employers and employees in their efforts to reduce the number of occupational safety and health hazards at their places of employment, and to stimulate employers and employ-

ees to institute new and to perfect existing programs for providing safe and healthful working conditions;

(2) by providing that employers and employees have separate but dependent responsibilities and rights with respect to achieving safe and healthful working conditions;

(3) by authorizing the Secretary of Labor to set mandatory occupational safety and health standards applicable to businesses affecting interstate commerce, and by creating an Occupational Safety and Health Review Commission for carrying out adjudicatory functions under this chapter;

(4) by building upon advances already made through employer and employee initiative for providing safe and healthful working conditions;

(5) by providing for research in the field of occupational safety and health, including the psychological factors involved, and by developing innovative methods, techniques, and approaches for dealing with occupational safety and health problems;

(6) by exploring ways to discover latent diseases, establishing causal connections between diseases and work in environmental conditions, and conducting other research relating to health problems, in recognition of the fact that occupational health standards present problems often different from those involved in occupational safety;

(7) by providing medical criteria which will assure insofar as practicable that no employee will suffer diminished health, functional capacity, or life expectancy as a result of his work experience;

(8) by providing for training programs to increase the number and competence of personnel engaged in the field of occupational safety and health;

(9) by providing for the development and promulgation of occupational safety and health standards;

(10) by providing an effective enforcement program which shall include a prohibition against giving advance notice of any inspection and sanctions for any individual violating this prohibition;

(11) by encouraging the States to assume the fullest responsibility for the administration and enforcement of their occupational safety and health laws by providing grants to the States to assist in identifying their needs and responsibilities in the area of occupational safety and health, to develop plans in accordance with the provisions of this chapter, to improve the administration and enforcement of State occupational safety and health laws, and to conduct experimental and demonstration projects in connection therewith;

(12) by providing for appropriate reporting procedures with respect to occupational safety and health which procedures will help achieve the objectives of this chapter and accurately describe the nature of the occupational safety and health problem;

(13) by encouraging joint labor-management efforts to reduce injuries and disease arising out of employment.

§ 652. Definitions

For the purposes of this chapter—

(1) The term "Secretary" mean the Secretary of Labor.

(2) The term "Commission" means the Occupational Safety and Health Review Commission established under this chapter.

(3) The term "commerce" means trade, traffic, commerce, transportation, or communication among the several States, or between a State and any place outside thereof, or within the District of Columbia, or a possession of the United States (other than the Trust Territory of the Pacific Islands), or between points in the same State but through a point outside thereof.

(4) The term "person" means one or more individuals, partnerships, associations, corporations, business trusts, legal representatives, or any organized group of persons.

(5) The term "employer" means a person engaged in a business affecting commerce who has employees, but does not include the United States (not including the United States Post Office) or any State or political subdivision of a State.

(6) The term "employee" means an employee of an employer who is employed in a business of his employer which affects commerce.

(7) The term "State" includes a State of the United States, the District of Columbia, Puerto Rico, the Virgin Islands, American Samoa, Guam, and the Trust Territory of the Pacific Islands.

(8) The term "occupational safety and health standard" means a standard which requires conditions, or the adoption or use of one or more practices, means, methods, operations, or processes, reasonably necessary or appropriate to provide safe or healthful employment and places of employment.

(9) The term "national consensus standard" means any occupational safety and health standard or modification thereof which (1) has been adopted and promulgated by a nationally recognized standards-producing organization under procedures whereby it can be determined by the Secretary that persons interested and affected by the scope or provisions of the standard have reached substantial agreement on its adoption, (2) was formulated in a manner which afforded an opportunity for diverse views to be considered and (3)

has been designated as such a standard by the Secretary, after consultation with other appropriate Federal agencies.

(10) The term "established Federal standard" means any operative occupational safety and health standard established by any agency of the United States and presently in effect, or contained in any Act of Congress in force on December 29, 1970.

(11) The term "Committee" means the National Advisory Committee on Occupational Safety and Health established under this chapter.

(12) The term "Director" means the Director of the National Institute for Occupational Safety and Health.

(13) The term "Institute" means the National Institute for Occupational Safety and Health established under this chapter.

(14) The term "Workmen's Compensation Commission" means the National Commission on State Workmen's Compensation Laws established under this chapter.

§ 653. Geographic applicability; judicial enforcement; applicability to existing standards; report to Congress on duplication and coordination of Federal laws; workmen's compensation law or common law or statutory rights, duties, or liabilities of employers and employees unaffected

(a) This chapter shall apply with respect to employment performed in a workplace in a State, the District of Columbia, the Commonwealth of Puerto Rico, the Virgin Islands, American Samoa, Guam, the Trust Territory of the Pacific Islands, Wake Island, Outer Continental Shelf lands defined in the Outer Continental Shelf Lands Act [43 U.S.C. § 1331 et seq.], Johnston Island, and the Canal Zone. The Secretary of the Interior shall, by regulation, provide for judicial enforcement of this chapter by the courts established for areas in which there are no United States district courts having jurisdiction.

(b)(1) Nothing in this chapter shall apply to working conditions of employees with respect to which other Federal agencies, and State agencies acting under section 2021 of Title 42, exercise statutory authority to prescribe or enforce standards or regulations affecting occupational safety or health.

(2) The safety and health standards promulgated under the Act of June 30, 1936, commonly known as the Walsh-Healey Act [41 U.S.C. § 35 et seq.], the Service Contract Act of 1965 [41 U.S.C. § 351 et seq.], Public Law 91–54, Act of August 9, 1969, Public Law 85–742, Act of August 23, 1958, and the National Foundation on Arts and Humanities Act [20 U.S.C. § 951 et seq.] are superseded on the effective date of corresponding standards, promulgated under this

chapter, which are determined by the Secretary to be more effective. Standards issued under the laws listed in this paragraph and in effect on or after the effective date of this chapter shall be deemed to be occupational safety and health standards issued under this chapter, as well as under such other Acts.

(3) The Secretary shall, within three years after the effective date of this chapter, report to the Congress his recommendations for legislation to avoid unnecessary duplication and to achieve coordination between this chapter and other Federal laws.

(4) Nothing in this chapter shall be construed to supersede or in any manner affect any workmen's compensation law or to enlarge or diminish or affect in any other manner the common law or statutory rights, duties, or liabilities of employers and employees under any law with respect to injuries, diseases, or death of employees arising out of, or in the course of, employment.

§ 654. Duties of employers and employees

(a) Each employer—

(1) shall furnish to each of his employees employment and a place of employment which are free from recognized hazards that are causing or are likely to cause death or serious physical harm to his employees;

(2) shall comply with occupational safety and health standards promulgated under this chapter.

(b) Each employee shall comply with occupational safety and health standards and all rules, regulations, and orders issued pursuant to this chapter which are applicable to his own actions and conduct.

§ 655. Standards

(a) Promulgation by Secretary of national consensus standards and established Federal standards; time for promulgation; conflicting standards. Without regard to chapter 5 of Title 5 or to the other subsections of this section, the Secretary shall, as soon as practicable during the period beginning with the effective date of this chapter and ending two years after such date, by rule promulgate as an occupational safety or health standard any national consensus standard, and any established Federal standard, unless he determines that the promulgation of such a standard would not result in improved safety or health for specifically designated employees. In the event of conflict among any such standards, the Secretary shall promulgate the standard which assures the greatest protection of the safety or health of the affected employees.

(b) Procedure for promulgation, modification, or revocation of standards. The Secretary may by rule promulgate, modify, or revoke any occupational safety or health standard in the following manner:

(1) Whenever the Secretary, upon the basis of information submitted to him in writing by an interested person, a representative of any organization of employers or employees, a nationally recognized standards-producing organization, the Secretary of Health and Human Services, the National Institute for Occupational Safety and Health, or a State or political subdivision, or on the basis of information developed by the Secretary or otherwise available to him, determines that a rule should be promulgated in order to serve the objectives of this chapter, the Secretary may request the recommendations of an advisory committee appointed under section 656 of this title. The Secretary shall provide such an advisory committee with any proposals of his own or of the Secretary of Health and Human Services, together with all pertinent factual information developed by the Secretary or the Secretary of Health and Human Services, or otherwise available, including the results of research, demonstrations, and experiments. An advisory committee shall submit to the Secretary its recommendations regarding the rule to be promulgated within ninety days from the date of its appointment or within such longer or shorter period as may be prescribed by the Secretary, but in no event for a period which is longer than two hundred and seventy days.

(2) The Secretary shall publish a proposed rule promulgating, modifying, or revoking an occupational safety or health standard in the Federal Register and shall afford interested persons a period of thirty days after publication to submit written data or comments. Where an advisory committee is appointed and the Secretary determines that a rule should be issued, he shall publish the proposed rule within sixty days after the submission of the advisory committee's recommendations or the expiration of the period prescribed by the Secretary for such submission.

(3) On or before the last day of the period provided for the submission of written data or comments under paragraph (2), any interested person may file with the Secretary written objections to the proposed rule, stating the grounds therefor and requesting a public hearing on such objections. Within thirty days after the last day for filing such objections, the Secretary shall publish in the Federal Register a notice specifying the occupational safety or health standard to which objections have been filed and a hearing requested, and specifying a time and place for such hearing.

(4) Within sixty days after the expiration of the period provided for the submission of written data or comments under paragraph (2), or within sixty days after the completion of any hearing held under paragraph (3), the Secretary shall issue a rule promulgating, modifying, or revoking an occupational safety or health standard or make a determination that a rule should not be issued. Such a rule may contain a provision delaying its effective date for such period (not in

excess of ninety days) as the Secretary determines may be necessary to insure that affected employers and employees will be informed of the existence of the standard and of its terms and that employers affected are given an opportunity to familiarize themselves and their employees with the existence of the requirements of the standard.

(5) The Secretary, in promulgating standards dealing with toxic materials or harmful physical agents under this subsection, shall set the standard which most adequately assures, to the extent feasible, on the basis of the best available evidence, that no employee will suffer material impairment of health or functional capacity even if such employee has regular exposure to the hazard dealt with by such standard for the period of his working life. Development of standards under this subsection shall be based upon research, demonstrations, experiments, and such other information as may be appropriate. In addition to the attainment of the highest degree of health and safety protection for the employee, other considerations shall be the latest available scientific data in the field, the feasibility of the standards, and experience gained under this and other health and safety laws. Whenever practicable, the standard promulgated shall be expressed in terms of objective criteria and of the performance desired.

(6)(A) Any employer may apply to the Secretary for a temporary order granting a variance from a standard or any provision thereof promulgated under this section. Such temporary order shall be granted only if the employer files an application which meets the requirements of clause (B) and establishes that

> (i) he is unable to comply with a standard by its effective date because of unavailability of professional or technical personnel or of materials and equipment needed to come into compliance with the standard or because necessary construction or alteration of facilities cannot be completed by the effective date,

> (ii) he is taking all available steps to safeguard his employees against the hazards covered by the standard, and

> (iii) he has an effective program for coming into compliance with the standard as quickly as practicable. Any temporary order issued under this paragraph shall prescribe the practices, means, methods, operations, and processes which the employer must adopt and use while the order is in effect and state in detail his program for coming into compliance with the standard. Such a temporary order may be granted only after notice to employees and an opportunity for a hearing: Provided, That the Secretary may issue one interim order to be effective until a decision is made on the basis of the hearing. No temporary order may be in effect for

longer than the period needed by the employer to achieve compliance with the standard or one year, whichever is shorter, except that such an order may be renewed not more than twice

(I) so long as the requirements of this paragraph are met and

(II) if an application for renewal is filed at least 90 days prior to the expiration date of the order. No interim renewal of an order may remain in effect for longer than 180 days.

(B) An application for a temporary order under this paragraph (6) shall contain:

(i) a specification of the standard or portion thereof from which the employer seeks a variance,

(ii) a representation by the employer, supported by representations from qualified persons having firsthand knowledge of the facts represented, that he is unable to comply with the standard or portion thereof and a detailed statement of the reasons therefor,

(iii) a statement of the steps he has taken and will take (with specific dates) to protect employees against the hazard covered by the standard,

(iv) a statement of when he expects to be able to comply with the standard and what steps he has taken and what steps he will take (with dates specified) to come into compliance with the standard, and

(v) a certification that he has informed his employees of the application by giving a copy thereof to their authorized representative, posting a statement giving a summary of the application and specifying where a copy may be examined at the place or places where notices to employees are normally posted, and by other appropriate means. A description of how employees have been informed shall be contained in the certification. The information to employees shall also inform them of their right to petition the Secretary for a hearing.

(C) The Secretary is authorized to grant a variance from any standard or portion thereof whenever he determines, or the Secretary of Health and Human Services certifies, that such variance is necessary to permit an employer to participate in an experiment approved by him or the Secretary of Health and Human Services designed to demonstrate or validate new and improved techniques to safeguard the health or safety of workers.

(7) Any standard promulgated under this subsection shall prescribe the use of labels or other appropriate forms of warning as are necessary to insure that employees are apprised of all hazards to which they are exposed, relevant symptoms and appropriate emergency treatment, and proper conditions and precautions of safe use or exposure. Where appropriate, such standard shall also prescribe suitable protective equipment and control or technological procedures to be used in connection with such hazards and shall provide for monitoring or measuring employee exposure at such locations and intervals, and in such manner as may be necessary for the protection of employees. In addition, where appropriate, any such standard shall prescribe the type and frequency of medical examinations or other tests which shall be made available, by the employer or at his cost, to employees exposed to such hazards in order to most effectively determine whether the health of such employees is adversely affected by such exposure. In the event such medical examinations are in the nature of research, as determined by the Secretary of Health and Human Services, such examinations may be furnished at the expense of the Secretary of Health and Human Services. The results of such examinations or tests shall be furnished only to the Secretary or the Secretary of Health and Human Services, and, at the request of the employee, to his physician. The Secretary, in consultation with the Secretary of Health and Human Services, may by rule promulgated pursuant to section 553 of Title 5, make appropriate modifications in the foregoing requirements relating to the use of labels or other forms of warning, monitoring or measuring, and medical examinations, as may be warranted by experience, information, or medical or technological developments acquired subsequent to the promulgation of the relevant standard.

(8) Whenever a rule promulgated by the Secretary differs substantially from an existing national consensus standard, the Secretary shall, at the same time, publish in the Federal Register a statement of the reasons why the rule as adopted will better effectuate the purposes of this chapter than the national consensus standard.

(c) Emergency temporary standards.

(1) The Secretary shall provide, without regard to the requirements of chapter 5 of Title 5, for an emergency temporary standard to take immediate effect upon publication in the Federal Register if he determines (A) that employees are exposed to grave danger from exposure to substances or agents determined to be toxic or physically harmful or from new hazards, and (B) that such emergency standard is necessary to protect employees from such danger.

(2) Such standard shall be effective until superseded by a standard promulgated in accordance with the procedures prescribed in paragraph (3) of this subsection.

(3) Upon publication of such standard in the Federal Register the Secretary shall commence a proceeding in accordance with subsection (b) of this section, and the standard as published shall also serve as a proposed rule for the proceeding. The Secretary shall promulgate a standard under this paragraph no later than six months after publication of the emergency standard as provided in paragraph (2) of this subsection.

(d) Variances from standards; procedure. Any affected employer may apply to the Secretary for a rule or order for a variance from a standard promulgated under this section. Affected employees shall be given notice of each such application and an opportunity to participate in a hearing. The Secretary shall issue such rule or order if he determines on the record, after opportunity for an inspection where appropriate and a hearing, that the proponent of the variance has demonstrated by a preponderance of the evidence that the conditions, practices, means, methods, operations, or processes used or proposed to be used by an employer will provide employment and places of employment to his employees which are as safe and healthful as those which would prevail if he complied with the standard. The rule or order so issued shall prescribe the conditions the employer must maintain, and the practices, means, methods, operations, and processes which he must adopt and utilize to the extent they differ from the standard in question. Such a rule or order may be modified or revoked upon application by an employer, employees, or by the Secretary on his own motion, in the manner prescribed for its issuance under this subsection at any time after six months from its issuance.

(e) Statement of reasons for Secretary's determinations; publication in Federal Register. Whenever the Secretary promulgates any standard, makes any rule, order, or decision, grants any exemption or extension of time, or compromises, mitigates, or settles any penalty assessed under this chapter, he shall include a statement of the reasons for such action, which shall be published in the Federal Register.

(f) Judicial review. Any person who may be adversely affected by a standard issued under this section may at any time prior to the sixtieth day after such standard is promulgated file a petition challenging the validity of such standard with the United States court of appeals for the circuit wherein such person resides or has his principal place of business, for a judicial review of such standard. A copy of the petition shall be forthwith transmitted by the clerk of the court to the Secretary. The filing of such petition shall not, unless otherwise ordered by the court, operate as a stay of the standard. The determinations of the Secretary shall be conclusive if supported by substantial evidence in the record considered as a whole.

(g) Priority for establishment of standards. In determining the priority for establishing standards under this section, the Secretary shall give

due regard to the urgency of the need for mandatory safety and health standards for particular industries, trades, crafts, occupations, businesses, workplaces or work environments. The Secretary shall also give due regard to the recommendations of the Secretary of Health and Human Services regarding the need for mandatory standards in determining the priority for establishing such standards.

* * *

§ 657. Inspections, investigations, and recordkeeping

(a) Authority of Secretary to enter, inspect, and investigate places of employment; time and manner. In order to carry out the purposes of this chapter, the Secretary, upon presenting appropriate credentials to the owner, operator, or agent in charge, is authorized—

(1) to enter without delay and at reasonable times any factory, plant, establishment, construction site, or other area, workplace or environment where work is performed by an employee of an employer; and

(2) to inspect and investigate during regular working hours and at other reasonable times, and within reasonable limits and in a reasonable manner, any such place of employment and all pertinent conditions, structures, machines, apparatus, devices, equipment, and materials therein, and to question privately any such employer, owner, operator, agent or employee.

(b) Attendance and testimony of witnesses and production of evidence; enforcement of subpoena. In making his inspections and investigations under this chapter the Secretary may require the attendance and testimony of witnesses and the production of evidence under oath. Witnesses shall be paid the same fees and mileage that are paid witnesses in the courts of the United States. In case of a contumacy, failure, or refusal of any person to obey such an order, any district court of the United States or the United States courts of any territory or possession, within the jurisdiction of which such person is found, or resides or transacts business, upon the application by the Secretary, shall have jurisdiction to issue to such person an order requiring such person to appear to produce evidence if, as, and when so ordered, and to give testimony relating to the matter under investigation or in question, and any failure to obey such order of the court may be punished by said court as a contempt thereof.

(c) Maintenance, preservation, and availability of records; issuance of regulations; scope of records; periodic inspections by employer; posting of notices by employer; notification of employee of corrective action.

(1) Each employer shall make, keep and preserve, and make available to the Secretary or the Secretary of Health and Human Services, such records regarding his activities relating to this chapter as

the Secretary, in cooperation with the Secretary of Health and Human Services, may prescribe by regulation as necessary or appropriate for the enforcement of this chapter or for developing information regarding the causes and prevention of occupational accidents and illnesses. In order to carry out the provisions of this paragraph such regulations may include provisions requiring employers to conduct periodic inspections. The Secretary shall also issue regulations requiring that employers, through posting of notices or other appropriate means, keep their employees informed of their protections and obligations under this chapter, including the provisions of applicable standards.

(2) The Secretary, in cooperation with the Secretary of Health and Human Services, shall prescribe regulations requiring employers to maintain accurate records of, and to make periodic reports on, work-related deaths, injuries and illnesses other than minor injuries requiring only first aid treatment and which do not involve medical treatment, loss of consciousness, restriction of work or motion, or transfer to another job.

(3) The Secretary, in cooperation with the Secretary of Health and Human Services, shall issue regulations requiring employers to maintain accurate records of employee exposures to potentially toxic materials or harmful physical agents which are required to be monitored or measured under section 655 of this title. Such regulations shall provide employees or their representatives with an opportunity to observe such monitoring or measuring, and to have access to the records thereof. Such regulations shall also make appropriate provision for each employee or former employee to have access to such records as will indicate his own exposure to toxic materials or harmful physical agents. Each employer shall promptly notify any employee who has been or is being exposed to toxic materials or harmful physical agents in concentrations or at levels which exceed those prescribed by an applicable occupational safety and health standard promulgated under section 655 of this title, and shall inform any employee who is being thus exposed of the corrective action being taken.

(d) *Obtaining of information.* Any information obtained by the Secretary, the Secretary of Health and Human Services, or a State agency under this chapter shall be obtained with a minimum burden upon employers, especially those operating small businesses. Unnecessary duplication of efforts in obtaining information shall be reduced to the maximum extent feasible.

(e) *Employer and authorized employee representatives to accompany Secretary or his authorized representative on inspection of workplace; consultation with employees where no authorized employee representative is present.* Subject to regulations issued by the Secretary, a representative

314

of the employer and a representative authorized by his employees shall be given an opportunity to accompany the Secretary or his authorized representative during the physical inspection of any workplace under subsection (a) of this section for the purpose of aiding such inspection. Where there is no authorized employee representative, the Secretary or his authorized representative shall consult with a reasonable number of employees concerning matters of health and safety in the workplace.

(f) Request for inspection by employees or representative of employees; grounds; procedure; determination of request; notification of Secretary or representative prior to or during any inspection of violations; procedure for review of refusal by representative of Secretary to issue citation for alleged violations.

(1) Any employees or representative of employees who believe that a violation of a safety or health standard exists that threatens physical harm, or that an imminent danger exists, may request an inspection by giving notice to the Secretary or his authorized representative of such violation or danger. Any such notice shall be reduced to writing, shall set forth with reasonable particularity the grounds for the notice, and shall be signed by the employees or representative of employees, and a copy shall be provided the employer or his agent no later than at the time of inspection, except that, upon the request of the person giving such notice, his name and the names of individual employees referred to therein shall not appear in such copy or on any record published, released, or made available pursuant to subsection (g) of this section. If upon receipt of such notification the Secretary determines there are reasonable grounds to believe that such violation or danger exists, he shall make a special inspection in accordance with the provisions of this section as soon as practicable, to determine if such violation or danger exists. If the Secretary determines there are no reasonable grounds to believe that a violation or danger exists he shall notify the employees or representative of the employees in writing of such determination.

(2) Prior to or during any inspection of a workplace, any employees or representative of employees employed in such workplace may notify the Secretary or any representative of the Secretary responsible for conducting the inspection, in writing, of any violation of this chapter which they have reason to believe exists in such workplace. The Secretary shall, by regulation, establish procedures for informal review of any refusal by a representative of the Secretary to issue a citation with respect to any such alleged violation and shall furnish the employees or representative of employees requesting such review a written statement of the reasons for the Secretary's final disposition of the case.

(g) Compilation, analysis, and publication of reports and information; rules and regulations.

(1) The Secretary and Secretary of Health and Human Services are authorized to compile, analyze, and publish, either in summary or detailed form, all reports or information obtained under this section.

(2) The Secretary and the Secretary of Health and Human Services shall each prescribe such rules and regulations as he may deem necessary to carry out their responsibilities under this chapter, including rules and regulations dealing with the inspection of an employer's establishment.

(h) Restrictions on the use of results of enforcement activities. The Secretary shall not use the results of enforcement activities, such as the number of citations issued or penalties assessed, to evaluate employees directly involved in enforcement activities under this chapter or to impose quotas or goals with regard to the results of such activities.

§ 658. Citations

(a) Authority to issue; grounds; contents; notice in lieu of citation for de minimis violations. If, upon inspection or investigation, the Secretary or his authorized representative believes that an employer has violated a requirement of section 654 of this title, of any standard, rule or order promulgated pursuant to section 655 of this title, or of any regulations prescribed pursuant to this chapter, he shall with reasonable promptness issue a citation to the employer. Each citation shall be in writing and shall describe with particularity the nature of the violation, including a reference to the provision of the chapter, standard, rule, regulation, or order alleged to have been violated. In addition, the citation shall fix a reasonable time for the abatement of the violation. The Secretary may prescribe procedures for the issuance of a notice in lieu of a citation with respect to de minimis violations which have no direct or immediate relationship to safety or health.

(b) Posting. Each citation issued under this section, or a copy or copies thereof, shall be prominently posted, as prescribed in regulations issued by the Secretary, at or near each place a violation referred to in the citation occurred.

(c) Time for issuance. No citation may be issued under this section after the expiration of six months following the occurrence of any violation.

§ 659. Enforcement procedures

(a) Notification of employer of proposed assessment of penalty subsequent to issuance of citation; time for notification of Secretary by employer of contest by employer of citation or proposed assessment; citation and proposed assessment as final order upon failure of employer to notify of contest and failure of employees to file notice. If, after an inspection or

investigation, the Secretary issues a citation under section 658(a) of this title, he shall, within a reasonable time after the termination of such inspection or investigation, notify the employer by certified mail of the penalty, if any, proposed to be assessed under section 666 of this title and that the employer has fifteen working days within which to notify the Secretary that he wishes to contest the citation or proposed assessment of penalty. If, within fifteen working days from the receipt of the notice issued by the Secretary the employer fails to notify the Secretary that he intends to contest the citation or proposed assessment of penalty, and no notice is filed by any employee or representative of employees under subsection (c) of this section within such time, the citation and the assessment, as proposed, shall be deemed a final order of the Commission and not subject to review by any court or agency.

(b) Notification of employer of failure to correct in allotted time period violation for which citation was issued and proposed assessment of penalty for failure to correct; time for notification of Secretary by employer of contest by employer of notification of failure to correct or proposed assessment; notification or proposed assessment as final order upon failure of employer to notify of contest. If the Secretary has reason to believe that an employer has failed to correct a violation for which a citation has been issued within the period permitted for its correction (which period shall not begin to run until the entry of a final order by the Commission in the case of any review proceedings under this section initiated by the employer in good faith and not solely for delay or avoidance of penalties), the Secretary shall notify the employer by certified mail of such failure and of the penalty proposed to be assessed under section 666 of this title by reason of such failure, and that the employer has fifteen working days within which to notify the Secretary that he wishes to contest the Secretary's notification or the proposed assessment of penalty. If, within fifteen working days from the receipt of notification issued by the Secretary, the employer fails to notify the Secretary that he intends to contest the notification or proposed assessment of penalty, the notification and assessment, as proposed, shall be deemed a final order of the Commission and not subject to review by any court or agency.

(c) Advisement of Commission by Secretary of notification of contest by employer of citation or notification or of filing of notice by any employee or representative of employees; hearing by Commission; orders of Commission and Secretary; rules of procedure. If an employer notifies the Secretary that he intends to contest a citation issued under section 658(a) of this title or notification issued under subsection (a) or (b) of this section, or if, within fifteen working days of the issuance of a citation under section 658(a) of this title, any employee or representative of employees files a notice with the Secretary alleging that the period of time fixed in the citation for the abatement of the violation is unreasonable, the Secretary shall immediately advise the Commission of such

317

notification, and the Commission shall afford an opportunity for a hearing (in accordance with section 554 of Title 5 but without regard to subsection (a)(3) of such section). The Commission shall thereafter issue an order, based on findings of fact, affirming, modifying, or vacating the Secretary's citation or proposed penalty, or directing other appropriate relief, and such order shall become final thirty days after its issuance. Upon a showing by an employer of a good faith effort to comply with the abatement requirements of a citation, and that abatement has not been completed because of factors beyond his reasonable control, the Secretary, after an opportunity for a hearing as provided in this subsection, shall issue an order affirming or modifying the abatement requirements in such citation. The rules of procedure prescribed by the Commission shall provide affected employees or representatives of affected employees an opportunity to participate as parties to hearings under this subsection.

§ 660. Judicial review

(a) Filing of petition by persons adversely affected or aggrieved; orders subject to review; jurisdiction; venue; procedure; conclusiveness of record and findings of Commission; appropriate relief; finality of judgment. Any person adversely affected or aggrieved by an order of the Commission issued under subsection (c) of section 659 of this title may obtain a review of such order in any United States court of appeals for the circuit in which the violation is alleged to have occurred or where the employer has its principal office, or in the Court of Appeals for the District of Columbia Circuit, by filing in such court within sixty days following the issuance of such order a written petition praying that the order be modified or set aside. A copy of such petition shall be forthwith transmitted by the clerk of the court to the Commission and to the other parties, and thereupon the Commission shall file in the court the record in the proceeding as provided in section 2112 of Title 28. Upon such filing, the court shall have jurisdiction of the proceeding and of the question determined therein, and shall have power to grant such temporary relief or restraining order as it deems just and proper, and to make and enter upon the pleadings, testimony, and proceedings set forth in such record a decree affirming, modifying, or setting aside in whole or in part, the order of the Commission and enforcing the same to the extent that such order is affirmed or modified. The commencement of proceedings under this subsection shall not, unless ordered by the court, operate as a stay of the order of the Commission. No objection that has not been urged before the Commission shall be considered by the court, unless the failure or neglect to urge such objection shall be excused because of extraordinary circumstances. The findings of the Commission with respect to questions of fact, if supported by substantial evidence on the record considered as a whole, shall be conclusive. If any party shall apply to the court for leave to adduce additional evidence and

shall show to the satisfaction of the court that such additional evidence is material and that there were reasonable grounds for the failure to adduce such evidence in the hearing before the Commission, the court may order such additional evidence to be taken before the Commission and to be made a part of the record. The Commission may modify its findings as to the facts, or make new findings, by reason of additional evidence so taken and filed, and it shall file such modified or new findings, which findings with respect to questions of fact, if supported by substantial evidence on the record considered as a whole, shall be conclusive, and its recommendations, if any, for the modification or setting aside of its original order. Upon the filing of the record with it, the jurisdiction of the court shall be exclusive and its judgment and decree shall be final, except that the same shall be subject to review by the Supreme Court of the United States, as provided in section 1254 of Title 28.

(b) Filing of petition by Secretary; orders subject to review; jurisdiction; venue; procedure; conclusiveness of record and findings of Commission; enforcement of orders; contempt proceedings. The Secretary may also obtain review or enforcement of any final order of the Commission by filing a petition for such relief in the United States court of appeals for the circuit in which the alleged violation occurred or in which the employer has its principal office, and the provisions of subsection (a) of this section shall govern such proceedings to the extent applicable. If no petition for review, as provided in subsection (a) of this section, is filed within sixty days after service of the Commission's order, the Commission's findings of fact and order shall be conclusive in connection with any petition for enforcement which is filed by the Secretary after the expiration of such sixty-day period. In any such case, as well as in the case of a noncontested citation or notification by the Secretary which has become a final order of the Commission under subsection (a) or (b) of section 659 of this title, the clerk of the court, unless otherwise ordered by the court, shall forthwith enter a decree enforcing the order and shall transmit a copy of such decree to the Secretary and the employer named in the petition. In any contempt proceeding brought to enforce a decree of a court of appeals entered pursuant to this subsection or subsection (a) of this section, the court of appeals may assess the penalties provided in section 666 of this title, in addition to invoking any other available remedies.

(c) Discharge or discrimination against employee for exercise of rights under this chapter; prohibition; procedure for relief.

(1) No person shall discharge or in any manner discriminate against any employee because such employee has filed any complaint or instituted or caused to be instituted any proceeding under or related to this chapter or has testified or is about to testify in any such proceeding or because of the exercise by such employee on behalf of himself or others of any right afforded by this chapter.

(2) Any employee who believes that he has been discharged or otherwise discriminated against by any person in violation of this subsection may, within thirty days after such violation occurs, file a complaint with the Secretary alleging such discrimination. Upon receipt of such complaint, the Secretary shall cause such investigation to be made as he deems appropriate. If upon such investigation, the Secretary determines that the provisions of this subsection have been violated, he shall bring an action in any appropriate United States district court against such person. In any such action the United States district courts shall have jurisdiction, for cause shown to restrain violations of paragraph (1) of this subsection and order all appropriate relief including rehiring or reinstatement of the employee to his former position with back pay.

(3) Within 90 days of the receipt of a complaint filed under this subsection the Secretary shall notify the complainant of his determination under paragraph (2) of this subsection.

§ 661. Occupational Safety and Health Review Commission

(a) Establishment; membership; appointment; Chairman. The Occupational Safety and Health Review Commission is hereby established. The Commission shall be composed of three members who shall be appointed by the President, by and with the advice and consent of the Senate, from among persons who by reason of training, education, or experience are qualified to carry out the functions of the Commission under this chapter. The President shall designate one of the members of the Commission to serve as Chairman.

(b) Terms of office; removal by President. The terms of members of the Commission shall be six years except that (1) the members of the Commission first taking office shall serve, as designated by the President at the time of appointment, one for a term of two years, one for a term of four years, and one for a term of six years, and (2) a vacancy caused by the death, resignation, or removal of a member prior to the expiration of the term for which he was appointed shall be filled only for the remainder of such unexpired term. A member of the Commission may be removed by the President for inefficiency, neglect of duty, or malfeasance in office.

* * *

(f) Quorum; official action. For the purpose of carrying out its functions under this chapter, two members of the Commission shall constitute a quorum and official action can be taken only on the affirmative vote of at least two members.

(g) Hearings and records open to public; promulgation of rules; applicability of Federal Rules of Civil Procedure. Every official act of the Commission shall be entered of record, and its hearings and records shall

be open to the public. The Commission is authorized to make such rules as are necessary for the orderly transaction of its proceedings. Unless the Commission has adopted a different rule, its proceedings shall be in accordance with the Federal Rules of Civil Procedure.

(h) Depositions and production of documentary evidence; fees. The Commission may order testimony to be taken by deposition in any proceeding pending before it at any state of such proceeding. Any person may be compelled to appear and depose, and to produce books, papers, or documents, in the same manner as witnesses may be compelled to appear and testify and produce like documentary evidence before the Commission. Witnesses whose depositions are taken under this subsection, and the persons taking such depositions, shall be entitled to the same fees as are paid for like services in the courts of the United States.

(i) Investigatory powers. For the purpose of any proceeding before the Commission, the provisions of section 161 of this title are hereby made applicable to the jurisdiction and powers of the Commission.

(j) Administrative law judges; determinations; report as final order of Commission. A administrative law judge appointed by the Commission shall hear, and make a determination upon, any proceeding instituted before the Commission and any motion in connection therewith, assigned to such administrative law judge by the Chairman of the Commission, and shall make a report of any such determination which constitutes his final disposition of the proceedings. The report of the administrative law judge shall become the final order of the Commission within thirty days after such report by the administrative law judge, unless within such period any Commission member has directed that such report shall be reviewed by the Commission.

* * *

§ 662. Injunction proceedings

(a) Petition by Secretary to restrain imminent dangers; scope of order. The United States district courts shall have jurisdiction, upon petition of the Secretary, to restrain any conditions or practices in any place of employment which are such that a danger exists which could reasonably be expected to cause death or serious physical harm immediately or before the imminence of such danger can be eliminated through the enforcement procedures otherwise provided by this chapter. Any order issued under this section may require such steps to be taken as may be necessary to avoid, correct, or remove such imminent danger and prohibit the employment or presence of any individual in locations or under conditions where such imminent danger exists, except individuals whose presence is necessary to avoid, correct, or remove such imminent danger or to maintain the capacity of a continuous process operation to resume normal operations without a complete cessation of operations, or where a

cessation of operations is necessary, to permit such to be accomplished in a safe and orderly manner.

(b) Appropriate injunctive relief or temporary restraining order pending outcome of enforcement proceeding; applicability of Rule 65 of Federal Rules of Civil Procedure. Upon the filing of any such petition the district court shall have jurisdiction to grant such injunctive relief or temporary restraining order pending the outcome of an enforcement proceeding pursuant to this chapter. The proceeding shall be as provided by Rule 65 of the Federal Rules, Civil Procedure, except that no temporary restraining order issued without notice shall be effective for a period longer than five days.

(c) Notification of affected employees and employers by inspector of danger and of recommendation to Secretary to seek relief. Whenever and as soon as an inspector concludes that conditions or practices described in subsection (a) of this section exist in any place of employment, he shall inform the affected employees and employers of the danger and that he is recommending to the Secretary that relief be sought.

(d) Failure of Secretary to seek relief; writ of mandamus. If the Secretary arbitrarily or capriciously fails to seek relief under this section, any employee who may be injured by reason of such failure, or the representative of such employees, might bring an action against the Secretary in the United States district court for the district in which the imminent danger is alleged to exist or the employer has its principal office, or for the District of Columbia, for a writ of mandamus to compel the Secretary to seek such an order and for such further relief as may be appropriate.

* * *

§ 665. Variations, tolerances, and exemptions from required provisions; procedure; duration

The Secretary, on the record, after notice and opportunity for a hearing may provide such reasonable limitations and may make such rules and regulations allowing reasonable variations, tolerances, and exemptions to and from any or all provisions of this chapter as he may find necessary and proper to avoid serious impairment of the national defense. Such action shall not be in effect for more than six months without notification to affected employees and an opportunity being afforded for a hearing.

§ 666. Civil and criminal penalties

(a) Willful or repeated violation. Any employer who willfully or repeatedly violates the requirements of section 654 of this title, any standard, rule, or order promulgated pursuant to section 655 of this title, or regulations prescribed pursuant to this chapter, may be assessed a

civil penalty of not more than $70,000 for each violation, but not less than $5,000 for each willful violation.

(b) Citation for serious violation. Any employer who has received a citation for a serious violation of the requirements of section 654 of this title, of any standard, rule, or order promulgated pursuant to section 655 of this title, or of any regulations prescribed pursuant to this chapter, shall be assessed a civil penalty of up to $7,000 for each such violation.

(c) Citation for violation determined not serious. Any employer who has received a citation for a violation of the requirements of section 654 of this title, of any standard, rule, or order promulgated pursuant to section 655 of this title, or of regulations prescribed pursuant to this chapter, and such violation is specifically determined not to be of a serious nature, may be assessed a civil penalty of up to $7,000 for each such violation.

(d) Failure to correct violation. Any employer who fails to correct a violation for which a citation has been issued under section 658(a) of this title within the period permitted for its correction (which period shall not begin to run until the date of the final order of the Commission in the case of any review proceeding under section 659 of this title initiated by the employer in good faith and not solely for delay or avoidance of penalties), may be assessed a civil penalty of not more than $7,000 for each day during which such failure or violation continues.

(e) Willful violation causing death to employee. Any employer who willfully violates any standard, rule, or order promulgated pursuant to section 655 of this title, or of any regulations prescribed pursuant to this chapter, and that violation caused death to any employee, shall, upon conviction, be punished by a fine of not more than $10,000 or by imprisonment for not more than six months, or by both; except that if the conviction is for a violation committed after a first conviction of such person, punishment shall be by a fine of not more than $20,000 or by imprisonment for not more than one year, or by both.

(f) Giving advance notice of inspection. Any person who gives advance notice of any inspection to be conducted under this chapter, without authority from the Secretary or his designees, shall, upon conviction, be punished by a fine of not more than $1,000 or by imprisonment for not more than six months, or by both.

(g) False statements, representations or certification. Whoever knowingly makes any false statement, representation, or certification in any application, record, report, plan, or other document filed or required to be maintained pursuant to this chapter shall, upon conviction, be punished by a fine of not more than $10,000, or by imprisonment for not more than six months, or by both.

(h) Omitted.

(i) Violation of posting requirements. Any employer who violates any of the posting requirements, as prescribed under the provisions of this

chapter, shall be assessed a civil penalty of up to $7,000 for each violation.

(j) Authority of Commission to assess civil penalties. The Commission shall have authority to assess all civil penalties provided in this section, giving due consideration to the appropriateness of the penalty with respect to the size of the business of the employer being charged, the gravity of the violation, the good faith of the employer, and the history of previous violations.

(k) Determination of serious violation. For purposes of this section, a serious violation shall be deemed to exist in a place of employment if there is a substantial probability that death or serious physical harm could result from a condition which exists, or from one or more practices, means, methods, operations, or processes which have been adopted or are in use, in such place of employment unless the employer did not, and could not with the exercise of reasonable diligence, know of the presence of the violation.

(l) Procedure for payment of civil penalties. Civil penalties owed under this chapter shall be paid to the Secretary for deposit into the Treasury of the United States and shall accrue to the United States and may be recovered in a civil action in the name of the United States brought in the United States district court for the district where the violation is alleged to have occurred or where the employer has its principal office.

§ 667. State jurisdiction and plans

(a) Assertion of State standards in absence of applicable Federal standards. Nothing in this chapter shall prevent any State agency or court from asserting jurisdiction under State law over any occupational safety or health issue with respect to which no standard is in effect under section 655 of this title.

(b) Submission of State plan for development and enforcement of State standards to preempt applicable Federal standards. Any State which, at any time, desires to assume responsibility for development and enforcement therein of occupational safety and health standards relating to any occupational safety or health issue with respect to which a Federal standard has been promulgated under section 655 of this title shall submit a State plan for the development of such standards and their enforcement.

(c) Conditions for approval of plan. The Secretary shall approve the plan submitted by a State under subsection (b) of this section, or any modification thereof, if such plan in his judgment—

(1) designates a State agency or agencies as the agency or agencies responsible for administering the plan throughout the State,

(2) provides for the development and enforcement of safety and health standards relating to one or more safety or health issues, which standards (and the enforcement of which standards) are or

will be at least as effective in providing safe and healthful employment and places of employment as the standards promulgated under section 655 of this title which relate to the same issues, and which standards, when applicable to products which are distributed or used in interstate commerce, are required by compelling local conditions and do not unduly burden interstate commerce,

(3) provides for a right of entry and inspection of all workplaces subject to this chapter which is at least as effective as that provided in section 657 of this title, and includes a prohibition on advance notice of inspections,

(4) contains satisfactory assurances that such agency or agencies have or will have the legal authority and qualified personnel necessary for the enforcement of such standards,

(5) gives satisfactory assurances that such State will devote adequate funds to the administration and enforcement of such standards,

(6) contains satisfactory assurances that such State will, to the extent permitted by its law, establish and maintain an effective and comprehensive occupational safety and health program applicable to all employees of public agencies of the State and its political subdivisions, which program is as effective as the standards contained in an approved plan,

(7) requires employers in the State to make reports to the Secretary in the same manner and to the same extent as if the plan were not in effect, and

(8) provides that the State agency will make such reports to the Secretary in such form and containing such information, as the Secretary shall from time to time require.

(d) Rejection of plan; notice and opportunity for hearing. If the Secretary rejects a plan submitted under subsection (b) of this section, he shall afford the State submitting the plan due notice and opportunity for a hearing before so doing.

(e) Discretion of Secretary to exercise authority over comparable standards subsequent to approval of State plans; duration; retention of jurisdiction by Secretary upon determination of enforcement of plan by State. After the Secretary approves a State plan submitted under subsection (b) of this section, he may, but shall not be required to, exercise his authority under sections 657, 658, 659, 662, and 666 of this title with respect to comparable standards promulgated under section 655 of this title, for the period specified in the next sentence. The Secretary may exercise the authority referred to above until he determines, on the basis of actual operations under the State plan, that the criteria set forth in subsection (c) of this section are being applied, but he shall not make such determination for at least three years after the plan's approval under subsection (c) of this section. Upon making the determination referred to in the preceding sentence, the provisions of

sections 654(a)(2), 657 (except for the purpose of carrying out subsection (f) of this section), 658, 659, 662, and 666 of this title, and standards promulgated under section 655 of this title, shall not apply with respect to any occupational safety or health issues covered under the plan, but the Secretary may retain jurisdiction under the above provisions in any proceeding commenced under section 658 or 659 of this title before the date of determination.

(f) Continuing evaluation by Secretary of State enforcement of approved plan; withdrawal of approval of plan by Secretary; grounds; procedure; conditions for retention of jurisdiction by State. The Secretary shall, on the basis of reports submitted by the State agency and his own inspections make a continuing evaluation of the manner in which each State having a plan approved under this section is carrying out such plan. Whenever the Secretary finds, after affording due notice and opportunity for a hearing, that in the administration of the State plan there is a failure to comply substantially with any provision of the State plan (or any assurance contained therein), he shall notify the State agency of his withdrawal of approval of such plan and upon receipt of such notice such plan shall cease to be in effect, but the State may retain jurisdiction in any case commenced before the withdrawal of the plan in order to enforce standards under the plan whenever the issues involved do not relate to the reasons for the withdrawal of the plan.

(g) Judicial review of Secretary's withdrawal of approval or rejection of plan; jurisdiction; venue; procedure; appropriate relief; finality of judgment. The State may obtain a review of a decision of the Secretary withdrawing approval of or rejecting its plan by the United States court of appeals for the circuit in which the State is located by filing in such court within thirty days following receipt of notice of such decision a petition to modify or set aside in whole or in part the action of the Secretary. A copy of such petition shall forthwith be served upon the Secretary, and thereupon the Secretary shall certify and file in the court the record upon which the decision complained of was issued as provided in section 2112 of Title 28. Unless the court finds that the Secretary's decision in rejecting a proposed State plan or withdrawing his approval of such a plan is not supported by substantial evidence the court shall affirm the Secretary's decision. The judgment of the court shall be subject to review by the Supreme Court of the United States upon certiorari or certification as provided in section 1254 of Title 28.

(h) Temporary enforcement of State standards. The Secretary may enter into an agreement with a State under which the State will be permitted to continue to enforce one or more occupational health and safety standards in effect in such State until final action is taken by the Secretary with respect to a plan submitted by a State under subsection (b) of this section, or two years from December 29, 1970, whichever is earlier.

* * *

MODEL STATE ADMINISTRATIVE PROCEDURE ACT (1981)

UNIFORM LAWS ANNOTATED
UNIFORM LAW COMMISSIONERS' MODEL STATE ADMINISTRATIVE PROCEDURE ACT (1981)

ARTICLE I. GENERAL PROVISIONS

ARTICLE II. PUBLIC ACCESS TO AGENCY LAW AND POLICY

ARTICLE III. RULE MAKING

CHAPTER I. ADOPTION AND EFFECTIVENESS OF RULES

ARTICLE I. GENERAL PROVISIONS

§ 1–101. [Short Title]

This Act may be cited as the [state] Administrative Procedure Act.

§ 1–102. [Definitions]

As used in this Act:

(1) "Agency" means a board, commission, department, officer, or other administrative unit of this State, including the agency head, and one or more members of the agency head or agency employees or other persons directly or indirectly purporting to act on behalf or under the authority of the agency head.   The term does not include the [legislature] or the courts [, or the governor] [, or the governor in the exercise of powers derived directly and exclusively from the constitution of this State].   The term does not include a political subdivision of the state or any of the administrative units of a political subdivision, but it does include a board, commission, department, officer, or other administrative unit created or appointed by joint or concerted action of an agency and one or more political subdivisions of the state or any of their units.   To the extent it purports to exercise authority subject to any provision of this Act, an administrative unit otherwise qualifying as an "agency" must be treated as a separate agency even if the unit is located within or subordinate to another agency.

(2) "Agency action" means:

(i) the whole or a part of a rule or an order;

(ii) the failure to issue a rule or an order; or

(iii) an agency's performance of, or failure to perform, any other duty, function, or activity, discretionary or otherwise.

(3) "Agency head" means an individual or body of individuals in whom the ultimate legal authority of the agency is vested by any provision of law.

(4) "License" means a franchise, permit, certification, approval, registration, charter, or similar form of authorization required by law.

(5) "Order" means an agency action of particular applicability that determines the legal rights, duties, privileges, immunities, or other legal interests of one or more specific persons. [The term does not include an "executive order" issued by the governor pursuant to Section 1-104 or 3-202.]

(6) "Party to agency proceedings," or "party" in context so indicating, means:

(i) a person to whom the agency action is specifically directed; or

(ii) a person named as a party to an agency proceeding or allowed to intervene or participate as a party in the proceeding.

(7) "Party to judicial review or civil enforcement proceedings," or "party" in context so indicating, means:

(i) a person who files a petition for judicial review or civil enforcement or

(ii) a person named as a party in a proceeding for judicial review or civil enforcement or allowed to participate as a party in the proceeding.

(8) "Person" means an individual, partnership, corporation, association, governmental subdivision or unit thereof, or public or private organization or entity of any character, and includes another agency.

(9) "Provision of law" means the whole or a part of the federal or state constitution, or of any federal or state (i) statute, (ii) rule of court, (iii) executive order, or (iv) rule of an administrative agency.

(10) "Rule" means the whole or a part of an agency statement of general applicability that implements, interprets, or prescribes (i) law or policy, or (ii) the organization, procedure, or practice requirements of an agency. The term includes the amendment, repeal, or suspension of an existing rule.

(11) "Rule making" means the process for formulation and adoption of a rule.

§ 1–103. [Applicability and Relation to Other Law]

(a) This Act applies to all agencies and all proceedings not expressly exempted.

(b) This Act creates only procedural rights and imposes only procedural duties. They are in addition to those created and imposed by other statutes. To the extent that any other statute would diminish a right created or duty imposed by this Act, the other statute is superseded by this Act, unless the other statute expressly provides otherwise.

(c) An agency may grant procedural rights to persons in addition to those conferred by this Act so long as rights conferred upon other persons by any provision of law are not substantially prejudiced.

§ 1–104. [Suspension of Act's Provisions When Necessary to Avoid Loss of Federal Funds or Services]

(a) To the extent necessary to avoid a denial of funds or services from the United States which would otherwise be available to the state, the [governor by executive order] [attorney general by rule] [may] [shall] suspend, in whole or in part, one or more provisions of this Act. The [governor by executive order] [attorney general by rule] shall declare the termination of a suspension as soon as it is no longer necessary to prevent the loss of funds or services from the United States.

[(b) An executive order issued under subsection (a) is subject to the requirements applicable to the adoption and effectiveness of a rule.]

(c) If any provision of this Act is suspended pursuant to this section, the [governor] [attorney general] shall promptly report the suspension to the [legislature]. The report must include recommendations concerning any desirable legislation that may be necessary to conform this Act to federal law.

§ 1–105. [Waiver]

Except to the extent precluded by another provision of law, a person may waive any right conferred upon that person by this Act.

§ 1–106. [Informal Settlements]

Except to the extent precluded by another provision of law, informal settlement of matters that may make unnecessary more elaborate proceedings under this Act is encouraged. Agencies shall establish by rule specific procedures to facilitate informal settlement of matters. This section does not require any party or other person to settle a matter pursuant to informal procedures.

§ 1–107. [Conversion of Proceedings]

(a) At any point in an agency proceeding the presiding officer or other agency official responsible for the proceeding:

(1) may convert the proceeding to another type of agency proceeding provided for by this Act if the conversion is appropriate, is in the public interest, and does not substantially prejudice the rights of any party; and

(2) if required by any provision of law, shall convert the proceeding to another type of agency proceeding provided for by this Act.

(b) A conversion of a proceeding of one type to a proceeding of another type may be effected only upon notice to all parties to the original proceeding.

(c) If the presiding officer or other agency official responsible for the original proceeding would not have authority over the new proceeding to which it is to be converted, that officer or official, in accordance with agency rules, shall secure the appointment of a successor to preside over or be responsible for the new proceeding.

(d) To the extent feasible and consistent with the rights of parties and the requirements of this Act pertaining to the new proceeding, the record of the original agency proceeding must be used in the new agency proceeding.

(e) After a proceeding is converted from one type to another, the presiding officer or other agency official responsible for the new proceeding shall:

(1) give such additional notice to parties or other persons as is necessary to satisfy the requirements of this Act pertaining to those proceedings;

(2) dispose of the matters involved without further proceedings if sufficient proceedings have already been held to satisfy the requirements of this Act pertaining to the new proceedings; and

(3) conduct or cause to be conducted any additional proceedings necessary to satisfy the requirements of this Act pertaining to those proceedings.

(f) Each agency shall adopt rules to govern the conversion of one type of proceeding to another. Those rules must include an enumeration of the factors to be considered in determining whether and under what circumstances one type of proceeding will be converted to another.

§ 1–108. [Effective Date]

This Act takes effect on [date] and does not govern proceedings pending on that date. This Act governs all agency proceedings, and all proceedings for judicial review or civil enforcement of agency action, commenced after that date. This Act also governs agency proceedings conducted on a remand from a court or another agency after the effective date of this Act.

§ 1-109. [Severability]

If any provision of this Act or the application thereof to any person or circumstance is held invalid, the invalidity does not affect other provisions or applications of the Act which can be given effect without the invalid provision or application, and for this purpose the provisions of this Act are severable.

ARTICLE II. PUBLIC ACCESS TO AGENCY LAW AND POLICY

§ 2-101. [Administrative Rules Editor; Publication, Compilation, Indexing, and Public Inspection of Rules]

(a) There is created, within the executive branch, an [administrative rules editor]. The governor shall appoint the [administrative rules editor] who shall serve at the pleasure of the governor.

(b) Subject to the provisions of this Act, the [administrative rules editor] shall prescribe a uniform numbering system, form, and style for all proposed and adopted rules caused to be published by that office [, and shall have the same editing authority with respect to the publication of rules as the [reviser of statutes] has with respect to the publication of statutes].

(c) The [administrative rules editor] shall cause the [administrative bulletin] to be published in pamphlet form [once each week]. For purposes of calculating adherence to time requirements imposed by this Act, an issue of the [administrative bulletin] is deemed published on the later of the date indicated in that issue or the date of its mailing. The [administrative bulletin] must contain:

  (1) notices of proposed rule adoption prepared so that the text of the proposed rule shows the text of any existing rule proposed to be changed and the change proposed;

  (2) newly filed adopted rules prepared so that the text of the newly filed adopted rule shows the text of any existing rule being changed and the change being made;

  (3) any other notices and materials designated by [law] [the administrative rules editor] for publication therein; and

  (4) an index to its contents by subject.

(d) The [administrative rules editor] shall cause the [administrative code] to be compiled, indexed by subject, and published [in loose-leaf form]. All of the effective rules of each agency must be published and indexed in that publication. The [administrative rules editor] shall also cause [loose-leaf] supplements to the [administrative code] to be published at least every [3 months]. [The loose-leaf supplements must be in a form suitable for insertion in the appropriate places in the permanent [administrative code] compilation.]

(e) The [administrative rules editor] may omit from the [administrative bulletin or code] any proposed or filed adopted rule the publication of which would be unduly cumbersome, expensive, or otherwise inexpedient, if:

> (1) knowledge of the rule is likely to be important to only a small class of persons;

> (2) on application to the issuing agency, the proposed or adopted rule in printed or processed form is made available at no more than its cost of reproduction; and

> (3) the [administrative bulletin or code] contains a notice stating in detail the specific subject matter of the omitted proposed or adopted rule and how a copy of the omitted material may be obtained.

(f) The [administrative bulletin and administrative code] must be furnished to [designated officials] without charge and to all subscribers at a cost to be determined by the [administrative rules editor]. Each agency shall also make available for public inspection and copying those portions of the [administrative bulletin and administrative code] containing all rules adopted or used by the agency in the discharge of its functions, and the index to those rules.

(g) Except as otherwise required by a provision of law, subsections (c) through (f) do not apply to rules governed by Section 3–116, and the following provisions apply instead:

> (1) Each agency shall maintain an official, current, and dated compilation that is indexed by subject, containing all of its rules within the scope of Section 3–116. Each addition to, change in, or deletion from the official compilation must also be dated, indexed, and a record thereof kept. Except for those portions containing rules governed by Section 3–116(2), the compilation must be made available for public inspection and copying. Certified copies of the full compilation must also be furnished to the [secretary of state, the administrative rules counsel, and members of the administrative rules review committee], and be kept current by the agency at least every [30] days.

> (2) A rule subject to the requirements of this subsection may not be relied on by an agency to the detriment of any person who does not have actual, timely knowledge of the contents of the rule until the requirements of paragraph (1) are satisfied. The burden of proving that knowledge is on the agency. This provision is also inapplicable to the extent necessary to avoid imminent peril to the public health, safety, or welfare.

§ **2–102.** [Public Inspection and Indexing of Agency Orders]

(a) In addition to other requirements imposed by any provision of law, each agency shall make all written final orders available for public inspection and copying and index them by name and subject. An agency shall delete from those orders identifying details to the extent required by any provision of law [or necessary to prevent a clearly unwarranted invasion of privacy or release of trade secrets]. In each case the justification for the deletion must be explained in writing and attached to the order.

(b) A written final order may not be relied on as precedent by an agency to the detriment of any person until it has been made available for public inspection and indexed in the manner described in subsection (a). This provision is inapplicable to any person who has actual timely knowledge of the order. The burden of proving that knowledge is on the agency.

§ 2–103. [Declaratory Orders]

(a) Any person may petition an agency for a declaratory order as to the applicability to specified circumstances of a statute, rule, or order within the primary jurisdiction of the agency. An agency shall issue a declaratory order in response to a petition for that order unless the agency determines that issuance of the order under the circumstances would be contrary to a rule adopted in accordance with subsection (b). However, an agency may not issue a declaratory order that would substantially prejudice the rights of a person who would be a necessary party and who does not consent in writing to the determination of the matter by a declaratory order proceeding.

(b) Each agency shall issue rules that provide for: (i) the form, contents, and filing of petitions for declaratory orders; (ii) the procedural rights of persons in relation to the petitions and (iii) the disposition of the petitions. Those rules must describe the classes of circumstances in which the agency will not issue a declaratory order and must be consistent with the public interest and with the general policy of this Act to facilitate and encourage agency issuance of reliable advice.

(c) Within [15] days after receipt of a petition for a declaratory order, an agency shall give notice of the petition to all persons to whom notice is required by any provision of law and may give notice to any other persons.

(d) Persons who qualify under Section 4–209(a)(2) and (3) and file timely petitions for intervention according to agency rules may intervene in proceedings for declaratory orders. Other provisions of Article IV apply to agency proceedings for declaratory orders only to the extent an agency so provides by rule or order.

(e) Within [30] days after receipt of a petition for a declaratory order an agency, in writing, shall:

   (1) issue an order declaring the applicability of the statute, rule, or order in question to the specified circumstances;

   (2) set the matter for specified proceedings;

(3) agree to issue a declaratory order by a specified time; or

(4) decline to issue a declaratory order, stating the reasons for its action.

(f) A copy of all orders issued in response to a petition for a declaratory order must be mailed promptly to petitioner and any other parties.

(g) A declaratory order has the same status and binding effect as any other order issued in an agency adjudicative proceeding. A declaratory order must contain the names of all parties to the proceeding on which it is based, the particular facts on which it is based, and the reasons for its conclusion.

(h) If an agency has not issued a declaratory order within [60] days after receipt of a petition therefor, the petition is deemed to have been denied.

§ 2–104. [Required Rule Making]

In addition to other rule-making requirements imposed by law, each agency shall:

(1) adopt as a rule a description of the organization of the agency which states the general course and method of its operations and where and how the public may obtain information or make submissions or requests;

(2) adopt rules of practice setting forth the nature and requirements of all formal and informal procedures available to the public, including a description of all forms and instructions that are to be used by the public in dealing with the agency; [and]

(3) as soon as feasible and to the extent practicable, adopt rules, in addition to those otherwise required by this Act, embodying appropriate standards, principles, and procedural safeguards that the agency will apply to the law it administers [; and] [.]

[(4) as soon as feasible and to the extent practicable, adopt rules to supersede principles of law or policy lawfully declared by the agency as the basis for its decisions in particular cases.]

§ 2–105. [Model Rules of Procedure]

In accordance with the rule-making requirements of this Act, the [attorney general] shall adopt model rules of procedure appropriate for use by as many agencies as possible. The model rules must deal with all general functions and duties performed in common by several agencies. Each agency shall adopt as much of the model rules as is practicable under its circumstances. To the extent an agency adopts the model rules, it shall do so in accordance with the rule-making requirements of this Act. Any agency adopting a rule of procedure that differs from the model rules shall include in the rule a finding stating the reasons why the relevant portions of the model rules were impracticable under the circumstances.

ARTICLE III.   RULE MAKING
CHAPTER I.   ADOPTION AND EFFECTIVENESS OF RULES

§ 3–101.   [Advice on Possible Rules before Notice of Proposed Rule Adoption]

(a) In addition to seeking information by other methods, an agency, before publication of a notice of proposed rule adoption under Section 3–103, may solicit comments from the public on a subject matter of possible rule making under active consideration within the agency by causing notice to be published in the [administrative bulletin] of the subject matter and indicating where, when, and how persons may comment.

(b) Each agency may also appoint committees to comment, before publication of a notice of proposed rule adoption under Section 3–103, on the subject matter of a possible rule making under active consideration within the agency. The membership of those committees must be published at least [annually] in the [administrative bulletin].

§ 3–102.   [Public Rule-making Docket]

(a) Each agency shall maintain a current, public rule-making docket.

(b) The rule-making docket [must] [may] contain a listing of the precise subject matter of each possible rule currently under active consideration within the agency for proposal under Section 3–103, the name and address of agency personnel with whom persons may communicate with respect to the matter, and an indication of the present status within the agency of that possible rule.

(c) The rule-making docket must list each pending rule-making proceeding. A rule-making proceeding is pending from the time it is commenced, by publication of a notice of proposed rule adoption, to the time it is terminated, by publication of a notice of termination or the rule becoming effective. For each rule-making proceeding, the docket must indicate:

(1) the subject matter of the proposed rule;

(2) a citation to all published notices relating to the proceeding;

(3) where written submissions on the proposed rule may be inspected;

(4) the time during which written submissions may be made;

(5) the names of persons who have made written requests for an opportunity to make oral presentations on the proposed rule, where

those requests may be inspected, and where and when oral presentations may be made;

(6) whether a written request for the issuance of a regulatory analysis of the proposed rule has been filed, whether that analysis has been issued, and where the written request and analysis may be inspected;

(7) the current status of the proposed rule and any agency determinations with respect thereto;

(8) any known timetable for agency decisions or other action in the proceeding;

(9) the date of the rule's adoption;

(10) the date of the rule's filing, indexing, and publication; and

(11) when the rule will become effective.

§ 3–103.   [Notice of Proposed Rule Adoption]

(a) At least [30] days before the adoption of a rule an agency shall cause notice of its contemplated action to be published in the [administrative bulletin].   The notice of proposed rule adoption must include:

(1) a short explanation of the purpose of the proposed rule;

(2) the specific legal authority authorizing the proposed rule;

(3) subject to Section 2–101(e), the text of the proposed rule;

(4) where, when, and how persons may present their views on the proposed rule; and

(5) where, when, and how persons may demand an oral proceeding on the proposed rule if the notice does not already provide for one.

(b) Within [3] days after its publication in the [administrative bulletin], the agency shall cause a copy of the notice of proposed rule adoption to be mailed to each person who has made a timely request to the agency for a mailed copy of the notice.   An agency may charge persons for the actual cost of providing them with mailed copies.

§ 3–104.   [Public Participation]

(a) For at least [30] days after publication of the notice of proposed rule adoption, an agency shall afford persons the opportunity to submit in writing, argument, data, and views on the proposed rule.

(b)(1) An agency shall schedule an oral proceeding on a proposed rule if, within [20] days after the published notice of proposed rule adoption, a written request for an oral proceeding is submitted by [the administrative rules review committee,] [the administrative rules counsel,] a political subdivision, an agency, or [25] persons. At that proceeding, persons may present oral argument, data, and views on the proposed rule.

(2) An oral proceeding on a proposed rule, if required, may not be held earlier than [20] days after notice of its location and time is published in the [administrative bulletin].

(3) The agency, a member of the agency, or another presiding officer designated by the agency, shall preside at a required oral proceeding on a proposed rule. If the agency does not preside, the presiding official shall prepare a memorandum for consideration by the agency summarizing the contents of the presentations made at the oral proceeding. Oral proceedings must be open to the public and be recorded by stenographic or other means.

(4) Each agency shall issue rules for the conduct of oral rule-making proceedings. Those rules may include provisions calculated to prevent undue repetition in the oral proceedings.

§ 3–105. [Regulatory Analysis]

(a) An agency shall issue a regulatory analysis of a proposed rule if, within [20] days after the published notice of proposed rule adoption, a written request for the analysis is filed in the office of the [secretary of state] by [the administrative rules review committee, the governor, a political subdivision, an agency, or [300] persons signing the request]. The [secretary of state] shall immediately forward to the agency a certified copy of the filed request.

(b) Except to the extent that the written request expressly waives one or more of the following, the regulatory analysis must contain:

(1) a description of the classes of persons who probably will be affected by the proposed rule, including classes that will bear the costs of the proposed rule and classes that will benefit from the proposed rule;

(2) a description of the probable quantitative and qualitative impact of the proposed rule, economic or otherwise, upon affected classes of persons;

(3) the probable costs to the agency and to any other agency of the implementation and enforcement of the proposed rule and any anticipated effect on state revenues;

(4) a comparison of the probable costs and benefits of the proposed rule to the probable costs and benefits of inaction;

(5) a determination of whether there are less costly methods or less intrusive methods for achieving the purpose of the proposed rule; and

(6) a description of any alternative methods for achieving the purpose of the proposed rule that were seriously considered by the agency and the reasons why they were rejected in favor of the proposed rule.

(c) Each regulatory analysis must include quantification of the data to the extent practicable and must take account of both short-term and long-term consequences.

(d) A concise summary of the regulatory analysis must be published in the [administrative bulletin] at least [10] days before the earliest of:

(1) the end of the period during which persons may make written submissions on the proposed rule;

(2) the end of the period during which an oral proceeding may be requested; or

(3) the date of any required oral proceeding on the proposed rule.

(e) The published summary of the regulatory analysis must also indicate where persons may obtain copies of the full text of the regulatory analysis and where, when, and how persons may present their views on the proposed rule and demand an oral proceeding thereon if one is not already provided.

(f) If the agency has made a good faith effort to comply with the requirements of subsections (a) through (c), the rule may not be invalidated on the ground that the contends of the regulatory analysis are insufficient or inaccurate.

§ 3-106. [Time and Manner of Rule Adoption]

(a) An agency may not adopt a rule until the period for making written submissions and oral presentations has expired.

(b) Within [180] days after the later of (i) the publication of the notice of proposed rule adoption, or (ii) the end of oral proceedings thereon, an agency shall adopt a rule pursuant to the rule-making proceeding or terminate the proceeding by publication of a notice to that effect in the [administrative bulletin].

(c) Before the adoption of a rule, an agency shall consider the written submissions, oral submissions or any memorandum summarizing oral submissions, and any regulatory analysis, provided for by this Chapter.

(d) Within the scope of its delegated authority, an agency may use its own experience, technical competence, specialized knowledge, and judgment in the adoption of a rule.

§ 3-107. [Variance between Adopted Rule and Published Notice of Proposed Rule Adoption]

(a) An agency may not adopt a rule that is substantially different from the proposed rule contained in the published notice of proposed rule adoption. However, an agency may terminate a rule-making proceeding and commence a new rule-making proceeding for the purpose of adopting a substantially different rule.

341

(b) In determining whether an adopted rule is substantially different from the published proposed rule upon which it is required to be based, the following must be considered:

(1) the extent to which all persons affected by the adopted rule should have understood that the published proposed rule would affect their interests;

(2) the extent to which the subject matter of the adopted rule or the issues determined by that rule are different from the subject matter or issues involved in the published proposed rule; and

(3) the extent to which the effects of the adopted rule differ from the effects of the published proposed rule had it been adopted instead.

§ 3–108. [General Exemption from Public Rule-making Procedures]

(a) To the extent an agency for good cause finds that any requirements of Sections 3–103 through 3–107 are unnecessary, impracticable, or contrary to the public interest in the process of adopting a particular rule, those requirements do not apply. The agency shall incorporate the required finding and a brief statement of its supporting reasons in each rule adopted in reliance upon this subsection.

(b) In an action contesting a rule adopted under subsection (a), the burden is upon the agency to demonstrate that any omitted requirements of Sections 3–103 through 3–107 were impracticable, unnecessary, or contrary to the public interest in the particular circumstances involved.

(c) Within [2] years after the effective date of a rule adopted under subsection (a), the [administrative rules review committee or the governor] may request the agency to hold a rule-making proceeding thereon according to the requirements of Sections 3–103 through 3–107. The request must be in writing and filed in the office of the [secretary of state]. The [secretary of state] shall immediately forward to the agency and to the [administrative rules editor] a certified copy of the request. Notice of the filing of the request must be published in the next issue of the [administrative bulletin]. The rule in question ceases to be effective [180] days after the request is filed. However, an agency, after the filing of the request, may subsequently adopt an identical rule in a rule-making proceeding conducted pursuant to the requirements of Sections 3–103 through 3–107.

§ 3–109. [Exemption for Certain Rules]

(a) An agency need not follow the provisions of Sections 3–103 through 3–108 in the adoption of a rule that only defines the meaning of a statute or other provision of law or precedent if the agency does not possess delegated authority to bind the courts to any extent with its definition. A rule adopted under this subsection must include a statement that it was adopted under this subsection when it is published in the [administrative bulletin], and there must be an indication to that effect adjacent to the rule when it is published in the [administrative code].

(b) A reviewing court shall determine wholly de novo the validity of a rule within the scope of subsection (a) that is adopted without complying with the provisions of Sections 3–103 through 3–108.

§ 3–110. [Concise Explanatory Statement]

(a) At the time it adopts a rule, an agency shall issue a concise explanatory statement containing:

(1) its reasons for adopting the rule; and

(2) an indication of any change between the text of the proposed rule contained in the published notice of proposed rule adoption and the text of the rule as finally adopted, with the reasons for any change.

(b) Only the reasons contained in the concise explanatory statement may be used by any party as justifications for the adoption of the rule in any proceeding in which its validity is at issue.

§ 3–111. [Contents, Style, and Form of Rule]

(a) Each rule adopted by an agency must contain the text of the rule and:

(1) the date the agency adopted the rule;

(2) a concise statement of the purpose of the rule;

(3) a reference to all rules repealed, amended, or suspended by the rule;

(4) a reference to the specific statutory or other authority authorizing adoption of the rule;

(5) any findings required by any provision of law as a prerequisite to adoption or effectiveness of the rule; and

(6) the effective date of the rule if other than that specified in Section 3–115(a).

[(b) To the extent feasible, each rule should be written in clear and concise language understandable to persons who may be affected by it.]

(c) An agency may incorporate, by reference in its rules and without publishing the incorporated matter in full, all or any part of a code, standard, rule, or regulation that has been adopted by an agency of the United States or of this state, another state, or by a nationally recognized organization or association, if incorporation of its text in agency rules would be unduly cumbersome, expensive, or otherwise inexpedient.

The reference in the agency rules must fully identify the incorporated matter by location, date, and otherwise, [and must state that the rule does not include any later amendments or editions of the incorporated matter]. An agency may incorporate by reference such matter in its rules only if the agency, organization, or association originally issuing that matter makes copies of it readily available to the public. The rules must state where copies of the incorporated matter are available at cost from the agency issuing the rule, and where copies are available from the agency of the United States, this State, another state, or the organization or association originally issuing that matter.

(d) In preparing its rules pursuant to this Chapter, each agency shall follow the uniform numbering system, form, and style prescribed by the [administrative rules editor].

§ 3-112. [Agency Rule-making Record]

(a) An agency shall maintain an official rule-making record for each rule it (i) proposes by publication in the [administrative bulletin] of a notice of proposed rule adoption, or (ii) adopts. The record and materials incorporated by reference must be available for public inspection.

(b) The agency rule-making record must contain:

(1) copies of all publications in the [administrative bulletin] with respect to the rule or the proceeding upon which the rule is based;

(2) copies of any portions of the agency's public rule-making docket containing entries relating to the rule or the proceeding upon which the rule is based;

(3) all written petitions, requests, submissions, and comments received by the agency and all other written materials considered by the agency in connection with the formulation, proposal, or adoption of the rule or the proceeding upon which the rule is based;

(4) any official transcript of oral presentations made in the proceeding upon which the rule is based or, if not transcribed, any tape recording or stenographic record of those presentations, and any memorandum prepared by a presiding official summarizing the contents of those presentations;

(5) a copy of any regulatory analysis prepared for the proceeding upon which the rule is based;

(6) a copy of the rule and explanatory statement filed in the office of the [secretary of state];

(7) all petitions for exceptions to, amendments of, or repeal or suspension of, the rule;

(8) a copy of any request filed pursuant to Section 3-108(c);

[(9) a copy of any objection to the rule filed by the [administrative rules review committee] pursuant to Section 3–204(d) and the agency's response;] and

(10) a copy of any filed executive order with respect to the rule.

(c) Upon judicial review, the record required by this section constitutes the official agency rule-making record with respect to a rule. Except as provided in Section 3–110(b) or otherwise required by a provision of law, the agency rule-making record need not constitute the exclusive basis for agency action on that rule or for judicial review thereof.

§ 3–113. [Invalidity of Rules Not Adopted According to Chapter; Time Limitation]

(a) A rule adopted after [date] is invalid unless adopted in substantial compliance with the provisions of Sections 3–102 through 3–108 and Sections 3–110 through 3–112. However, inadvertent failure to mail a notice of proposed rule adoption to any person as required by Section 3–103(b) does not invalidate a rule.

(b) An action to contest the validity of a rule on the grounds of its noncompliance with any provision of Sections 3–102 through 3–108 or Sections 3–110 through 3–112 must be commenced within [2] years after the effective date of the rule.

§ 3–114. [Filing of Rules]

(a) An agency shall file in the office of the [secretary of state] each rule it adopts and all rules existing on the effective date of this Act that have not previously been filed. The filing must be done as soon after adoption of the rule as is practicable. At the time of filing, each rule adopted after the effective date of this Act must have attached to it the explanatory statement required by Section 3–110. The [secretary of state] shall affix to each rule and statement a certification of the time and date of filing and keep a permanent register open to public inspection of all filed rules and attached explanatory statements. In filing a rule, each agency shall use a standard form prescribed by the [secretary of state].

(b) The [secretary of state] shall transmit to the [administrative rules editor], [administrative rules counsel], and to the members of the [administrative rules review committee] a certified copy of each filed rule as soon after its filing as is practicable.

§ 3–115. [Effective Date of Rules]

(a) Except to the extent subsection (b) or (c) provides otherwise, each rule adopted after the effective date of this Act becomes effective [30] days after the later of (i) its filing in the office of the [secretary of state] or (ii) its publication and indexing in the [administrative bulletin].

(b)(1) A rule becomes effective on a date later than that established by subsection (a) if a later date is required by another statute or specified in the rule.

(2) A rule may become effective immediately upon its filing or any subsequent date earlier than that established by subsection (a) if the agency establishes such an effective date and finds that:

(i) it is required by constitution, statute, or court order;

(ii) the rule only confers a benefit or removes a restriction on the public or some segment thereof;

(iii) the rule only delays the effective date of another rule that is not yet effective; or

(iv) the earlier effective date is necessary because of imminent peril to the public health, safety, or welfare.

(3) The finding and a brief statement of the reasons therefor required by paragraph (2) must be made a part of the rule. In any action contesting the effective date of a rule made effective under paragraph (2), the burden is on the agency to justify its finding.

(4) Each agency shall make a reasonable effort to make known to persons who may be affected by it a rule made effective before publication and indexing under this subsection.

(c) This section does not relieve an agency from compliance with any provision of law requiring that some or all of its rules be approved by other designated officials or bodies before they become effective.

§ 3–116.   [Special Provision for Certain Classes of Rules]

Except to the extent otherwise provided by any provision of law, Sections 3–102 through 3–115 are inapplicable to:

(1) a rule concerning only the internal management of an agency which does not directly and substantially affect the procedural or substantive rights or duties of any segment of the public;

(2) a rule that establishes criteria or guidelines to be used by the staff of an agency in performing audits, investigations, or inspections, settling commercial disputes, negotiating commercial arrangements, or in the defense, prosecution, or settlement of cases, if disclosure of the criteria or guidelines would:

(i) enable law violators to avoid detection;

(ii) facilitate disregard of requirements imposed by law; or

(iii) give a clearly improper advantage to persons who are in an adverse position to the state;

(3) a rule that only establishes specific prices to be charged for particular goods or services sold by an agency;

(4) a rule concerning only the physical servicing, maintenance, or care of agency owned or operated facilities or property;

(5) a rule relating only to the use of a particular facility or property owned, operated, or maintained by the state or any of its subdivisions, if the substance of the rule is adequately indicated by means of signs or signals to persons who use the facility or property;

(6) a rule concerning only inmates of a correctional or detention facility, students enrolled in an educational institution, or patients admitted to a hospital, if adopted by that facility, institution, or hospital;

(7) a form whose contents or substantive requirements are prescribed by rule or statute, and instructions for the execution or use of the form;

(8) an agency budget; [or]

(9) an opinion of the attorney general [; or] [.]

(10) [the terms of a collective bargaining agreement.]

§ 3–117. [Petition for Adoption of Rule]

Any person may petition an agency requesting the adoption of a rule. Each agency shall prescribe by rule the form of the petition and the procedure for its submission, consideration, and disposition. Within [60] days after submission of a petition, the agency shall either (i) deny the petition in writing, stating its reasons therefor, (ii) initiate rule-making proceedings in accordance with this Chapter, or (iii) if otherwise lawful, adopt a rule.

CHAPTER II. REVIEW OF AGENCY RULES

§ 3–201. [Review by Agency]

At least [annually], each agency shall review all of its rules to determine whether any new rule should be adopted. In conducting that review, each agency shall prepare a written report summarizing its findings, its supporting reasons, and any proposed course of action. For each rule, the [annual] report must include, at least once every [7] years, a concise statement of:

(1) the rule's effectiveness in achieving its objectives, including a summary of any available data supporting the conclusions reached;

(2) criticisms of the rule received during the previous [7] years, including a summary of any petitions for waiver of the rule tendered to the agency or granted by it; and

(3) alternative solutions to the criticisms and the reasons they were rejected or the changes made in the rule in response to those criticisms and the reasons for the changes. A copy of the [annual]

report must be sent to the [administrative rules review committee and the administrative rules counsel] and be available for public inspection.

[§ 3–202. [Review by Governor; Administrative Rules Counsel]]

(a) To the extent the agency itself would have authority, the governor may rescind or suspend all or a severable portion of a rule of an agency. In exercising this authority, the governor shall act by an executive order that is subject to the provisions of this Act applicable to the adoption and effectiveness of a rule.

(b) The governor may summarily terminate any pending rule-making proceeding by an executive order to that effect, stating therein the reasons for the action. The executive order must be filed in the office of the [secretary of state], which shall promptly forward a certified copy to the agency and the [administrative rules editor]. An executive order terminating a rule-making proceeding becomes effective on [the date it is filed] and must be published in the next issue of the [administrative bulletin].

(c) There is created, within the office of the governor, an [administrative rules counsel] to advise the governor in the execution of the authority vested under this Article. The governor shall appoint the [administrative rules counsel] who shall serve at the pleasure of the governor.

[§ 3–203. [Administrative Rules Review Committee]]

There is created the ["administrative rules review committee"] of the [legislature]. The committee must be [bipartisan] and composed of [3] senators appointed by the [president of the senate] and [3] representatives appointed by the [speaker of the house]. Committee members must be appointed within [30] days after the convening of a regular legislative session. The term of office is [2] years while a member of the [legislature] and begins on the date of appointment to the committee. While a member of the [legislature], a member of the committee whose term has expired shall serve until a successor is appointed. A vacancy on the committee may be filled at any time by the original appointing authority for the remainder of the term. The committee shall choose a chairman from its membership for a [2]-year term and may employ staff it considers advisable.

§ 3–204. [Review by Administrative Rules Review Committee]

(a) The [administrative rules review committee] shall selectively review possible, proposed, or adopted rules and prescribe appropriate committee procedures for that purpose. The committee may receive and investigate complaints from members of the public with respect to possible, proposed, or adopted rules and hold public proceedings on those complaints.

(b) Committee meetings must be open to the public. Subject to procedures established by the committee, persons may present oral argument, data, or views at those meetings. The committee may require a representative of an agency whose possible, proposed, or adopted rule is under examination to attend a committee meeting and answer relevant questions. The committee may also communicate to the agency its comments on any possible, proposed, or adopted rule and require the agency to respond to them in writing. Unless impracticable, in advance of each committee meeting notice of the time and place of the meeting and the specific subject matter to be considered must be published in the [administrative bulletin].

(c) The committee may recommend enactment of a statute to improve the operation of an agency. The committee may also recommend that a particular rule be superseded in whole or in part by statute. The [speaker of the house and the president of the senate] shall refer those recommendations to the appropriate standing committees. This subsection does not preclude any committee of the legislature from reviewing a rule on its own motion or recommending that it be superseded in whole or in part by statute.

[(d)(1) If the committee objects to all or some portion of a rule because the committee considers it to be beyond the procedural or substantive authority delegated to the adopting agency, the committee may file that objection in the office of the [secretary of state]. The filed objection must contain a concise statement of the committee's reasons for its action.]

(2) The [secretary of state] shall affix to each objection a certification of the date and time of its filing and as soon thereafter as practicable shall transmit a certified copy thereof to the agency issuing the rule in question, the [administrative rules editor, and the administrative rules counsel]. The [secretary of state] shall also maintain a permanent register open to public inspection of all objections by the committee.

(3) The [administrative rules editor] shall publish and index an objection filed pursuant to this subsection in the next issue of the [administrative bulletin] and indicate its existence adjacent to the rule in question when that rule is published in the [administrative code]. In case of a filed objection by the committee to a rule that is subject to the requirements of Section 2–101(g), the agency shall indicate the existence of that objection adjacent to the rule in the official compilation referred to in that subsection.

(4) Within [14] days after the filing of an objection by the committee to a rule, the issuing agency shall respond in writing to the commit-

tee. After receipt of the response, the committee may withdraw or modify its objection.

[(5) After the filing of an objection by the committee that is not subsequently withdrawn, the burden is upon the agency in any proceeding for judicial review or for enforcement of the rule to establish that the whole or portion of the rule objected to is within the procedural and substantive authority delegated to the agency.]

(6) The failure of the [administrative rules review committee] to object to a rule is not an implied legislative authorization of its procedural or substantive validity.

(e) The committee may recommend to an agency that it adopt a rule. [The committee may also require an agency to publish notice of the committee's recommendation as a proposed rule of the agency and to allow public participation thereon, according to the provisions of Sections 3–103 through 3–104. An agency is not required to adopt the proposed rule.]

(f) The committee shall file an annual report with the [presiding officer] of each house and the governor.

ARTICLE IV. ADJUDICATIVE PROCEEDINGS
CHAPTER I. AVAILABILITY OF ADJUDICATIVE PROCEEDINGS; APPLICATIONS; LICENSES

§ 4–101. [Adjudicative Proceedings; When Required; Exceptions]

(a) An agency shall conduct an adjudicative proceeding as the process for formulating and issuing an order, unless the order is a decision:

(1) to issue or not to issue a complaint, summons, or similar accusation;

(2) to initiate or not to initiate an investigation, prosecution, or other proceeding before the agency, another agency, or a court; or

(3) under Section 4–103, not to conduct an adjudicative proceeding.

(b) This Article applies to rule-making proceedings only to the extent that another statute expressly so requires.

§ 4–102. [Adjudicative Proceedings; Commencement]

(a) An agency may commence an adjudicative proceeding at any time with respect to a matter within the agency's jurisdiction.

(b) An agency shall commence an adjudicative proceeding upon the application of any person, unless:

(1) the agency lacks jurisdiction of the subject matter;

(2) resolution of the matter requires the agency to exercise discretion within the scope of Section 4–101(a);

(3) a statute vests the agency with discretion to conduct or not to conduct an adjudicative proceeding before issuing an order to resolve the matter and, in the exercise of that discretion, the agency has determined not to conduct an adjudicative proceeding;

(4) resolution of the matter does not require the agency to issue an order that determines the applicant's legal rights, duties, privileges, immunities, or other legal interests;

(5) the matter was not timely submitted to the agency; or

(6) the matter was not submitted in a form substantially complying with any applicable provision of law.

(c) An application for an agency to issue an order includes an application for the agency to conduct appropriate adjudicative proceedings, whether or not the applicant expressly requests those proceedings.

(d) An adjudicative proceeding commences when the agency or a presiding officer:

(1) notifies a party that a pre-hearing conference, hearing, or other stage of an adjudicative proceeding will be conducted; or

(2) begins to take action on a matter that appropriately may be determined by an adjudicative proceeding, unless this action is:

(i) an investigation for the purpose of determining whether an adjudicative proceeding should be conducted; or

(ii) a decision which, under Section 4–101(a), the agency may make without conducting an adjudicative proceeding.

§ 4–103. [Decision Not to Conduct Adjudicative Proceeding]

If an agency decides not to conduct an adjudicative proceeding in response to an application, the agency shall furnish the applicant a copy of its decision in writing, with a brief statement of the agency's reasons and of any administrative review available to the applicant.

§ 4–104. [Agency Action on Applications]

(a) Except to the extent that the time limits in this subsection are inconsistent with limits established by another statute for any stage of the proceedings, an agency shall process an application for an order, other than a declaratory order, as follows:

(1) Within [30] days after receipt of the application, the agency shall examine the application, notify the applicant of any apparent errors or omissions, request any additional information the agency wishes to obtain and is permitted by law to require, and notify the applicant of the name, official title, mailing address and telephone number of

an agency member or employee who may be contacted regarding the application.

(2) Except in situations governed by paragraph (3), within [90] days after receipt of the application or of the response to a timely request made by the agency pursuant to paragraph (1), the agency shall:

    (i) approve or deny the application, in whole or in part, on the basis of emergency or summary adjudicative proceedings, if those proceedings are available under this Act for disposition of the matter;

    (ii) commence a formal adjudicative hearing or a conference adjudicative hearing in accordance with this Act; or

    (iii) dispose of the application in accordance with Section 4–103.

(3) If the application pertains to subject matter that is not available when the application is filed but may be available in the future, including an application for housing or employment at a time no vacancy exists, the agency may proceed to make a determination of eligibility within the time provided in paragraph (2). If the agency determines that the applicant is eligible, the agency shall maintain the application on the agency's list of eligible applicants as provided by law and, upon request, shall notify the applicant of the status of the application.

(b) If a timely and sufficient application has been made for renewal of a license with reference to any activity of a continuing nature, the existing license does not expire until the agency has taken final action upon the application for renewal or, if the agency's action is unfavorable, until the last day for seeking judicial review of the agency's action or a later date fixed by the reviewing court.

§ 4–105. [Agency Action Against Licensees]

An agency may not revoke, suspend, modify, annul, withdraw, or amend a license unless the agency first gives notice and an opportunity for an appropriate adjudicative proceeding in accordance with this Act or other statute. This section does not preclude an agency from (i) taking immediate action to protect the public interest in accordance with Section 4–501 or (ii) adopting rules, otherwise within the scope of its authority, pertaining to a class of licensees, including rules affecting the existing licenses of a class of licensees.

CHAPTER II. FORMAL ADJUDICATIVE HEARING

§ 4–201. [Applicability]

An adjudicative proceeding is governed by this chapter, except as otherwise provided by:

    (1) a statute other than this Act;

(2) a rule that adopts the procedures for the conference adjudicative hearing or summary adjudicative proceeding in accordance with the standards provided in this Act for those proceedings;

(3) Section 4–501 pertaining to emergency adjudicative proceedings; or

(4) Section 2–103 pertaining to declaratory proceedings.

§ 4–202. [Presiding Officer, Disqualification, Substitution]

(a) The agency head, one or more members of the agency head, one or more administrative law judges assigned by the office of administrative hearings in accordance with Section 4–301 [, or, unless prohibited by law, one or more other persons designated by the agency head], in the discretion of the agency head, may be the presiding officer.

(b) Any person serving or designated to serve alone or with others as presiding officer is subject to disqualification for bias, prejudice, interest, or any other cause provided in this Act or for which a judge is or may be disqualified.

(c) Any party may petition for the disqualification of a person promptly after receipt of notice indicating that the person will preside or promptly upon discovering facts establishing grounds for disqualification, whichever is later.

(d) A person whose disqualification is requested shall determine whether to grant the petition, stating facts and reasons for the determination.

(e) If a substitute is required for a person who is disqualified or becomes unavailable for any other reason, the substitute must be appointed by:

(1) the governor, if the disqualified or unavailable person is an elected official; or

(2) the appointing authority, if the disqualified or unavailable person is an appointed official.

(f) Any action taken by a duly-appointed substitute for a disqualified or unavailable person is as effective as if taken by the latter.

§ 4–203. [Representation]

(a) Any party may participate in the hearing in person or, if the party is a corporation or other artificial person, by a duly authorized representative.

(b) Whether or not participating in person, any party may be advised and represented at the party's own expense by counsel or, if permitted by law, other representative.

§ 4–204. [Pre-hearing Conference—Availability, Notice]

The presiding officer designated to conduct the hearing may determine, subject to the agency's rules, whether a pre-hearing conference will be conducted. If the conference is conducted:

(1) The presiding officer shall promptly notify the agency of the determination that a pre-hearing conference will be conducted. The agency shall assign or request the office of administrative hearings to assign a presiding officer for the pre-hearing conference, exercising the same discretion as is provided by Section 4–202 concerning the selection of a presiding officer for a hearing.

(2) The presiding officer for the pre-hearing conference shall set the time and place of the conference and give reasonable written notice to all parties and to all persons who have filed written petitions to intervene in the matter. The agency shall give notice to other persons entitled to notice under any provision of law.

(3) The notice must include:

(i) the names and mailing addresses of all parties and other persons to whom notice is being given by the presiding officer;

(ii) the name, official title, mailing address, and telephone number of any counsel or employee who has been designated to appear for the agency;

(iii) the official file or other reference number, the name of the proceeding, and a general description of the subject matter;

(iv) a statement of the time, place, and nature of the pre-hearing conference;

(v) a statement of the legal authority and jurisdiction under which the pre-hearing conference and the hearing are to be held;

(vi) the name, official title, mailing address and telephone number of the presiding officer for the pre-hearing conference;

(vii) a statement that at the pre-hearing conference the proceeding, without further notice, may be converted into a conference adjudicative hearing or a summary adjudicative proceeding for disposition of the matter as provided by this Act; and

(viii) a statement that a party who fails to attend or participate in a pre-hearing conference, hearing, or other state of an adjudicative proceeding may be held in default under this Act.

(4) The notice may include any other matter that the presiding officer considers desirable to expedite the proceedings.

§ 4–205. [Pre-hearing Conference—Procedure and Pre-hearing Order]

(a) The presiding officer may conduct all or part of the pre-hearing conference by telephone, television, or other electronic means if each participant in the conference has an opportunity to participate in, to hear, and, if technically feasible, to see the entire proceeding while it is taking place.

(b) The presiding officer shall conduct the pre-hearing conference, as may be appropriate, to deal with such matters as conversion of the proceeding to another type, exploration of settlement possibilities, preparation of stipulations, clarification of issues, rulings on identity and limitation of the number of witnesses, objections to proffers of evidence, determination of the extent to which direct evidence, rebuttal evidence, or cross-examination will be presented in written form, and the extent to which telephone, television, or other electronic means will be used as a substitute for proceedings in person, order of presentation of evidence and cross-examination, rulings regarding issuance of subpoenas, discovery orders and protective orders, and such other matters as will promote the orderly and prompt conduct of the hearing. The presiding officer shall issue a pre-hearing order incorporating the matters determined at the pre-hearing conference.

(c) If a pre-hearing conference is not held, the presiding officer for the hearing may issue a pre-hearing order, based on the pleadings, to regulate the conduct of the proceedings.

§ 4–206. [Notice of Hearing]

(a) The presiding officer for the hearing shall set the time and place of the hearing and give reasonable written notice to all parties and to all persons who have filed written petitions to intervene in the matter.

(b) The notice must include a copy of any pre-hearing order rendered in the matter.

(c) To the extent not included in a pre-hearing order accompanying it, the notice must include:

(1) the names and mailing addresses of all parties and other persons to whom notice is being given by the presiding officer;

(2) the name, official title, mailing address and telephone number of any counsel or employee who has been designated to appear for the agency;

(3) the official file or other reference number, the name of the proceeding, and a general description of the subject matter;

(4) a statement of the time, place, and nature of the hearing;

(5) a statement of the legal authority and jurisdiction under which the hearing is to be held;

(6) the name, official title, mailing address, and telephone number of the presiding officer;

(7) a statement of the issues involved and, to the extent known to the presiding officer, of the matters asserted by the parties; and

(8) a statement that a party who fails to attend or participate in a pre-hearing conference, hearing, or other stage of an adjudicative proceeding may be held in default under this Act.

(d) The notice may include any other matters the presiding officer considers desirable to expedite the proceedings.

(e) The agency shall give notice to persons entitled to notice under any provision of law who have not been given notice by the presiding officer. Notice under this subsection may include all types of information provided in subsections (a) through (d) or may consist of a brief statement indicating the subject matter, parties, time, place, and nature of the hearing, manner in which copies of the notice to the parties may be inspected and copied, and name and telephone number of the presiding officer.

§ 4–207. [Pleadings, Briefs, Motions, Service]

(a) The presiding officer, at appropriate stages of the proceedings, shall give all parties full opportunity to file pleadings, motions, objections and offers of settlement.

(b) The presiding officer, at appropriate stages of the proceedings, may give all parties full opportunity to file briefs, proposed findings of fact and conclusions of law, and proposed initial or final orders.

(c) A party shall serve copies of any filed item on all parties, by mail or any other means prescribed by agency rule.

§ 4–208. [Default]

(a) If a party fails to attend or participate in a pre-hearing conference, hearing, or other stage of an adjudicative proceeding, the presiding officer may serve upon all parties written notice of a proposed default order, including a statement of the grounds.

(b) Within [7] days after service of a proposed default order, the party against whom it was issued may file a written motion requesting that the proposed default order be vacated and stating the grounds relied upon. During the time within which a party may file a written motion under this subsection, the presiding officer may adjourn the proceedings or conduct them without the participation of the party against whom a proposed default order was issued, having due regard for the interests of justice and the orderly and prompt conduct of the proceedings.

(c) The presiding officer shall either issue or vacate the default order promptly after expiration of the time within which the party may file a written motion under subsection (b).

(d) After issuing a default order, the presiding officer shall conduct any further proceedings necessary to complete the adjudication without the participation of the party in default and shall determine all issues in the adjudication, including those affecting the defaulting party.

§ 4–209. [Intervention]

(a) The presiding officer shall grant a petition for intervention if:

(1) the petition is submitted in writing to the presiding officer, with copies mailed to all parties named in the presiding officer's notice of the hearing, at least [3] days before the hearing;

(2) the petition states facts demonstrating that the petitioner's legal rights, duties, privileges, immunities, or other legal interests may be substantially affected by the proceeding or that the petitioner qualifies as an intervener under any provision of law; and

(3) the presiding officer determines that the interests of justice and the orderly and prompt conduct of the proceedings will not be impaired by allowing the intervention.

(b) The presiding officer may grant a petition for intervention at any time, upon determining that the intervention sought is in the interests of justice and will not impair the orderly and prompt conduct of the proceedings.

(c) If a petitioner qualifies for intervention, the presiding officer may impose conditions upon the intervener's participation in the proceedings, either at the time that intervention is granted or at any subsequent time. Conditions may include:

(1) limiting the intervener's participation to designated issues in which the intervener has a particular interest demonstrated by the petition;

(2) limiting the intervener's use of discovery, cross-examination, and other procedures so as to promote the orderly and prompt conduct of the proceedings; and

(3) requiring 2 or more interveners to combine their presentations of evidence and argument, cross-examination, discovery, and other participation in the proceedings.

(d) The presiding officer, at least [24 hours] before the hearing, shall issue an order granting or denying each pending petition for intervention, specifying any conditions, and briefly stating the reasons for the order. The presiding officer may modify the order at any time, stating the reasons for the modification. The presiding officer shall promptly give notice of an order granting, denying, or modifying intervention to the petitioner for intervention and to all parties.

§ 4–210.   [Subpoenas, Discovery and Protective Orders]

(a) The presiding officer [at the request of any party shall, and upon the presiding officer's own motion,] may issue subpoenas, discovery orders and protective orders, in accordance with the rules of civil procedure.

(b) Subpoenas and orders issued under this section may be enforced pursuant to the provisions of this Act on civil enforcement of agency action.

§ 4–211.   [Procedure at Hearing]

At a hearing:

(1) The presiding officer shall regulate the course of the proceedings in conformity with any pre-hearing order.

(2) To the extent necessary for full disclosure of all relevant facts and issues, the presiding officer shall afford to all parties the opportunity to respond, present evidence and argument, conduct cross-examination, and submit rebuttal evidence, except as restricted by a limited grant of intervention or by the pre-hearing order.

(3) The presiding officer may give nonparties an opportunity to present oral or written statements. If the presiding officer proposes to consider a statement by a nonparty, the presiding officer shall give all parties an opportunity to challenge or rebut it and, on motion of any party, the presiding officer shall require the statement to be given under oath or affirmation.

(4) The presiding officer may conduct all or part of the hearing by telephone, television, or other electronic means, if each participant in the hearing has an opportunity to participate in, to hear, and, if technically feasible, to see the entire proceeding while it is taking place.

(5) The presiding officer shall cause the hearing to be recorded at the agency's expense. The agency is not required, at its expense, to prepare a transcript, unless required to do so by a provision of law. Any party, at the party's expense, may cause a reporter approved by the agency to prepare a transcript from the agency's record, or cause additional recordings to be made during the hearing if the making of the additional recordings does not cause distraction or disruption.

(6) The hearing is open to public observation, except for the parts that the presiding officer states to be closed pursuant to a provision of law expressly authorizing closure. To the extent that a hearing is conducted by telephone, television, or other electronic means, and is not closed, the availability of public observation is satisfied by giving members of the public an opportunity, at reasonable times, to hear

or inspect the agency's record, and to inspect any transcript obtained by the agency.

§ 4–212. [Evidence, Official Notice]

(a) Upon proper objection, the presiding officer shall exclude evidence that is irrelevant, immaterial, unduly repetitious, or excludable on constitutional or statutory grounds or on the basis of evidentiary privilege recognized in the courts of this state. In the absence of proper objection, the presiding officer may exclude objectionable evidence. Evidence may not be excluded solely because it is hearsay.

(b) All testimony of parties and witnesses must be made under oath or affirmation.

(c) Statements presented by nonparties in accordance with Section 4–211(3) may be received as evidence.

(d) Any part of the evidence may be received in written form if doing so will expedite the hearing without substantial prejudice to the interests of any party.

(e) Documentary evidence may be received in the form of a copy or excerpt. Upon request, parties must be given an opportunity to compare the copy with the original if available.

(f) Official notice may be taken of (i) any fact that could be judicially noticed in the courts of this State, (ii) the record of other proceedings before the agency, (iii) technical or scientific matters within the agency's specialized knowledge, and (iv) codes or standards that have been adopted by an agency of the United States, of this State or of another state, or by a nationally recognized organization or association. Parties must be notified before or during the hearing, or before the issuance of any initial or final order that is based in whole or in part on facts or material noticed, of the specific facts or material noticed and the source thereof, including any staff memoranda and data, and be afforded an opportunity to contest and rebut the facts or material so noticed.

§ 4–213. [Ex parte Communications]

(a) Except as provided in subsection (b) or unless required for the disposition of ex parte matters specifically authorized by statute, a presiding officer serving in an adjudicative proceeding may not communicate, directly or indirectly, regarding any issue in the proceeding, while the proceeding is pending, with any party, with any person who has a direct or indirect interest in the outcome of the proceeding, or with any person who presided at a previous stage of the proceeding, without notice and opportunity for all parties to participate in the communication.

(b) A member of a multi-member panel of presiding officers may communicate with other members of the panel regarding a matter pending before the panel, and any presiding officer may receive aid from staff assistants if the assistants do not (i) receive ex parte communications of a type that the presiding officer would be prohibited from receiving or (ii) furnish, augment, diminish, or modify the evidence in the record.

(c) Unless required for the disposition of ex parte matters specifically authorized by statute, no party to an adjudicative proceeding, and no person who has a direct or indirect interest in the outcome of the proceeding or who presided at a previous stage of the proceeding, may communicate, directly or indirectly, in connection with any issue in that proceeding, while the proceeding is pending, with any person serving as presiding officer, without notice and opportunity for all parties to participate in the communication.

(d) If, before serving as presiding officer in an adjudicative proceeding, a person receives an ex parte communication of a type that could not properly be received while serving, the person, promptly after starting to serve, shall disclose the communication in the manner prescribed in subsection (e).

(e) A presiding officer who receives an ex parte communication in violation of this section shall place on the record of the pending matter all written communications received, all written responses to the communications, and a memorandum stating the substance of all oral communications received, all responses made, and the identity of each person from whom the presiding officer received an ex parte communication, and shall advise all parties that these matters have been placed on the record. Any party desiring to rebut the ex parte communication must be allowed to do so, upon requesting the opportunity for rebuttal within [10] days after notice of the communication.

(f) If necessary to eliminate the effect of an ex parte communication received in violation of this section, a presiding officer who receives the communication may be disqualified and the portions of the record pertaining to the communication may be sealed by protective order.

(g) The agency shall, and any party may, report any willful violation of this section to appropriate authorities for any disciplinary proceedings provided by law. In addition, each agency by rule may provide for appropriate sanctions, including default, for any violations of this section.

§ 4–214. [Separation of Functions]

(a) A person who has served as investigator, prosecutor or advocate in an adjudicative proceeding or in its pre-adjudicative stage may not serve as presiding officer or assist or advise a presiding officer in the same proceeding.

(b) A person who is subject to the authority, direction, or discretion of one who has served as investigator, prosecutor, or advocate in an adjudicative proceeding or in its pre-adjudicative stage may not serve as presiding officer or assist or advise a presiding officer in the same proceeding.

(c) A person who has participated in a determination of probable cause or other equivalent preliminary determination in an adjudicative proceeding may serve as presiding officer or assist or advise a presiding officer in the same proceeding, unless a party demonstrates grounds for disqualification in accordance with Section 4–202.

(d) A person may serve as presiding officer at successive stages of the same adjudicative proceeding, unless a party demonstrates grounds for disqualification in accordance with Section 4–202.

§ 4–215. [Final Order, Initial Order]

(a) If the presiding officer is the agency head, the presiding officer shall render a final order.

(b) If the presiding officer is not the agency head, the presiding officer shall render an initial order, which becomes a final order unless reviewed in accordance with Section 4–216.

(c) A final order or initial order must include, separately stated, findings of fact, conclusions of law, and policy reasons for the decision if it is an exercise of the agency's discretion, for all aspects of the order, including the remedy prescribed and, if applicable, the action taken on a petition for stay of effectiveness. Findings of fact, if set forth in language that is no more than mere repetition or paraphrase of the relevant provision of law, must be accompanied by a concise and explicit statement of the underlying facts of record to support the findings. If a party has submitted proposed findings of fact, the order must include a ruling on the proposed findings. The order must also include a statement of the available procedures and time limits for seeking reconsideration or other administrative relief. An initial order must include a statement of any circumstances under which the initial order, without further notice, may become a final order.

(d) Findings of fact must be based exclusively upon the evidence of record in the adjudicative proceeding and on matters officially noticed in that proceeding. Findings must be based upon the kind of evidence on which reasonably prudent persons are accustomed to rely in the conduct of their serious affairs and may be based upon such evidence even if it would be inadmissible in a civil trial. The presiding officer's experience, technical competence, and specialized knowledge may be utilized in evaluating evidence.

(e) If a person serving or designated to serve as presiding officer becomes unavailable, for any reason, before rendition of the final order or initial order, a substitute presiding officer must be appointed as provided in Section 4–202. The substitute presiding officer shall use any existing record and may conduct any further proceedings appropriate in the interests of justice.

(f) The presiding officer may allow the parties a designated amount of time after conclusion of the hearing for the submission of proposed findings.

(g) A final order or initial order pursuant to this section must be rendered in writing within [90] days after conclusion of the hearing or after submission of proposed findings in accordance with subsection (f) unless this period is waived or extended with the written consent of all parties or for good cause shown.

(h) The presiding officer shall cause copies of the final order or initial order to be delivered to each party and to the agency head.

§ 4–216. [Review of Initial Order; Exceptions to Reviewability]

(a) The agency head, upon its own motion may, and upon appeal by any party shall, review an initial order, except to the extent that:

   (1) a provision of law precludes or limits agency review of the initial order; or

   (2) the agency head, in the exercise of discretion conferred by a provision of law,

      (i) determines to review some but not all issues, or not to exercise any review,

      (ii) delegates its authority to review the initial order to one or more persons, or

      (iii) authorizes one or more persons to review the initial order, subject to further review by the agency head.

(b) A petition for appeal from an initial order must be filed with the agency head, or with any person designated for this purpose by rule of the agency, within [10] days after rendition of the initial order. If the agency head on its own motion decides to review an initial order, the agency head shall give written notice of its intention to review the initial order within [10] days after its rendition. The [10]-day period for a party to file a petition for appeal or for the agency head to give notice of its intention to review an initial order on the agency head's own motion is tolled by the submission of a timely petition for reconsideration of the initial order pursuant to Section 4–218, and a new [10]-day period starts to run upon disposition of the petition for reconsideration. If an initial order is subject both to a timely petition for reconsideration and to a petition for appeal or to review by the agency head on its own motion, the petition for reconsideration must be disposed of first, unless the agency head determines that action on the petition for reconsideration has been unreasonably delayed.

(c) The petition for appeal must state its basis. If the agency head on its own motion gives notice of its intent to review an initial order, the agency head shall identity the issues that it intends to review.

(d) The presiding officer for the review of an initial order shall exercise all the decision-making power that the presiding officer would have had to render a final order had the presiding officer presided over the hearing, except to the extent that the issues subject to review are limited by a provision of law or by the presiding officer upon notice to all parties.

(e) The presiding officer shall afford each party an opportunity to present briefs and may afford each party an opportunity to present oral argument.

(f) Before rendering a final order, the presiding officer may cause a transcript to be prepared, at the agency's expense, of such portions of the proceeding under review as the presiding officer considers necessary.

(g) The presiding officer may render a final order disposing of the proceeding or may remand the matter for further proceedings with instructions to the person who rendered the initial order. Upon remanding a matter, the presiding officer may order such temporary relief as is authorized and appropriate.

(h) A final order or an order remanding the matter for further proceedings must be rendered in writing within [60] days after receipt of briefs and oral argument unless that period is waived or extended with the written consent of all parties or for good cause shown.

(i) A final order or an order remanding the matter for further proceedings under this section must identify any difference between this order and the initial order and must include, or incorporate by express reference to the initial order, all the matters required by Section 4–215(c).

(j) The presiding officer shall cause copies of the final order or order remanding the matter for further proceedings to be delivered to each party and to the agency head.

§ 4–217. [Stay]

A party may submit to the presiding officer a petition for stay of effectiveness of an initial or final order within [7] days after its rendition unless otherwise provided by statute or stated in the initial or final order. The presiding officer may take action on the petition for stay, either before or after the effective date of the initial or final order.

§ 4–218. [Reconsideration]

Unless otherwise provided by statute or rule:

> (1) Any party, within [10] days after rendition of an initial or final order, may file a petition for reconsideration, stating the specific

grounds upon which relief is requested. The filing of the petition is not a prerequisite for seeking administrative or judicial review.

(2) The petition must be disposed of by the same person or persons who rendered the initial or final order, if available.

(3) The presiding officer shall render a written order denying the petition, granting the petition and dissolving or modifying the initial or final order, or granting the petition and setting the matter for further proceedings. The petition may be granted, in whole or in part, only if the presiding officer states, in the written order, findings of fact, conclusions of law, and policy reasons for the decision if it is an exercise of the agency's discretion, to justify the order. The petition is deemed to have been denied if the presiding officer does not dispose of it within [20] days after the filing of the petition.

§ 4–219. [Review by Superior Agency]

If, pursuant to statute, an agency may review the final order of another agency, the review is deemed to be a continuous proceeding as if before a single agency. The final order of the first agency is treated as an initial order and the second agency functions as though it were reviewing an initial order in accordance with Section 4–216.

§ 4–220. [Effectiveness of Orders]

(a) Unless a later date is stated in a final order or a stay is granted, a final order is effective [10] days after rendition, but:

(1) a party may not be required to comply with a final order unless the party has been served with or has actual knowledge of the final order;

(2) a nonparty may not be required to comply with a final order unless the agency has made the final order available for public inspection and copying or the nonparty has actual knowledge of the final order.

(b) Unless a later date is stated in an initial order or a stay is granted, the time when an initial order becomes a final order in accordance with Section 4–215 is determined as follows:

(1) when the initial order is rendered, if administrative review is unavailable;

(2) when the agency head renders an order stating, after a petition for appeal has been filed, that review will not be exercised, if discretion is available to make a determination to this effect; or

(3) [10] days after rendition of the initial order, if no party has filed a petition for appeal and the agency head has not given written notice of its intention to exercise review.

(c) Unless a later date is stated in an initial order or a stay is granted, an initial order that becomes a final order in accordance with subsection (b) and Section 4–215 is effective [10] days after becoming a final order, but:

(1) a party may not be required to comply with the final order unless the party has been served with or has actual knowledge of the initial order or of an order stating that review will not be exercised; and

(2) a nonparty may not be required to comply with the final order unless the agency has made the initial order available for public inspection and copying or the nonparty has actual knowledge of the initial order or of an order stating that review will not be exercised.

(d) This section does not preclude an agency from taking immediate action to protect the public interest in accordance with Section 4–501.

§ 4–221. [Agency Record]

(a) An agency shall maintain an official record of each adjudicative proceeding under this Chapter.

(b) The agency record consists only of:

(1) notices of all proceedings;

(2) any pre-hearing order;

(3) any motions, pleadings, briefs, petitions, requests, and intermediate rulings;

(4) evidence received or considered;

(5) a statement of matters officially noticed;

(6) proffers of proof and objections and rulings thereon;

(7) proposed findings, requested orders, and exceptions;

(8) the record prepared for the presiding officer at the hearing, together with any transcript of all or part of the hearing considered before final disposition of the proceeding;

(9) any final order, initial order, or order on reconsideration;

(10) staff memoranda or data submitted to the presiding officer, unless prepared and submitted by personal assistants and not inconsistent with Section 4–213(b); and

(11) matters placed on the record after an ex parte communication.

(c) Except to the extent that this Act or another statute provides otherwise, the agency record constitutes the exclusive basis for agency action in adjudicative proceedings under this Chapter and for judicial review thereof.

CHAPTER III. OFFICE OF ADMINISTRATIVE HEARINGS

§ 4–301. [Office of Administrative Hearings—Creation, Powers, Duties]

(a) There is created the office of administrative hearings within the [Department of _____], to be headed by a director appointed by the governor [and confirmed by the senate].

(b) The office shall employ administrative law judges as necessary to conduct proceedings required by this Act or other provision of law. [Only a person admitted to practice law in [this State] [a jurisdiction in the United States] may be employed as an administrative law judge.]

(c) If the office cannot furnish one of its administrative law judges in response to an agency request, the director shall designate in writing a full-time employee of an agency other than the requesting agency to serve as administrative law judge for the proceeding, but only with the consent of the employing agency. The designee must possess the same qualifications required of administrative law judges employed by the office.

(d) The director may furnish administrative law judges on a contract basis to any governmental entity to conduct any proceeding not subject to this Act.

(e) The office may adopt rules:

> (1) to establish further qualifications for administrative law judges, procedures by which candidates will be considered for employment, and the manner in which public notice of vacancies in the staff of the office will be given;

> (2) to establish procedures for agencies to request and for the director to assign administrative law judges; however, an agency may neither select nor reject any individual administrative law judge for any proceeding except in accordance with this Act;

> (3) to establish procedures and adopt forms, consistent with this Act, the model rules of procedure, and other provisions of law, to govern administrative law judges;

> (4) to establish standards and procedures for the evaluation, training, promotion, and discipline of administrative law judges; and

> (5) to facilitate the performance of the responsibilities conferred upon the office by this Act.

(f) The director may:

> (1) maintain a staff of reporters and other personnel; and

> (2) implement the provisions of this section and rules adopted under its authority.

366

CHAPTER IV. CONFERENCE ADJUDICATIVE HEARING

§ 4–401. [Conference Adjudicative Hearing—Applicability]

A conference adjudicative hearing may be used if its use in the circumstances does not violate any provision of law and the matter is entirely within one or more categories for which the agency by rule had adopted this chapter[; however, those categories may include only the following:

(1) a matter in which there is no disputed issue of material fact; or

(2) a matter in which there is a disputed issue of material fact, if the matter involves only:

(i) a monetary amount of not more than [$1,000];

(ii) a disciplinary sanction against a prisoner;

(iii) a disciplinary sanction against a student which does not involve expulsion from an academic institution or suspension for more than [10] days;

(iv) a disciplinary sanction against a public employee which does not involve discharge from employment or suspension for more than [10] days;

(v) a disciplinary sanction against a licensee which does not involve revocation, suspension, annulment, withdrawal, or amendment of a license; or (vi)....]

§ 4–402. [Conference Adjudicative Hearing—Procedures]

The procedures of this Act pertaining to formal adjudicative hearings apply to a conference adjudicative hearing, except to the following extent:

(1) If a matter is initiated as a conference adjudicative hearing, no pre-hearing conference may be held.

(2) The provisions of Section 4–210 do not apply to conference adjudicative hearings insofar as those provisions authorize the issuance and enforcement of subpoenas and discovery orders, but do apply to conference adjudicative hearings insofar as those provisions authorize the presiding officer to issue protective orders at the request of any party or upon the presiding officer's motion.

(3) Paragraphs (1), (2) and (3) of Section 4–211 do not apply; but,

(i) the presiding officer shall regulate the course of the proceedings,

(ii) only the parties may testify and present written exhibits, and

(iii) the parties may offer comments on the issues.

§ 4–403. [Conference Adjudicative Hearing—Proposed Proof]

(a) If the presiding officer has reason to believe that material facts are in dispute, the presiding officer may require any party to state the identity of the witnesses or other sources through whom the party would propose to present proof if the proceeding were converted to a formal adjudicative hearing, but if disclosure of any fact, allegation, or source is privileged or expressly prohibited by any provision of law, the presiding officer may require the party to indicate that confidential facts, allegations, or sources are involved, but not to disclose the confidential facts, allegations, or sources.

(b) If a party has reason to believe that essential facts must be obtained in order to permit an adequate presentation of the case, the party may inform the presiding officer regarding the general nature of the facts and the sources from whom the party would propose to obtain those facts if the proceeding were converted to a formal adjudicative hearing.

CHAPTER V. EMERGENCY AND SUMMARY ADJUDICATIVE PROCEEDINGS

§ 4–501. [Emergency Adjudicative Proceedings]

(a) An agency may use emergency adjudicative proceedings in a situation involving an immediate danger to the public health, safety, or welfare requiring immediate agency action.

(b) The agency may take only such action as is necessary to prevent or avoid the immediate danger to the public health, safety, or welfare that justifies use of emergency adjudication.

(c) The agency shall render an order, including a brief statement of findings of fact, conclusions of law, and policy reasons for the decision if it is an exercise of the agency's discretion, to justify the determination of an immediate danger and the agency's decision to take the specific action.

(d) The agency shall give such notice as is practicable to persons who are required to comply with the order. The order is effective when rendered.

(e) After issuing an order pursuant to this section, the agency shall proceed as quickly as feasible to complete any proceedings that would be required if the matter did not involve an immediate danger.

(f) The agency record consists of any documents regarding the matter that were considered or prepared by the agency. The agency shall maintain these documents as its official record.

(g) Unless otherwise required by a provision of law, the agency record need not constitute the exclusive basis for agency action in emergency adjudicative proceedings or for judicial review thereof.

§ 4–502. [Summary Adjudicative Proceedings—Applicability]

An agency may use summary adjudicative proceedings if:

(1) the use of those proceedings in the circumstances does not violate any provision of law;

(2) the protection of the public interest does not require the agency to give notice and an opportunity to participate to persons other than the parties; and

(3) the matter is entirely within one or more categories for which the agency by rule has adopted this section and Sections 4–503 to 4–506 [; however, those categories may include only the following:

(i) a monetary amount of not more than [$100];

(ii) a reprimand, warning, disciplinary report, or other purely verbal sanction without continuing impact against a prisoner, student, public employee, or licensee;

(iii) the denial of an application after the applicant has abandoned the application;

(iv) the denial of an application for admission to an educational institution or for employment by an agency;

(v) the denial, in whole or in part, of an application if the applicant has an opportunity for administrative review in accordance with Section 4–504;

(vi) a matter that is resolved on the sole basis of inspections, examinations, or tests;

(vii) the acquisition, leasing, or disposal of property or the procurement of goods or services by contract;

(viii) any matter having only trivial potential impact upon the affected parties; and (ix) . . . .]

§ 4–503. [Summary Adjudicative Proceedings—Procedures]

(a) The agency head, one or more members of the agency head, one or more administrative law judges assigned by the office of administrative hearings in accordance with Section 4–301 [, or, unless prohibited by law, one or more other persons designated by the agency head], in the discretion of the agency head, may be the presiding officer. Unless prohibited by law, a person exercising authority over the matter is the presiding officer.

(b) If the proceeding involves a monetary matter or a reprimand, warning, disciplinary report, or other sanction:

(1) the presiding officer, before taking action, shall give each party an opportunity to be informed of the agency's view of the matter and to explain the party's view of the matter; and

(2) the presiding officer, at the time any unfavorable action is taken, shall give each party a brief statement of findings of fact, conclusions of law, and policy reasons for the decision if it is an exercise of the agency's discretion, to justify the action, and a notice of any available administrative review.

(c) An order rendered in a proceeding that involves a monetary matter must be in writing. An order in any other summary adjudicative proceeding may be oral or written.

(d) The agency, by reasonable means, shall furnish to each party notification of the order in a summary adjudicative proceeding. Notification must include at least a statement of the agency's action and a notice of any available administrative review.

§ 4–504. [Administrative Review of Summary Adjudicative Proceedings—Applicability]

Unless prohibited by any provision of law, an agency, on its own motion, may conduct administrative review of an order resulting from summary adjudicative proceedings, and shall conduct this review upon the written or oral request of a party if the agency receives the request within [10] days after furnishing notification under Section 4–503(d).

§ 4–505. [Administrative Review of Summary Adjudicative Proceedings—Procedures]

Unless otherwise provided by statute [or rule]:

(1) An agency need not furnish notification of the pendency of administrative review to any person who did not request the review, but the agency may not take any action on review less favorable to any party than the original order without giving that party notice and an opportunity to explain that party's view of the matter.

(2) The reviewing officer, in the discretion of the agency head, may be any person who could have presided at the summary adjudicative proceeding, but the reviewing officer must be one who is authorized to grant appropriate relief upon review.

(3) The reviewing officer shall give each party an opportunity to explain the party's view of the matter unless the party's view is apparent from the written materials in the file submitted to the reviewing officer. The reviewing officer shall make any inquiries necessary to ascertain whether the proceeding must be converted to a conference adjudicative hearing or a formal adjudicative hearing.

(4) The reviewing officer may render an order disposing of the proceeding in any manner that was available to the presiding officer at the summary adjudicative proceeding or the reviewing officer may remand the matter for further proceedings, with or without conver-

sion to a conference adjudicative hearing or a formal adjudicative hearing.

(5) If the order under review is or should have been in writing, the order on review must be in writing, including a brief statement of findings of fact, conclusions of law, and policy reasons for the decision if it is an exercise of the agency's discretion, to justify the order, and a notice of any further available administrative review.

(6) A request for administrative review is deemed to have been denied if the reviewing officer does not dispose of the matter or remand it for further proceedings within [20] days after the request is submitted.

§ 4–506. [Agency Record of Summary Adjudicative Proceedings and Administrative Review]

(a) The agency record consists of any documents regarding the matter that were considered or prepared by the presiding officer for the summary adjudicative proceeding or by the reviewing officer for any review. The agency shall maintain these documents as its official record.

(b) Unless otherwise required by a provision of law, the agency record need not constitute the exclusive basis for agency action in summary adjudicative proceedings or for judicial review thereof.

ARTICLE V. JUDICIAL REVIEW AND ENFORCEMENT
CHAPTER I. JUDICIAL REVIEW

§ 5–101. [Relationship Between this Act and Other Law on Judicial Review and Other Judicial Remedies]

This Act establishes the exclusive means of judicial review of agency action, but:

(1) The provisions of this Act for judicial review do not apply to litigation in which the sole issue is a claim for money damages or compensation and the agency whose action is at issue does not have statutory authority to determine the claim.

(2) Ancillary procedural matters, including intervention, class actions, consolidation, joinder, severance, transfer, protective orders, and other relief from disclosure of privileged or confidential material, are governed, to the extent not inconsistent with this Act, by other applicable law.

(3) If the relief available under other sections of this Act is not equal or substantially equivalent to the relief otherwise available under law, the relief otherwise available and the related procedures supersede and supplement this Act to the extent necessary for their effectuation. The applicable provisions of this Act and other law must be combined to govern a single proceeding or, if the court

orders, 2 or more separate proceedings, with or without transfer to other courts, but no type of relief may be sought in a combined proceeding after expiration of the time limit for doing so.

§ 5–102.   [Final Agency Action Reviewable]

(a) A person who qualifies under this Act regarding (i) standing (Section 5–106), (ii) exhaustion of administrative remedies (Section 5–107), and (iii) time for filing the petition for review (Section 5–108), and other applicable provisions of law regarding bond, compliance, and other preconditions is entitled to judicial review of final agency action, whether or not the person has sought judicial review of any related non-final agency action.

(b) For purposes of this section and Section 5–103:

(1) "Final agency action" means the whole or a part of any agency action other than non-final agency action;

(2) "Non-final agency action" means the whole or a part of an agency determination, investigation, proceeding, hearing, conference, or other process that the agency intends or is reasonably believed to intend to be preliminary, preparatory, procedural, or intermediate with regard to subsequent agency action of that agency or another agency.

§ 5–103.   [Non-final Agency Action Reviewable]

A person is entitled to judicial review of non-final agency action only if:

(1) it appears likely that the person will qualify under Section 5–102 for judicial review of the related final agency action; and

(2) postponement of judicial review would result in an inadequate remedy or irreparable harm disproportionate to the public benefit derived from postponement.

§ 5–104.   [Jurisdiction, Venue] [ALTERNATIVE A]

(a) The [trial court of general jurisdiction] shall conduct judicial review.

(b) Venue is in the [district] [that includes the state capital] [where the petitioner resides or maintains a principal place of business] unless otherwise provided by law.

§ 5–105.   [Form of Action]

Judicial review is initiated by filing a petition for review in [the appropriate] court. A petition may seek any type of relief available under Sections 5–101(3) and 5–117.

§ 5-106. [Standing]

(a) The following persons have standing to obtain judicial review of final or non-final agency action:

(1) a person to whom the agency action is specifically directed;

(2) a person who was a party to the agency proceedings that led to the agency action;

(3) if the challenged agency action is a rule, a person subject to that rule;

(4) a person eligible for standing under another provision of law; or

(5) a person otherwise aggrieved or adversely affected by the agency action. For purposes of this paragraph, no person has standing as one otherwise aggrieved or adversely affected unless:

(i) the agency action has prejudiced or is likely to prejudice that person;

(ii) that person's asserted interests are among those that the agency was required to consider when it engaged in the agency action challenged; and

(iii) a judgment in favor of that person would substantially eliminate or redress the prejudice to that person caused or likely to be caused by the agency action. [(b) A standing committee of the legislature which is required to exercise general and continuing oversight over administrative agencies and procedures may petition for judicial review of any rule or intervene in any litigation arising from agency action.]

§ 5-107. [Exhaustion of Administrative Remedies]

A person may file a petition for judicial review under this Act only after exhausting all administrative remedies available within the agency whose action is being challenged and within any other agency authorized to exercise administrative review, but:

(1) a petitioner for judicial review of a rule need not have participated in the rule-making proceeding upon which that rule is based, or have petitioned for its amendment or repeal;

(2) a petitioner for judicial review need not exhaust administrative remedies to the extent that this Act or any other statute states that exhaustion is not required; or

(3) the court may relieve a petitioner of the requirement to exhaust any or all administrative remedies, to the extent that the administrative remedies are inadequate, or requiring their exhaustion would result in irreparable harm disproportionate to the public benefit derived from requiring exhaustion.

§ 5–108.   [Time for Filing Petition for Review]

Subject to other requirements of this Act or of another statute:

(1) A petition for judicial review of a rule may be filed at any time, except as limited by Section 3–113(b).

(2) A petition for judicial review of an order is not timely unless filed within [30] days after rendition of the order, but the time is extended during the pendency of the petitioner's timely attempts to exhaust administrative remedies, if the attempts are not clearly frivolous or repetitious.

(3) A petition for judicial review of agency action other than a rule or order is not timely unless filed within [30] days after the agency action, but the time is extended:

(i) during the pendency of the petitioner's timely attempts to exhaust administrative remedies, if the attempts are not clearly frivolous or repetitious; and

(ii) during any period that the petitioner did not know and was under no duty to discover, or did not know and was under a duty to discover but could not reasonably have discovered, that the agency had taken the action or that the agency action had a sufficient effect to confer standing upon the petitioner to obtain judicial review under this Act.

§ 5–109.   [Petition for Review—Filing and Contents]

(a) A petition for review must be filed with the clerk of the court.

(b) A petition for review must set forth:

(1) the name and mailing address of the petitioner;

(2) the name and mailing address of the agency whose action is at issue;

(3) identification of the agency action at issue, together with a duplicate copy, summary, or brief description of the agency action;

(4) identification of persons who were parties in any adjudicative proceedings that led to the agency action;

(5) facts to demonstrate that the petitioner is entitled to obtain judicial review;

(6) the petitioner's reasons for believing that relief should be granted; and

(7) a request for relief, specifying the type and extent of relief requested.

§ 5–110. [Petition for Review—Service and Notification]

(a) A petitioner for judicial review shall serve a copy of the petition upon the agency in the manner provided by [statute] [the rules of civil procedure].

(b) The petitioner shall use means provided by [statute] [the rules of civil procedure] to give notice of the petition for review to all other parties in any adjudicative proceedings that led to the agency action.

§ 5–111. [Stay and Other Temporary Remedies Pending Final Disposition]

(a) Unless precluded by law, the agency may grant a stay on appropriate terms or other temporary remedies during the pendency of judicial review.

(b) A party may file a motion in the reviewing court, during the pendency of judicial review, seeking interlocutory review of the agency's action on an application for stay or other temporary remedies.

(c) If the agency has found that its action on an application for stay or other temporary remedies is justified to protect against a substantial threat to the public health, safety, or welfare, the court may not grant relief unless it finds that:

> (1) the applicant is likely to prevail when the court finally disposes of the matter;

> (2) without relief the applicant will suffer irreparable injury;

> (3) the grant of relief to the applicant will not substantially harm other parties to the proceedings; and

> (4) the threat to the public health, safety, or welfare relied on by the agency is not sufficiently serious to justify the agency's action in the circumstances.

(d) If subsection (c) does not apply, the court shall grant relief if it finds, in its independent judgment, that the agency's action on the application for stay or other temporary remedies was unreasonable in the circumstances.

(e) If the court determines that relief should be granted from the agency's action on an application for stay or other temporary remedies, the court may remand the matter to the agency with directions to deny a stay, to grant a stay on appropriate terms, or to grant other temporary remedies, or the court may issue an order denying a stay, granting a stay on appropriate terms, or granting other temporary remedies.

§ 5–112. [Limitation on New Issues]

A person may obtain judicial review of an issue that was not raised before the agency, only to the extent that:

(1) the agency did not have jurisdiction to grant an adequate remedy based on a determination of the issue;

(2) the person did not know and was under no duty to discover, or did not know and was under a duty to discover but could not reasonably have discovered, facts giving rise to the issue;

(3) the agency action subject to judicial review is a rule and the person has not been a party in adjudicative proceedings which provided an adequate opportunity to raise the issue;

(4) the agency action subject to judicial review is an order and the person was not notified of the adjudicative proceeding in substantial compliance with this Act; or

(5) the interests of justice would be served by judicial resolution of an issue arising from:

> (i) a change in controlling law occurring after the agency action; or

> (ii) agency action occurring after the person exhausted the last feasible opportunity for seeking relief from the agency.

§ 5-113. [Judicial Review of Facts Confined to Record for Judicial Review and Additional Evidence Taken Pursuant to Act]

Judicial review of disputed issues of fact must be confined to the agency record for judicial review as defined in this Act, supplemented by additional evidence taken pursuant to this Act.

§ 5-114. [New Evidence Taken by Court or Agency Before Final Disposition]

(a) The court [(if Alternative B of Section 5-104 is adopted), assisted by a referee, master, trial court judge as provided in Section 5-104(c),] may receive evidence, in addition to that contained in the agency record for judicial review, only if it relates to the validity of the agency action at the time it was taken and is needed to decide disputed issues regarding:

(1) improper constitution as a decision-making body, or improper motive or grounds for disqualification, of those taking the agency action;

(2) unlawfulness of procedure or of decision-making process; or

(3) any material fact that was not required by any provision of law to be determined exclusively on an agency record of a type reasonably suitable for judicial review.

(b) The court may remand a matter to the agency, before final disposition of a petition for review, with directions that the agency conduct fact-finding and other proceedings the court considers necessary and that the agency take such further action on the basis thereof as the court directs, if:

(1) the agency was required by this Act or any other provision of law to base its action exclusively on a record of a type reasonably suitable for judicial review, but the agency failed to prepare or preserve an adequate record;

(2) the court finds that (i) new evidence has become available that relates to the validity of the agency action at the time it was taken, that one or more of the parties did not know and was under no duty to discover, or did not know and was under a duty to discover but could not reasonably have discovered, until after the agency action, and (ii) the interests of justice would be served by remand to the agency;

(3) the agency improperly excluded or omitted evidence from the record; or

(4) a relevant provision of law changed after the agency action and the court determines that the new provision may control the outcome.

§ 5–115. [Agency Record for Judicial Review—Contents, Preparation, Transmittal, Cost]

(a) Within [_____] days after service of the petition, or within further time allowed by the court or by other provision of law, the agency shall transmit to the court the original or a certified copy of the agency record for judicial review of the agency action, consisting of any agency documents expressing the agency action, other documents identified by the agency as having been considered by it before its action and used as a basis for its action, and any other material described in this Act as the agency record for the type of agency action at issue, subject to the provisions of this section.

(b) If part of the record has been preserved without a transcript, the agency shall prepare a transcript for inclusion in the record transmitted to the court, except for portions that the parties stipulate to omit in accordance with subsection (d).

(c) The agency shall charge the petitioner with the reasonable cost of preparing any necessary copies and transcripts for transmittal to the court. [A failure by the petitioner to pay any of this cost to the agency does not relieve the agency from the responsibility for timely preparation of the record and transmittal to the court.]

(d) By stipulation of all parties to the review proceedings, the record may be shortened, summarized, or organized.

(e) The court may tax the cost of preparing transcripts and copies for the record:

(1) against a party who unreasonably refuses to stipulate to shorten, summarize, or organize the record;

(2) as provided by Section 5–117; or

(3) in accordance with any other provision of law.

(f) Additions to the record pursuant to Section 5–114 must be made as ordered by the court.

(g) The court may require or permit subsequent corrections or additions to the record.

§ 5–116.   [Scope of Review; Grounds for Invalidity]

(a) Except to the extent that this Act or another statute provides otherwise:

(1) The burden of demonstrating the invalidity of agency action is on the party asserting invalidity; and

(2) The validity of agency action must be determined in accordance with the standards of review provided in this section, as applied to the agency action at the time it was taken.

(b) The court shall make a separate and distinct ruling on each material issue on which the court's decision is based.

(c) The court shall grant relief only if it determines that a person seeking judicial relief has been substantially prejudiced by any one or more of the following:

(1) The agency action, or the statute or rule on which the agency action is based, is unconstitutional on its face or as applied.

(2) The agency has acted beyond the jurisdiction conferred by any provision of law.

(3) The agency has not decided all issues requiring resolution.

(4) The agency has erroneously interpreted or applied the law.

(5) The agency has engaged in an unlawful procedure or decision-making process, or has failed to follow prescribed procedure.

(6) The persons taking the agency action were improperly constituted as a decision-making body, motivated by an improper purpose, or subject to disqualification.

(7) The agency action is based on a determination of fact, made or implied by the agency, that is not supported by evidence that is substantial when viewed in light of the whole record before the court, which includes the agency record for judicial review, supplemented by any additional evidence received by the court under this Act.

(8) The agency action is:

(i) outside the range of discretion delegated to the agency by any provision of law;

(ii) agency action, other than a rule, that is inconsistent with a rule of the agency; [or]

(iii) agency action, other than a rule, that is inconsistent with the agency's prior practice unless the agency justifies the inconsistency by stating facts and reasons to demonstrate a fair and rational basis for the inconsistency. [; or] [.]

(iv) [otherwise unreasonable, arbitrary or capricious.]

§ 5–117. [Type of Relief]

(a) The court may award damages or compensation only to the extent expressly authorized by another provision of law.

(b) The court may grant other appropriate relief, whether mandatory, injunctive, or declaratory; preliminary or final; temporary or permanent; equitable or legal. In granting relief, the court may order agency action required by law, order agency exercise of discretion required by law, set aside or modify agency action, enjoin or stay the effectiveness of agency action, remand the matter for further proceedings, render a declaratory judgment, or take any other action that is authorized and appropriate.

(c) The court may also grant necessary ancillary relief to redress the effects of official action wrongfully taken or withheld, but the court may award attorney's fees or witness fees only to the extent expressly authorized by other law.

(d) If the court sets aside or modifies agency action or remands the matter to the agency for further proceedings, the court may make any interlocutory order it finds necessary to preserve the interests of the parties and the public pending further proceedings or agency action.

[§ 5–118.   [Review by Higher Court]]

Decisions on petitions for review of agency action are reviewable by the [appellate court] as in other civil cases.

CHAPTER II. CIVIL ENFORCEMENT

§ 5–201.   [Petition by Agency for Civil Enforcement of Rule or Order]

(a) In addition to other remedies provided by law, an agency may seek enforcement of its rule or order by filing a petition for civil enforcement in the [trial court of general jurisdiction.]

(b) The petition must name, as defendants, each alleged violator against whom the agency seeks to obtain civil enforcement.

(c) Venue is determined as in other civil cases.

(d) A petition for civil enforcement filed by an agency may request, and the court may grant, declaratory relief, temporary or permanent injunctive relief, any other civil remedy provided by law, or any combination of the foregoing.

§ 5–202. [Petition by Qualified Person for Civil Enforcement of Agency's Order]

(a) Any person who would qualify under this Act as having standing to obtain judicial review of an agency's failure to enforce its order may file a petition for civil enforcement of that order, but the action may not be commenced:

> (1) until at least [60] days after the petitioner has given notice of the alleged violation and of the petitioner's intent to seek civil enforcement to the head of the agency concerned, to the attorney general, and to each alleged violator against whom the petitioner seeks civil enforcement;

> (2) if the agency has filed and is diligently prosecuting a petition for civil enforcement of the same order against the same defendant; or

> (3) if a petition for review of the same order has been filed and is pending in court.

(b) The petition must name, as defendants, the agency whose order is sought to be enforced and each alleged violator against whom the petitioner seeks civil enforcement.

(c) The agency whose order is sought to be enforced may move to dismiss on the grounds that the petition fails to qualify under this section or that enforcement would be contrary to the policy of the agency. The court shall grant the motion to dismiss unless the petitioner demonstrates that (i) the petition qualifies under this section and (ii) the agency's failure to enforce its order is based on an exercise of discretion that is improper on one or more of the grounds provided in Section 5–116(c)(8).

(d) Except to the extent expressly authorized by law, a petition for civil enforcement filed under this section may not request, and the court may not grant any monetary payment apart from taxable costs.

§ 5–203. [Defenses; Limitation on New Issues and New Evidence]

A defendant may assert, in a proceeding for civil enforcement:

> (1) that the rule or order sought to be enforced is invalid on any of the grounds stated in Section 5–116. If that defense is raised, the court may consider issues and receive evidence only within the limitations provided by Sections 5–112, 5–113, and 5–114; and

(2) any of the following defenses on which the court, to the extent necessary for the determination of the matter, may consider new issues or take new evidence:

> (i) the rule or order does not apply to the party;

> (ii) the party has not violated the rule or order;

> (iii) the party has violated the rule or order but has subsequently complied, but a party who establishes this defense is not necessarily relieved from any sanction provided by law for past violations; or

> (iv) any other defense allowed by law.

§ 5–204. [Incorporation of Certain Provisions on Judicial Review]

Proceedings for civil enforcement are governed by the following provisions of this Act on judicial review, as modified where necessary to adapt them to those proceedings:

(1) Section 5–101(2) (ancillary procedural matters); and

(2) Section 5–115 (agency record for judicial review—contents, preparation, transmittal, cost.)

§ 5–205. [Review by Higher Court]

Decisions on petitions for civil enforcement are reviewable by the [appellate court] as in other civil cases.

MODEL STATE ADMINISTRATIVE PROCEDURE ACT (1961)

UNIFORM LAWS ANNOTATED

UNIFORM LAW COMMISSIONERS' MODEL STATE ADMINISTRATIVE PROCEDURE ACT (1961)

§ 1. [Definitions]

As used in this Act:

(1) "agency" means each state [board, commission, department, or officer], other than the legislature or the courts, authorized by law to make rules or to determine contested cases;

(2) "contested case" means a proceeding, including but not restricted to ratemaking, [price fixing], and licensing, in which the legal rights, duties, or privileges of a party are required by law to be determined by an agency after an opportunity for hearing;

(3) "license" includes the whole or part of any agency permit, certificate, approval, registration, charter, or similar form of permission required by law, but it does not include a license required solely for revenue purposes;

(4) "licensing" includes the agency process respecting the grant, denial, renewal, revocation, suspension, annulment, withdrawal, or amendment of a license;

(5) "party" means each person or agency named or admitted as a party, or properly seeking and entitled as of right to be admitted as a party;

(6) "persons" means any individual, partnership, corporation, association, governmental subdivision, or public or private organization of any character other than an agency;

(7) "rule" means each agency statement of general applicability that implements, interprets, or prescribes law or policy, or describes the organization, procedure, or practice requirements of any agency. The term includes the amendment or repeal of a prior rule, but does not include (A) statements concerning only the internal management of an agency and not affecting private rights or procedures available to the public, or (B) declaratory rulings issued pursuant to Section 8, or (C) intra-agency memoranda.

§ 2. [Public Information; Adoption of Rules; Availability of Rules and Orders]

(a) In addition to other rule-making requirements imposed by law, each agency shall:

> (1) adopt as a rule a description of its organization, stating the general course and method of its operations and the methods whereby the public may obtain information or make submissions or requests;

> (2) adopt rules of practice setting forth the nature and requirements of all formal and informal procedures available, including a description of all forms and instructions used by the agency;

> (3) make available for public inspection all rules and all other written statements of policy or interpretations formulated, adopted, or used by the agency in the discharge of its functions;

> (4) make available for public inspection all final orders, decisions, and opinions.

(b) No agency rule, order, or decision is valid or effective against any person or party, nor may it be invoked by the agency for any purpose, until it has been made available for public inspection as herein required. This provision is not applicable in favor of any person or party who has actual knowledge thereof.

§ 3. [Procedure for Adoption of Rules]

(a) Prior to the adoption, amendment, or repeal of any rule, the agency shall:

(1) give at least 20 days' notice of its intended action. The notice shall include a statement of either the terms or substance of the intended action or a description of the subjects and issues involved, and the time when, the place where, and the manner in which interested persons may present their views thereon. The notice shall be mailed to all persons who have made timely request of the agency for advance notice of its rule-making proceedings and shall be published in [here insert the medium of publication appropriate for the adopting state];

(2) afford all interested persons reasonable opportunity to submit data, views, or arguments, orally or in writing. In case of substantive rules, opportunity for oral hearing must be granted if requested by 25 persons, by a governmental subdivision or agency, or by an association having not less than 25 members. The agency shall consider fully all written and oral submissions respecting the proposed rule. Upon adoption of a rule, the agency, if requested to do so by an interested person either prior to adoption or within 30 days thereafter, shall issue a concise statement of the principal reasons for and against its adoption, incorporating therein its reasons for overruling the considerations urged against its adoption.

(b) If an agency finds that an imminent peril to the public health, safety, or welfare requires adoption of a rule upon fewer than 20 days' notice and states in writing its reasons for that finding, it may proceed without prior notice or hearing or upon any abbreviated notice and hearing that it finds practicable, to adopt an emergency rule. The rule may be effective for a period of not longer than 120 days [renewable once for a period not exceeding (4) days], but the adoption of an identical rule under subsections (a)(1) and (a)(2) of this Section is not precluded.

(c) No rule hereafter adopted is valid unless adopted in substantial compliance with this Section. A proceeding to contest any rule on the ground of non-compliance with the procedural requirements of this Section must be commenced within 2 years from the effective date of the rule.

§ 4. [Filing and Taking Effect of Rules]

(a) Each agency shall file in the office of the [Secretary of State] a certified copy of each rule adopted by it, including all rules existing on the effective date of this Act. The [Secretary of State] shall keep a permanent register of the rules open to public inspection.

(b) Each rule hereafter adopted is effective 20 days after filing, except that:

(1) if a later date is required by statute or specified in the rule, the later date is the effective date;

(2) subject to applicable constitutional or statutory provisions, an emergency rule becomes effective immediately upon filing with the [Secretary of State], or at a stated date less than 20 days thereafter, if the agency finds that this effective date is necessary because of imminent peril to the public health, safety, or welfare. The agency's finding and a brief statement of the reasons therefor shall be filed with the rule. The agency shall take appropriate measures to make emergency rules known to the persons who may be affected by them.

§ 5. [Publication of Rules]

(a) The [Secretary of State] shall compile, index, and publish all effective rules adopted by each agency. Compilations shall be supplemented or revised as often as necessary [and at least once every 2 years].

(b) The [Secretary of State] shall publish a [monthly] bulletin setting forth the text of all rules filed during the preceding [month] excluding rules in effect upon the adoption of this Act.

(c) The [Secretary of State] may omit from the bulletin or compilation any rule the publication of which would be unduly cumbersome, expensive, or otherwise inexpedient, if the rule in printed or processed form is made available on application to the adopting agency, and if the bulletin or compilation contains a notice stating the general subject matter of the omitted rule and stating how a copy thereof may be obtained.

(d) Bulletins and compilations shall be made available upon request to [agencies and officials of this State] free of charge and to other persons at prices fixed by the [Secretary of State] to cover mailing and publication costs.

§ 6. [Petition for Adoption of Rules]

An interested person may petition an agency requesting the promulgation, amendment, or repeal of a rule. Each agency shall prescribe by rule the form for petitions and the procedure for their submission, consideration, and disposition. Within 30 days after submission of a petition, the agency either shall deny the petition in writing (stating its reasons for the denials) or shall initiate rule-making proceedings in accordance with Section 3.

§ 7. [Declaratory Judgment on Validity or Applicability of Rules]

The validity or applicability of a rule may be determined in an action for declaratory judgment in the [District Court of . . . County], if it is alleged that the rule, or its threatened application, interferes with or impairs, or threatens to interfere with or impair, the legal rights or privileges of the plaintiff. The agency shall be made a party to the action. A declaratory judgment may be rendered whether or not the plaintiff has requested the agency to pass upon the validity or applicability of the rule in question.

§ 8. [Declaratory Rulings by Agencies]

Each agency shall provide by rule for the filing and prompt disposition of petitions for declaratory rulings as to the applicability of any statutory provision or of any rule or order of the agency. Rulings disposing of petitions have the same status as agency decisions or orders in contested cases.

§ 9. [Contested Cases; Notice; Hearing; Records]

(a) In a contested case, all parties shall be afforded an opportunity for hearing after reasonable notice.

(b) The notice shall include:

    (1) a statement of the time, place, and nature of the hearing;

    (2) a statement of the legal authority and jurisdiction under which the hearing is to be held;

    (3) a reference to the particular sections of the statutes and rules involved;

    (4) a short and plain statement of the matters asserted. If the agency or other party is unable to state the matters in detail at the time the notice is served, the initial notice may be limited to a statement of the issues involved. Thereafter upon application a more definite and detailed statement shall be furnished.

(c) Opportunity shall be afforded all parties to respond and present evidence and argument on all issues involved.

(d) Unless precluded by law, informal disposition may be made of any contested case by stipulation, agreed settlement, consent order, or default.

(e) The record in a contested case shall include:

    (1) all pleadings, motions, intermediate rulings;

    (2) evidence received or considered;

    (3) a statement of matters officially noticed;

    (4) questions and offers of proof, objections, and rulings thereon;

    (5) proposed findings and exceptions;

    (6) any decision, opinion, or report by the officer presiding at the hearing;

    (7) all staff memoranda or data submitted to the hearing officer or members of the agency in connection with their consideration of the case.

(f) Oral proceedings or any part thereof shall be transcribed on request of any party.

(g) Findings of fact shall be based exclusively on the evidence and on matters officially noticed.

§ 10. [Rules of Evidence; Official Notice]

In contested cases:

(1) irrelevant, immaterial, or unduly repetitious evidence shall be excluded. The rules of evidence as applied in [non-jury] civil cases in the [District Courts of this State] shall be followed. When necessary to ascertain facts not reasonably susceptible of proof under those rules, evidence not admissible thereunder may be admitted (except where precluded by statute) if it is of a type commonly relied upon by reasonably prudent men in the conduct of their affairs. Agencies shall give effect to the rules of privilege recognized by law. Objections to evidentiary offers may be made and shall be noted in the record. Subject to these requirements, when a hearing will be expedited and the interests of the parties will not be prejudiced substantially, any part of the evidence may be received in written form;

[(2) documentary evidence may be received in the form of copies or excerpts, if the original is not readily available. Upon request, parties shall be given an opportunity to compare the copy with the original;]

(3) a party may conduct cross-examinations required for a full and true disclosure of the facts;

(4) notice may be taken of judicially cognizable facts. In addition, notice may be taken of generally recognized technical or scientific facts within the agency's specialized knowledge. Parties shall be notified either before or during the hearing, or by reference in preliminary reports or otherwise, of the material noticed, including any staff memoranda or data, and they shall be afforded an opportunity to contest the material so noticed. The agency's experience, technical competence, and specialized knowledge may be utilized in the evaluation of the evidence.

§ 11. [Examination of Evidence by Agency]

When in a contested case a majority of the officials of the agency who are to render the final decision have not heard the case or read the record, the decision, if adverse to a party to the proceeding other than the agency itself, shall not be made until a proposal for decision is served upon the parties, and an opportunity is afforded to each party adversely affected to file exceptions and present briefs and oral argument to the officials who are to render the decision. The proposal for decision shall contain a statement of the reasons therefor and of each issue of fact or law necessary to the proposed decision, prepared by the person who conducted the hearing or one who has read the record. The parties by written stipulation may waive compliance with this section.

§ 12. [Decisions and Orders]

A final decision or order adverse to a party in a contested case shall be in writing or stated in the record. A final decision shall include findings of fact and conclusions of law, separately stated. Findings of fact, if set forth in statutory language, shall be accompanied by a concise and explicit statement of the underlying facts supporting the findings. If, in accordance with agency rules, a party submitted proposed findings of fact, the decision shall include a ruling upon each proposed finding. Parties shall be notified either personally or by mail of any decision or order. Upon request a copy of the decision or order shall be delivered or mailed forthwith to each party and to his attorney of record.

§ 13. [Ex Parte Consultations]

Unless required for the disposition of ex parte matters authorized by law, members or employees of an agency assigned to render a decision or to make findings of fact and conclusions of law in a contested case shall not communicate, directly or indirectly, in connection with any issue of fact, with any person or party, nor, in connection with any issue of law, with any party or his representative, except upon notice and opportunity for all parties to participate. An agency member

(1) may communicate with other members of the agency, and

(2) may have the aid and advice of one or more personal assistants.

§ 14. [Licenses]

(a) When the grant, denial, or renewal of a license is required to be preceded by notice and opportunity for hearing, the provisions of this Act concerning contested cases apply.

(b) When a licensee has made timely and sufficient application for the renewal of a license or a new license with reference to any activity of a continuing nature, the existing license does not expire until the application has been finally determined by the agency, and, in case the application is denied or the terms of the new license limited, until the last day for seeking review of the agency order or a later date fixed by order of the reviewing court.

(c) No revocation, suspension, annulment, or withdrawal of any license is lawful unless, prior to the institution of agency proceedings, the agency gave notice by mail to the licensee of facts or conduct which warrant the intended action, and the licensee was given an opportunity to show compliance with all lawful requirements for the retention of the license. If the agency finds that public health, safety, or welfare imperatively requires emergency action, and incorporates a finding to that effect in its order, summary suspension of a license may be ordered pending proceedings for revocation or other action. These proceedings shall be promptly instituted and determined.

§ 15. [Judicial Review of Contested Cases]

(a) A person who has exhausted all administrative remedies available within the agency and who is aggrieved by a final decision in a contested case is entitled to judicial review under this Act. This Section does not limit utilization of or the scope of judicial review available under other means of review, redress, relief, or trial de novo provided by law. A preliminary, procedural, or intermediate agency action or ruling is immediately reviewable if review of the final agency decision would not provide an adequate remedy.

(b) Proceedings for review are instituted by filing a petition in the [District Court of the _____ County] within [30] days after [mailing notice of] the final decision of the agency or, if a rehearing is requested, within [30] days after the decision thereon. Copies of the petition shall be served upon the agency and all parties of record.

(c) The filing of the petition does not itself stay enforcement of the agency decision. The agency may grant, or the reviewing court may order, a stay upon appropriate terms.

(d) Within [30] days after the service of the petition, or within further time allowed by the court, the agency shall transmit to the reviewing court the original or a certified copy of the entire record of the proceeding under review. By stipulation of all parties to the review proceedings, the record may be shortened. A party unreasonably refusing to stipulate to limit the record may be taxed by the court for the additional costs. The court may require or permit subsequent corrections or additions to the record.

(e) If, before the date set for hearing, application is made to the court for leave to present additional evidence, and it is shown to the satisfaction of the court that the additional evidence is material and that there were good reasons for failure to present it in the proceeding before the agency, the court may order that the additional evidence be taken before the agency upon conditions determined by the court. The agency may modify its findings and decision by reason of the additional evidence and shall file that evidence and any modifications, new findings, or decisions with the reviewing court.

(f) The review shall be conducted by the court without a jury and shall be confined to the record. In cases of alleged irregularities in procedure before the agency, not shown in the record, proof thereon may be taken in the court. The court, upon request, shall hear oral argument and receive written briefs.

(g) The court shall not substitute its judgment for that of the agency as to the weight of the evidence on questions of fact. The court may affirm the decision of the agency or remand the case for further proceedings. The court may reverse or modify the decision if substantial rights of the appellant have been prejudiced because the administrative findings, inferences, conclusions, or decisions are:

    (1) in violation of constitutional or statutory provisions;

    (2) in excess of the statutory authority of the agency;

    (3) made upon unlawful procedure;

    (4) affected by other error of law;

    (5) clearly erroneous in view of the reliable, probative, and substantial evidence on the whole record; or

    (6) arbitrary or capricious or characterized by abuse of discretion or clearly unwarranted exercise of discretion.

§ 16. [Appeals]

An aggrieved party may obtain a review of any final judgment of the [District Court] under this Act by appeal to the [Supreme Court]. The appeal shall be taken as in other civil cases.

[§ 17. [Severability]

If any provision of this Act or the application thereof to any person or circumstance is held invalid, the invalidity does not affect other provisions or applications of the Act which can be given effect without the invalid provision or application, and for this purpose the provisions of this Act are severable.]

§ 18. [Repealed]

§ 19. [Time of Taking Effect and Scope of Application]

This Act takes effect .... and (except as to proceedings then pending) applies to all agencies and agency proceedings not expressly exempted.

CALIFORNIA CODE OF CIVIL PROCEDURE

PART 3. OF SPECIAL PROCEEDINGS OF A CIVIL NATURE
TITLE 1. OF WRITS OF REVIEW, MANDATE, AND PROHIBITION
CHAPTER 2. WRIT OF MANDATE

§ 1094.5. Review of administrative orders or decisions; filing record; extent of injury; abuse of discretion; relevant evidence; judgment; stay; disposal of administrative records

(a) Where the writ is issued for the purpose of inquiring into the validity of any final administrative order or decision made as the result of a proceeding in which by law a hearing is required to be given, evidence is required to be taken, and discretion in the determination of facts is vested in the inferior tribunal, corporation, board, or officer, the case shall be heard by the court sitting without a jury. All or part of the record of the proceedings before the inferior tribunal, corporation, board, or officer may be filed with the petition, may be filed with respondent's points and authorities, or may be ordered to be filed by the court. Except when otherwise prescribed by statute, the cost of preparing the record shall be borne by the petitioner. Where the petitioner has proceeded pursuant to Section 68511.3 of the Government Code and the Rules of Court implementing that section and where the transcript is necessary to a proper review of the administrative proceedings, the cost of preparing the transcript shall be borne by the respondent. Where the party seeking the writ has proceeded pursuant to Section 1088.5, the administrative record shall be filed as expeditiously as possible, and may be filed with the petition, or by the respondent after payment of the costs by the petitioner, where required, or as otherwise directed by the court. If the expense of preparing all or any part of the record has been borne by the prevailing party, the expense shall be taxable as costs.

(b) The inquiry in such a case shall extend to the questions whether the respondent has proceeded without, or in excess of jurisdiction; whether there was a fair trial; and whether there was any prejudicial abuse of discretion. Abuse of discretion is established if the respondent has not proceeded in the manner required by law, the order or decision is not supported by the findings, or the findings are not supported by the evidence.

(c) Where it is claimed that the findings are not supported by the evidence, in cases in which the court is authorized by law to exercise its independent judgment on the evidence, abuse of discretion is established if the court determines that the findings are not supported by the weight of the evidence. In all other cases, abuse of discretion is established if the court determines that the findings are not supported by substantial evidence in the light of the whole record.

(d) Notwithstanding subdivision (c), in cases arising from private hospital boards or boards of directors of districts organized pursuant to The Local Hospital District Law, Division 23 (commencing with Section 32000) of the Health and Safety Code or governing bodies of municipal hospitals formed pursuant to Article 7 (commencing with Section 37600) or Article 8 (commencing with Section 37650) of Chapter 5 of Division 3 of Title 4 of the Government Code, abuse of discretion is established if the court determines that the findings are not supported by substantial evidence in the light of the whole record. However, in all cases in which the petition alleges discriminatory actions prohibited by Section 1316 of the Health and Safety Code, and the plaintiff makes a preliminary showing of substantial evidence in support of that allegation, the court shall exercise its independent judgment on the evidence and abuse of discretion shall be established if the court determines that the findings are not supported by the weight of the evidence.

(e) Where the court finds that there is relevant evidence that, in the exercise of reasonable diligence, could not have been produced or that was improperly excluded at the hearing before respondent, it may enter judgment as provided in subdivision (f) remanding the case to be reconsidered in the light of that evidence; or, in cases in which the court is authorized by law to exercise its independent judgment on the evidence, the court may admit the evidence at the hearing on the writ without remanding the case.

(f) The court shall enter judgment either commanding respondent to set aside the order or decision, or denying the writ. Where the judgment commands that the order or decision be set aside, it may order the reconsideration of the case in the light of the court's opinion and judgment and may order respondent to take such further action as is specially enjoined upon it by law, but the judgment shall not limit or control in any way the discretion legally vested in the respondent.

(g) Except as provided in subdivision (h), the court in which proceedings under this section are instituted may stay the operation of the administrative order or decision pending the judgment of the court, or until the filing of a notice of appeal from the judgment or until the expiration of the time for filing the notice, whichever occurs first. However, no such stay shall be imposed or continued if the court is satisfied that it is against the public interest. The application for the stay shall be accompanied by proof of service of a copy of the application on the respondent. Service shall be made in the manner provided by Title 5 (commencing with Section 405) of Part 2 or Chapter 5 (commencing with Section 1010) of Title 14 of Part 2. If an appeal is taken from a denial of the writ, the order or decision of the agency shall not be stayed except upon the order of the court to which the appeal is taken. However, in cases where a stay is in effect at the time of filing the notice of appeal, the stay shall be continued by operation of law for a period of 20 days from the filing of the notice. If an appeal is taken from the granting of the writ, the order or decision of the agency is stayed pending the determination of the appeal unless the court to which the appeal is taken shall otherwise order. Where any final administrative order or decision is the subject of proceedings under this section, if the petition shall have been filed while the penalty imposed is in full force and effect, the determination shall not be considered to have become moot in cases where the penalty imposed by the administrative agency has been completed or complied with during the pendency of the proceedings.

(h)(1) The court in which proceedings under this section are instituted may stay the operation of the administrative order or decision of any licensed hospital or any state agency made after a hearing required by statute to be conducted under the Administrative Procedure Act, as set forth in Chapter 5 (commencing with Section 11500) of Part 1 of Division 3 of Title 2 of the Government Code, conducted by the agency itself or an administrative law judge on the staff of the Office of Administrative Hearings pending the judgment of the court, or until the filing of a notice of appeal from the judgment or until the expiration of the time for filing the notice, whichever occurs first. However, the stay shall not be imposed or continued unless the court is satisfied that the public interest will not suffer and that the licensed hospital or agency is unlikely to prevail ultimately on the merits. The application for the stay shall be accompanied by proof of service of a copy of the application on the respondent. Service shall be made in the manner provided by Title 5 (commencing with Section 405) of Part 2 or Chapter 5 (commencing with Section 1010) of Title 14 of Part 2.

(2) The standard set forth in this subdivision for obtaining a stay shall apply to any administrative order or decision of an agency that issues licenses pursuant to Division 2 (commencing with Section 500) of the Business and Professions Code or pursuant to the Osteopathic Initiative Act or the Chiropractic Initiative Act. With respect to orders or decisions of other state agencies, the standard in this subdivision shall apply only when the agency has adopted the proposed decision of the administrative law judge in its entirety or has adopted the proposed decision but reduced the proposed penalty pursuant to subdivision (b) of Section 11517 of the Government Code; otherwise the standard in subdivision (g) shall apply.

(3) If an appeal is taken from a denial of the writ, the order or decision of the hospital or agency shall not be stayed except upon the order of the court to which the appeal is taken. However, in cases where a stay is in effect at the time of filing the notice of appeal, the stay shall be continued by operation of law for a period of 20 days from the filing of the notice. If an appeal is taken from

the granting of the writ, the order or decision of the hospital or agency is stayed pending the determination of the appeal unless the court to which the appeal is taken shall otherwise order. Where any final administrative order or decision is the subject of proceedings under this section, if the petition shall have been filed while the penalty imposed is in full force and effect, the determination shall not be considered to have become moot in cases where the penalty imposed by the administrative agency has been completed or complied with during the pendency of the proceedings.

(i) Any administrative record received for filing by the clerk of the court may be disposed of as provided in Sections 1952, 1952.2, and 1952.3.

(j) Effective January 1, 1996, this subdivision shall apply to state employees in State Bargaining Unit 5. This subdivision shall apply to state employees in State Bargaining Unit 8. For purposes of this section, the court is not authorized to review any disciplinary decisions reached pursuant to Section 19576.1 or 19576.5 of the Government Code.

(k) This section shall not apply to state employees in State Bargaining Unit 11 disciplined or rejected on probation for positive drug test results who expressly waive appeal to the State Personnel Board and invoke arbitration proceedings pursuant to a State Bargaining Unit 11 collective bargaining agreement. [This subsection was held unconstitutional in the case of *State Personnel Bd. v. Department of Personnel Admin.* (2005) 36 Cal.Rptr.3d 142, 37 Cal.4th 512, 123 P.3d 169.]

CALIFORNIA GOVERNMENT CODE

TITLE 2. GOVERNMENT OF THE STATE OF CALIFORNIA

DIVISION 3. EXECUTIVE DEPARTMENT

PART 1. STATE DEPARTMENTS AND AGENCIES

CHAPTER 3.5. ADMINISTRATIVE REGULATIONS
AND RULEMAKING

ARTICLE 1. GENERAL

CALIFORNIA GOVERNMENT CODE

CHAPTER 5. ADMINISTRATIVE ADJUDICATION: FORMAL HEARING

ARTICLE I. GENERAL

§ 11340. Legislative finding and declaration

The Legislature finds and declares as follows:

(a) There has been an unprecedented growth in the number of administrative regulations in recent years.

(b) The language of many regulations is frequently unclear and unnecessarily complex, even when the complicated and technical nature of the subject matter is taken into account. The language is often confusing to the persons who must comply with the regulations.

(c) Substantial time and public funds have been spent in adopting regulations, the necessity for which has not been established.

(d) The imposition of prescriptive standards upon private persons and entities through regulations where the establishment of performance standards could reasonably be expected to produce the same result has placed an unnecessary burden on California citizens and discouraged innovation, research, and development of improved means of achieving desirable social goals.

(e) There exists no central office in state government with the power and duty to review regulations to ensure that they are written in a comprehensible manner, are authorized by statute, and are consistent with other law.

(f) Correcting the problems that have been caused by the unprecedented growth of regulations in California requires the direct involvement of the Legislature as well as that of the executive branch of state government.

(g) The complexity and lack of clarity in many regulations put small businesses, which do not have the resources to hire experts to assist them, at a distinct disadvantage.

§ 11340.1. Legislative Intent

(a) The Legislature therefore declares that it is in the public interest to establish an Office of Administrative Law which shall be charged with the orderly review of adopted regulations. It is the intent of the Legislature that the purpose of such review shall be to reduce the number of administrative regulations and to improve the quality of those regulations which are adopted. It is the intent of the Legislature that agencies shall actively seek to reduce the unnecessary regulatory burden on private individuals and entities by substituting performance standards for prescriptive standards wherever performance standards can be reasonably expected to be as effective and less burdensome, and that this substitution shall be considered during the course of the agency rulemaking process. It is the intent of the Legislature that neither the Office of Administrative Law nor the court should substitute its judgment for that of the rulemaking agency as expressed in the substantive content of adopted regulations. It is the intent of the Legislature that while the Office of Administrative Law will be part of the executive branch of state government, that the office work closely with, and upon request report directly to, the Legislature in order to accomplish regulatory reform in California.

(b) It is the intent of the Legislature that the California Code of Regulations made available on the Internet by the office pursuant to Section 11344 include complete authority and reference citations and history notes.

§ 11340.2. Establishment of office; director and deputy director

(a) The Office of Administrative Law is hereby established in state government. The office shall be under the direction and control of an executive officer who shall be known as the director. There shall also be a deputy director. The director's term and the deputy director's term of office shall be coterminous with that of the appointing power, except that they shall be subject to reappointment.

(b) The director and deputy director shall have the same qualifications as a hearing officer and shall be appointed by the Governor subject to the confirmation of the Senate.

* * *

§ 11340.5. Agency guidelines, criteria, bulletins, manuals, instructions, orders, standards of general application or other rules: adoption as regulation; filing; determination of status as regulation

(a) No state agency shall issue, utilize, enforce, or attempt to enforce any guideline, criterion, bulletin, manual, instruction, order, standard of general application, or other rule, which is a regulation as defined in Section 11342.600, unless the guideline, criterion, bulletin, manual, instruction, order, standard of general application, or other rule has been adopted as a regulation and filed with the Secretary of State pursuant to this chapter.

(b) If the office is notified of, or on its own, learns of the issuance, enforcement of, or use of, an agency guideline, criterion, bulletin, manual, instruction, order, standard of general application, or other rule that has not been adopted as a regulation and filed with the Secretary of State pursuant to this chapter, the office may issue a determination as to whether the guideline, criterion, bulletin, manual, instruction, order, standard of general application, or other rule, is a regulation as defined in Section 11342.600.

(c) The office shall do all of the following:

(1) File its determination upon issuance with the Secretary of State.

(2) Make its determination known to the agency, the Governor, and the Legislature.

(3) Publish its determination in the California Regulatory Notice Register within 15 days of the date of issuance.

(4) Make its determination available to the public and the courts.

(d) Any interested person may obtain judicial review of a given determination by filing a written petition requesting that the determination of the office be modified or set aside. A petition shall be filed with the court within 30 days of the date the determination is published.

(e) A determination issued by the office pursuant to this section shall not be considered by a court, or by an administrative agency in an adjudicatory proceeding if all of the following occurs:

(1) The court or administrative agency proceeding involves the party that sought the determination from the office.

(2) The proceeding began prior to the party's request for the office's determination.

(3) At issue in the proceeding is the question of whether the guideline, criterion, bulletin, manual, instruction, order, standard of general application, or other rule that is the legal basis for the adjudicatory action is a regulation as defined in Section 11342.600.

§ 11340.6.   Petition for adoption or repeal; contents

Except where the right to petition for adoption of a regulation is restricted by statute to a designated group or where the form of procedure for such a petition is otherwise prescribed by statute, any interested person may petition a state agency requesting the adoption, amendment, or repeal of a regulation as provided in Article 5 (commencing with Section 11346). This petition shall state the following clearly and concisely:

(a) The substance or nature of the regulation, amendment, or repeal requested.

(b) The reason for the request.

(c) Reference to the authority of the state agency to take the action requested.

§ 11340.7.   Petition for adoption, amendment or repeal; relief; reconsideration; decision

(a) Upon receipt of a petition requesting the adoption, amendment, or repeal of a regulation pursuant to Article 5 (commencing with Section 11346), a state agency shall notify the petitioner in writing of the receipt and shall within 30 days deny the petition indicating why the agency has reached its decision on the merits of the petition in writing or schedule the matter for public hearing in accordance with the notice and hearing requirements of that article.

(b) A state agency may grant or deny the petition in part, and may grant any other relief or take any other action as it may determine to be warranted by the petition and shall notify the petitioner in writing of this action.

(c) Any interested person may request a reconsideration of any part or all of a decision of any agency on any petition submitted. The request shall be submitted in accordance with Section 11340.6 and include the reason or reasons why an agency should reconsider its previous decision no later than 60 days after the date of the decision involved. The agency's reconsideration of any matter relating to a petition shall be subject to subdivision (a).

(d) Any decision of a state agency denying in whole or in part or granting in whole or in part a petition requesting the adoption, amendment, or repeal of a regulation pursuant to Article 5 (commencing with Section 11346) shall be in writing and shall be transmitted to the Office of Administrative Law for publication in the California Regulatory Notice Register at the earliest practicable date. The decision shall identify the agency, the party submitting the petition, the provisions of the California Code of Regulations requested to be affected, reference to authority to take the action requested, the reasons supporting the agency determination, an agency contact person, and the right of interested persons to obtain a copy of the petition from the agency.

ARTICLE 5. PUBLIC PARTICIPATION: PROCEDURE FOR ADOPTION OF REGULATIONS

§ 11346. Purpose; application; construction

(a) It is the purpose of this chapter to establish basic minimum procedural requirements for the adoption, amendment, or repeal of administrative regulations. Except as provided in Section 11346.1, the provisions of this chapter are applicable to the exercise of any quasi-legislative power conferred by any statute heretofore or hereafter enacted, but nothing in this chapter repeals or diminishes additional requirements imposed by any statute. This chapter shall not be superseded or modified by any subsequent legislation except to the extent that the legislation shall do so expressly.

(b) An agency that is considering adopting, amending, or repealing a regulation may consult with interested persons before initiating regulatory action pursuant to this article.

§ 11346.2. Notification of proposed agency action; public information

Every agency subject to this chapter shall prepare, submit to the office with the notice of the proposed action as described in Section 11346.5, and make available to the public upon request, all of the following:

(a) A copy of the express terms of the proposed regulation.

(1) The agency shall draft the regulation in plain, straightforward language, avoiding technical terms as much as possible, and using a coherent and easily readable style. The agency shall draft the regulation in plain English.

(2) The agency shall include a notation following the express terms of each California Code of Regulations section, listing the specific statutes or other provisions of law authorizing the adoption of the regulation and listing the specific statutes or other provisions of law being implemented, interpreted, or made specific by that section in the California Code of Regulations.

(3) The agency shall use underline or italics to indicate additions to, and strikeout to indicate deletions from, the California Code of Regulations.

(b) An initial statement of reasons for proposing the adoption, amendment, or repeal of a regulation. This statement of reasons shall include, but not be limited to, all of the following:

(1) A statement of the specific purpose of each adoption, amendment, or repeal and the rationale for the determination by the agency that each adoption, amendment, or repeal is reasonably necessary to carry out the purpose for which it is proposed. Where the adoption or amendment of a regulation would mandate the use of specific technologies or equipment, a statement of the reasons why the agency believes these mandates or prescriptive standards are required.

(2) An identification of each technical, theoretical, and empirical study, report, or similar document, if any, upon which the agency relies in proposing the adoption, amendment, or repeal of a regulation.

(3) (A) A description of reasonable alternatives to the regulation and the agency's reasons for rejecting those alternatives. In the case of a regulation that would mandate the use of specific technologies or equipment or prescribe specific actions or procedures, the imposition of performance standards shall be considered as an alternative.

(B) A description of reasonable alternatives to the regulation that would lessen any adverse impact on small business and the agency's reasons for rejecting those alternatives.

(C) Notwithstanding subparagraph (A) or (B), an agency is not required to artificially construct alternatives, describe unreasonable alternatives, or justify why it has not described alternatives.

(4) Facts, evidence, documents, testimony, or other evidence on which the agency relies to support an initial determination that the action will not have a significant adverse economic impact on business.

(5) A department, board, or commission within the Environmental Protection Agency, the Resources Agency, or the Office of the State Fire Marshal shall describe its efforts, in connection with a proposed rulemaking action, to avoid unnecessary duplication or conflicts with federal regulations contained in the Code of Federal Regulations addressing the same issues. These agencies may adopt regulations different from federal regulations contained in the Code of Federal Regulations addressing the same issues upon a finding of one or more of the following justifications:

(A) The differing state regulations are authorized by law.

(B) The cost of differing state regulations is justified by the benefit to human health, public safety, public welfare, or the environment.

(c) A state agency that adopts or amends a regulation mandated by federal law or regulations, the provisions of which are identical to a previously adopted or amended federal regulation, shall be deemed to have complied with subdivision (b) if a statement to the effect that a federally mandated regulation or amendment to a regulation is being proposed, together with a citation to where an explanation of the provisions of the regulation can be found, is included in the notice of proposed adoption or amendment prepared pursuant to Section 11346.5. However, the agency shall comply fully with this chapter with respect to any provisions in the regulation that the agency proposes to adopt or amend that are different from the corresponding provisions of the federal regulation.

§ 11346.3. Action with potential or significant adverse economic impact on small businesses or individuals; potential cost impact; exemption from reporting

(a) State agencies proposing to adopt, amend, or repeal any administrative regulation shall assess the potential for adverse economic impact on California business enterprises and individuals, avoiding the imposition of unnecessary or unreasonable regulations or reporting, recordkeeping, or compliance requirements. For purposes of this subdivision, assessing the potential for adverse economic impact shall require agencies, when proposing to adopt, amend, or repeal a regulation, to adhere to the following requirements, to the extent that these requirements do not conflict with other state or federal laws:

(1) The proposed adoption, amendment, or repeal of a regulation shall be based on adequate information concerning the need for, and consequences of, proposed governmental action.

(2) The state agency, prior to submitting a proposal to adopt, amend, or repeal a regulation to the office, shall consider the proposal's impact on business, with consideration of industries affected including the ability of California businesses to compete with businesses in other states. For purposes of evaluating the impact on the ability of California businesses to compete with businesses in other states, an agency shall consider, but not be limited to, information supplied by interested parties.

It is not the intent of this section to impose additional criteria on agencies, above that which exists in current law, in assessing adverse economic impact on California business enterprises, but only to assure that the assessment is made early in the process of initiation and development of a proposed adoption, amendment, or repeal of a regulation.

(b)(1) All state agencies proposing to adopt, amend, or repeal any administrative regulations shall assess whether and to what extent it will affect the following:

(A) The creation or elimination of jobs within the State of California.

(B) The creation of new businesses or the elimination of existing businesses within the State of California.

(C) The expansion of businesses currently doing business within the State of California.

(2) This subdivision does not apply to the University of California, the Hastings College of the Law, or the Fair Political Practices Commission.

(3) Information required from state agencies for the purpose of completing the assessment may come from existing state publications.

(c) No administrative regulation adopted on or after January 1, 1993, that requires a report shall apply to businesses, unless the state agency adopting the regulation makes a finding that it is necessary for the health, safety, or welfare of the people of the state that the regulation apply to businesses.

§ 11346.4. Notice of proposed action; methods; effective period; notice of changes after completion and approval; refusal to publish; regulatory notice register

(a) At least 45 days prior to the hearing and close of the public comment period on the adoption, amendment, or repeal of a regulation, notice of the proposed action shall be:

(1) Mailed to every person who has filed a request for notice of regulatory actions with the state agency. Each state agency shall give a person filing a request for notice of regulatory actions the option of being notified of all proposed regulatory actions or being notified of regulatory actions concerning one or more particular programs of the state agency.

(2) In cases in which the state agency is within a state department, mailed or delivered to the director of the department.

(3) Mailed to a representative number of small business enterprises or their representatives that are likely to be affected by the proposed action. "Representative" for the purposes of this paragraph includes, but is not limited to, a trade association, industry association, professional association, or any other business group or association of any kind that represents a business enterprise or employees of a business enterprise.

(4) When appropriate in the judgment of the state agency, mailed to any person or group of persons whom the agency believes to be interested in the proposed action and published in the form and manner as the state agency shall prescribe.

(5) Published in the California Regulatory Notice Register as prepared by the office for each state agency's notice of regulatory action.

(6) Posted on the state agency's website if the agency has a website.

(b) The effective period of a notice issued pursuant to this section shall not exceed one year from the date thereof. If the adoption, amendment, or repeal of a regulation proposed in the notice is not completed and transmitted to the office within the period of one year, a notice of the proposed action shall again be issued pursuant to this article.

(c) Once the adoption, amendment, or repeal is completed and approved by the office, no further adoption, amendment, or repeal to the noticed regulation shall be made without subsequent notice being given.

(d) The office may refuse to publish a notice submitted to it if the agency has failed to comply with this article.

(e) The office shall make the California Regulatory Notice Register available to the public and state agencies at a nominal cost that is consistent with a policy of encouraging the widest possible notice distribution to interested persons.

(f) Where the form or manner of notice is prescribed by statute in any particular case, in addition to filing and mailing notice as required by this section, the notice shall be published, posted, mailed, filed, or otherwise publicized as prescribed by that statute. The failure to mail notice to any person as provided in this section shall not invalidate any action taken by a state agency pursuant to this article.

§ 11346.45. Public discussions of proposed regulations

(a) In order to increase public participation and improve the quality of regulations, state agencies proposing to adopt regulations shall, prior to publication of the notice required by Section 11346.5, involve parties who would be subject to the proposed regulations in public discussions regarding those proposed regulations, when the proposed regulations involve complex proposals or a large number of proposals that cannot easily be reviewed during the comment period.

(b) This section does not apply to a state agency in any instance where that state agency is required to implement federal law and regulations for which there is little or no discretion on the part of the state to vary.

§ 11346.5. Notice of proposed adoption, amendment or repeal; contents; availability to public

(a) The notice of proposed adoption, amendment, or repeal of a regulation shall include the following:

(1) A statement of the time, place, and nature of proceedings for adoption, amendment, or repeal of the regulation.

(2) Reference to the authority under which the regulation is proposed and a reference to the particular code sections or other provisions of law that are being implemented, interpreted, or made specific.

(3) An informative digest drafted in plain English in a format similar to the Legislative Counsel's digest on legislative bills. The informative digest shall include the following:

(A) A concise and clear summary of existing laws and regulations, if any, related directly to the proposed action and of the effect of the proposed action.

(B) If the proposed action differs substantially from an existing comparable federal regulation or statute, a brief description of the significant differences and the full citation of the federal regulations or statutes.

(C) A policy statement overview explaining the broad objectives of the regulation and, if appropriate, the specific objectives.

(4) Any other matters as are prescribed by statute applicable to the specific state agency or to any specific regulation or class of regulations.

(5) A determination as to whether the regulation imposes a mandate on local agencies or school districts and, if so, whether the mandate requires state reimbursement pursuant to Part 7 (commencing with Section 17500) of Division 4.

(6) An estimate, prepared in accordance with instructions adopted by the Department of Finance, of the cost or savings to any state

agency, the cost to any local agency or school district that is required to be reimbursed under Part 7 (commencing with Section 17500) of Division 4, other nondiscretionary cost or savings imposed on local agencies, and the cost or savings in federal funding to the state. For purposes of this paragraph, "cost or savings" means additional costs or savings, both direct and indirect, that a public agency necessarily incurs in reasonable compliance with regulations.

(7) If a state agency, in proposing to adopt, amend, or repeal any administrative regulation, makes an initial determination that the action may have a significant, statewide adverse economic impact directly affecting business, including the ability of California businesses to compete with businesses in other states, it shall include the following information in the notice of proposed action:

(A) Identification of the types of businesses that would be affected.

(B) A description of the projected reporting, recordkeeping, and other compliance requirements that would result from the proposed action.

(C) The following statement: "The (name of agency) has made an initial determination that the (adoption/amendment/repeal) of this regulation may have a significant, statewide adverse economic impact directly affecting business, including the ability of California businesses to compete with businesses in other states. The (name of agency) (has/has not) considered proposed alternatives that would lessen any adverse economic impact on business and invites you to submit proposals. Submissions may include the following considerations:

(i) The establishment of differing compliance or reporting requirements or timetables that take into account the resources available to businesses.

(ii) Consolidation or simplification of compliance and reporting requirements for businesses.

(iii) The use of performance standards rather than prescriptive standards.

(iv) Exemption or partial exemption from the regulatory requirements for businesses."

(8) If a state agency, in adopting, amending, or repealing any administrative regulation, makes an initial determination that the action will not have a significant, statewide adverse economic impact directly affecting business, including the ability of California businesses to compete with businesses in other states, it shall make a declaration to that effect in the notice of proposed action. In making this declaration, the agency shall provide in the record facts, evidence, documents, testimony, or other evidence upon which the

agency relies to support its initial determination. An agency's initial determination and declaration that a proposed adoption, amendment, or repeal of a regulation may have or will not have a significant, adverse impact on businesses, including the ability of California businesses to compete with businesses in other states, shall not be grounds for the office to refuse to publish the notice of proposed action.

(9) A description of all cost impacts, known to the agency at the time the notice of proposed action is submitted to the office, that a representative private person or business would necessarily incur in reasonable compliance with the proposed action. If no cost impacts are known to the agency, it shall state the following: "The agency is not aware of any cost impacts that a representative private person or business would necessarily incur in reasonable compliance with the proposed action."

(10) A statement of the results of the assessment required by subdivision (b) of Section 11346.3.

(11) The finding prescribed by subdivision (c) of Section 11346.3, if required.

(12) A statement that the action would have a significant effect on housing costs, if a state agency, in adopting, amending, or repealing any administrative regulation, makes an initial determination that the action would have that effect. In addition, the agency officer designated in paragraph (14), shall make available to the public, upon request, the agency's evaluation, if any, of the effect of the proposed regulatory action on housing costs.

(13) A statement that the adopting agency must determine that no reasonable alternative considered by the agency or that has otherwise been identified and brought to the attention of the agency would be more effective in carrying out the purpose for which the action is proposed or would be as effective and less burdensome to affected private persons than the proposed action.

(14) The name and telephone number of the agency representative and designated backup contact person to whom inquiries concerning the proposed administrative action may be directed.

(15) The date by which comments submitted in writing must be received to present statements, arguments, or contentions in writing relating to the proposed action in order for them to be considered by the state agency before it adopts, amends, or repeals a regulation.

(16) Reference to the fact that the agency proposing the action has prepared a statement of the reasons for the proposed action, has available all the information upon which its proposal is based, and has available the express terms of the proposed action, pursuant to subdivision (b).

(17) A statement that if a public hearing is not scheduled, any interested person or his or her duly authorized representative may request, no later than 15 days prior to the close of the written comment period, a public hearing pursuant to Section 11346.8.

(18) A statement indicating that the full text of a regulation changed pursuant to Section 11346.8 will be available for at least 15 days prior to the date on which the agency adopts, amends, or repeals the resulting regulation.

(19) A statement explaining how to obtain a copy of the final statement of reasons once it has been prepared pursuant to subdivision (a) of Section 11346.9.

(20) If the agency maintains an Internet web site or other similar forum for the electronic publication or distribution of written material, a statement explaining how materials published or distributed through that forum can be accessed.

(b) The agency representative designated in paragraph (14) of subdivision (a) shall make available to the public upon request the express terms of the proposed action. The representative shall also make available to the public upon request the location of public records, including reports, documentation, and other materials, related to the proposed action. If the representative receives an inquiry regarding the proposed action that the representative cannot answer, the representative shall refer the inquiry to another person in the agency for a prompt response.

(c) This section shall not be construed in any manner that results in the invalidation of a regulation because of the alleged inadequacy of the notice content or the summary or cost estimates, or the alleged inadequacy or inaccuracy of the housing cost estimates, if there has been substantial compliance with those requirements.

§ 11346.8.   Hearing; actions affecting regulations; public notification; conditions

(a) If a public hearing is held, both oral and written statements, arguments, or contentions, shall be permitted. The agency may impose reasonable limitations on oral presentations. If a public hearing is not scheduled, the state agency shall, consistent with Section 11346.4, afford any interested person or his or her duly authorized representative, the opportunity to present statements, arguments or contentions in writing. In addition, a public hearing shall be held if, no later than 15 days prior to the close of the written comment period, an interested person or his or her duly authorized representative submits in writing to the state agency, a request to hold a public hearing. The state agency shall, to the extent practicable, provide notice of the time, date, and place of the hearing by mailing the notice to every person who has filed a request for notice thereby with the state agency. The state agency shall consider all relevant matter presented to it before adopting, amending, or repealing any regulation.

(b) In any hearing under this section, the state agency or its duly authorized representative shall have authority to administer oaths or affirmations. An agency may continue or postpone a hearing from time to time to the time and at the place as it determines. If a hearing is continued or postponed, the state agency shall provide notice to the public as to when it will be resumed or rescheduled.

(c) No state agency may adopt, amend, or repeal a regulation which has been changed from that which was originally made available to the public pursuant to Section 11346.5, unless the change is (1) nonsubstantial or solely grammatical in nature, or (2) sufficiently related to the original text that the public was adequately placed on notice that the change could result from the originally proposed regulatory action. If a sufficiently related change is made, the full text of the resulting adoption, amendment, or repeal, with the change clearly indicated, shall be made available to the public for at least 15 days before the agency adopts, amends, or repeals the resulting regulation. Any written comments received regarding the change must be responded to in the final statement of reasons required by Section 11346.9.

(d) No state agency shall add any material to the record of the rulemaking proceeding after the close of the public hearing or comment period, unless the agency complies with Section 11347.1. This subdivision does not apply to material prepared pursuant to Section 11346.9.

(e) If a comment made at a public hearing raises a new issue concerning a proposed regulation and a member of the public requests additional time to respond to the new issue before the state agency takes final action, it is the intent of the Legislature that rulemaking agencies consider granting the request for additional time if, under the circumstances, granting the request is practical and does not unduly delay action on the regulation.

§ 11346.9. Final statement of reasons; updated informative digest; adoption or amendment of federal regulations

Every agency subject to this chapter shall do the following:

(a) Prepare and submit to the office with the adopted regulation a final statement of reasons that shall include all of the following:

(1) An update of the information contained in the initial statement of reasons. If the update identifies any data or any technical, theoretical or empirical study, report, or similar document on which the agency is relying in proposing the adoption, amendment, or repeal of a regulation that was not identified in the initial statement of reasons, or which was otherwise not identified or made available

for public review prior to the close of the public comment period, the agency shall comply with Section 11347.1.

(2) A determination as to whether adoption, amendment, or repeal of the regulation imposes a mandate on local agencies or school districts. If the determination is that adoption, amendment, or repeal of the regulation would impose a local mandate, the agency shall state whether the mandate is reimbursable pursuant to Part 7 (commencing with Section 17500) of Division 4. If the agency finds that the mandate is not reimbursable, it shall state the reasons for that finding.

(3) A summary of each objection or recommendation made regarding the specific adoption, amendment, or repeal proposed, together with an explanation of how the proposed action has been changed to accommodate each objection or recommendation, or the reasons for making no change. This requirement applies only to objections or recommendations specifically directed at the agency's proposed action or to the procedures followed by the agency in proposing or adopting the action. The agency may aggregate and summarize repetitive or irrelevant comments as a group, and may respond to repetitive comments or summarily dismiss irrelevant comments as a group. For the purposes of this paragraph, a comment is "irrelevant" if it is not specifically directed at the agency's proposed action or to the procedures followed by the agency in proposing or adopting the action.

(4) A determination with supporting information that no alternative considered by the agency would be more effective in carrying out the purpose for which the regulation is proposed or would be as effective and less burdensome to affected private persons than the adopted regulation.

(5) An explanation setting forth the reasons for rejecting any proposed alternatives that would lessen the adverse economic impact on small businesses.

(b) Prepare and submit to the office with the adopted regulation an updated informative digest containing a clear and concise summary of the immediately preceding laws and regulations, if any, relating directly to the adopted, amended, or repealed regulation and the effect of the adopted, amended, or repealed regulation. The informative digest shall be drafted in a format similar to the Legislative Counsel's Digest on legislative bills.

(c) A state agency that adopts or amends a regulation mandated by federal law or regulations, the provisions of which are identical to a previously adopted or amended federal regulation, shall be deemed to have complied with this section if a statement to the effect that a federally mandated regulation or amendment to a regulation is being proposed, together with a citation to where an explanation of the provisions of the regulation can be found, is included in the notice of proposed adoption or amendment prepared pursuant to Section 11346.5. However, the agency shall comply fully with this chapter with respect to any provisions in the regulation which the agency proposes to adopt or amend that are different from the corresponding provisions of the federal regulation.

(d) If an agency determines that a requirement of this section can be satisfied by reference to an agency statement made pursuant to Sections 11346.2 to 11346.5, inclusive, the agency may satisfy the requirement by incorporating the relevant statement by reference.

§11347. Failure to proceed with proposed action; notice for publication

(a) If, after publication of a notice of proposed action pursuant to Section 11346.4, but before the notice of proposed action becomes ineffective pursuant to subdivision (b) of that section, an agency decides not to proceed with the proposed action, it shall deliver notice of its decision to the office for publication in the California Regulatory Notice Register.

(b) Publication of a notice under this section terminates the effect of the notice of proposed action referred to in the notice. Nothing in this section precludes an agency from proposing a new regulatory action that is similar or identical to a regulatory action that was previously the subject of a notice published under this section.

§11347.1. Rulemaking; documents made available

(a) An agency that adds any technical, theoretical, or empirical study, report, or similar document to the rulemaking file after publication of the notice of proposed action and relies on the document in proposing the action shall make the document available as required by this section.

(b) At least 15 calendar days before the proposed action is adopted by the agency, the agency shall mail to all of the following persons a notice identifying the added document and stating the place and business hours that the document is available for public inspection:

   (1) Persons who testified at the public hearing.

   (2) Persons who submitted written comments at the public hearing.

   (3) Persons whose comments were received by the agency during the public comment period.

   (4) Persons who requested notification from the agency of the availability of changes to the text of the proposed regulation.

(c) The document shall be available for public inspection at the location described in the notice for at least 15 calendar days before the proposed action is adopted by the agency.

413

(d) Written comments on the document or information received by the agency during the availability period shall be summarized and responded to in the final statement of reasons as provided in Section 11346.9.

(e) The rulemaking file shall contain a statement confirming that the agency complied with the requirements of this section and stating the date on which the notice was mailed.

(f) If there are no persons in categories listed in subdivision (b), then the rulemaking file shall contain a confirming statement to that effect.

§ 11347.3. File of rulemaking proceeding

(a) Every agency shall maintain a file of each rulemaking that shall be deemed to be the record for that rulemaking proceeding. Commencing no later than the date that the notice of the proposed action is published in the California Regulatory Notice Register, and during all subsequent periods of time that the file is in the agency's possession, the agency shall make the file available to the public for inspection and copying during regular business hours.

(b) The rulemaking file shall include:

(1) Copies of any petitions received from interested persons proposing the adoption, amendment, or repeal of the regulation, and a copy of any decision provided for by subdivision (d) of Section 11340.7, which grants a petition in whole or in part.

(2) All published notices of proposed adoption, amendment, or repeal of the regulation, and an updated informative digest, the initial statement of reasons, and the final statement of reasons.

(3) The determination, together with the supporting data required by paragraph (5) of subdivision (a) of Section 11346.5.

(4) The determination, together with the supporting data required by paragraph (8) of subdivision (a) of Section 11346.5.

(5) The estimate, together with the supporting data and calculations, required by paragraph (6) of subdivision (a) of Section 11346.5.

(6) All data and other factual information, any studies or reports, and written comments submitted to the agency in connection with the adoption, amendment, or repeal of the regulation.

(7) All data and other factual information, technical, theoretical, and empirical studies or reports, if any, on which the agency is relying in the adoption, amendment, or repeal of a regulation, including any cost impact estimates as required by Section 11346.3.

(8) A transcript, recording, or minutes of any public hearing connected with the adoption, amendment, or repeal of the regulation.

414

(9) The date on which the agency made the full text of the proposed regulation available to the public for 15 days prior to the adoption, amendment, or repeal of the regulation, if required to do so by subdivision (c) of Section 11346.8.

(10) The text of regulations as originally proposed and the modified text of regulations, if any, that were made available to the public prior to adoption.

(11) Any other information, statement, report, or data that the agency is required by law to consider or prepare in connection with the adoption, amendment, or repeal of a regulation.

(12) An index or table of contents that identifies each item contained in the rulemaking file. The index or table of contents shall include an affidavit or a declaration under penalty of perjury in the form specified by Section 2015.5 of the Code of Civil Procedure by the agency official who has compiled the rulemaking file, specifying the date upon which the record was closed, and that the file or the copy, if submitted, is complete.

(c) Every agency shall submit to the office with the adopted regulation, the rulemaking file or a complete copy of the rulemaking file.

(d) The rulemaking file shall be made available by the agency to the public, and to the courts in connection with the review of the regulation.

(e) Upon filing a regulation with the Secretary of State pursuant to Section 11349.3, the office shall return the related rulemaking file to the agency, after which no item contained in the file shall be removed, altered, or destroyed or otherwise disposed of. The agency shall maintain the file unless it elects to transmit the file to the State Archives pursuant to subdivision (f).

(f) The agency may transmit the rulemaking file to the State Archives. The file shall include instructions that the Secretary of State shall not remove, alter, or destroy or otherwise dispose of any item contained in the file. Pursuant to Section 12223.5, the Secretary of State may designate a time for the delivery of the rulemaking file to the State Archives in consideration of document processing or storage limitations.

§ 11348. Rulemaking records; currency and location

Each agency subject to this chapter shall keep its rulemaking records on all of that agency's pending rulemaking actions, in which the notice has been published in the California Regulatory Notice Register, current and in one central location.

ARTICLE 6. REVIEW OF PROPOSED REGULATIONS

§ 11349. Definitions

The following definitions govern the interpretation of this chapter:

(a) "Necessity" means the record of the rulemaking proceeding demonstrates by substantial evidence the need for a regulation to effectuate the purpose of the statute, court decision, or other provision of law that the regulation implements, interprets, or makes specific, taking into account the totality of the record. For purposes of this standard, evidence includes, but is not limited to, facts, studies, and expert opinion.

(b) "Authority" means the provision of law which permits or obligates the agency to adopt, amend, or repeal a regulation.

(c) "Clarity" means written or displayed so that the meaning of regulations will be easily understood by those persons directly affected by them.

(d) "Consistency" means being in harmony with, and not in conflict with or contradictory to, existing statutes, court decisions, or other provisions of law.

(e) "Reference" means the statute, court decision, or other provision of law which the agency implements, interprets, or makes specific by adopting, amending, or repealing a regulation.

(f) "Nonduplication" means that a regulation does not serve the same purpose as a state or federal statute or another regulation. This standard requires that an agency proposing to amend or adopt a regulation must identify any state or federal statute or regulation which is overlapped or duplicated by the proposed regulation and justify any overlap or duplication. This standard is not intended to prohibit state agencies from printing relevant portions of enabling legislation in regulations when the duplication is necessary to satisfy the clarity standard in paragraph (3) of subdivision (a) of Section 11349.1. This standard is intended to prevent the indiscriminate incorporation of statutory language in a regulation.

§ 11349.1. Review of regulations

(a) The office shall review all regulations adopted, amended, or repealed pursuant to the procedure specified in Article 5 (commencing with Section 11346) and submitted to it for publication in the California Code of Regulations Supplement and for transmittal to the Secretary of State and make determinations using all of the following standards:

    (1) Necessity.

    (2) Authority.

    (3) Clarity.

    (4) Consistency.

    (5) Reference.

    (6) Nonduplication.

In reviewing regulations pursuant to this section, the office shall restrict its review to the regulation and the record of the rulemaking proceeding.

The office shall approve the regulation or order of repeal if it complies with the standards set forth in this section and with this chapter.

(b) In reviewing proposed regulations for the criteria in subdivision (a), the office may consider the clarity of the proposed regulation in the context of related regulations already in existence.

(c) The office shall adopt regulations governing the procedures it uses in reviewing regulations submitted to it. The regulations shall provide for an orderly review and shall specify the methods, standards, presumptions, and principles the office uses, and the limitations it observes, in reviewing regulations to establish compliance with the standards specified in subdivision (a). The regulations adopted by the office shall ensure that it does not substitute its judgment for that of the rulemaking agency as expressed in the substantive content of adopted regulations.

(d) The office shall return any regulation subject to this chapter to the adopting agency if any of the following occur:

(1) The adopting agency has not prepared the estimate required by paragraph (6) of subdivision (a) of Section 11346.5 and has not included the data used and calculations made and the summary report of the estimate in the file of the rulemaking.

(2) The agency has not complied with Section 11346.3.

(3) The adopting agency has prepared the estimate required by paragraph (6) of subdivision (a) of Section 11346.5, the estimate indicates that the regulation will result in a cost to local agencies or school districts that is required to be reimbursed under Part 7 (commencing with Section 17500) of Division 4, and the adopting agency fails to do any of the following:

(A) Cite an item in the Budget Act for the fiscal year in which the regulation will go into effect as the source from which the Controller may pay the claims of local agencies or school districts.

(B) Cite an accompanying bill appropriating funds as the source from which the Controller may pay the claims of local agencies or school districts.

(C) Attach a letter or other documentation from the Department of Finance which states that the Department of Finance has approved a request by the agency that funds be included in the Budget Bill for the next following fiscal year to reimburse local agencies or school districts for the costs mandated by the regulation.

(D) Attach a letter or other documentation from the Department of Finance which states that the Department of Finance has authorized the augmentation of the amount available for expenditure under the agency's appropriation in the Budget Act which is for reimbursement pursuant to Part 7 (commencing with Section 17500) of Division 4 to local agencies or school districts from the unencumbered balances of other appropriations in the Budget Act and that this augmentation is sufficient to reimburse local agencies or school districts for their costs mandated by the regulation.

(e) The office shall notify the Department of Finance of all regulations returned pursuant to subdivision (d).

(f) The office shall return a rulemaking file to the submitting agency if the file does not comply with subdivisions (a) and (b) of Section 11347.3. Within three state working days of the receipt of a rulemaking file, the office shall notify the submitting agency of any deficiency identified. If no notice of deficiency is mailed to the adopting agency within that time, a rulemaking file shall be deemed submitted as of the date of its original receipt by the office. A rulemaking file shall not be deemed submitted until each deficiency identified under this subdivision has been corrected.

This subdivision shall not limit the review of regulations under this article, including, but not limited to, the conformity of rulemaking files to subdivisions (a) and (b) of Section 11347.3.

§ 11349.2. Rulemaking file; material added

An agency may add material to a rulemaking file that has been submitted to the office for review pursuant to this article if addition of the material does not violate other requirements of this chapter.

§ 11349.3. Approval or disapproval; return upon request of agency

(a) The office shall either approve a regulation submitted to it for review and transmit it to the Secretary of State for filing or disapprove it within 30 working days after the regulation has been submitted to the office for review. If the office fails to act within 30 days, the regulation shall be deemed to have been approved and the office shall transmit it to the Secretary of State for filing.

(b) If the office disapproves a regulation, it shall return it to the adopting agency within the 30–day period specified in subdivision (a) accompanied by a notice specifying the reasons for disapproval. Within seven calendar days of the issuance of the notice, the office shall provide the adopting agency with a written decision detailing the reasons for disapproval. No regulation shall be disapproved except for failure to comply with the standards set forth in Section 11349.1 or for failure to comply with this chapter.

§ 11349.4. Returned regulations; readoption; limited review

(a) A regulation returned to an agency because of failure to meet the standards of Section 11349.1, because of an agency's failure to comply with this chapter may be rewritten and resubmitted within 120 days of the agency's receipt of the written opinion required by subdivision (b) of Section 11349.3 without complying with the notice and public hearing requirements of Sections 11346.4, 11346.5, and 11346.8 unless the substantive provisions of the regulation have been significantly changed. If the regulation has been significantly changed or was not submitted within 120 days of receipt of the written opinion, the agency shall comply with Article 5 (commencing with Section 11346) and readopt the regulation. The director of the office may, upon a showing of good cause, grant an extension to the 120-day time period specified in this subdivision.

(b) Upon resubmission of a disapproved regulation to the office pursuant to subdivision (a), the office shall only review the resubmitted regulation for those reasons expressly identified in the written opinion required by subdivision (b) of Section 11349.3, or for those issues arising as a result of a substantial change to a provision of the resubmitted regulation or as a result of intervening statutory changes or intervening court orders or decisions.

(c) When an agency resubmits a withdrawn or disapproved regulation to the office it shall identify the prior withdrawn or disapproved regulation by date of submission to the office, shall specify the portion of the prior rulemaking record that should be included in the resubmission, and shall submit to the office a copy of the prior rulemaking record if that record has been returned to the agency by the office.

(d) The office shall expedite the review of a regulation submitted without significant substantive change.

§ 11349.5. Review by Governor of decision by office of administrative law; written request for review; contents; delivery; response; written decision; publication; overruling decision of office

(a) To initiate a review of a decision by the office, the agency shall file a written Request for Review with the Governor's Legal Affairs Secretary within 10 days of receipt of the written opinion provided by the office pursuant to subdivision (b) of Section 11349.3. The Request for Review shall include a complete statement as to why the agency believes the decision is incorrect and should be overruled. Along with the Request for Review, the agency shall submit all of the following:

(1) The office's written decision detailing the reasons for disapproval required by subdivision (b) of Section 11349.3.

(2) Copies of all regulations, notices, statements, and other documents which were submitted to the office.

(b) A copy of the agency's Request for Review shall be delivered to the office on the same day it is delivered to the Governor's office. The office shall file its written response to the agency's request with the Governor's Legal Affairs Secretary within 10 days and deliver a copy of its response to the agency on the same day it is delivered to the Governor's office.

(c) The Governor's office shall provide the requesting agency and the office with a written decision within 15 days of receipt of the response by the office to the agency's Request for Review. Upon receipt of the decision, the office shall publish in the California Regulatory Notice Register the agency's Request for Review, the office's response thereto, and the decision of the Governor's office.

(d) The time requirements set by subdivisions (a) and (b) may be shortened by the Governor's office for good cause.

(e) The Governor may overrule the decision of the office disapproving a proposed regulation, an order repealing an emergency regulation adopted pursuant to subdivision (b) of Section 11346.1, or a decision refusing to allow the readoption of an emergency regulation pursuant to Section 11346.1. In that event, the office shall immediately transmit the regulation to the Secretary of State for filing.

(f) Upon overruling the decision of the office, the Governor shall immediately transmit to the Committees on Rules of both houses of the Legislature a statement of his or her reasons for overruling the decision of the office, along with copies of the adopting agency's initial statement of reasons issued pursuant to Section 11346.2 and the office's statement regarding the disapproval of a regulation issued pursuant to subdivision (b) of Section 11349.3. The Governor's action and the reasons therefor shall be published in the California Regulatory Notice Register.

§ 11349.6. Emergency regulations

(a) If the adopting agency has complied with Sections 11346.2 to 11347.3, inclusive, prior to the adoption of the regulation as an emergency, the office shall approve or disapprove the regulation in accordance with this article.

(b) Emergency regulations adopted pursuant to subdivision (b) of Section 11346.1 shall be reviewed by the office within 10 calendar days after their submittal to the office. After posting a notice of the filing of a proposed emergency regulation on its Internet Web site, the office shall allow interested persons five calendar days to submit comments on the proposed emergency regulations unless the emergency situation clearly poses such an immediate serious harm that delaying action to allow public comment would be inconsistent with the public interest. The office shall disapprove the emergency regulations if it determines that the situation addressed by the regulations is not an emergency, or if it determines that the regulation fails to meet the standards set forth in Section 11349.1, or if it determines the agency failed to comply with Section 11346.1.

(c) If the office considers any information not submitted to it by the rulemaking agency when determining whether to file emergency regulations, the office shall provide the rulemaking agency with an opportunity to rebut or comment upon that information.

(d) Within 30 working days of the filing of a certificate of compliance, the office shall review the regulation and hearing record and approve or order the repeal of an emergency regulation if it determines that the regulation fails to meet the standards set forth in Section 11349.1, or if it determines that the agency failed to comply with this chapter.

ARTICLE 8. JUDICIAL REVIEW

§ 11350. Declaratory relief; grounds for declaration of invalidity

(a) Any interested person may obtain a judicial declaration as to the validity of any regulation or order of repeal by bringing an action for declaratory relief in the superior court in accordance with the Code of Civil Procedure. The right to judicial determination shall not be affected by the failure either to petition or to seek reconsideration of a petition filed pursuant to Section 11340.7 before the agency promulgating the regulation or order of repeal. The regulation or order of repeal may be declared to be invalid for a substantial failure to comply with this chapter, or, in the case of an emergency regulation or order of repeal, upon the ground that the facts recited in the finding of emergency prepared pursuant to subdivision (b) of Section 11346.1 do not constitute an emergency within the provisions of Section 11346.1.

(b) In addition to any other ground that may exist, a regulation or order of repeal may be declared invalid if either of the following exists:

(1) The agency's determination that the regulation is reasonably necessary to effectuate the purpose of the statute, court decision, or other provision of law that is being implemented, interpreted, or made specific by the regulation is not supported by substantial evidence.

(2) The agency declaration pursuant to paragraph (8) of subdivision (a) of Section 11346.5 is in conflict with substantial evidence in the record.

(c) The approval of a regulation or order of repeal by the office or the Governor's overruling of a decision of the office disapproving a regulation or order of repeal shall not be considered by a court in any action for declaratory relief brought with respect to a regulation or order of repeal.

(d) In a proceeding under this section, a court may only consider the following evidence:

(1) The rulemaking file prepared under Section 11347.3.

(2) The finding of emergency prepared pursuant to subdivision (b) of Section 11346.1.

(3) An item that is required to be included in the rulemaking file but is not included in the rulemaking file, for the sole purpose of proving its omission.

(4) Any evidence relevant to whether a regulation used by an agency is required to be adopted under this chapter.

§ 11350.3. Judicial declaration as to validity of regulation disapproved or ordered repealed; action for declaratory relief

Any interested person may obtain a judicial declaration as to the validity of a regulation or order of repeal which the office has disapproved pursuant to Section 11349.3, or 11349.6, or of a regulation that has been ordered repealed pursuant to Section 11349.7 by bringing an action for declaratory relief in the superior court in accordance with the Code of Civil Procedure. The court may declare the regulation valid if it determines that the regulation meets the standards set forth in Section 11349.1 and that the agency has complied with this chapter. If the court so determines, it may order the office to immediately file the regulation with the Secretary of State.

CHAPTER 4.5 ADMINISTRATIVE ADJUDICATION: GENERAL PROVISIONS
ARTICLE 2. DEFINITIONS

* * *

§ 11405.20. Adjudicative proceeding

"Adjudicative proceeding" means an evidentiary hearing for determination of facts pursuant to which an agency formulates and issues a decision.

* * *

§ 11405.50. Decision

(a) "Decision" means an agency action of specific application that determines a legal right, duty, privilege, immunity, or other legal interest of a particular person.

(b) Nothing in this section limits any of the following:

(1) The precedential effect of a decision under Section 11425.60.

(2) The authority of an agency to make a declaratory decision pursuant to Article 14 (commencing with Section 11465.10).

§ 11405.60. Party

"Party" includes the agency that is taking action, the person to which the agency action is directed, and any other person named as a party or allowed to appear or intervene in the proceeding. If the agency that is taking action and the agency that is conducting the adjudicative proceeding are separate agencies, the agency that is taking action is a party and the agency that is conducting the adjudicative proceeding is not a party.

* * *

§ 11405.80. Presiding officer

"Presiding officer" means the agency head, member of the agency head, administrative law judge, hearing officer, or other person who presides in an adjudicative proceeding.

ARTICLE 3. APPLICATION OF CHAPTER

§ 11410.10. Evidentiary hearing required

This chapter applies to a decision by an agency if, under the federal or state Constitution or a federal or state statute, an evidentiary hearing for determination of facts is required for formulation and issuance of the decision.

* * *

§ 11410.50. Adjudicative proceeding under Chapter 5

This chapter applies to an adjudicative proceeding required to be conducted under Chapter 5 (commencing with Section 11500) unless the statutes relating to the proceeding provide otherwise.

* * *

ARTICLE 4. GOVERNING PROCEDURE

§ 11415.10. Statutes and regulations; Administrative Procedure Act

(a) The governing procedure by which an agency conducts an adjudicative proceeding is determined by the statutes and regulations applicable to that proceeding. If no other governing procedure is provided by statute or regulation, an agency may conduct an adjudicative proceeding under the administrative adjudication provisions of the Administrative Procedure Act.

(b) This chapter supplements the governing procedure by which an agency conducts an adjudicative proceeding.

* * *

§ 11415.60. Decision by settlement

(a) An agency may formulate and issue a decision by settlement, pursuant to an agreement of the parties, without conducting an adjudicative proceeding. Subject to subdivision (c), the settlement may be on any terms the parties determine are appropriate. Notwithstanding any other provision of law, no evidence of an offer of compromise or settlement made in settlement negotiations is admissible in an adjudicative proceeding or civil action, whether as affirmative evidence, by way of impeachment, or for any other purpose.

(b) A settlement may be made before or after issuance of an agency pleading, except that in an adjudicative proceeding to determine whether an occupational license should be revoked, suspended, limited, or conditioned, a settlement may not be made before issuance of the agency pleading. A settlement may be made before, during, or after the hearing.

(c) A settlement is subject to any necessary agency approval. An agency head may delegate the power to approve a settlement. The terms of a settlement may not be contrary to statute or regulation, except that the settlement may include sanctions the agency would otherwise lack power to impose.

ARTICLE 5.   ALTERNATIVE DISPUTE RESOLUTION

§ 11420.10. Referral of proceedings

(a) An agency, with the consent of all the parties, may refer a dispute that is the subject of an adjudicative proceeding for resolution by any of the following means:

(1) Mediation by a neutral mediator.

(2) Binding arbitration by a neutral arbitrator. An award in a binding arbitration is subject to judicial review in the manner provided in Chapter 4 (commencing with Section 1285) of Title 9 of Part 3 of the Code of Civil Procedure.

(3) Nonbinding arbitration by a neutral arbitrator. The arbitrator's decision in a nonbinding arbitration is final unless within 30 days after the arbitrator delivers the award to the agency head a party requests that the agency conduct a de novo adjudicative proceeding. If the decision in the de novo proceeding is not more favorable to the

party electing the de novo proceeding, the party shall pay the costs and fees specified in Section 1141.21 of the Code of Civil Procedure insofar as applicable in the adjudicative proceeding.

(b) If another statute requires mediation or arbitration in an adjudicative proceeding, that statute prevails over this section.

(c) This section does not apply in an adjudicative proceeding to the extent an agency by regulation provides that this section is not applicable in a proceeding of the agency.

§ 11420.20. Model regulations; contents

(a) The Office of Administrative Hearings shall adopt and promulgate model regulations for alternative dispute resolution under this article. The model regulations govern alternative dispute resolution by an agency under this article, except to the extent the agency by regulation provides inconsistent rules or provides that the model regulations are not applicable in a proceeding of the agency.

(b) The model regulations shall include provisions for selection and compensation of a mediator or arbitrator, qualifications of a mediator or arbitrator, and confidentiality of the mediation or arbitration proceeding.

* * *

ARTICLE 6. ADMINISTRATIVE ADJUDICATION BILL OF RIGHTS

§ 11425.10. Governing procedures; requirements

(a) The governing procedure by which an agency conducts an adjudicative proceeding is subject to all of the following requirements:

(1) The agency shall give the person to which the agency action is directed notice and an opportunity to be heard, including the opportunity to present and rebut evidence.

(2) The agency shall make available to the person to which the agency action is directed a copy of the governing procedure, including a statement whether Chapter 5 (commencing with Section 11500) is applicable to the proceeding.

(3) The hearing shall be open to public observation as provided in Section 11425.20.

(4) The adjudicative function shall be separated from the investigative, prosecutorial, and advocacy functions within the agency as provided in Section 11425.30.

(5) The presiding officer is subject to disqualification for bias, prejudice, or interest as provided in Section 11425.40.

(6) The decision shall be in writing, be based on the record, and include a statement of the factual and legal basis of the decision as provided in Section 11425.50.

(7) A decision may not be relied on as precedent unless the agency designates and indexes the decision as precedent as provided in Section 11425.60.

(8) Ex parte communications shall be restricted as provided in Article 7 (commencing with Section 11430.10).

(9) Language assistance shall be made available as provided in Article 8 (commencing with Section 11435.05) by an agency described in Section 11018 or 11435.15.

(b) The requirements of this section apply to the governing procedure by which an agency conducts an adjudicative proceeding without further action by the agency, and prevail over a conflicting or inconsistent provision of the governing procedure, subject to Section 11415.20. The governing procedure by which an agency conducts an adjudicative proceeding may include provisions equivalent to, or more protective of the rights of the person to which the agency action is directed than, the requirements of this section.

§ 11425.20. Open hearings; exceptions

(a) A hearing shall be open to public observation. Nothing in this subdivision limits the authority of the presiding officer to order closure of a hearing or make other protective orders to the extent necessary or proper for any of the following purposes:

(1) To satisfy the United States Constitution, the California Constitution, federal or state statute, or other law, including but not limited to laws protecting privileged, confidential, or other protected information.

(2) To ensure a fair hearing in the circumstances of the particular case.

(3) To conduct the hearing, including the manner of examining witnesses, in a way that is appropriate to protect a minor witness or a witness with a developmental disability, as defined in Section 4512 of the Welfare and Institutions Code, from intimidation or other harm, taking into account the rights of all persons.

(b) To the extent a hearing is conducted by telephone, television, or other electronic means, subdivision (a) is satisfied if members of the public have an opportunity to do both of the following:

(1) At reasonable times, hear or inspect the agency's record, and inspect any transcript obtained by the agency.

(2) Be physically present at the place where the presiding officer is conducting the hearing.

(c) This section does not apply to a prehearing conference, settlement conference, or proceedings for alternative dispute resolution other than binding arbitration.

§ 11425.30. Presiding officer; disqualification

(a) A person may not serve as presiding officer in an adjudicative proceeding in any of the following circumstances:

(1) The person has served as investigator, prosecutor, or advocate in the proceeding or its preadjudicative stage.

(2) The person is subject to the authority, direction, or discretion of a person who has served as investigator, prosecutor, or advocate in the proceeding or its preadjudicative stage.

(b) Notwithstanding subdivision (a):

(1) A person may serve as presiding officer at successive stages of an adjudicative proceeding.

(2) A person who has participated only as a decisionmaker or as an advisor to a decisionmaker in a determination of probable cause or other equivalent preliminary determination in an adjudicative proceeding or its preadjudicative stage may serve as presiding officer in the proceeding.

(c) The provisions of this section governing separation of functions as to the presiding officer also govern separation of functions as to the agency head or other person or body to which the power to hear or decide in the proceeding is delegated.

§ 11425.40. Bias, prejudice or interest

(a) The presiding officer is subject to disqualification for bias, prejudice, or interest in the proceeding.

(b) It is not alone or in itself grounds for disqualification, without further evidence of bias, prejudice, or interest, that the presiding officer:

(1) Is or is not a member of a racial, ethnic, religious, sexual, or similar group and the proceeding involves the rights of that group.

(2) Has experience, technical competence, or specialized knowledge of, or has in any capacity expressed a view on, a legal, factual, or policy issue presented in the proceeding.

(3) Has as a lawyer or public official participated in the drafting of laws or regulations or in the effort to pass or defeat laws or regulations, the meaning, effect, or application of which is in issue in the proceeding.

(c) The provisions of this section governing disqualification of the presiding officer also govern disqualification of the agency head or other person or body to which the power to hear or decide in the proceeding is delegated.

(d) An agency that conducts an adjudicative proceeding may provide by regulation for peremptory challenge of the presiding officer.

§ 11425.50. Written decision; contents

(a) The decision shall be in writing and shall include a statement of the factual and legal basis for the decision.

(b) The statement of the factual basis for the decision may be in the language of, or by reference to, the pleadings. If the statement is no more than mere repetition or paraphrase of the relevant statute or regulation, the statement shall be accompanied by a concise and explicit statement of the underlying facts of record that support the decision. If the factual basis for the decision includes a determination based substantially on the credibility of a witness, the statement shall identify any specific evidence of the observed demeanor, manner, or attitude of the witness that supports the determination, and on judicial review the court shall give great weight to the determination to the extent the determination identifies the observed demeanor, manner, or attitude of the witness that supports it.

(c) The statement of the factual basis for the decision shall be based exclusively on the evidence of record in the proceeding and on matters officially noticed in the proceeding. The presiding officer's experience, technical competence, and specialized knowledge may be used in evaluating evidence.

(d) Nothing in this section limits the information that may be contained in the decision, including a summary of evidence relied on.

(e) A penalty may not be based on a guideline, criterion, bulletin, manual, instruction, order, standard of general application or other rule subject to Chapter 3.5 (commencing with Section 11340) unless it has been adopted as a regulation pursuant to Chapter 3.5 (commencing with Section 11340).

§ 11425.60. Precedent; designation; index

(a) A decision may not be expressly relied on as precedent unless it is designated as a precedent decision by the agency.

(b) An agency may designate as a precedent decision a decision or part of a decision that contains a significant legal or policy determination of general application that is likely to recur. Designation of a decision or part of a decision as a precedent decision is not rulemaking and need not be done under Chapter 3.5 (commencing with Section 11340). An agency's designation of a decision or part of a decision, or failure to designate a decision or part of a decision, as a precedent decision is not subject to judicial review.

(c) An agency shall maintain an index of significant legal and policy determinations made in precedent decisions. The index shall be updated not less frequently than annually, unless no precedent decision has been designated since the last preceding update. The index shall be made available to the public by subscription, and its availability shall be publicized annually in the California Regulatory Notice Register.

(d) This section applies to decisions issued on or after July 1, 1997. Nothing in this section precludes an agency from designating as a precedent decision a decision issued before July 1, 1997.

ARTICLE 7. EX PARTE COMMUNICATIONS

§ 11430.10. Pending proceedings

(a) While the proceeding is pending there shall be no communication, direct or indirect, regarding any issue in the proceeding, to the presiding officer from an employee or representative of an agency that is a party or from an interested person outside the agency, without notice and opportunity for all parties to participate in the communication.

(b) Nothing in this section precludes a communication, including a communication from an employee or representative of an agency that is a party, made on the record at the hearing.

(c) For the purpose of this section, a proceeding is pending from the issuance of the agency's pleading, or from an application for an agency decision, whichever is earlier.

§ 11430.20. Permissible communications

A communication otherwise prohibited by Section 11430.10 is permissible in any of the following circumstances:

(a) The communication is required for disposition of an ex parte matter specifically authorized by statute.

(b) The communication concerns a matter of procedure or practice, including a request for a continuance, that is not in controversy.

§ 11430.30. Permissible communications from employees or representatives of agencies

A communication otherwise prohibited by Section 11430.10 from an employee or representative of an agency that is a party to the presiding officer is permissible in any of the following circumstances:

(a) The communication is for the purpose of assistance and advice to the presiding officer from a person who has not served as investigator, prosecutor, or advocate in the proceeding or its preadjudicative stage. An assistant or advisor may evaluate the evidence in the record but shall not furnish, augment, diminish, or modify the evidence in the record.

(b) The communication is for the purpose of advising the presiding officer concerning a settlement proposal advocated by the advisor.

(c) The communication is for the purpose of advising the presiding officer concerning any of the following matters in an adjudicative proceeding that is nonprosecutorial in character:

(1) The advice involves a technical issue in the proceeding and the advice is necessary for, and is not otherwise reasonably available to, the presiding officer, provided the content of the advice is disclosed on the record and all parties are given an opportunity to address it in the manner provided in Section 11430.50.

(2) The advice involves an issue in a proceeding of the San Francisco Bay Conservation and Development Commission, California Tahoe Regional Planning Agency, Delta Protection Commission, Water Resources Control Board, or a regional water quality control board.

§ 11430.40. Communications received prior to serving as presiding officer; disclosure

If, while the proceeding is pending but before serving as presiding officer, a person receives a communication of a type that would be in violation of this article if received while serving as presiding officer, the person, promptly after starting to serve, shall disclose the content of the communication on the record and give all parties an opportunity to address it in the manner provided in Section 11430.50.

§ 11430.50. Violations; duty of presiding officer

(a) If a presiding officer receives a communication in violation of this article, the presiding officer shall make all of the following a part of the record in the proceeding:

(1) If the communication is written, the writing and any written response of the presiding officer to the communication.

(2) If the communication is oral, a memorandum stating the substance of the communication, any response made by the presiding officer, and the identity of each person from whom the presiding officer received the communication.

(b) The presiding officer shall notify all parties that a communication described in this section has been made a part of the record.

(c) If a party requests an opportunity to address the communication within 10 days after receipt of notice of the communication:

(1) The party shall be allowed to comment on the communication.

(2) The presiding officer has discretion to allow the party to present evidence concerning the subject of the communication, including discretion to reopen a hearing that has been concluded.

§ 11430.60. Disqualification of presiding officer

Receipt by the presiding officer of a communication in violation of this article may be grounds for disqualification of the presiding officer. If the presiding officer is disqualified, the portion of the record pertaining to the ex parte communication may be sealed by protective order of the disqualified presiding officer.

§ 11430.70. Agency heads or other persons with power to hear or decide

(a) Subject to subdivision (b), the provisions of this article governing ex parte communications to the presiding officer also govern ex parte communications in an adjudicative proceeding to the agency head or other person or body to which the power to hear or decide in the proceeding is delegated.

(b) An ex parte communication to the agency head or other person or body to which the power to hear or decide in the proceeding is delegated is permissible in an individualized ratemaking proceeding if the content of the communication is disclosed on the record and all parties are given an opportunity to address it in the manner provided in Section 11430.50.

§ 11430.80. Communications between presiding officer and agency head regarding the merits of any issue

(a) There shall be no communication, direct or indirect, while a proceeding is pending regarding the merits of any issue in the proceeding, between the presiding officer and the agency head or other person or body to which the power to hear or decide in the proceeding is delegated.

(b) This section does not apply where the agency head or other person or body to which the power to hear or decide in the proceeding is delegated serves as both presiding officer and agency head, or where the presiding officer does not issue a decision in the proceeding.

ARTICLE 9. GENERAL PROCEDURAL PROVISIONS

§ 11440.10. Authority of agency head following decision

(a) The agency head may do any of the following with respect to a decision of the presiding officer or the agency:

(1) Determine to review some but not all issues, or not to exercise any review.

(2) Delegate its review authority to one or more persons.

(3) Authorize review by one or more persons, subject to further review by the agency head.

(b) By regulation an agency may mandate review, or may preclude or limit review, of a decision of the presiding officer or the agency.

* * *

§ 11440.30. Conduct of hearing by electronic means

(a) The presiding officer may conduct all or part of a hearing by telephone, television, or other electronic means if each participant in the hearing has an opportunity to participate in and to hear the entire proceeding while it is taking place and to observe exhibits.

(b) The presiding officer may not conduct all or part of a hearing by telephone, television, or other electronic means if a party objects.

* * *

ARTICLE 10. INFORMAL HEARING

§ 11445.10. Informal hearing procedure; legislative findings and declarations

(a) Subject to the limitations in this article, an agency may conduct an adjudicative proceeding under the informal hearing procedure provided in this article.

(b) The Legislature finds and declares the following:

(1) The informal hearing procedure is intended to satisfy due process and public policy requirements in a manner that is simpler and more expeditious than hearing procedures otherwise required by statute, for use in appropriate circumstances.

(2) The informal hearing procedure provides a forum in the nature of a conference in which a party has an opportunity to be heard by the presiding officer.

(3) The informal hearing procedure provides a forum that may accommodate a hearing where by regulation or statute a member of the public may participate without appearing or intervening as a party.

§ 11445.20. Proceedings

Subject to Section 11445.30, an agency may use an informal hearing procedure in any of the following proceedings, if in the circumstances its use does not violate another statute or the federal or state Constitution:

(a) A proceeding where there is no disputed issue of material fact.

(b) A proceeding where there is a disputed issue of material fact, if the matter is limited to any of the following:

(1) A monetary amount of not more than one thousand dollars ($1,000).

(2) A disciplinary sanction against a student that does not involve expulsion from an academic institution or suspension for more than 10 days.

(3) A disciplinary sanction against an employee that does not involve discharge from employment, demotion, or suspension for more than 5 days.

(4) A disciplinary sanction against a licensee that does not involve an actual revocation of a license or an actual suspension of a license for more than five days. Nothing in this section precludes an agency from imposing a stayed revocation or a stayed suspension of a license in an informal hearing.

(c) A proceeding where, by regulation, the agency has authorized use of an informal hearing.

(d) A proceeding where an evidentiary hearing for determination of facts is not required by statute but where the agency determines the federal or state Constitution may require a hearing.

§ 11445.30. Notice of hearing; objection

(a) The notice of hearing shall state the agency's selection of the informal hearing procedure.

(b) Any objection of a party to use of the informal hearing procedure shall be made in the party's pleading.

(c) An objection to use of the informal hearing procedure shall be resolved by the presiding officer before the hearing on the basis of the pleadings and any written submissions in support of the pleadings. An objection to use of the informal hearing procedure in a disciplinary proceeding involving an occupational license shall be resolved in favor of the licensee.

§ 11445.40. Hearing procedures applicable; authority of presiding officer

(a) Except as provided in this article, the hearing procedures otherwise required by statute for an adjudicative proceeding apply to an informal hearing.

(b) In an informal hearing the presiding officer shall regulate the course of the proceeding. The presiding officer shall permit the parties and may permit others to offer written or oral comments on the issues. The presiding officer may limit the use of witnesses, testimony, evidence, and argument, and may limit or eliminate the use of pleadings, intervention, discovery, prehearing conferences, and rebuttal.

§ 11445.50. Denial of use of informal hearing procedure; cross examination; judicial review

(a) The presiding officer may deny use of the informal hearing procedure, or may convert an informal hearing to a formal hearing after an informal hearing is commenced, if it appears to the presiding officer that cross-examination is necessary for proper determination of the matter and that the delay, burden, or complication due to allowing cross-examination in the informal hearing will be more than minimal.

(b) An agency, by regulation, may specify categories of cases in which cross-examination is deemed not necessary for proper determination of the matter under the informal hearing procedure. The presiding officer may allow cross-examination of witnesses in an informal hearing notwithstanding an agency regulation if it appears to the presiding officer that in the circumstances cross-examination is necessary for proper determination of the matter.

(c) The actions of the presiding officer under this section are not subject to judicial review.

§ 11445.60. Material facts in dispute; presentation of proof

(a) If the presiding officer has reason to believe that material facts are in dispute, the presiding officer may require a party to state the identity of the witnesses or other sources through which the party would propose to present proof if the proceeding were converted to a formal or other applicable hearing procedure. If disclosure of a fact, allegation, or source is privileged or expressly prohibited by a regulation, statute, or the federal or state Constitution, the presiding officer may require the party to indicate that confidential facts, allegations, or sources are involved, but not to disclose the confidential facts, allegations, or sources.

(b) If a party has reason to believe that essential facts must be obtained in order to permit an adequate presentation of the case, the party may inform the presiding officer regarding the general nature of the facts and the sources from which the party would propose to obtain the facts if the proceeding were converted to a formal or other applicable hearing procedure.

CHAPTER 5.   ADMINISTRATIVE ADJUDICATION: FORMAL HEARING

§ 11500. Definitions

In this chapter unless the context or subject matter otherwise requires:

(a) "Agency" includes the state boards, commissions, and officers to which this chapter is made applicable by law, except that wherever the word "agency" alone is used the power to act may be delegated by the agency, and wherever the words "agency itself" are used the power to act shall not be delegated unless the statutes relating to the particular agency authorize the delegation of the agency's power to hear and decide.

(b) "Party" includes the agency, the respondent, and any person, other than an officer or an employee of the agency in his or her official capacity, who has been allowed to appear or participate in the proceeding.

(c) "Respondent" means any person against whom an accusation is filed pursuant to Section 11503 or against whom a statement of issues is filed pursuant to Section 11504.

(d) "Administrative law judge" means an individual qualified under Section 11502.

(e) "Agency member" means any person who is a member of any agency to which this chapter is applicable and includes any person who himself or herself constitutes an agency.

§ 11501. Application of chapter; application of other law

(a) This chapter applies to any agency as determined by the statutes relating to that agency.

(b) This chapter applies to an adjudicative proceeding of an agency created on or after July 1, 1997, unless the statutes relating to the proceeding provide otherwise.

(c) Chapter 4.5 (commencing with Section 11400) applies to an adjudicative proceeding required to be conducted under this chapter, unless the statutes relating to the proceeding provide otherwise.

§ 11502. Administrative law judges; duties; appointment; qualifications

(a) All hearings of state agencies required to be conducted under this chapter shall be conducted by administrative law judges on the staff of the Office of Administrative Hearings. This subdivision applies to a hearing required to be conducted under this chapter that is conducted under the informal hearing or emergency decision procedure provided in Chapter 4.5 (commencing with Section 11400).

(b) The Director of the Office of Administrative Hearings has power to appoint a staff of administrative law judges for the office as provided in Section 11370.3. Each administrative law judge shall have been admitted to practice law in this state for at least five years immediately preceding his or her appointment and shall possess any additional qualifications established by the State Personnel Board for the particular class of position involved.

§ 11503. Revocation, suspension, limitation, or condition of a right, authority, license or privilege; accusation; contents; verification

A hearing to determine whether a right, authority, license or privilege should be revoked, suspended, limited or conditioned shall be initiated by filing an accusation. The accusation shall be a written statement of charges which shall set forth in ordinary and concise language the acts or omissions with which the respondent is charged, to the end that the respondent will be able to prepare his defense. It shall specify the statutes and rules which the respondent is alleged to have violated, but shall not consist merely of charges phrased in the language of such statutes and rules. The accusation shall be verified unless made by a public officer acting in his official capacity or by an employee of the agency before which the proceeding is to be held. The verification may be on information and belief.

* * *

§ 11505. Service of accusation; notice of defense; request for hearing; discovery; postponement

(a) Upon the filing of the accusation the agency shall serve a copy thereof on the respondent as provided in subdivision (c). The agency may include with the accusation any information which it deems appropriate, but it shall include a post card or other form entitled Notice of Defense which, when signed by or on behalf of the respondent and returned to the agency, will acknowledge service of the accusation and constitute a notice of defense under Section 11506. The copy of the accusation shall include or be accompanied by (1) a statement that respondent may request a hearing by filing a notice of defense as provided in Section 11506 within 15 days after service upon the respondent of the accusation, and that failure to do so will constitute a waiver of the respondent's right to a hearing, and (2) copies of Sections 11507.5, 11507.6, and 11507.7.

(b) The statement to respondent shall be substantially in the following form:

> Unless a written request for a hearing signed by or on behalf of the person named as respondent in the accompanying accusation is delivered or mailed to the agency within 15 days after the accusation was personally served on you or mailed to you, (here insert name of agency) may proceed upon the accusation without a hearing. The request for a hearing may be made by delivering or mailing the enclosed form entitled Notice of Defense, or by delivering or mailing a notice of defense as provided by Section 11506 of the Government Code to: (here insert name and address of agency). You may, but need not, be represented by counsel at any or all stages of these proceedings.

436

If you desire the names and addresses of witnesses or an opportunity to inspect and copy the items mentioned in Section 11507.6 of the Government Code in the possession, custody or control of the agency, you may contact: (here insert name and address of appropriate person).

The hearing may be postponed for good cause. If you have good cause, you are obliged to notify the agency or, if an administrative law judge has been assigned to the hearing, the Office of Administrative Hearings, within 10 working days after you discover the good cause. Failure to give notice within 10 days will deprive you of a postponement.

(c) The accusation and all accompanying information may be sent to the respondent by any means selected by the agency. But no order adversely affecting the rights of the respondent shall be made by the agency in any case unless the respondent shall have been served personally or by registered mail as provided herein, or shall have filed a notice of defense or otherwise appeared. Service may be proved in the manner authorized in civil actions. Service by registered mail shall be effective if a statute or agency rule requires the respondent to file the respondent's address with the agency and to notify the agency of any change, and if a registered letter containing the accusation and accompanying material is mailed, addressed to the respondent at the latest address on file with the agency.

§ 11506. Notice of defense; grounds; right to hearing

(a) Within 15 days after service of the accusation the respondent may file with the agency a notice of defense in which the respondent may:

(1) Request a hearing.

(2) Object to the accusation upon the ground that it does not state acts or omissions upon which the agency may proceed.

(3) Object to the form of the accusation on the ground that it is so indefinite or uncertain that the respondent cannot identify the transaction or prepare a defense.

(4) Admit the accusation in whole or in part.

(5) Present new matter by way of defense.

(6) Object to the accusation upon the ground that, under the circumstances, compliance with the requirements of a regulation would result in a material violation of another regulation enacted by another department affecting substantive rights.

(b) Within the time specified respondent may file one or more notices of defense upon any or all of these grounds but all of these notices shall be filed within that period unless the agency in its discretion authorizes the filing of a later notice.

(c) The respondent shall be entitled to a hearing on the merits if the respondent files a notice of defense, and the notice shall be deemed a specific denial of all parts of the accusation not expressly admitted. Failure to file a notice of defense shall constitute a waiver of respondent's right to a hearing, but the agency in its discretion may nevertheless grant a hearing. Unless objection is taken as provided in paragraph (3) of subdivision (a), all objections to the form of the accusation shall be deemed waived.

(d) The notice of defense shall be in writing signed by or on behalf of the respondent and shall state the respondent's mailing address. It need not be verified or follow any particular form.

(e) As used in this section, "file," "files," "filed," or "filing" means "delivered or mailed" to the agency as provided in Section 11505.

* * *

§ 11507.5. Discovery; exclusive provisions

The provisions of Section 11507.6 provide the exclusive right to and method of discovery as to any proceeding governed by this chapter.

§ 11507.6. Request for discovery; statements; writings; investigative reports

After initiation of a proceeding in which a respondent or other party is entitled to a hearing on the merits, a party, upon written request made to another party, prior to the hearing and within 30 days after service by the agency of the initial pleading or within 15 days after the service of an additional pleading, is entitled to (1) obtain the names and addresses of witnesses to the extent known to the other party, including, but not limited to, those intended to be called to testify at the hearing, and (2) inspect and make a copy of any of the following in the possession or custody or under the control of the other party:

(a) A statement of a person, other than the respondent, named in the initial administrative pleading, or in any additional pleading, when it is claimed that the act or omission of the respondent as to this person is the basis for the administrative proceeding;

(b) A statement pertaining to the subject matter of the proceeding made by any party to another party or person;

(c) Statements of witnesses then proposed to be called by the party and of other persons having personal knowledge of the acts, omissions or events which are the basis for the proceeding, not included in (a) or (b) above;

(d) All writings, including, but not limited to, reports of mental, physical and blood examinations and things which the party then proposes to offer in evidence;

(e) Any other writing or thing which is relevant and which would be admissible in evidence;

(f) Investigative reports made by or on behalf of the agency or other party pertaining to the subject matter of the proceeding, to the extent that these reports (1) contain the names and addresses of witnesses or of persons having personal knowledge of the acts, omissions or events which are the basis for the proceeding, or (2) reflect matters perceived by the investigator in the course of his or her investigation, or (3) contain or include by attachment any statement or writing described in (a) to (e), inclusive, or summary thereof.

For the purpose of this section, "statements" include written statements by the person signed or otherwise authenticated by him or her, stenographic, mechanical, electrical or other recordings, or transcripts thereof, of oral statements by the person, and written reports or summaries of these oral statements.

Nothing in this section shall authorize the inspection or copying of any writing or thing which is privileged from disclosure by law or otherwise made confidential or protected as the attorney's work product.

§ 11507.7. Motion to compel discovery

(a) Any party claiming the party's request for discovery pursuant to Section 11507.6 has not been complied with may serve and file with the administrative law judge a motion to compel discovery, naming as respondent the party refusing or failing to comply with Section 11507.6. The motion shall state facts showing the respondent party failed or refused to comply with Section 11507.6, a description of the matters sought to be discovered, the reason or reasons why the matter is discoverable under that section, that a reasonable and good faith attempt to contact the respondent for an informal resolution of the issue has been made, and the ground or grounds of respondent's refusal so far as known to the moving party.

(b) The motion shall be served upon respondent party and filed within 15 days after the respondent party first evidenced failure or refusal to comply with Section 11507.6 or within 30 days after request was made and the party has failed to reply to the request, or within another time provided by stipulation, whichever period is longer.

(c) The hearing on the motion to compel discovery shall be held within 15 days after the motion is made, or a later time that the administrative law judge may on the judge's own motion for good cause determine. The respondent party shall have the right to serve and file a written answer or other response to the motion before or at the time of the hearing.

(d) Where the matter sought to be discovered is under the custody or control of the respondent party and the respondent party asserts that the matter is not a discoverable matter under the provisions of Section 11507.6, or is privileged against disclosure under those provisions, the administrative law judge may order lodged with it matters provided in subdivision (b) of Section 915 of the Evidence Code and examine the matters in accordance with its provisions.

(e) The administrative law judge shall decide the case on the matters examined in camera, the papers filed by the parties, and such oral argument and additional evidence as the administrative law judge may allow.

(f) Unless otherwise stipulated by the parties, the administrative law judge shall no later than 15 days after the hearing make its order denying or granting the motion. The order shall be in writing setting forth the matters the moving party is entitled to discover under Section 11507.6. A copy of the order shall forthwith be served by mail by the administrative law judge upon the parties. Where the order grants the motion in whole or in part, the order shall not become effective until 10 days after the date the order is served. Where the order denies relief to the moving party, the order shall be effective on the date it is served.

§ 11508. Time and place of hearing

(a) The agency shall consult the office, and subject to the availability of its staff, shall determine the time and place of the hearing. The hearing shall be held at a hearing facility maintained by the office in Sacramento, Oakland, Los Angeles, or San Diego and shall be held at the facility that is closest to the location where the transaction occurred or the respondent resides.

(b) Notwithstanding subdivision (a), the hearing may be held at either of the following places:

(1) A place selected by the agency that is closer to the location where the transaction occurred or the respondent resides.

(2) A place within the state selected by agreement of the parties.

(c) The respondent may move for, and the administrative law judge has discretion to grant or deny, a change in the place of the hearing. A motion for a change in the place of the hearing shall be made within 10 days after service of the notice of hearing on the respondent.

Unless good cause is identified in writing by the administrative law judge, hearings shall be held in a facility maintained by the office.

§ 11509. Notice of hearing

The agency shall deliver or mail a notice of hearing to all parties at least 10 days prior to the hearing. The hearing shall not be prior to the expiration of the time within which the respondent is entitled to file a notice of defense.

The notice to respondent shall be substantially in the following form but may include other information:

You are hereby notified that a hearing will be held before [here insert name of agency] at [here insert place of hearing] on the _____ day of _____, 19__, at the hour of _____, upon the charges made in the accusation served upon you. If you object to the place of hearing, you must notify the presiding officer within 10 days after this notice is served on you. Failure to notify the presiding officer within 10 days will deprive you of a change in the place of the hearing. You may be present at the hearing. You have the right to be represented by an attorney at your own expense. You are not entitled to the appointment of an attorney to represent you at public expense. You are entitled to represent yourself without legal counsel. You may present any relevant evidence, and will be given full opportunity to cross-examine all witnesses testifying against you. You are entitled to the issuance of subpoenas to compel the attendance of witnesses and the production of books, documents or other things by applying to [here insert appropriate office of agency].

§ 11511. Depositions

On verified petition of any party, an administrative law judge or, if an administrative law judge has not been appointed, an agency may order that the testimony of any material witness residing within or without the state be taken by deposition in the manner prescribed by law for depositions in civil actions under Title 4 (commencing with Section 2016.010) of Part 4 of the Code of Civil Procedure. The petition shall set forth the nature of the pending proceeding; the name and address of the witness whose testimony is desired; a showing of the materiality of the testimony; a showing that the witness will be unable or cannot be compelled to attend; and shall request an order requiring the witness to appear and testify before an officer named in the petition for that purpose. The petitioner shall serve notice of hearing and a copy of the petition on the other parties at least 10 days before the hearing. Where the witness resides outside the state and where the administrative law judge or agency has ordered the taking of the testimony by deposition, the agency shall obtain an order of court to that effect by filing a petition therefor in the superior court in Sacramento County. The proceedings thereon shall be in accordance with the provisions of Section 11189.

§ 11511.5. Prehearing conference; subject matter; prehearing order

(a) On motion of a party or by order of an administrative law judge, the administrative law judge may conduct a prehearing conference. The administrative law judge shall set the time and place for the prehearing conference, and shall give reasonable written notice to all parties.

(b) The prehearing conference may deal with one or more of the following matters:

(1) Exploration of settlement possibilities.

(2) Preparation of stipulations.

(3) Clarification of issues.

(4) Rulings on identity and limitation of the number of witnesses.

(5) Objections to proffers of evidence.

(6) Order of presentation of evidence and cross-examination.

(7) Rulings regarding issuance of subpoenas and protective orders.

(8) Schedules for the submission of written briefs and schedules for the commencement and conduct of the hearing.

(9) Exchange of witness lists and of exhibits or documents to be offered in evidence at the hearing.

(10) Motions for intervention.

(11) Exploration of the possibility of using alternative dispute resolution provided in Article 5 (commencing with Section 11420.10) of, or the informal hearing procedure provided in Article 10 (commencing with Section 11445.10) of, Chapter 4.5, and objections to use of the informal hearing procedure. Use of alternative dispute resolution or of the informal hearing procedure is subject to subdivision (d).

(12) Any other matters as shall promote the orderly and prompt conduct of the hearing.

(c) The administrative law judge may conduct all or part of the prehearing conference by telephone, television, or other electronic means if each participant in the conference has an opportunity to participate in and to hear the entire proceeding while it is taking place.

(d) With the consent of the parties, the prehearing conference may be converted immediately into alternative dispute resolution or an informal hearing. With the consent of the parties, the proceeding may be converted into alternative dispute resolution to be conducted at another time. With the consent of the agency, the proceeding may be converted into an informal hearing to be conducted at another time subject to the right of a party to object to use of the informal hearing procedure as provided in Section 11445.30.

(e) The administrative law judge shall issue a prehearing order incorporating the matters determined at the prehearing conference. The administrative law judge may direct one or more of the parties to prepare a prehearing order.

§ 11511.7. Settlement conferences

(a) The administrative law judge may order the parties to attend and participate in a settlement conference. The administrative law judge shall set the time and place for the settlement conference, and shall give reasonable written notice to all parties.

(b) The administrative law judge at the settlement conference shall not preside as administrative law judge at the hearing unless otherwise stipulated by the parties. The administrative law judge may conduct all or part of the settlement conference by telephone, television, or other electronic means if each participant in the conference has an opportunity to participate in and to hear the entire proceeding while it is taking place.

§ 11512. Presiding officer; participation of agency in hearing; conduct of hearing; disqualification of administrative law judge or agency member; reporter; proposed decision

(a) Every hearing in a contested case shall be presided over by an administrative law judge. The agency itself shall determine whether the administrative law judge is to hear the case alone or whether the agency itself is to hear the case with the administrative law judge.

(b) When the agency itself hears the case, the administrative law judge shall preside at the hearing, rule on the admission and exclusion of evidence, and advise the agency on matters of law; the agency itself shall exercise all other powers relating to the conduct of the hearing but may delegate any or all of them to the administrative law judge. When the administrative law judge alone hears a case, he or she shall exercise all powers relating to the conduct of the hearing. A ruling of the administrative law judge admitting or excluding evidence is subject to review in the same manner and to the same extent as the administrative law judge's proposed decision in the proceeding.

(c) An administrative law judge or agency member shall voluntarily disqualify himself or herself and withdraw from any case in which there are grounds for disqualification, including disqualification under Section 11425.40. The parties may waive the disqualification by a writing that recites the grounds for disqualification. A waiver is effective only when signed by all parties, accepted by the administrative law judge or agency member, and included in the record. Any party may request the disqualification of any administrative law judge or agency member by filing an affidavit, prior to the taking of evidence at a hearing, stating with particularity the grounds upon which it is claimed that the administrative law judge or agency member is disqualified. Where the request concerns an agency member, the issue shall be determined by the other members of the agency. Where the request concerns the administrative law judge, the issue shall be determined by the agency itself if the agency itself hears the case with the administrative law judge, otherwise the issue shall be determined by the administrative law judge. No agency member shall withdraw voluntarily or be subject to disqualification if his or her disqualification would prevent the existence of a quorum qualified to act in the particular case, except that a substitute qualified to act may be appointed by the appointing authority.

(d) The proceedings at the hearing shall be reported by a stenographic reporter. However, upon the consent of all the parties, the proceedings may be reported electronically.

(e) Whenever, after the agency itself has commenced to hear the case with an administrative law judge presiding, a quorum no longer exists, the administrative law judge who is presiding shall complete the hearing as if sitting alone and shall render a proposed decision in accordance with subdivision (b) of Section 11517.

§ 11513.   Evidence; examination of witnesses

(a) Oral evidence shall be taken only on oath or affirmation.

(b) Each party shall have these rights: to call and examine witnesses, to introduce exhibits; to cross-examine opposing witnesses on any matter relevant to the issues even though that matter was not covered in the direct examination; to impeach any witness regardless of which party first called him or her to testify; and to rebut the evidence against him or her. If respondent does not testify in his or her own behalf he or she may be called and examined as if under cross-examination.

(c) The hearing need not be conducted according to technical rules relating to evidence and witnesses, except as hereinafter provided. Any relevant evidence shall be admitted if it is the sort of evidence on which responsible persons are accustomed to rely in the conduct of serious affairs, regardless of the existence of any common law or statutory rule which might make improper the admission of the evidence over objection in civil actions.

(d) Hearsay evidence may be used for the purpose of supplementing or explaining other evidence but over timely objection shall not be sufficient in itself to support a finding unless it would be admissible over objection in civil actions. An objection is timely if made before submission of the case or on reconsideration.

(e) The rules of privilege shall be effective to the extent that they are otherwise required by statute to be recognized at the hearing.

(f) The presiding officer has discretion to exclude evidence if its probative value is substantially outweighed by the probability that its admission will necessitate undue consumption of time.

* * *

§ 11515. Official notice

In reaching a decision official notice may be taken, either before or after submission of the case for decision, of any generally accepted technical or scientific matter within the agency's special field, and of any fact which may be judicially noticed by the courts of this State. Parties present at the hearing shall be informed of the matters to be noticed, and those matters shall be noted in the record, referred to therein, or appended thereto. Any such party shall be given a reasonable opportunity on request to refute the officially noticed matters by evidence or by written or oral presentation of authority, the manner of such refutation to be determined by the agency.

* * *

§ 11517. Contested case; original hearing; agency or administrative law judge

(a) A contested case may be originally heard by the agency itself and subdivision (b) shall apply. Alternatively, at the discretion of the agency, an administrative law judge may originally hear the case alone and subdivision (c) shall apply.

(b) If a contested case is originally heard before an agency itself, all of the following provisions apply:

(1) An administrative law judge shall be present during the consideration of the case and, if requested, shall assist and advise the agency in the conduct of the hearing.

(2) No member of the agency who did not hear the evidence shall vote on the decision.

(3) The agency shall issue its decision within 100 days of submission of the case.

(c)(1) If a contested case is originally heard by an administrative law judge alone, he or she shall prepare within 30 days after the case is submitted to him or her a proposed decision in a form that may be adopted by the agency as the final decision in the case. Failure of the administrative law judge to deliver a proposed decision within the time required does not prejudice the rights of the agency in the case. Thirty days after the receipt by the agency of the proposed decision, a copy of the proposed decision shall be filed by the agency as a public record and a copy shall be served by the agency on each party and his or her attorney. The filing and service is not an adoption of a proposed decision by the agency.

(2) Within 100 days of receipt by the agency of the administrative law judge's proposed decision, the agency may act as prescribed in subparagraphs (A) to (E), inclusive. If the agency fails to act as prescribed in subparagraphs (A) to (E), inclusive, within 100 days of

receipt of the proposed decision, the proposed decision shall be deemed adopted by the agency. The agency may do any of the following:

(A) Adopt the proposed decision in its entirety.

(B) Reduce or otherwise mitigate the proposed penalty and adopt the balance of the proposed decision.

(C) Make technical or other minor changes in the proposed decision and adopt it as the decision. Action by the agency under this paragraph is limited to a clarifying change or a change of a similar nature that does not affect the factual or legal basis of the proposed decision.

(D) Reject the proposed decision and refer the case to the same administrative law judge if reasonably available, otherwise to another administrative law judge, to take additional evidence. If the case is referred to an administrative law judge pursuant to this subparagraph, he or she shall prepare a revised proposed decision, as provided in paragraph (1), based upon the additional evidence and the transcript and other papers that are part of the record of the prior hearing. A copy of the revised proposed decision shall be furnished to each party and his or her attorney as prescribed in this subdivision.

(E) Reject the proposed decision, and decide the case upon the record, including the transcript, or upon an agreed statement of the parties, with or without taking additional evidence. By stipulation of the parties, the agency may decide the case upon the record without including the transcript. If the agency acts pursuant to this subparagraph, all of the following provisions apply:

(i) A copy of the record shall be made available to the parties. The agency may require payment of fees covering direct costs of making the copy.

(ii) The agency itself shall not decide any case provided for in this subdivision without affording the parties the opportunity to present either oral or written argument before the agency itself. If additional oral evidence is introduced before the agency itself, no agency member may vote unless the member heard the additional oral evidence.

(iii) The authority of the agency itself to decide the case under this subdivision includes authority to decide some but not all issues in the case.

(iv) If the agency elects to proceed under this subparagraph, the agency shall issue its final decision not later than 100 days after rejection of the proposed decision. If the agency elects to proceed under this subparagraph, and has

ordered a transcript of the proceedings before the administrative law judge, the agency shall issue its final decision
not later than 100 days after receipt of the transcript. If the
agency finds that a further delay is required by special
circumstance, it shall issue an order delaying the decision
for no more than 30 days and specifying the reasons therefor. The order shall be subject to judicial review pursuant to
Section 11523.

(d) The decision of the agency shall be filed immediately by the agency
as a public record and a copy shall be served by the agency on each party
and his or her attorney.

* * *

§ **11519.** Effective date of decision; stay of execution; notification; restitution

(a) The decision shall become effective 30 days after it is delivered or
mailed to respondent unless: a reconsideration is ordered within that
time, or the agency itself orders that the decision shall become effective
sooner, or a stay of execution is granted.

(b) A stay of execution may be included in the decision or if not included
therein may be granted by the agency at any time before the decision
becomes effective. The stay of execution provided herein may be accompanied by an express condition that respondent comply with specified
terms of probation; provided, however, that the terms of probation shall
be just and reasonable in the light of the findings and decision.

(c) If respondent was required to register with any public officer, a
notification of any suspension or revocation shall be sent to the officer
after the decision has become effective.

(d) As used in subdivision (b), specified terms of probation may include
an order of restitution. Where restitution is ordered and paid pursuant
to the provisions of this subdivision, the amount paid shall be credited to
any subsequent judgment in a civil action.

(e) The person to which the agency action is directed may not be
required to comply with a decision unless the person has been served
with the decision in the manner provided in Section 11505 or has actual
knowledge of the decision.

(f) A nonparty may not be required to comply with a decision unless the
agency has made the decision available for public inspection and copying
or the nonparty has actual knowledge of the decision.

(g) This section does not preclude an agency from taking immediate
action to protect the public interest in accordance with Article 13
(commencing with Section 11460.10) of Chapter 4.5.

* * *

§ 11523. Judicial review

Judicial review may be had by filing a petition for a writ of mandate in accordance with the provisions of the Code of Civil Procedure, subject, however, to the statutes relating to the particular agency. Except as otherwise provided in this section, the petition shall be filed within 30 days after the last day on which reconsideration can be ordered. The right to petition shall not be affected by the failure to seek reconsideration before the agency. On request of the petitioner for a record of the proceedings, the complete record of the proceedings, or the parts thereof as are designated by the petitioner in the request, shall be prepared by the Office of Administrative Hearings or the agency and shall be delivered to the petitioner, within 30 days after the request, which time shall be extended for good cause shown, upon the payment of the cost for the preparation of the transcript, the cost for preparation of other portions of the record and for certification thereof. The complete record includes the pleadings, all notices and orders issued by the agency, any proposed decision by an administrative law judge, the final decision, a transcript of all proceedings, the exhibits admitted or rejected, the written evidence and any other papers in the case. If the petitioner, within 10 days after the last day on which reconsideration can be ordered, requests the agency to prepare all or any part of the record, the time within which a petition may be filed shall be extended until 30 days after its delivery to him or her. The agency may file with the court the original of any document in the record in lieu of a copy thereof. If petitioner prevails in overturning the administrative decision following judicial review, the agency shall reimburse the petitioner for all costs of transcript preparation, compilation of the record, and certification.

FLORIDA PUBLIC RECORDS LAW

TITLE X. PUBLIC OFFICERS, EMPLOYEES, AND RECORDS
CHAPTER 119. PUBLIC RECORDS

§ 119.01. General state policy on public records

(1) It is the policy of this state that all state, county, and municipal records are open for personal inspection and copying by any person. Providing access to public records is a duty of each agency.

(2)(a) Automation of public records must not erode the right of access to those records. As each agency increases its use of and dependence on electronic recordkeeping, each agency must provide reasonable public access to records electronically maintained and must ensure that exempt or confidential records are not disclosed except as otherwise permitted by law.

(b) When designing or acquiring an electronic recordkeeping system, an agency must consider whether such system is capable of providing data in some common format such as, but not limited to, the American Standard Code for Information Interchange.

(c) An agency may not enter into a contract for the creation or maintenance of a public records database if that contract impairs the ability of the public to inspect or copy the public records of the agency, including public records that are on-line or stored in an electronic recordkeeping system used by the agency.

(d) Subject to the restrictions of copyright and trade secret laws and public records exemptions, agency use of proprietary software must not diminish the right of the public to inspect and copy a public record.

(e) Providing access to public records by remote electronic means is an additional method of access that agencies should strive to provide to the extent feasible. If an agency provides access to public records by remote electronic means, such access should be provided in the most cost-effective and efficient manner available to the agency providing the information.

(f) Each agency that maintains a public record in an electronic recordkeeping system shall provide to any person, pursuant to this chapter, a copy of any public record in that system which is not exempted by law from public disclosure. An agency must provide a copy of the record in the medium requested if the agency maintains the record in that medium, and the agency may charge a fee in accordance with this chapter. For the purpose of satisfying a public records request, the fee to be charged by an agency if it elects to provide a copy of a public record in a medium not routinely used by the agency, or if it elects to compile information not routinely developed or maintained by the agency or that requires a substantial amount of manipulation or programming, must be in accordance with § 119.07(4).

(3) If public funds are expended by an agency in payment of dues or membership contributions for any person, corporation, foundation, trust, association, group, or other organization, all the financial, business, and membership records of that person, corporation, foundation, trust, association, group, or other organization which pertain to the public agency are public records and subject to the provisions of § 119.07.

§ 119.011. Definitions

As used in this chapter, the term:

(1) "Actual cost of duplication" means the cost of the material and supplies used to duplicate the public record, but does not include labor cost or overhead cost associated with such duplication.

(2) "Agency" means any state, county, district, authority, or municipal officer, department, division, board, bureau, commission, or other separate unit of government created or established by law including, for the purposes of this chapter, the Commission on Ethics, the Public Service Commission, and the Office of Public Counsel, and any other public or private agency, person, partnership, corporation, or business entity acting on behalf of any public agency.

(3)(a) "Criminal intelligence information" means information with respect to an identifiable person or group of persons collected by a criminal justice agency in an effort to anticipate, prevent, or monitor possible criminal activity.

(b) "Criminal investigative information" means information with respect to an identifiable person or group of persons compiled by a criminal justice agency in the course of conducting a criminal investigation of a specific act or omission, including, but not limited to, information derived from laboratory tests, reports of investigators or informants, or any type of surveillance.

(c) "Criminal intelligence information" and "criminal investigative information" shall not include:

1. The time, date, location, and nature of a reported crime.

2. The name, sex, age, and address of a person arrested or of the victim of a crime except as provided in § 119.071(2)(h).

3. The time, date, and location of the incident and of the arrest.

4. The crime charged.

5. Documents given or required by law or agency rule to be given to the person arrested, except as provided in § 119.071(2)(h), and, except that the court in a criminal case may order that certain information required by law or agency rule to be given to the person arrested be maintained in a confidential manner and exempt from the provisions of § 119.07(1) until released at trial if it is found that the release of such information would:

    a. Be defamatory to the good name of a victim or witness or would jeopardize the safety of such victim or witness; and

    b. Impair the ability of a state attorney to locate or prosecute a codefendant.

6. Informations and indictments except as provided in § 905.26.

(d) The word "active" shall have the following meaning:

1. Criminal intelligence information shall be considered "active" as long as it is related to intelligence gathering conducted with a reasonable, good faith belief that it will lead to detection of ongoing or reasonably anticipated criminal activities.

2. Criminal investigative information shall be considered "active" as long as it is related to an ongoing investigation which is

continuing with a reasonable, good faith anticipation of securing an arrest or prosecution in the foreseeable future.

In addition, criminal intelligence and criminal investigative information shall be considered "active" while such information is directly related to pending prosecutions or appeals. The word "active" shall not apply to information in cases which are barred from prosecution under the provisions of § 775.15 or other statute of limitation.

(4) "Criminal justice agency" means:

(a) Any law enforcement agency, court, or prosecutor;

(b) Any other agency charged by law with criminal law enforcement duties;

(c) Any agency having custody of criminal intelligence information or criminal investigative information for the purpose of assisting such law enforcement agencies in the conduct of active criminal investigation or prosecution or for the purpose of litigating civil actions under the Racketeer Influenced and Corrupt Organization Act, during the time that such agencies are in possession of criminal intelligence information or criminal investigative information pursuant to their criminal law enforcement duties; or

(d) The Department of Corrections.

(5) "Custodian of public records" means the elected or appointed state, county, or municipal officer charged with the responsibility of maintaining the office having public records, or his or her designee.

(6) "Data processing software" means the programs and routines used to employ and control the capabilities of data processing hardware, including, but not limited to, operating systems, compilers, assemblers, utilities, library routines, maintenance routines, applications, and computer networking programs.

(7) "Duplicated copies" means new copies produced by duplicating, as defined in § 283.30.

(8) "Exemption" means a provision of general law which provides that a specified record or meeting, or portion thereof, is not subject to the access requirements of § 119.07(1), § 286.011, or § 24, Art. I of the State Constitution.

(9) "Information technology resources" means data processing hardware and software and services, communications, supplies, personnel, facility resources, maintenance, and training.

(10) "Proprietary software" means data processing software that is protected by copyright or trade secret laws.

(11) "Public records" means all documents, papers, letters, maps, books, tapes, photographs, films, sound recordings, data processing software, or other material, regardless of the physical form, characteristics, or means

of transmission, made or received pursuant to law or ordinance or in connection with the transaction of official business by any agency.

(12) "Redact" means to conceal from a copy of an original public record, or to conceal from an electronic image that is available for public viewing, that portion of the record containing exempt or confidential information.

(13) "Sensitive," for purposes of defining agency-produced software that is sensitive, means only those portions of data processing software, including the specifications and documentation, which are used to:

(a) Collect, process, store, and retrieve information that is exempt from § 119.07(1);

(b) Collect, process, store, and retrieve financial management information of the agency, such as payroll and accounting records; or

(c) Control and direct access authorizations and security measures for automated systems.

§ 119.021. Custodial requirements; maintenance, preservation, and retention of public records

(1) Public records shall be maintained and preserved as follows:

(a) All public records should be kept in the buildings in which they are ordinarily used.

(b) Insofar as practicable, a custodian of public records of vital, permanent, or archival records shall keep them in fireproof and waterproof safes, vaults, or rooms fitted with noncombustible materials and in such arrangement as to be easily accessible for convenient use.

(c)1. Record books should be copied or repaired, renovated, or rebound if worn, mutilated, damaged, or difficult to read.

2. Whenever any state, county, or municipal records are in need of repair, restoration, or rebinding, the head of the concerned state agency, department, board, or commission; the board of county commissioners of such county; or the governing body of such municipality may authorize that such records be removed from the building or office in which such records are ordinarily kept for the length of time required to repair, restore, or rebind them.

3. Any public official who causes a record book to be copied shall attest and certify under oath that the copy is an accurate copy of the original book. The copy shall then have the force and effect of the original.

(2)(a) The Division of Library and Information Services of the Department of State shall adopt rules to establish retention schedules and a disposal process for public records.

(b) Each agency shall comply with the rules establishing retention schedules and disposal processes for public records which are adopted by the records and information management program of the division.

(c) Each public official shall systematically dispose of records no longer needed, subject to the consent of the records and information management program of the division in accordance with § 257.36.

(d) The division may ascertain the condition of public records and shall give advice and assistance to public officials to solve problems related to the preservation, creation, filing, and public accessibility of public records in their custody. Public officials shall assist the division by preparing an inclusive inventory of categories of public records in their custody. The division shall establish a time period for the retention or disposal of each series of records. Upon the completion of the inventory and schedule, the division shall, subject to the availability of necessary space, staff, and other facilities for such purposes, make space available in its records center for the filing of semicurrent records so scheduled and in its archives for noncurrent records of permanent value, and shall render such other assistance as needed, including the microfilming of records so scheduled.

(3) Agency orders that comprise final agency action and that must be indexed or listed pursuant to § 120.53 have continuing legal significance; therefore, notwithstanding any other provision of this chapter or any provision of chapter 257, each agency shall permanently maintain records of such orders pursuant to the applicable rules of the Department of State.

(4)(a) Whoever has custody of any public records shall deliver, at the expiration of his or her term of office, to his or her successor or, if there be none, to the records and information management program of the Division of Library and Information Services of the Department of State, all public records kept or received by him or her in the transaction of official business.

(b) Whoever is entitled to custody of public records shall demand them from any person having illegal possession of them, who must forthwith deliver the same to him or her. Any person unlawfully possessing public records must within 10 days deliver such records to the lawful custodian of public records unless just cause exists for failing to deliver such records.

§ 119.07.   Inspection and copying of records; photographing public records; fees; exemptions

(1)(a) Every person who has custody of a public record shall permit the record to be inspected and copied by any person desiring to do so, at any reasonable time, under reasonable conditions, and under supervision by the custodian of the public records.

(b) A person who has custody of a public record who asserts that an exemption applies to a part of such record shall redact that portion of the record to which an exemption has been asserted and validly applies, and such person shall produce the remainder of such record for inspection and copying.

(c) If the person who has custody of a public record contends that all or part of the record is exempt from inspection and copying, he or she shall state the basis of the exemption that he or she contends is applicable to the record, including the statutory citation to an exemption created or afforded by statute.

(d) If requested by the person seeking to inspect or copy the record, the custodian of public records shall state in writing and with particularity the reasons for the conclusion that the record is exempt or confidential.

(e) In any civil action in which an exemption to this section is asserted, if the exemption is alleged to exist under or by virtue of § 119.071(1)(d) or (f), (2)(d),(e), or (f), or (4)(c), the public record or part thereof in question shall be submitted to the court for an inspection in camera. If an exemption is alleged to exist under or by virtue of § 119.071(2)(c), an inspection in camera is discretionary with the court. If the court finds that the asserted exemption is not applicable, it shall order the public record or part thereof in question to be immediately produced for inspection or copying as requested by the person seeking such access.

(f) Even if an assertion is made by the custodian of public records that a requested record is not a public record subject to public inspection or copying under this subsection, the requested record shall, nevertheless, not be disposed of for a period of 30 days after the date on which a written request to inspect or copy the record was served on or otherwise made to the custodian of public records by the person seeking access to the record. If a civil action is instituted within the 30–day period to enforce the provisions of this section with respect to the requested record, the custodian of public records may not dispose of the record except by order of a court of competent jurisdiction after notice to all affected parties.

(g) The absence of a civil action instituted for the purpose stated in paragraph (e) does not relieve the custodian of public records of the duty to maintain the record as a public record if the record is in fact a public record subject to public inspection and copying under this subsection and does not otherwise excuse or exonerate the custodian of public records from any unauthorized or unlawful disposition of such record.

(2)(a) As an additional means of inspecting or copying public records, a custodian of public records may provide access to public records by remote electronic means, provided exempt or confidential information is not disclosed.

(b) The custodian of public records shall provide safeguards to protect the contents of public records from unauthorized remote electronic access or alteration and to prevent the disclosure or modification of those portions of public records which are exempt or confidential from subsection (1) or § 24, Art. I of the State Constitution.

(c) Unless otherwise required by law, the custodian of public records may charge a fee for remote electronic access, granted under a contractual arrangement with a user, which fee may include the direct and indirect costs of providing such access. Fees for remote electronic access provided to the general public shall be in accordance with the provisions of this section.

(3)(a) Any person shall have the right of access to public records for the purpose of making photographs of the record while such record is in the possession, custody, and control of the custodian of public records.

(b) This subsection applies to the making of photographs in the conventional sense by use of a camera device to capture images of public records but excludes the duplication of microfilm in the possession of the clerk of the circuit court where a copy of the microfilm may be made available by the clerk.

(c) Photographing public records shall be done under the supervision of the custodian of public records, who may adopt and enforce reasonable rules governing the photographing of such records.

(d) Photographing of public records shall be done in the room where the public records are kept. If, in the judgment of the custodian of public records, this is impossible or impracticable, photographing shall be done in another room or place, as nearly adjacent as possible to the room where the public records are kept, to be determined by the custodian of public records. Where provision of another room or place for photographing is required, the expense of providing the same shall be paid by the person desiring to photograph the public record pursuant to paragraph (4)(e).

(4) The custodian of public records shall furnish a copy or a certified copy of the record upon payment of the fee prescribed by law. If a fee is not prescribed by law, the following fees are authorized:

(a)1. Up to 15 cents per one-sided copy for duplicated copies of not more than 14 inches by 8 1/2 inches;

2. No more than an additional 5 cents for each two-sided copy; and

3. For all other copies, the actual cost of duplication of the public record.

(b) The charge for copies of county maps or aerial photographs supplied by county constitutional officers may also include a reasonable charge for the labor and overhead associated with their duplication.

(c) An agency may charge up to $1 per copy for a certified copy of a public record.

(d) If the nature or volume of public records requested to be inspected or copied pursuant to this subsection is such as to require extensive use of information technology resources or extensive clerical or supervisory assistance by personnel of the agency involved, or both, the agency may charge, in addition to the actual cost of duplication, a special service charge, which shall be reasonable and shall be based on the cost incurred for such extensive use of information technology resources or the labor cost of the personnel providing the service that is actually incurred by the agency or attributable to the agency for the clerical and supervisory assistance required, or both.

(e)1. Where provision of another room or place is necessary to photograph public records, the expense of providing the same shall be paid by the person desiring to photograph the public records.

2. The custodian of public records may charge the person making the photographs for supervision services at a rate of compensation to be agreed upon by the person desiring to make the photographs and the custodian of public records. If they fail to agree as to the appropriate charge, the charge shall be determined by the custodian of public records.

(5) When ballots are produced under this section for inspection or examination, no persons other than the supervisor of elections or the supervisor's employees shall touch the ballots. If the ballots are being examined before the end of the contest period in § 102.168, the supervisor of elections shall make a reasonable effort to notify all candidates by telephone or otherwise of the time and place of the inspection or examination. All such candidates, or their representatives, shall be allowed to be present during the inspection or examination.

(6) Nothing in this chapter shall be construed to exempt from subsection (1) a public record that was made a part of a court file and that is not specifically closed by order of court, except as provided in § 119.071(1)(d) and (f), (2)(d), (e), and (f), and (4)(c) and except information or records that may reveal the identity of a person who is a victim of a sexual offense as provided in § 119.071(2)(h).

(7) An exemption contained in this chapter or in any other general or special law shall not limit the access of the Auditor General, the Office of

Program Policy Analysis and Government Accountability, or any state, county, municipal, university, board of community college, school district, or special district internal auditor to public records when such person states in writing that such records are needed for a properly authorized audit, examination, or investigation. Such person shall maintain the exempt or confidential status of that public record and shall be subject to the same penalties as the custodian of that record for public disclosure of such record.

(8) An exemption from this section does not imply an exemption from § 286.011. The exemption from § 286.011 must be expressly provided.

(9) The provisions of this section are not intended to expand or limit the provisions of Rule 3.220, Florida Rules of Criminal Procedure, regarding the right and extent of discovery by the state or by a defendant in a criminal prosecution or in collateral postconviction proceedings. This section may not be used by any inmate as the basis for failing to timely litigate any postconviction action.

§ 119.071. General exemptions from inspection or copying of public records

(1) **Agency administration.**—

(a) Examination questions and answer sheets of examinations administered by a governmental agency for the purpose of licensure, certification, or employment are exempt from § 119.07(1) and § 24(a), Art. I of the State Constitution. A person who has taken such an examination has the right to review his or her own completed examination.

(b) 1. a. Sealed bids or proposals received by an agency pursuant to invitations to bid or requests for proposals are exempt from § 119.07(1) and § 24(a), Art. I of the State Constitution until such time as the agency provides notice of a decision or intended decision pursuant to § 120.57(3)(a) or within 10 days after bid or proposal opening, whichever is earlier.

b. If an agency rejects all bids or proposals submitted in response to an invitation to bid or request for proposals and the agency concurrently provides notice of its intent to reissue the invitation to bid or request for proposals, the rejected bids or proposals remain exempt from § 119.07(1) and § 24(a), Art. I of the State Constitution until such time as the agency provides notice of a decision or intended decision pursuant to § 120.57(3)(a) concerning the reissued invitation to bid or request for proposals or until the agency withdraws the reissued invitation to bid or request for proposals. This sub-subparagraph is subject to the Open Government Sunset Review Act in accordance with § 119.15 and shall stand repealed on October 2, 2011,

458

unless reviewed and saved from repeal through reenactment by the Legislature.

2. a. A competitive sealed reply in response to an invitation to negotiate, as defined in § 287.012, is exempt from § 119.07(1) and § 24(a), Art. I of the State Constitution until such time as the agency provides notice of a decision or intended decision pursuant to § 120.57(3)(a) or until 20 days after the final competitive sealed replies are all opened, whichever occurs earlier.

b. If an agency rejects all competitive sealed replies in response to an invitation to negotiate and concurrently provides notice of its intent to reissue the invitation to negotiate and reissues the invitation to negotiate within 90 days after the notice of intent to reissue the invitation to negotiate, the rejected replies remain exempt from § 119.07(1) and § 24(a), Art. I of the State Constitution until such time as the agency provides notice of a decision or intended decision pursuant to § 120.57(3)(a) concerning the reissued invitation to negotiate or until the agency withdraws the reissued invitation to negotiate. A competitive sealed reply is not exempt for longer than 12 months after the initial agency notice rejecting all replies.

c. This subparagraph is subject to the Open Government Sunset Review Act in accordance with § 119.15 and shall stand repealed on October 2, 2011, unless reviewed and saved from repeal through reenactment by the Legislature.

(c) Any financial statement that an agency requires a prospective bidder to submit in order to prequalify for bidding or for responding to a proposal for a road or any other public works project is exempt from § 119.07(1) and § 24(a), Art. I of the State Constitution.

(d) 1. A public record that was prepared by an agency attorney (including an attorney employed or retained by the agency or employed or retained by another public officer or agency to protect or represent the interests of the agency having custody of the record) or prepared at the attorney's express direction, that reflects a mental impression, conclusion, litigation strategy, or legal theory of the attorney or the agency, and that was prepared exclusively for civil or criminal litigation or for adversarial administrative proceedings, or that was prepared in anticipation of imminent civil or criminal litigation or imminent adversarial administrative proceedings, is exempt from § 119.07(1) and § 24(a), Art. I of the State Constitution until the conclusion of the litigation or adversarial administrative proceedings. For purposes of capital collateral litigation as set forth in § 27.7001, the Attorney General's office is entitled to claim this exemption for those public records prepared for

459

direct appeal as well as for all capital collateral litigation after direct appeal until execution of sentence or imposition of a life sentence.

   2.   This exemption is not waived by the release of such public record to another public employee or officer of the same agency or any person consulted by the agency attorney. When asserting the right to withhold a public record pursuant to this paragraph, the agency shall identify the potential parties to any such criminal or civil litigation or adversarial administrative proceedings. If a court finds that the document or other record has been improperly withheld under this paragraph, the party seeking access to such document or record shall be awarded reasonable attorney's fees and costs in addition to any other remedy ordered by the court.

(e) Any videotape or video signal that, under an agreement with an agency, is produced, made, or received by, or is in the custody of, a federally licensed radio or television station or its agent is exempt from § 119.07(1).

(f) Data processing software obtained by an agency under a licensing agreement that prohibits its disclosure and which software is a trade secret, as defined in § 812.081, and agency-produced data processing software that is sensitive are exempt from § 119.07(1) and § 24(a), Art. I of the State Constitution. The designation of agency-produced software as sensitive shall not prohibit an agency head from sharing or exchanging such software with another public agency.

(2) Agency investigations.—

(a) All criminal intelligence and criminal investigative information received by a criminal justice agency prior to January 25, 1979, is exempt from § 119.07(1) and § 24(a), Art. I of the State Constitution.

(b) Whenever criminal intelligence information or criminal investigative information held by a non-Florida criminal justice agency is available to a Florida criminal justice agency only on a confidential or similarly restricted basis, the Florida criminal justice agency may obtain and use such information in accordance with the conditions imposed by the providing agency.

(c) 1.   Active criminal intelligence information and active criminal investigative information are exempt from § 119.07(1) and § 24(a), Art. I of the State Constitution.

   2.   A request of a law enforcement agency to inspect or copy a public record that is in the custody of another agency, the custodian's response to the request, and any information that would identify the public record that was requested by the law enforcement agency or provided by the custodian are exempt

from § 119.07(1) and § 24(a), Art. I of the State Constitution, during the period in which the information constitutes criminal intelligence information or criminal investigative information that is active. This exemption is remedial in nature, and it is the intent of the Legislature that the exemption be applied to requests for information received before, on, or after the effective date of this subparagraph. The law enforcement agency shall give notice to the custodial agency when the criminal intelligence information or criminal investigative information is no longer active, so that the custodian's response to the request and information that would identify the public record requested are available to the public. This subparagraph is subject to the Open Government Sunset Review Act in accordance with § 119.15 and shall stand repealed October 2, 2007, unless reviewed and saved from repeal through reenactment by the Legislature.

(d) Any information revealing surveillance techniques or procedures or personnel is exempt from § 119.07(1) and § 24(a), Art. I of the State Constitution. Any comprehensive inventory of state and local law enforcement resources compiled pursuant to part I, chapter 23, and any comprehensive policies or plans compiled by a criminal justice agency pertaining to the mobilization, deployment, or tactical operations involved in responding to emergencies, as defined in § 252.34(3), are exempt from § 119.07(1) and § 24(a), Art. I of the State Constitution and unavailable for inspection, except by personnel authorized by a state or local law enforcement agency, the office of the Governor, the Department of Legal Affairs, the Department of Law Enforcement, or the Department of Community Affairs as having an official need for access to the inventory or comprehensive policies or plans.

(e) Any information revealing the substance of a confession of a person arrested is exempt from § 119.07(1) and § 24(a), Art. I of the State Constitution, until such time as the criminal case is finally determined by adjudication, dismissal, or other final disposition.

(f) Any information revealing the identity of a confidential informant or a confidential source is exempt from § 119.07(1) and § 24(a), Art. I of the State Constitution.

(g) When the alleged victim chooses not to file a complaint and requests that records of the complaint remain confidential, all records relating to an allegation of employment discrimination are confidential and exempt from § 119.07(1) and § 24(a), Art. I of the State Constitution.

(h) 1. Any criminal intelligence information or criminal investigative information including the photograph, name, address, or other fact or information which reveals the identity of the victim of the

461

crime of sexual battery as defined in chapter 794; the identity of the victim of a lewd or lascivious offense committed upon or in the presence of a person less than 16 years of age, as defined in chapter 800; or the identity of the victim of the crime of child abuse as defined by chapter 827 and any criminal intelligence information or criminal investigative information or other criminal record, including those portions of court records and court proceedings, which may reveal the identity of a person who is a victim of any sexual offense, including a sexual offense proscribed in chapter 794, chapter 800, or chapter 827, is exempt from § 119.07(1) and § 24(a), Art. I of the State Constitution.

    2. In addition to subparagraph 1., any criminal intelligence information or criminal investigative information that is a photograph, videotape, or image of any part of the body of the victim of a sexual offense prohibited under chapter 794, chapter 800, or chapter 827, regardless of whether the photograph, videotape, or image identifies the victim, is confidential and exempt from § 119.07(1) and § 24(a), Art. I of the State Constitution. This exemption applies to photographs, videotapes, or images held as criminal intelligence information or criminal investigative information before, on, or after the effective date of the exemption.

(i) Any criminal intelligence information or criminal investigative information that reveals the personal assets of the victim of a crime, other than property stolen or destroyed during the commission of the crime, is exempt from § 119.07(1) and § 24(a), Art. I of the State Constitution.

(j) 1. Any document that reveals the identity, home or employment telephone number, home or employment address, or personal assets of the victim of a crime and identifies that person as the victim of a crime, which document is received by any agency that regularly receives information from or concerning the victims of crime, is exempt from § 119.07(1) and § 24(a), Art. I of the State Constitution. Any information not otherwise held confidential or exempt from § 119.07(1) which reveals the home or employment telephone number, home or employment address, or personal assets of a person who has been the victim of sexual battery, aggravated child abuse, aggravated stalking, harassment, aggravated battery, or domestic violence is exempt from § 119.07(1) and § 24(a), Art. I of the State Constitution, upon written request by the victim, which must include official verification that an applicable crime has occurred. Such information shall cease to be exempt 5 years after the receipt of the written request. Any state or federal agency that is authorized to have access to such documents by any provision of law shall be granted such access in the furtherance of such agency's statutory duties, notwithstanding this section.

2. a. Any information in a videotaped statement of a minor who is alleged to be or who is a victim of sexual battery, lewd acts, or other sexual misconduct proscribed in chapter 800 or in § 794.011, § 827.071, § 847.012, § 847.0125, § 847.013, § 847.0133, or § 847.0145, which reveals that minor's identity, including, but not limited to, the minor's face; the minor's home, school, church, or employment telephone number; the minor's home, school, church, or employment address; the name of the minor's school, church, or place of employment; or the personal assets of the minor; and which identifies that minor as the victim of a crime described in this subparagraph, held by a law enforcement agency, is confidential and exempt from § 119.07(1) and § 24(a), Art. I of the State Constitution. Any governmental agency that is authorized to have access to such statements by any provision of law shall be granted such access in the furtherance of the agency's statutory duties, notwithstanding the provisions of this section.

b. A public employee or officer who has access to a videotaped statement of a minor who is alleged to be or who is a victim of sexual battery, lewd acts, or other sexual misconduct proscribed in chapter 800 or in § 794.011, § 827.071, § 847.012, § 847.0125, § 847.013, § 847.0133, or § 847.0145 may not willfully and knowingly disclose videotaped information that reveals the minor's identity to a person who is not assisting in the investigation or prosecution of the alleged offense or to any person other than the defendant, the defendant's attorney, or a person specified in an order entered by the court having jurisdiction of the alleged offense. A person who violates this provision commits a misdemeanor of the first degree, punishable as provided in § 775.082 or § 775.083.

(3) Security.—

(a) 1. As used in this paragraph, the term "security system plan" includes all:

a. Records, information, photographs, audio and visual presentations, schematic diagrams, surveys, recommendations, or consultations or portions thereof relating directly to the physical security of the facility or revealing security systems;

b. Threat assessments conducted by any agency or any private entity;

c. Threat response plans;

d. Emergency evacuation plans;

e. Sheltering arrangements; or

f.   Manuals for security personnel, emergency equipment, or security training.

..   A security system plan or portion thereof for:

a.   Any property owned by or leased to the state or any of its political subdivisions; or

b.   Any privately owned or leased property

held by an agency is confidential and exempt from § 119.07(1) and § 24(a), Art. I of the State Constitution. This exemption is remedial in nature, and it is the intent of the Legislature that this exemption apply to security system plans held by an agency before, on, or after the effective date of this paragraph.

3.   Information made confidential and exempt by this paragraph may be disclosed by the custodian of public records to:

a.   The property owner or leaseholder; or

b.   Another state or federal agency to prevent, detect, guard against, respond to, investigate, or manage the consequences of any attempted or actual act of terrorism, or to prosecute those persons who are responsible for such attempts or acts.

(b) Building plans, blueprints, schematic drawings, and diagrams, including draft, preliminary, and final formats, which depict the internal layout and structural elements of a building, arena, stadium, water treatment facility, or other structure owned or operated by an agency are exempt from § 119.07(1) and § 24(a), Art. I of the State Constitution. This exemption applies to building plans, blueprints, schematic drawings, and diagrams, including draft, preliminary, and final formats, which depict the internal layout and structural elements of a building, arena, stadium, water treatment facility, or other structure owned or operated by an agency before, on, or after the effective date of this act. Information made exempt by this paragraph may be disclosed to another governmental entity if disclosure is necessary for the receiving entity to perform its duties and responsibilities; to a licensed architect, engineer, or contractor who is performing work on or related to the building, arena, stadium, water treatment facility, or other structure owned or operated by an agency; or upon a showing of good cause before a court of competent jurisdiction. The entities or persons receiving such information shall maintain the exempt status of the information. This paragraph is subject to the Open Government Sunset Review Act in accordance with § 119.15 and shall stand repealed on October 2, 2007, unless reviewed and reenacted by the Legislature.

(c) Building plans, blueprints, schematic drawings, and diagrams, including draft, preliminary, and final formats, which depict the internal layout or structural elements of an attractions and recreation facility, entertainment or resort complex, industrial complex, retail and service development, office development, or hotel or motel development, which documents are held by an agency are exempt from § 119.07(1) and § 24(a), Art. I of the State Constitution. This exemption applies to any such documents held by an agency before, on, or after the effective date of this act. Information made exempt by this paragraph may be disclosed to another governmental entity if disclosure is necessary for the receiving entity to perform its duties and responsibilities; to the owner or owners of the structure in question or the owner's legal representative; or upon a showing of good cause before a court of competent jurisdiction. As used in this paragraph, the term:

1. "Attractions and recreation facility" means any sports, entertainment, amusement, or recreation facility, including, but not limited to, a sports arena, stadium, racetrack, tourist attraction, amusement park, or pari-mutuel facility that:

    a. For single-performance facilities:

        (I) Provides single-performance facilities; or

        (II) Provides more than 10,000 permanent seats for spectators.

    b. For serial-performance facilities:

        (I) Provides parking spaces for more than 1,000 motor vehicles; or

        (II) Provides more than 4,000 permanent seats for spectators.

2. "Entertainment or resort complex" means a theme park comprised of at least 25 acres of land with permanent exhibitions and a variety of recreational activities, which has at least 1 million visitors annually who pay admission fees thereto, together with any lodging, dining, and recreational facilities located adjacent to, contiguous to, or in close proximity to the theme park, as long as the owners or operators of the theme park, or a parent or related company or subsidiary thereof, has an equity interest in the lodging, dining, or recreational facilities or is in privity therewith. Close proximity includes an area within a 5–mile radius of the theme park complex.

3. "Industrial complex" means any industrial, manufacturing, processing, distribution, warehousing, or wholesale facility or plant, as well as accessory uses and structures, under common ownership which:

    a. Provides onsite parking for more than 250 motor vehicles;

    b.   Encompasses 500,000 square feet or more of gross floor area; or

    c.   Occupies a site of 100 acres or more, but excluding wholesale facilities or plants that primarily serve or deal onsite with the general public.

4.   "Retail and service development" means any retail, service, or wholesale business establishment or group of establishments which deals primarily with the general public onsite and is operated under one common property ownership, development plan, or management that:

    a.   Encompasses more than 400,000 square feet of gross floor area; or

    b.   Provides parking spaces for more than 2,500 motor vehicles.

5.   "Office development" means any office building or park operated under common ownership, development plan, or management that encompasses 300,000 or more square feet of gross floor area.

6.   "Hotel or motel development" means any hotel or motel development that accommodates 350 or more units.

This exemption does not apply to comprehensive plans or site plans, or amendments thereto, which are submitted for approval or which have been approved under local land development regulations, local zoning regulations, or development-of-regional-impact review.

(4) Agency personnel information.—

(a) 1.   The social security numbers of all current and former agency employees which numbers are contained in agency employment records are exempt from § 119.07(1) and § 24(a), Art. I of the State Constitution.

    2.   An agency that is the custodian of a social security number specified in subparagraph 1. and that is not the employing agency shall maintain the exempt status of the social security number only if the employee or the employing agency of the employee submits a written request for confidentiality to the custodial agency. However, upon a request by a commercial entity as provided in subparagraph (5)(a)5., the custodial agency shall release the last four digits of the exempt social security number, except that a social security number provided in a lien filed with the Department of State shall be released in its entirety. This subparagraph is subject to the Open Government Sunset Review Act in accordance with § 119.15 and shall stand repealed on October 2, 2009, unless reviewed and saved from repeal through reenactment by the Legislature.

(b) Medical information pertaining to a prospective, current, or former officer or employee of an agency which, if disclosed, would identify that officer or employee is exempt from § 119.07(1) and § 24(a), Art. I of the State Constitution. However, such information may be disclosed if the person to whom the information pertains or the person's legal representative provides written permission or pursuant to court order.

(c) Any information revealing undercover personnel of any criminal justice agency is exempt from § 119.07(1) and § 24(a), Art. I of the State Constitution.

(d) 1. The home addresses, telephone numbers, social security numbers, and photographs of active or former law enforcement personnel, including correctional and correctional probation officers, personnel of the Department of Children and Family Services whose duties include the investigation of abuse, neglect, exploitation, fraud, theft, or other criminal activities, personnel of the Department of Health whose duties are to support the investigation of child abuse or neglect, and personnel of the Department of Revenue or local governments whose responsibilities include revenue collection and enforcement or child support enforcement; the home addresses, telephone numbers, social security numbers, photographs, and places of employment of the spouses and children of such personnel; and the names and locations of schools and day care facilities attended by the children of such personnel are exempt from § 119.07(1). The home addresses, telephone numbers, and photographs of firefighters certified in compliance with § 633.35; the home addresses, telephone numbers, photographs, and places of employment of the spouses and children of such firefighters; and the names and locations of schools and day care facilities attended by the children of such firefighters are exempt from § 119.07(1). The home addresses and telephone numbers of justices of the Supreme Court, district court of appeal judges, circuit court judges, and county court judges; the home addresses, telephone numbers, and places of employment of the spouses and children of justices and judges; and the names and locations of schools and day care facilities attended by the children of justices and judges are exempt from § 119.07(1). The home addresses, telephone numbers, social security numbers, and photographs of current or former state attorneys, assistant state attorneys, statewide prosecutors, or assistant statewide prosecutors; the home addresses, telephone numbers, social security numbers, photographs, and places of employment of the spouses and children of current or former state attorneys, assistant state attorneys, statewide prosecutors, or assistant statewide prosecutors; and the names and locations of schools and day care facilities attended by the children of current or former state attorneys, assistant state attorneys, statewide prosecutors, or assistant statewide prosecutors are exempt from § 119.07(1) and § 24(a), Art. I of the State Constitution.

2. The home addresses, telephone numbers, and photographs of current or former human resource, labor relations, or employee relations directors, assistant directors, managers, or assistant managers of any local government agency or water management district whose duties include hiring and firing employees, labor contract negotiation, administration, or other personnel-related duties; the names, home addresses, telephone numbers, and places of employment of the spouses and children of such personnel; and the names and locations of schools and day care facilities attended by the children of such personnel are exempt from § 119.07(1) and § 24(a), Art. I of the State Constitution.

3. The home addresses, telephone numbers, social security numbers, and photographs of current or former United States attorneys and assistant United States attorneys; the home addresses, telephone numbers, social security numbers, photographs, and places of employment of the spouses and children of current or former United States attorneys and assistant United States attorneys; and the names and locations of schools and day care facilities attended by the children of current or former United States attorneys and assistant United States attorneys are exempt from § 119.07(1) and § 24(a), Art. I of the State Constitution. This subparagraph is subject to the Open Government Sunset Review Act in accordance with § 119.15 and shall stand repealed on October 2, 2009, unless reviewed and saved from repeal through reenactment by the Legislature.

4. The home addresses, telephone numbers, social security numbers, and photographs of current or former judges of United States Courts of Appeal, United States district judges, and United States magistrate judges; the home addresses, telephone numbers, social security numbers, photographs, and places of employment of the spouses and children of current or former judges of United States Courts of Appeal, United States district judges, and United States magistrate judges; and the names and locations of schools and day care facilities attended by the children of current or former judges of United States Courts of Appeal, United States district judges, and United States magistrate judges are exempt from § 119.07(1) and § 24(a), Art. I of the State Constitution. This subparagraph is subject to the Open Government Sunset Review Act in accordance with § 119.15 and shall stand repealed on October 2, 2009, unless reviewed and saved from repeal through reenactment by the Legislature.

5.   The home addresses, telephone numbers, and photographs of current or former code enforcement officers; the names, home addresses, telephone numbers, and places of employment of the spouses and children of such personnel; and the names and locations of schools and day care facilities attended by the children of such personnel are exempt from § 119.07(1) and § 24(a), Art. I of the State Constitution.

6.   The home addresses, telephone numbers, places of employment, and photographs of current or former guardians ad litem, as defined in § 39.820, and the names, home addresses, telephone numbers, and places of employment of the spouses and children of such persons, are exempt from § 119.07(1) and § 24(a), Art. I of the State Constitution, if the guardian ad litem provides a written statement that the guardian ad litem has made reasonable efforts to protect such information from being accessible through other means available to the public. This subparagraph is subject to the Open Government Sunset Review Act in accordance with § 119.15 and shall stand repealed on October 2, 2010, unless reviewed and saved from repeal through reenactment by the Legislature.

7.   The home addresses, telephone numbers, and photographs of current or former juvenile probation officers, juvenile probation supervisors, detention superintendents, assistant detention superintendents, senior juvenile detention officers, juvenile detention officer supervisors, juvenile detention officers, house parents I and II, house parent supervisors, group treatment leaders, group treatment leader supervisors, rehabilitation therapists, and social services counselors of the Department of Juvenile Justice; the names, home addresses, telephone numbers, and places of employment of spouses and children of such personnel; and the names and locations of schools and day care facilities attended by the children of such personnel are exempt from § 119.07(1) and § 24(a), Art. I of the State Constitution. This subparagraph is subject to the Open Government Sunset Review Act in accordance with § 119.15 and shall stand repealed on October 2, 2011, unless reviewed and saved from repeal through reenactment by the Legislature.

8.   An agency that is the custodian of the personal information specified in subparagraph 1., subparagraph 2., subparagraph 3., subparagraph 4., subparagraph 5., subparagraph 6., or subparagraph 7. and that is not the employer of the officer, employee, justice, judge, or other person specified in subparagraph 1., subparagraph 2., subparagraph 3., subparagraph 4., subparagraph 5., subparagraph 6., or subparagraph 7. shall maintain the exempt status of the personal information only if the officer, employee, justice, judge, other person, or employing agency of

the designated employee submits a written request for maintenance of the exemption to the custodial agency.

(5) Other personal information.—

(a) 1.   The Legislature acknowledges that the social security number was never intended to be used for business purposes but was intended to be used solely for the administration of the federal Social Security System. The Legislature is further aware that over time this unique numeric identifier has been used extensively for identity verification purposes and other legitimate consensual purposes. The Legislature is also cognizant of the fact that the social security number can be used as a tool to perpetuate fraud against a person and to acquire sensitive personal, financial, medical, and familial information, the release of which could cause great financial or personal harm to an individual. The Legislature intends to monitor the commercial use of social security numbers held by state agencies in order to maintain a balanced public policy.

2.   An agency may not collect an individual's social security number unless authorized by law to do so or unless the collection of the social security number is otherwise imperative for the performance of that agency's duties and responsibilities as prescribed by law. Social security numbers collected by an agency must be relevant to the purpose for which collected and may not be collected until and unless the need for social security numbers has been clearly documented. An agency that collects social security numbers shall also segregate that number on a separate page from the rest of the record, or as otherwise appropriate, in order that the social security number be more easily redacted, if required, pursuant to a public records request. An agency collecting a person's social security number shall, upon that person's request, at the time of or prior to the actual collection of the social security number by that agency, provide that person with a statement of the purpose or purposes for which the social security number is being collected and used. Social security numbers collected by an agency may not be used by that agency for any purpose other than the purpose stated. Social security numbers collected by an agency before May 13, 2002, shall be reviewed for compliance with this subparagraph. If the collection of a social security number before May 13, 2002, is found to be unwarranted, the agency shall immediately discontinue the collection of social security numbers for that purpose.

3.   Effective October 1, 2002, all social security numbers held by an agency are confidential and exempt from § 119.07(1) and § 24(a), Art. I of the State Constitution. This exemption applies

to all social security numbers held by an agency before, on, or after the effective date of this exemption.

4. Social security numbers may be disclosed to another governmental entity or its agents, employees, or contractors if disclosure is necessary for the receiving entity to perform its duties and responsibilities. The receiving governmental entity and its agents, employees, and contractors shall maintain the confidential and exempt status of the numbers.

5. An agency may not deny a commercial entity engaged in the performance of a commercial activity, which, for purposes of this paragraph, means an activity that provides a product or service that is available from a private source, or its agents, employees, or contractors access to social security numbers, provided the social security numbers will be used only in the normal course of business for legitimate business purposes, and provided the commercial entity makes a written request for social security numbers, verified as provided in § 92.525, legibly signed by an authorized officer, employee, or agent of the commercial entity. The verified written request must contain the commercial entity's name, business mailing and location addresses, business telephone number, and a statement of the specific purposes for which it needs the social security numbers and how the social security numbers will be used in the normal course of business for legitimate business purposes. The aggregate of these requests shall serve as the basis for the agency report required in subparagraph 8. An agency may request any other information reasonably necessary to verify the identity of the entity requesting the social security numbers and the specific purposes for which the numbers will be used; however, an agency has no duty to inquire beyond the information contained in the verified written request. A legitimate business purpose includes verification of the accuracy of personal information received by a commercial entity in the normal course of its business; use in a civil, criminal, or administrative proceeding; use for insurance purposes; use in law enforcement and investigation of crimes; use in identifying and preventing fraud; use in matching, verifying, or retrieving information; and use in research activities. A legitimate business purpose does not include the display or bulk sale of social security numbers to the general public or the distribution of such numbers to any customer that is not identifiable by the distributor.

6. Any person who makes a false representation in order to obtain a social security number pursuant to this paragraph, or any person who willfully and knowingly violates this paragraph, commits a felony of the third degree, punishable as provided in § 775.082 or § 775.083. Any public officer who violates this

paragraph is guilty of a noncriminal infraction, punishable by a fine not exceeding $500. A commercial entity that provides access to public records containing social security numbers in accordance with this paragraph is not subject to the penalty provisions of this subparagraph.

7.   a.   On or after October 1, 2002, a person preparing or filing a document to be recorded in the official records by the county recorder as provided for in chapter 28 may not include any person's social security number in that document, unless otherwise expressly required by law. If a social security number is or has been included in a document presented to the county recorder for recording in the official records of the county before, on, or after October 1, 2002, it may be made available as part of the official record available for public inspection and copying.

b.   Any person, or his or her attorney or legal guardian, has the right to request that a county recorder remove, from an image or copy of an official record placed on a county recorder's publicly available Internet website or a publicly available Internet website used by a county recorder to display public records or otherwise made electronically available to the general public by such recorder, his or her social security number contained in that official record. The request must be made in writing, legibly signed by the requester and delivered by mail, facsimile, or electronic transmission, or delivered in person, to the county recorder. The request must specify the identification page number that contains the social security number to be redacted. The county recorder has no duty to inquire beyond the written request to verify the identity of a person requesting redaction. A fee may not be charged for the redaction of a social security number pursuant to such request.

c.   A county recorder shall immediately and conspicuously post signs throughout his or her offices for public viewing and shall immediately and conspicuously post, on any Internet website or remote electronic site made available by the county recorder and used for the ordering or display of official records or images or copies of official records, a notice stating, in substantially similar form, the following:

(I) On or after October 1, 2002, any person preparing or filing a document for recordation in the official records may not include a social security number in such document, unless required by law.

(II) Any person has a right to request a county recorder to remove, from an image or copy of an official record placed on a county recorder's publicly available Internet website or on a publicly available Internet website used by a county recorder to display public records or otherwise made electronically available to the general public, any social security number contained in an official record. Such request must be made in writing and delivered by mail, facsimile, or electronic transmission, or delivered in person, to the county recorder. The request must specify the identification page number that contains the social security number to be redacted. A fee may not be charged for the redaction of a social security number pursuant to such a request.

d. Until January 1, 2008, if a social security number, made confidential and exempt pursuant to this paragraph, or a complete bank account, debit, charge, or credit card number made exempt pursuant to paragraph (b) is or has been included in a court file, such number may be included as part of the court record available for public inspection and copying unless redaction is requested by the holder of such number, or by the holder's attorney or legal guardian, in a signed, legibly written request specifying the case name, case number, document heading, and page number. The request must be delivered by mail, facsimile, electronic transmission, or in person to the clerk of the circuit court. The clerk of the circuit court does not have a duty to inquire beyond the written request to verify the identity of a person requesting redaction. A fee may not be charged for the redaction of a social security number or a bank account, debit, charge, or credit card number pursuant to such request. The clerk of the circuit court has no liability for the inadvertent release of confidential and exempt social security numbers or exempt bank account, debit, charge, or credit card numbers, unknown to the clerk of the circuit court in court records filed with the clerk of the circuit court on or before January 1, 2008.

e. Any person who prepares or files a document to be recorded in the official records by the county recorder as provided in chapter 28 may not include a person's social security number or complete bank account, debit, charge, or credit card number in that document unless otherwise expressly required by law. Until January 1, 2008, if a social security number or a complete bank account, debit, charge, or credit card number is or has been included in a document presented to the county recorder for recording in the official records of the county, such number may be made available as part of the official record available for public inspection and copying. Any person, or his or her attorney or legal guardian, may request that a county recorder remove from an image or copy of an official record placed on a county recorder's publicly available Internet website, or a publicly available Internet website used by a county recorder to display public records outside the office or otherwise made electronically available outside the county recorder's office to the general public, his or her social security number or complete account, debit, charge, or credit card number contained in that official record. Such request must be legibly written, signed by the requester, and delivered by mail, facsimile, electronic transmission, or in person to the county recorder. The request must specify the identification page number of the document that contains the number to be redacted. The county recorder does not have a duty to inquire beyond the written request to verify the identity of a person requesting redaction. A fee may not be charged for redacting such numbers. If the county recorder accepts or stores official records in an electronic format, the county recorder must use his or her best efforts to redact all social security numbers and complete bank account, debit, charge, or credit card numbers from electronic copies of the official record. The use of an automated program for redaction shall be deemed the best effort and complies with the requirements of this sub-subparagraph. The county recorder is not liable for the inadvertent release of confidential and exempt social security numbers, or exempt bank account, debit, charge, or credit card numbers, filed with the county recorder on or before January 1, 2008.

f.   Subparagraphs 5. and 6. do not apply to the clerks of the court or the county recorder with respect to circuit court records and official records.

g.   On January 1, 2008, and thereafter, the clerk of the circuit court and the county recorder must keep complete bank account, debit, charge, and credit card numbers exempt as provided for in paragraph (b), and must keep social security numbers confidential and exempt as provided for in subparagraph 3., without any person having to request redaction.

8.   Beginning January 31, 2004, and each January 31 thereafter, every agency must file a report with the Secretary of State, the President of the Senate, and the Speaker of the House of Representatives listing the identity of all commercial entities that have requested social security numbers during the preced-

ing calendar year and the specific purpose or purposes stated by each commercial entity regarding its need for social security numbers. If no disclosure requests were made, the agency shall so indicate.

9. Any affected person may petition the circuit court for an order directing compliance with this paragraph.

10. This paragraph does not supersede any other applicable public records exemptions existing prior to May 13, 2002, or created thereafter.

11. This paragraph is subject to the Open Government Sunset Review Act in accordance with § 119.15 and shall stand repealed October 2, 2007, unless reviewed and saved from repeal through reenactment by the Legislature.

(b) Bank account numbers and debit, charge, and credit card numbers held by an agency are exempt from § 119.07(1) and § 24(a), Art. I of the State Constitution. This exemption applies to bank account numbers and debit, charge, and credit card numbers held by an agency before, on, or after the effective date of this exemption. This paragraph is subject to the Open Government Sunset Review Act in accordance with § 119.15 and shall stand repealed on October 2, 2007, unless reviewed and saved from repeal through reenactment by the Legislature.

(c) Any information that would identify or help to locate a child who participates in government-sponsored recreation programs or camps or the parents or guardians of such child, including, but not limited to, the name, home address, telephone number, social security number, or photograph of the child; the names and locations of schools attended by such child; and the names, home addresses, and social security numbers of parents or guardians of such child is exempt from § 119.07(1) and § 24(a), Art. I of the State Constitution. Information made exempt pursuant to this paragraph may be disclosed by court order upon a showing of good cause. This exemption applies to records held before, on, or after the effective date of this exemption.

(d) All records supplied by a telecommunications company, as defined by § 364.02, to an agency which contain the name, address, and telephone number of subscribers are confidential and exempt from § 119.07(1) and § 24(a), Art. I of the State Constitution.

(e) Any information provided to an agency for the purpose of forming ridesharing arrangements, which information reveals the identity of an individual who has provided his or her name for ridesharing, as defined in § 341.031, is exempt from § 119.07(1) and § 24(a), Art. I of the State Constitution.

(f) Medical history records and information related to health or property insurance provided to the Department of Community Affairs, the Florida Housing Finance Corporation, a county, a municipality, or a local housing finance agency by an applicant for or a participant in a federal, state, or local housing assistance program are confidential and exempt from § 119.07(1) and § 24(a), Art. I of the State Constitution. Governmental entities or their agents shall have access to such confidential and exempt records and information for the purpose of auditing federal, state, or local housing programs or housing assistance programs. Such confidential and exempt records and information may be used in any administrative or judicial proceeding, provided such records are kept confidential and exempt unless otherwise ordered by a court.

(g) 1.   Biometric identification information held by an agency before, on, or after the effective date of this exemption is exempt from § 119.07(1) and § 24(a), Art. I of the State Constitution. As used in this paragraph, the term "biometric identification information" means:

    a.   Any record of friction ridge detail;

    b.   Fingerprints;

    c.   Palm prints; and

    d.   Footprints.

2.   This paragraph is subject to the Open Government Sunset Review Act in accordance with § 119.15 and shall stand repealed on October 2, 2011, unless reviewed and saved from repeal through reenactment by the Legislature.

§ 119.0711.   Executive branch agency exemptions from inspection or copying of public records

(1) All complaints and other records in the custody of any agency in the executive branch of state government which relate to a complaint of discrimination relating to race, color, religion, sex, national origin, age, handicap, or marital status in connection with hiring practices, position classifications, salary, benefits, discipline, discharge, employee performance, evaluation, or other related activities are exempt from § 119.07(1) and § 24(a), Art. I of the State Constitution until a finding is made relating to probable cause, the investigation of the complaint becomes inactive, or the complaint or other record is made part of the official record of any hearing or court proceeding. This provision shall not affect any function or activity of the Florida Commission on Human Relations. Any state or federal agency that is authorized to have access to such complaints or records by any provision of law shall be granted such access in the furtherance of such agency's statutory duties.

(2) When an agency of the executive branch of state government seeks to acquire real property by purchase or through the exercise of the power

of eminent domain, all appraisals, other reports relating to value, offers, and counteroffers must be in writing and are exempt from § 119.07(1) and § 24(a), Art. I of the State Constitution until execution of a valid option contract or a written offer to sell that has been conditionally accepted by the agency, at which time the exemption shall expire. The agency shall not finally accept the offer for a period of 30 days in order to allow public review of the transaction. The agency may give conditional acceptance to any option or offer subject only to final acceptance by the agency after the 30–day review period. If a valid option contract is not executed, or if a written offer to sell is not conditionally accepted by the agency, then the exemption shall expire at the conclusion of the condemnation litigation of the subject property. An agency of the executive branch may exempt title information, including names and addresses of property owners whose property is subject to acquisition by purchase or through the exercise of the power of eminent domain, from § 119.07(1) and § 24(a), Art. I of the State Constitution to the same extent as appraisals, other reports relating to value, offers, and counteroffers. For the purpose of this subsection, the term "option contract" means an agreement of an agency of the executive branch of state government to purchase real property subject to final agency approval. This subsection has no application to other exemptions from § 119.07(1) which are contained in other provisions of law and shall not be construed to be an express or implied repeal thereof.

§ 119.0712. Executive branch agency-specific exemptions from inspection or copying of public records

(1) **Department of health.**—All personal identifying information contained in records relating to an individual's personal health or eligibility for health-related services held by the Department of Health are confidential and exempt from § 119.07(1) and § 24(a), Art. I of the State Constitution, except as otherwise provided in this subsection. Information made confidential and exempt by this subsection shall be disclosed:

(a) With the express written consent of the individual or the individual's legally authorized representative.

(b) In a medical emergency, but only to the extent necessary to protect the health or life of the individual.

(c) By court order upon a showing of good cause.

(d) To a health research entity, if the entity seeks the records or data pursuant to a research protocol approved by the department, maintains the records or data in accordance with the approved protocol, and enters into a purchase and data-use agreement with the department, the fee provisions of which are consistent with § 119.07(4). The department may deny a request for records or data if the protocol provides for intrusive follow-back contacts, has not been approved by a human studies institutional review board, does not plan for the destruction of confidential records after the research is concluded, is administratively burdensome, or does not have scientific merit. The agreement must restrict the release of any information that would permit the identification of persons, limit the use of records or data to the approved research protocol, and prohibit any other use of the records or data. Copies of records or data issued pursuant to this paragraph remain the property of the department.

(2) Department of highway safety and motor vehicles.—Personal information contained in a motor vehicle record that identifies the subject of that record is exempt from § 119.07(1) and § 24(a), Art. I of the State Constitution except as provided in this section. Personal information includes, but is not limited to, the subject's social security number, driver identification number, name, address, telephone number, and medical or disability information. For purposes of this subsection, personal information does not include information relating to vehicular crashes, driving violations, and driver's status. For purposes of this subsection, the term "motor vehicle record" means any record that pertains to a motor vehicle operator's permit, motor vehicle title, motor vehicle registration, or identification card issued by the Department of Highway Safety and Motor Vehicles. Personal information contained in motor vehicle records exempted by this subsection shall be released by the department for any of the following uses:

(a) For use in connection with matters of motor vehicle or driver safety and theft; motor vehicle emissions; motor vehicle product alterations, recalls, or advisories; performance monitoring of motor vehicles and dealers by motor vehicle manufacturers; and removal of nonowner records from the original owner records of motor vehicle manufacturers, to carry out the purposes of the Automobile Information Disclosure Act, the Motor Vehicle Information and Cost Saving Act, the National Traffic and Motor Vehicle Safety Act of 1966, the Anti–Car Theft Act of 1992, and the Clean Air Act.

(b) For use by any government agency, including any court or law enforcement agency, in carrying out its functions, or any private person or entity acting on behalf of a federal, state, or local agency in carrying out its functions.

(c) For use in connection with matters of motor vehicle or driver safety and theft; motor vehicle emissions; motor vehicle product alterations, recalls, or advisories; performance monitoring of motor vehicles, motor vehicle parts, and dealers; motor vehicle market research activities, including survey research; and removal of nonowner records from the original owner records of motor vehicle manufacturers.

(d) For use in the normal course of business by a legitimate business or its agents, employees, or contractors, but only:

1. To verify the accuracy of personal information submitted by the individual to the business or its agents, employees, or contractors; and

2. If such information as so submitted is not correct or is no longer correct, to obtain the correct information, but only for the purposes of preventing fraud by, pursuing legal remedies against, or recovering on a debt or security interest against, the individual.

(e) For use in connection with any civil, criminal, administrative, or arbitral proceeding in any court or agency or before any self-regulatory body for:

1. Service of process by any certified process server, special process server, or other person authorized to serve process in this state.

2. Investigation in anticipation of litigation by an attorney licensed to practice law in this state or the agent of the attorney; however, the information may not be used for mass commercial solicitation of clients for litigation against motor vehicle dealers.

3. Investigation by any person in connection with any filed proceeding; however, the information may not be used for mass commercial solicitation of clients for litigation against motor vehicle dealers.

4. Execution or enforcement of judgments and orders.

5. Compliance with an order of any court.

(f) For use in research activities and for use in producing statistical reports, so long as the personal information is not published, redisclosed, or used to contact individuals.

(g) For use by any insurer or insurance support organization, or by a self-insured entity, or its agents, employees, or contractors, in connection with claims investigation activities, anti-fraud activities, rating, or underwriting.

(h) For use in providing notice to the owners of towed or impounded vehicles.

(i) For use by any licensed private investigative agency or licensed security service for any purpose permitted under this subsection. Personal information obtained based on an exempt driver's record may not be provided to a client who cannot demonstrate a need based on a police report, court order, or business or personal relationship with the subject of the investigation.

(j) For use by an employer or its agent or insurer to obtain or verify information relating to a holder of a commercial driver's license that is required under 49 U.S.C. §§ 31301 et seq.

(k) For use in connection with the operation of private toll transportation facilities.

(*l*) For bulk distribution for surveys, marketing, or solicitations when the department has obtained the express consent of the person to whom such personal information pertains.

(m) For any use if the requesting person demonstrates that he or she has obtained the written consent of the person who is the subject of the motor vehicle record.

(n) For any other use specifically authorized by state law, if such use is related to the operation of a motor vehicle or public safety.

(o) For any other use if the person to whom the information pertains has given express consent on a form prescribed by the department. Such consent shall remain in effect until it is revoked by the person on a form prescribed by the department.

The restrictions on disclosure of personal information provided by this subsection shall not in any way affect the use of organ donation information on individual driver licenses or affect the administration of organ donation initiatives in this state. Personal information exempted from public disclosure according to this subsection may be disclosed by the Department of Highway Safety and Motor Vehicles to an individual, firm, corporation, or similar business entity whose primary business interest is to resell or redisclose the personal information to persons who are authorized to receive such information. Prior to the department's disclosure of personal information, such individual, firm, corporation, or similar business entity must first enter into a contract with the department regarding the care, custody, and control of the personal information to ensure compliance with the federal Driver's Privacy Protection Act of 1994 and applicable state laws. An authorized recipient of personal information contained in a motor vehicle record, except a recipient under paragraph (*l*), may contract with the Department of Highway Safety and Motor Vehicles to resell or redisclose the information for any use permitted under this section. However, only authorized recipients of personal information under paragraph (*l*) may resell or redisclose personal information pursuant to paragraph (*l*). Any authorized recipient who resells or rediscloses personal information shall maintain, for a period of 5 years, records identifying each person or entity that receives the personal information and the permitted purpose for which it will be used. Such records shall be made available for inspection upon request by the department. The department shall adopt rules to carry out the purposes of this subsection and the federal Driver's Privacy Protection Act of 1994, 18 U.S.C. §§ 2721 et seq. Rules adopted by the department shall provide for the payment of applicable fees and, prior to the disclosure of personal information pursuant to this subsection, shall require the meeting of conditions by the requesting person for the purposes of obtaining reasonable assurance concerning the identity of such requesting person, and, to the extent required, assurance that the use will be only as authorized or that the consent of the person who is the subject of the personal information has been obtained. Such conditions may include, but need not be limited to, the making and filing of a written application in such form and containing such information and certification requirements as the department requires.

§ 119.0713. Local government agency exemptions from inspection or copying of public records

(1) All complaints and other records in the custody of any unit of local government which relate to a complaint of discrimination relating to race, color, religion, sex, national origin, age, handicap, marital status, sale or rental of housing, the provision of brokerage services, or the financing of housing are exempt from § 119.07(1) and § 24(a), Art. I of the State Constitution until a finding is made relating to probable cause, the investigation of the complaint becomes inactive, or the complaint or other record is made part of the official record of any hearing or court proceeding. This provision shall not affect any function or activity of the Florida Commission on Human Relations. Any state or federal agency that is authorized to have access to such complaints or records by any provision of law shall be granted such access in the furtherance of such agency's statutory duties. This subsection shall not be construed to modify or repeal any special or local act.

(2) All personal identifying information contained in records relating to a person's health held by local governmental entities for the purpose of determining eligibility for paratransit services under Title II of the Americans with Disabilities Act or eligibility for the transportation disadvantaged program as provided in part I of chapter 427 is confidential and exempt from § 119.07(1) and § 24(a), Art. I of the State Constitution, except as otherwise provided in this subsection. This exemption applies to personal identifying information contained in such records held by local governmental entities before, on, or after the effective date of this exemption. Information made confidential and exempt by this subsection shall be disclosed:

(a) With the express written consent of the individual or the individual's legally authorized representative;

(b) In a medical emergency, but only to the extent necessary to protect the health or life of the individual;

(c) By court order upon a showing of good cause; or

(d) For the purpose of determining eligibility for paratransit services if the individual or the individual's legally authorized representative has filed an appeal or petition before an administrative body of a local government or a court.

(3) The audit report of an internal auditor prepared for or on behalf of a unit of local government becomes a public record when the audit becomes final. As used in this subsection, the term "unit of local government" means a county, municipality, special district, local agency, authority, consolidated city-county government, or any other local governmental body or public body corporate or politic authorized or created by general or special law. An audit becomes final when the audit report is presented to the unit of local government. Audit workpapers and notes related to such audit report are confidential and exempt from § 119.07(1) and § 24(a), Art. I of the State Constitution until the audit is completed and the audit report becomes final.

(4) Any data, record, or document used directly or solely by a municipally owned utility to prepare and submit a bid relative to the sale, distribution, or use of any service, commodity, or tangible personal property to any customer or prospective customer is exempt from § 119.07(1) and § 24(a), Art. I of the State Constitution. This exemption commences when a municipal utility identifies in writing a specific bid to which it intends to respond. This exemption no longer applies when the contract for sale, distribution, or use of the service, commodity, or tangible personal property is executed, a decision is made not to execute such contract, or the project is no longer under active consideration. The exemption in this subsection includes the bid documents actually furnished in response to the request for bids. However, the exemption for the bid documents submitted no longer applies after the bids are opened by the customer or prospective customer.

§ 119.10.   Violation of chapter; penalties

(1) Any public officer who:

    (a) Violates any provision of this chapter commits a noncriminal infraction, punishable by fine not exceeding $500.

    (b) Knowingly violates the provisions of § 119.07(1) is subject to suspension and removal or impeachment and, in addition, commits a misdemeanor of the first degree, punishable as provided in § 775.082 or § 775.083.

(2) Any person who willfully and knowingly violates:

    (a) Any of the provisions of this chapter commits a misdemeanor of the first degree, punishable as provided in § 775.082 or § 775.083.

    (b) Section 119.105 commits a felony of the third degree, punishable as provided in § 775.082, § 775.083, or § 775.084.

§ 119.105.   Protection of victims of crimes or accidents

Police reports are public records except as otherwise made exempt or confidential. Every person is allowed to examine nonexempt or nonconfidential police reports. A person who comes into possession of exempt or confidential information contained in police reports may not use that information for any commercial solicitation of the victims or relatives of the victims of the reported crimes or accidents and may not knowingly disclose such information to any third party for the purpose of such solicitation during the period of time that information remains exempt or confidential. This section does not prohibit the publication of such information to the general public by any news media legally entitled to possess that information or the use of such information for any other data collection or analysis purposes by those entitled to possess that information.

§ 119.11. Accelerated hearing; immediate compliance

(1) Whenever an action is filed to enforce the provisions of this chapter, the court shall set an immediate hearing, giving the case priority over other pending cases.

(2) Whenever a court orders an agency to open its records for inspection in accordance with this chapter, the agency shall comply with such order within 48 hours, unless otherwise provided by the court issuing such order, or unless the appellate court issues a stay order within such 48–hour period.

(3) A stay order shall not be issued unless the court determines that there is a substantial probability that opening the records for inspection will result in significant damage.

(4) Upon service of a complaint, counterclaim, or cross-claim in a civil action brought to enforce the provisions of this chapter, the custodian of the public record that is the subject matter of such civil action shall not transfer custody, alter, destroy, or otherwise dispose of the public record sought to be inspected and examined, notwithstanding the applicability of an exemption or the assertion that the requested record is not a public record subject to inspection and examination under § 119.07(1), until the court directs otherwise. The person who has custody of such public record may, however, at any time permit inspection of the requested record as provided in § 119.07(1) and other provisions of law.

§ 119.12. Attorney's fees

If a civil action is filed against an agency to enforce the provisions of this chapter and if the court determines that such agency unlawfully refused to permit a public record to be inspected or copied, the court shall assess and award, against the agency responsible, the reasonable costs of enforcement including reasonable attorneys' fees.

FLORIDA OPEN MEETINGS LAW

TITLE XIX. PUBLIC BUSINESS
CHAPTER 286. PUBLIC BUSINESS;
MISCELLANEOUS PROVISIONS

§ 286.011. Public meetings and records; public inspection; criminal and civil penalties

(1) All meetings of any board or commission of any state agency or authority or of any agency or authority of any county, municipal corporation, or political subdivision, except as otherwise provided in the Constitution, at which official acts are to be taken are declared to be public meetings open to the public at all times, and no resolution, rule, or formal action shall be considered binding except as taken or made at such meeting. The board or commission must provide reasonable notice of all such meetings.

(2) The minutes of a meeting of any such board or commission of any such state agency or authority shall be promptly recorded, and such records shall be open to public inspection. The circuit courts of this state shall have jurisdiction to issue injunctions to enforce the purposes of this section upon application by any citizen of this state.

(3) (a) Any public officer who violates any provision of this section is guilty of a noncriminal infraction, punishable by fine not exceeding $500.

(b) Any person who is a member of a board or commission or of any state agency or authority of any county, municipal corporation, or political subdivision who knowingly violates the provisions of this section by attending a meeting not held in accordance with the provisions hereof is guilty of a misdemeanor of the second degree, punishable as provided in § 775.082 or § 75.083.

(c) Conduct which occurs outside the state which would constitute a knowing violation of this section is a misdemeanor of the second degree, punishable as provided in § 775.082 or § 775.083.

(4) Whenever an action has been filed against any board or commission of any state agency or authority or any agency or authority of any county, municipal corporation, or political subdivision to enforce the provisions of this section or to invalidate the actions of any such board, commission, agency, or authority, which action was taken in violation of this section, and the court determines that the defendant or defendants to such action acted in violation of this section, the court shall assess a reasonable attorney's fee against such agency, and may assess a reasonable attorney's fee against the individual filing such an action if the court finds it was filed in bad faith or was frivolous. Any fees so assessed

may be assessed against the individual member or members of such board or commission; provided, that in any case where the board or commission seeks the advice of its attorney and such advice is followed, no such fees shall be assessed against the individual member or members of the board or commission. However, this subsection shall not apply to a state attorney or his or her duly authorized assistants or any officer charged with enforcing the provisions of this section.

(5) Whenever any board or commission of any state agency or authority or any agency or authority of any county, municipal corporation, or political subdivision appeals any court order which has found said board, commission, agency, or authority to have violated this section, and such order is affirmed, the court shall assess a reasonable attorney's fee for the appeal against such board, commission, agency, or authority. Any fees so assessed may be assessed against the individual member or members of such board or commission; provided, that in any case where the board or commission seeks the advice of its attorney and such advice is followed, no such fees shall be assessed against the individual member or members of the board or commission.

(6) All persons subject to subsection (1) are prohibited from holding meetings at any facility or location which discriminates on the basis of sex, age, race, creed, color, origin, or economic status or which operates in such a manner as to unreasonably restrict public access to such a facility.

(7) Whenever any member of any board or commission of any state agency or authority or any agency or authority of any county, municipal corporation, or political subdivision is charged with a violation of this section and is subsequently acquitted, the board or commission is authorized to reimburse said member for any portion of his or her reasonable attorney's fees.

(8) Notwithstanding the provisions of subsection (1), any board or commission of any state agency or authority or any agency or authority of any county, municipal corporation, or political subdivision, and the chief administrative or executive officer of the governmental entity, may meet in private with the entity's attorney to discuss pending litigation to which the entity is presently a party before a court or administrative agency, provided that the following conditions are met:

(a) The entity's attorney shall advise the entity at a public meeting that he or she desires advice concerning the litigation.

(b) The subject matter of the meeting shall be confined to settlement negotiations or strategy sessions related to litigation expenditures.

(c) The entire session shall be recorded by a certified court reporter. The reporter shall record the times of commencement and termination of the session, all discussion and proceedings, the names of all persons present at any time, and the names of all persons speaking. No portion of the session shall be off the record. The court reporter's notes shall be fully transcribed and filed with the entity's clerk within a reasonable time after the meeting.

(d) The entity shall give reasonable public notice of the time and date of the attorney-client session and the names of persons who will be attending the session. The session shall commence at an open meeting at which the persons chairing the meeting shall announce the commencement and estimated length of the attorney-client session and the names of the persons attending. At the conclusion of the attorney-client session, the meeting shall be reopened, and the person chairing the meeting shall announce the termination of the session.

(e) The transcript shall be made part of the public record upon conclusion of the litigation.

†